African
Historiographies

Volume 12
SAGE SERIES ON AFRICAN MODERNIZATION AND DEVELOPMENT

Bogumil Jewsiewicki
David Newbury
Editors

African
Historiographies

What History
for Which Africa?

SAGE PUBLICATIONS Beverly Hills London New Delhi

For information address:

SAGE Publications, Inc.
275 South Beverly Drive
Beverly Hills, California 90212

SAGE Publications India Pvt. Ltd.   SAGE Publications Ltd
M-32 Market   28 Banner Street
Greater Kailash I   London EC1Y 8QE
New Delhi 110 048 India   England

Printed in the United States of America

Library of Congress Cataloging in Publication Data

Main entry under title:

African historiographies.

(Sage series on African modernization and
development; v. 12)
    Bibliography: p.
    1. Africa—Historiography—Addresses, essays,
lectures.   I. Jewsiewicki, Bogumil.   II. Newbury,
David S.   III. Series.
DT19.C86   1985   960'.072   85-8113
ISBN 0-8039-2498-4

FIRST PRINTING

Contents

Preface   7

Introduction: One Historiography
    or Several? A Requiem for Africanism
      BOGUMIL JEWSIEWICKI   9

PART I.   THE EPISTEMOLOGY OF AFRICAN STUDIES

1. African Historians and Africanist Historians
      NDAYWEL E NZIÈM   20

2. Knowledge and Perceptions of the African Past
      JAN VANSINA   28

3. Epistemological Ethnocentrism in African Studies
      WYATT MacGAFFEY   42

PART II.   THE HISTORIOGRAPHY OF ORAL DISCOURSE

4. Profile of a Historiography: Oral Tradition
    and Historical Research in Africa
      HENRI MONIOT   50

5. The Past in the Present: Notes on
    Oral Archaeology
      JEAN BAZIN   59

6. Confronting the Unequal Exchange of the Oral
    and the Written
      JEAN-PIERRE CHRÉTIEN   75

7. African History and the Rule of Evidence:
    Is Declaring Victory Enough?
      DAVID HENIGE   91

8. Afterthoughts on the Historiography of
    Oral Tradition
      JAN VANSINA   105

PART III.   AFRICA FROM THE OUTSIDE: FROM
                 IMPERIAL HISTORIOGRAPHY, TO
                 AFRICANIST HISTORIOGRAPHY,
                 AND BEYOND

9. The Idea of Progress in the Revision
    of African History, 1960-1970
      CAROLINE NEALE   112

10. Decolonization in Africa: A New British
      Historiographical Debate?
      MICHAEL TWADDLE   123

11. Africanist Historiography in France
   and Belgium: Traditions and Trends
   CATHERINE COQUERY-VIDROVITCH
   and BOGUMIL JEWSIEWICKI   139

12. Africanist Historical Studies in the
   United States: Metamorphosis or Metastasis?
   DAVID NEWBURY   151

13. The Historiography of South Africa:
   Recent Developments
   SHULA MARKS   165

PART IV.   AFRICA FROM WITHIN:
           NATIONAL HISTORIOGRAPHIES

14. Marxian Method and Historical Process in
   Contemporary Ethiopia
   ROBERT S. LOVE   179

15. Nigerian Academic Historians
   E. J. ALAGOA   189

16. Nigeria: The Ibandan School and Its Critics
   PAUL E. LOVEJOY   197

17. Senegalese Historiography: Present Practices
   and Future Perspectives
   MOHAMED MBODJ and MAMADOU DIOUF   207

18. The Development of Senegalese Historiography
   MARTIN A. KLEIN   215

19. Historical Research in Zaire: Present Status
   and Future Perspectives
   MUMBANZA MWA BAWELE and SABAKINU KIVILU   224

PART V.   WHICH WAY OUT? TRENDS IN THE
          DEVELOPING HISTORIOGRAPHIES OF AFRICA

20. The Method of "Histoire Immédiate":
   Its Application to Africa
   BENOIT VERHAEGEN   236

21. Dar es Salaam and the Postnationalist
   Historiography of Africa
   HENRY SLATER   249

22. Populist Political Action: Historical
   Understanding and Political Analysis in Africa
   JEAN-FRANÇOIS BAYART   261

23. Toward a Responsible African Historiography
   CHRISTOPHE WONDJI   269

References   279

About the Contributors   317

Preface

The chapters in this volume were written as part of a larger project originally conceived in 1980. In the initial stages this was envisaged as an opportunity for those interested in reviewing the development of Central African historiography over the recent past to meet and discuss their common preoccupations. Thanks to Peter Gutkind's suggestion, the project became a more ambitious adventure, and came to include participants from many different regions of the continent (and outside Africa) and from diverse intellectual traditions. From the beginning it was seen as important that African scholars be included at the center of this critical reassessment of the existing historiography. The invitation sent to more than thirty colleagues in April of 1981 proposed joining efforts to reflect on the social and political conditions prevailing in the production of African history, and shaping the evolution of historical practice on and of black Africa. This was based on the premise that knowledge of the past serves our understanding of the present, and conditions our imagination in dealing with the future.

Except for the Introduction and the contributions of Alagoa, Bayart, Marks, Newbury, and Twaddle, the chapters included here were discussed at the Thirteenth Annual Conference of the Canadian Association of African Studies held at Laval University in Québec City in May 1983. Financial assistance from the Canadian International Development Agency, the International Development Research Center, the Social Science Research Council of Canada, the Fonds HCAR of Québec, the Québec government, and the Ministère des Affaires Etrangères of France is gratefully acknowledged. We also particularly wish to express our thanks to Peter Gutkind for his original stimulus and constant encouragement. We dedicate this volume to him on the occasion of his retirement.

Given the strict page limitation imposed on the work, the editors have had to reduce the total manuscript by some 30 percent. We are grateful to the contributors for their forbearance in accepting the rather draconian reductions in their original texts. Working in constant contact with the authors, we have tried to make the volume more a work of collaboration and dialogue than a simple collection of separate papers, while at the same time remaining faithful to the ideas of each individual contributor. With the exception of several pages of the chapter by Jean Bazin, translated by C. Aubin-Sugy, all translations were undertaken by David Newbury, with grateful acknowledgment to Wesleyan University and Bowdoin College for providing facilities during the preparation of the translations. The Social Science Research Council of Canada and the History Department of Laval University have provided financial assistance for typing and duplicating the several versions of the individual chapters of this volume.

—*Bogumil Jewsiewicki*
David Newbury

INTRODUCTION
One Historiography or Several?
A Requiem for Africanism

BOGUMIL JEWSIEWICKI

If history as we practice it today is simultaneously both reconstruction of the past and project for the future, this volume is, at least in part, an imposture. As Ndaywel notes, the Africanist historian and the African historian fully share neither the same responsibilities nor the same existential constraints. And yet, the lost unity between these two sets of practitioners is partially reestablished by the social location associated with the production of Africanist discourse: In some respects African academics are closer to their colleagues in western universities than to the peasants of their "own" national society.

There is a striking contrast between the approaches adopted by university historians, of whatever nationality, and by historical narrators, whether performing in an urban bar or in a village ceremony (Jewsiewicki, 1984). Even while addressing the same issues, the two categories of narrator do not say the same things, because the discourse of the former must be directed primarily to an audience outside the historical actors. The discourse of a narrator of social facts who performs before "the people" (Bourdieu, 1983) to earn a living must first elicit a reaction among the social actors, a reaction that must find

Author's Note: I wish to express my thanks to V. Y. Mudimbe, D. Henige, D. Cordell, H. Moniot, J. Gregory, and D. Newbury for their comments on an earlier version of this chapter.

its resonance in the collective consciousness. Irrelevance in this context carries a heavy price, because it cuts off the performers from their living, although irrelevance upheld by state power, as illustrated in the case of Zairean "authenticity," can be transformed into a strategic tool (Thompson, 1978a; Legendre, 1982).

I

A New Copernican Revolution: The Decolonization of History [Sahli, cited in each issue of *Africa Zamani*].

Discourse based on Weberian rationalism and evolutionist historicism unifies participants at a level beyond the quarrels over a particular field of action. The type of analysis illustrated by the work of Cheikh Anta Diop is indicative of the broad scale on which such analyses take place. Many Western historians who would be prepared to argue the questions relating to pharonic negritude, were the debate to be carried out in its own terms, do not do so because they do not want to offend the sensitivities of their African colleagues. Diop's discourse divides African historians into unconditional supporters or opponents (for instance, see Obenga, 1980; Temu and Swai, 1981), but full debate is never engaged in by either group. From Laroui to Said in the Middle East, but also in many other cases (Berto, 1980; Larzac, 1971), historical and political experience show that calling for the decolonization of history is at the very least ambiguous (Rabinow, 1984). Lacking any social content, the greater the ambiguities in the Negro-Egyptian debate, the more the goal of "decolonization" reinforces rather than weakens Africanist epistemology.

Similarly, from their commitment to construct a veritable monument of respectability the authors of the UNESCO *General History* (1981) have avoided the essential questions, and focused instead on the simple chronological primacy of black civilization and its unity (Jewsiewicki, 1981a). As the inverse of the ideology of black inferiority, Diop's paradigm communicates essentially within the same epistemological framework, even if at the same time it reestablishes a degree of equilibrium to earlier arguments. But as with the colonial ethnographic corpus (Copans, 1980a, 1980b; Mudimbe, 1982b) and the "ethnosciences" (such as "ethnohistory" or "ethnophilosophy"; Houtondji, 1977; Mudimbe, 1984), this paradigm retains a slight "Odeur du Père" (Mudimbe, 1982a). Although useful for the political mobilization of the anticolonial struggle of the 1960s, Diop's paradigm lost its relevance once the problems of race gave way to questions of social struggle, and proletarianization.

As with negritude, the subtle charm of Africanist epistemology is to affirm the social unity of the intellectuals, to leap over the racial barrier, without touching the social order and without challenging the political order in any fundamental way. It forms an integral part of the Africanist struggles to convince Western academe that Africa truly has a scientific history (Deschamps, 1970; Ki-Zerbo, 1972; UNESCO, 1981) as if the past of the societies of Africa might be null and void if it were to lack a "university" history (Kipre, 1979; Vansina, 1978b). These recent monuments of African academic history differ from Diop's enterprise only in their scholarly tone, not in their epistemological nature.

I do not wish to trivialize the intellectual achievements of either of these approaches; along with the contributors to the present volume, I seek only to inquire into the relevance of this "dialogue of the deaf" that the African peasant tries to engage in today with the intellectual, concerning the ultimate goals of independence. Not that the peasants wish the return of the colonizer; flag independence is for them only the highest stage of colonialism. They need neither Egyptian antiquities nor the consolation of the discourse of negritude, which assures them that "Shaka was their Napolean." To negotiate the true goals of independence they need to know why the state has no skin color and why exploitation has no fragrance other than that of their own sweat; they need to know how their consent to such structures of domination was (and continues to be) obtained. And they need to know that their ancestors and they themselves rarely, if ever, struggled against change in itself but almost always struggled against the social costs that have been so gratuitously bestowed on the peasants. Yet on all these points Africanist knowledge is silent.

In the end, Africanist understanding has produced an Other; it has constructed its own Africa and provided it with an appropriate past (Fabian, 1983a; Jewsiewicki, 1981a). This is hardly exceptional, neither by reference to other exotic Others (Valensi, 1979; Said, 1978; Lucas and Vatin, 1982) nor relative to other "domesticated" Others: peasants, workers, or women. Even as the industrial expansion broke down differentiation, and homogenized different fragments, and rationalized status and space, scientific endeavor classified, labled and ordered the world around it in terms of the "utility" of the various components for the "progress" of humanity. Thus social identities, whether ethnic or regional, result at least in part from scholarly classifications objectified by the ongoing processes of internal under-development and interiorized by those concerned. An ideology of scientific production results neither from myopia nor from the deaf-ness of the intellectuals but from the unwillingness to see and analyze the social conditions of the production of knowledge and the political conditions of its consumption. The "archaeology of this knowledge" (Foucault, 1973) has yet to be undertaken (see Chapters 2 and 3).

Who then consumes Africanist historiography? Stengers (1979b) has noted that in the middle of the stormy discussions of the neo-colonial remnants in African historiography, there appeared the first overview of Zairean history by a Zairean; there, somewhat to his surprise, instead of the expected references to Rodney, he found an entire Belgian historical bibliography. The popularization of univer-sity knowledge, especially through the national school system, as-sures stability and continuity from one state to another (Ferro, 1983) even if one wishes the opposite (Collectif, 1977). Even if today the Hamitic myth is dead and buried in scholarly circles, "the temptation to trace one's ancestry to a supposedly superior race has been great" (Kiwanuka, 1977: 32).

To avoid the risks of mummifying the discipline, it is time to move beyond our obsession with the demons of the past, beyond dusting off yet again Hegel's forgotten passage or Trevor-Roper's famous phrase. It does not suffice simply to place a new grid of reading on earlier concepts; in the haste to open all the doors with the single key to understanding, for example, the concept of mode of production was emptied of almost all explanatory value. Moreover, the social reality of Africa continues to be described in terms of tribe and clan drawn directly from the material of the West reflected in the mirror of the "savage" (Vansina, 1980). Debate on the structures of social inequality is only possible if the pertinent historical categories of social and economic dependence are defined first.

Since in Africanist studies, perhaps even more than elsewhere, the search for values relevant to research was more important than the analysis of social reality, the ideology of a group was taken and reproduced as a charter of the legitimate social relations; an academic diploma conferred was really a "diploma of historical respectability": The Africanist was that person "whom we employ to get the better of Africans" (Fyfe, 1976: 4). This is also the reason African and Africanist studies had beliefs, magic, and symbolism but no ideology before their "discovery" by Augé (1977)—a "discovery" as banal as it was fundamental for Africanists (see Chapter 3). The local political powers in colonial Africa certainly had everything to gain in adapting themselves to the image that the colonial "civilizers" had of them (see Chapter 6). There was established at this level a subtle exchange of silent complicity; Africanist studies are still nourished today with concepts drawn from the past, the permanence of which still surprises us (see Chapters 2 and 9).

History for whom? Which history? These are the questions I asked three years ago when I launched the project. Indeed, "all philosophies of history are anthropologies. So are all theories of history. All philosophies of history suggest a way of life. So do all theories of history" (Heller, 1982: 231). Thus the path of those historians who analyze the past of a society from within disgresses from the path of those who approach it from the outside: "Making sense of something means to insert phenomena, experience, and the like into our world; it means to transform the unknown into the known, the inexplicable into the explicable, and to reinforce or alter the world by meaningful actions of various provenance" (Heller, 1982: 64).

II

Fifteen years ago the most advanced theoretical discussion, the most "daring" for the times, focused on sources; Did they even exist? What were they? Were they utilizable? Today we are concerned with the philosophy and epistemology of African history—the linguist is tempted to refer to the meta-history of African history; that is we are at the point where it is probably best no longer to speak of "African history" but simply of history, as it applies to Africa [Alexandre, 1976: 5].

We cannot share by intellectual choice either a historical present or a historical conscience with the actors. A true social project, which implies not only a vision but also social action, is situated at the intersection of the historical present, of historical consciousness, and of the collective memory—the expressions of past and present objectifications of real life retained through time, in which one is recognized as sharing a group's present past. This is the process essential to the production of historiographies, each with its own social locus of production. There is a difference between those who practice Africanism only as a professional career and those who live out the present history of Africa (see Chapter 1). Although this difference is not limited to the possibility of "opting out," the critical distinction occurs where opting out is not an option.

To this last aspect there is recognizably both a present and a narration of the past for which the academic world disputes the relative merits of the character of historical oral and written archives or of myth (de Heusch, 1982; Vansina, 1983; *Social Analysis,* 1980). Historical practice has been based on the assumption of the respectability of archives, presumed to be the only way of deducing historicity from narrative (Hobsbawm and Ranger, 1983) as if there had been only a single time and a single space flowing in the unique consciousness of the past (see Chapter 5). The recognition by oral historiography (Henige, 1982b) that oral narrative is also a historical discourse and therefore a social project (see Chapter 6) can put an end to the initial anthropological reactions to historical analyses, especially in the light of recent works recognizing the multiplicity of the uses of the social readings of the past. Thus it becomes increasingly difficult to attribute to the mode of transmission (Goody, 1977b), rather than to the sociopolitical structures of production, the imposition of a model, of a classification, of the "authority of the world" (Legendre, 1982). Given that the distinction between orality and writing is above all a question of the sociopolitical field, there is between the two neither a radical separation nor a specificity other than epistemological in nature. Since historicity is an action of a given society applied to itself, the political leadership is identified with this historicity and tries to appropriate it. The critical role of the historian is to expose this deception by bringing into evidence the multidimensionality of the creation of historicity. Beyond the battles and enthronement ceremonies, the multidimensionality of historical production is situated in the struggles of social groups for the management of inequality. Thus it is that political analysis in Africa discovers history (see Chapter 22).

III

The faithful phantom of Africanism can be represented in the two sides of a coin: with the state on one side (the legal symbol) and the nation (Anderson, 1983) on the other. Whether one tries to ignore it, work within it, or adore it, history, whether written or publicly recited, does not escape the state (see Bony and Wondji, 1979; Person,

1980); in fact, the understanding of the past becomes history in its confrontation with constituted political power. Thus contemporary national historiographies in Africa cannot be judged independently of the political phenomenon of the state-nation in its global dimension, and in its fatal separation from local social forces. Since to recount the past is to present the political crises of the present, African national historiography reflects as much the marginalization of civil societies and the atrophy of the political society as the fragility of the state (under the clamor of military exercises), underscoring the importance of its integration in the world system (Wallerstein, 1974). The integration of western epistemology conditions African historiography within the network of one or another aspect of the western university system. For each national historiography these ties are more important than the relations with the historiographies and historical practice of neighboring countries (see Chapters 14, 18, and 21). The unfortunate linguistic division is only the audible side of the capture of the infrastructures of research and of teaching in the former metropolitan powers and of the profound polarization of African intellectuals.

The institutional and methodological reproduction of metropolitan historiography haunts francophone Africa (Kaba, 1974; Iroko, 1977). The historiographies of the anglophone countries (see Chapters 13, 15, 16, and 21) are clearly older and professionally more secure, with their specialized journals and associations. They have the advantage of a North American alternative (see Chapter 12) for pursuing their scholarship, and benefit from the tradition (fragile as it may be, as the Kenyan case proves) of the autonomy of the university and of extramural teaching. The historiographies that are potentially the most innovative, as in the cases of Tanzania and Zaïre (see Chapters 19 and 21), are those for which the integration into the former metropolitan system is weak, the relationship with the local state structures the most direct, and the external influences the most diversified. Older "national" historiographies have adopted the maximum distance relative to power and to the society by placing themselves under the umbrella of metropolitan institutions: Nigeria, Senegal, the Ivory Coast, Kenya. But they are not entirely sheltered from social crisis, as has been recently shown in the case of Kenya and as the appearance of Marxist paradigms in Nigeria, Zambia, and Senegal illustrates.

If the originality and vitality of a historiography are in any way related to the depth of social crisis prevailing at a given time (see Chapter 20), then the recent advances made in the historiographies of

South Africa, Mozambique, or Zimbabwe (Phimister, 1984) should not be so surprising. The South African case (see Chapter 13) illustrates the case of the transfer of a historiography elaborated in the 1970s outside Africa, even though marked with a fundamental reorientation to meet the particular South African context. The imperative of joining the political debate directly, under the threat of otherwise producing a sterile historiography of little significance, means that it is in Mozambique (Gray, 1981; Centro de Estudos Africanos, 1982) and South Africa that the *History Workshop* approach (Pfordresher, 1984) is the most vigorous. This historiography seeks to remain close to the interests and perspectives of the rural people and the urban proletariat rather than to a more specialized university audience; in turn it seems to have found a significant African audience. The internal circulation of seminar papers, and local bulletins, and attempts to establish inexpensive local historical publications with a wide circulation, are signs of the vitality of this school; they seem to be taking seriously the challenge that Africa write its own history.

In order to confront the forms of Africanism that teach us more of western intellectual history and more of western relations with Africa than of African societies themselves, we need in Africa historiographies that are methodologically sound and confident in their value and power. Such approaches can only liberate themselves from Western epistemological orientations if they are fully involved with the larger world and fully take account of social change (Gutkind, 1977). Unfortunately, under present conditions of research and writing in Africa, these can only be national in orientation, perhaps a fatal flaw in achieving the goal set out here. But African historiographies are sorely in need of a climate of true debate, even of overt internal conflicts both within and especially between the various national historiographies; their social relevance depends on it. However, in bringing to their professional activities the range of social commitment that such historiographical development requires, African historians often bring into question even their very physical survival.

Instead, African societies have been included within historical discourse only as mere guardians of "oral archives" at the most, while historical discourse returns to them in the most alienated forms of official "university" history. The rewards from the production of Africanist discourse for Africa must be simultaneously fatal for Africanism and salutary for African historiographies and the peoples of Africa. African societies today, rich in past experience but poor in economic resources, cannot permit themselves the luxury of simple gratuitous historiographical production. Because of its alliance with state structures separated from the true needs and concerns of the people, the historiography of the savants is, in Africa as elsewhere, the dominant form by which the past is described. But such an alliance also requires the creation of myths which pretend to be exclusive truths and portray themselves as capable of overcoming all other means of understanding the past. Although derived from the West in the baggage of anthropological understanding (Fabian, 1983b), Africanism is no longer purely a western form of understanding. It is inseparable from the institutional and material reproduction of the linkages which tie African states (and hence also African societies and economies) to the West; is it possible to propose another form of discourse without touching the very foundations of the fragile legitimacy of the State itself? Lacking the firm basis necessary to maintain a discourse responsible to local needs and demands, there is the risk that the development of such a new form of historical understanding will simply produce new forms of integration to a revived Africanism.

PART I

THE EPISTEMOLOGY OF AFRICAN STUDIES

1

AFRICAN HISTORIANS
AND AFRICANIST HISTORIANS

NDAYWEL È NZIEM

**If, as some would
hold,** African historical awareness should serve as an instrument of
liberation, as a lever of progress, or as a means of action contributing
to development, then consideration of the type of researcher best able
to undertake fieldwork becomes crucial to the practice of African
history (Biobaku, 1959; Ki-Zerbo, 1961; Ndaywel, 1980). Here, no
less than in other fields of knowledge, satisfactory scholarly research
cannot be simply "interesting," contributing exclusively to the intellectual stimulation of a small educated class. What is at stake is
more important than that: If we are to believe the Africans, at least,
African history is being asked to contribute in a concrete manner to
the search for solutions to current questions and for the development
of the social, economic, and political well-being of the population
(Boubou Hama and Ki-Zerbo, 1980).

In the past, the conventional Africanist position was stated directly. As far as research was concerned, it was claimed, it was
dangerous to try to perform the functions of both "beetle" and "en-
tomologist." The second role, the only one accepted as "scientific,"
risked being invalidated by the first. Hence the golden rule was that of
"distance" between the observer and the observed. Africanist historians, it was assumed, had the advantage over their African colleagues of never confusing "mythical time" with "scientific time";[1]
there was no danger that the foreigner would fall prisoner to the
allegorical universe of the griot or of the traditionalist, as the African
was likely to do. Apparently young Africans initiated into the social

sciences could never undertake research similar to that of their teachers nor bring a scientific approach to the study of their own societies of origin or instruct others in such an approach. Africans were incapable of achieving such a level of objective scholarship as long as they insisted on staying in the field.

Once a class of educated Africans had emerged, however, another opinion took shape, taking as its point of departure quite the opposite point of view. It was assumed that there could be no true flowering of African history as long as there were no African historians. The first task that fell to the African historian, according to this point of view, was that of "correcting" what had already been said and written by Africanist historians: to reestablish the truth, to defalsify what had already been done, to point out the mistakes that had been committed (Diop, 1955, 1981). African students thus believed themselves obliged to concentrate on the problems identified by outsiders, to set right these mistakes or to correct these "fundamental errors."

But two such different conceptions, Africanist and African, could not persist for very long without developing a third, more conciliatory approach, and one, in fact, more realistic, emerging from the observation that the supposed barriers separating Africanists from their African colleagues were not so formidable as had been supposed (Moniot, 1970; 1974). Increasingly it came to be realized that specific characteristics applied to the "native" and the "nonnative" could also end up being shared, to some degree. If the distance separating "outsiders" from the object of their studies guaranteed their objectivity, "natives" too often found themselves "outsiders" when approaching an African society; separated from their mental universe of origin, they were no longer capable of grasping the elements of their own heritage by introspection alone. In other cases, the mental distance between nonnatives and African society was blurred and the "outsiders," in spite of their foreign origins, acquired a partisan stance, favorable or unfavorable, that clouded their vision of the object. This was often the case of Africanists so acculturated that they acquired a point of view similar to that of the natives; they unconsciously came to see the society under study as the archetype, the "model" on which their understanding of other societies in the same region was organized.

But ultimately this apparent conjunction of African and Africanist approaches was deceptive. To the African and the Africanist correspond two specific historical discourses, the differences of which are based on the practitioners' different positions with regard to history.

The one adopts a double role as observer and actor; the other assumes uniquely an observer's position. That makes all the difference. The perception of the dimension of actor as well as observer necessarily introduces a globalist point of view to the approach to history. Because Africans seek an improvement in the actor's social and economic conditions, every activity must be evaluated relative to the social goals pursued. From this perspective it is urgent to transcend the academic monograph to arrive at a general and coherent view of the history of the peoples of Africa in order to instruct the present generation and help them to seize the intelligible lines of their evolution.

To be sure, not all research should simply be inserted into a single coherent project of development. But at least we might avoid the situation in which historical research appears to be carried out in an anarchic manner and seek to reduce the conspicuous waste that characterizes it now. Seen from Africa, in fact, recent research seems to have been pursued without any apparent concern for the efficiency with which resources are used. Young American researchers willingly choose to undertake "fieldwork" in Africa that requires considerable logistical support and supplementary effort to learn the local languages and to absorb the local culture, in order better to grasp the unfolding of events reported to them. In Africa, on the other hand, just the opposite preoccupations are apparent: far from concentrating on using their accumulated skills in the local languages and cultures, African researchers seek instead to learn a variety of European languages in order to travel abroad, to go and decode the language of a few archival documents.

Africanist tradition is based on a classical scholarly tradition that utilizes, among other things, the organization of colloquia and seminars as means of action. Particularly in Africanist fields these seminars are held at great expense, given that they are by definition interdisciplinary and of continental, if not global, scope. But has the proliferation of such conferences really contributed to advancing the goals of research? Might not some of these resources have been better used to advance research projects or publications in Africa or to develop programs to encourage greater cooperation between Africanist and African researchers? A glance at the contributions of the major Africanist conferences gives the impression that we are simply repeating ourselves without really advancing the field in any resolute fashion: Conceptual frameworks occupy a larger place there than the search for solutions to the problems at hand. Scholarly progress is without doubt advanced, but for Africa, real and living Africa, there is no resultant increase in productivity. If the choice of an Africanist career requires a minimum of commitment to the African cause— even though such a commitment is clearly no utopia—it must be expected that such a commitment should assume greater importance and that the search for contemporary Africa should become the principal stimulus to research.

Even if historical sources are infinite, as Marc Bloch (1974) has written, they are certainly not all of equal importance. In the division of labor between African and Africanist historians, sources of African origin are best exploited by African historians. The corpus of oral traditions must be established by them and published with the necessary annotations so that they may be equally intelligible to specialists situated abroad who may be drawn to use them. Local archives must also be made the object of systematic exploitation. In addition to the preoccupation with unearthing raw materials, there is a need for greater care in their interpretation and use as a guide to the understanding of local history. It is obvious that this is what historians must strive to achieve now in Africa, where oral traditions have been studied sufficiently in terms of their possibilities and limitations.

The Africanist contribution—especially that found in universities outside Africa—should take on an entirely different role. A rich documentation on African history is still buried in European and American archival depositories, as well as in certain private collections. Even though a few such documents have achieved some circulation, this is often of a very limited scope; certainly they have not sufficiently reached African scholarly milieux. If only to gain access to the existing written documentation on Zaïre, it is necessary to master French and English for recent studies; Flemish is needed to consult certain important works dating from the colonial period. Moreover, to do a complete job Portuguese and Italian are needed to consult the oldest narrative sources relating to the western coast, and an acquaintance with Arabic might be useful in understanding the social and cultural realities of eastern Zaïre, especially during the nineteenth century. Such an accumulation of linguistic competence is practically impossible for one person to achieve, especially for Zaïreans, who must also maintain and even extend their skills in a variety of local languages to assure a continuing contact with the realities of their field of research. One might hope for greater effort on the part of non-Africans to provide properly annotated translations of certain texts and thus to facilitate access to them.

In this context the ethnographic documentation of Zaïre raises a particular problem. Data drawn from oral and ethnographic sources results from two different types of collection. The most recent type is that done by the local people, for the most part undertaken by researchers, usually students preparing doctoral dissertations or master's theses. But there exists another form: the systematic collection of local data by colonial administrators (often in the form of responses to official questionnaires) currently found scattered in a variety of archival depositories in the form of *rapports d'enquêtes*. To evaluate them better, what is called for is a systematic analysis of the complete corpus of these materials, comparing them one to another, and at least in some cases complementing them with oral inquiries of their authors, who are probably still alive, former missionaries and colonial authorities now returned to Europe (Ndaywel, 1976). This work is of great urgency because very few of these people have written of their experiences in the field and their numbers are decreasing every year: "Each time an old man dies a library is lost." In Europe as in Africa this phrase elicits the same response: The maxim is more often repeated than put into practice.

Even in assessing the contacts between Europe and Africa, it is obvious that there is still much to be done. If "colonial history" has been written, "the history of colonization" remains yet to be written along the lines of a new vision, one resolutely attentive to the local peoples for whom colonization constitutes an important aspect of their history. Here, too, a certain number of colonial actors are still alive whose recollections might be recorded and used as relevant items to explain, clarify, or provide greater subtlety to present understanding. Research on colonial biographies is needed, but must not be limited to the histories of the colonial elite; it must include all levels of colonial society regardless of their roles, large or small. In this fashion they can serve as collective witness, eventually faced with the other testimonies based on local autobiographical narratives. The use of "outside" sources, we are coming to realize, has until now been accomplished only in a partial manner.

But the simple accumulation of information of all sorts, gathered from "outside" and from "inside," raises the fundamental problem of the type of approach considered. This question of interpretation leads directly to the choice of writing history. Does there exist any truly African vision of history that has begun to formulate a theoretical framework of its own? There is no doubt whatsoever that there is a place for an African concept of history, which would provide for the reassessment of the facts of African history and world history as seen resolutely from the African perspective. Such a truly "African" history, in its selection and its formulation, can be different, even divergent, from a "European" history of Africa; the emphasis should be placed not on the cult of the difference, but on the free exercise and consequences of different specializations. Similarly, there is an "African" history of Europe and "African" history of America, different from the European history of Europe and America. An African history of Africa provides one history of Africa, just as does a European history of Africa; both serve as components of an eventual comprehensive and unified history of Africa.

But does there exist a truly African history of Africa? Does there exist a new perspective of history to be suggested? This brings us back to a more general consideration of the theoretical sterility, with regard to the practice of the social sciences, on the part of Africans themselves. It is deplorable that they remain dependent on theories essentially of Western origin; they remain "consumers" of ideas developed elsewhere and exporters of the field data needed in European and American universities to establish scholarly syntheses. But at least on the basis of experience in Zaïre, the reality is not as hopeless as some forms of African criticisms would imply. It is a fact that "African studies" is currently going through a period of fundamental reassessment (Schwarz, 1980). The discredit placed until now on anthropology alone has ramifications that apply to the entire range of social sciences, where history, taking the place of a moribund anthropology, now assumes the greatest importance.

But it is curious that even where everyone is pointing a finger at African studies Africans themselves remain quiet. Their silence is astonishing. They are accused of dogmatism, a lack of productivity, of methodologial sterility. But one should not lose sight of the fact that for Africanists, as we have already mentioned, African history is no more than a scholarly discipline, a field of thought, a profession practiced, which allows a social insertion in another context entirely—the European or American university, which in fact has nothing to do with this history itself, or at least is only indirectly involved with it. Africans, however, live in an entirely different situation. For them African history is not just a research and teaching field. In Africa, historians who study African history live it too, and they have to put up with the consequences and the setbacks of history, in the most intimate and personal manner. That makes all the difference. Africanists can change their field: If unsatisfied with Zaïre, they can try to become specialists on Senegal or Sierra Leone. They can even retool themselves and immerse themselves in another reality entirely: China, Canada, India. African historians, however, do not have the chance of such mobility. Even were they to become specialists on India or China, they still, in spite of everything else, would experience African history no less. That is the principal characteristic of African historians. They do not engage in a cult of theory. Instead, by their very proximity to the "empirical field," they tend to maintain a sense of proportion, refusing to treat theory as an endeavor of pure erudition not clearly tied to the problems of praxis. The problems Africans perceive as being "true" problems often are different from what Africanist scholars inform them are the "true" problems. The oustanding example of this is the interest Pharaonic Egypt holds for African historians. This is clearly a line of research that must be accounted for in Africa. But it is clear that this approach appears almost inexplicable in the eyes of Africanists. Criticisms arise from every direction to pass judgment on the possibility and the validity of such an approach. Even the most accommodating Africanist opinion concludes that this is nothing more than a "surrealist" digression, a means of avoiding the true problems of African history (Vellut, 1980; Jewsiewicki, 1979b). In fact, despite the polemics surrounding the issue, this preoccupation with Pharaonic Egypt is a fundamental part of African history. We cannot pretend to construct contemporary African societies from nothing. It is necessary to assure African historical studies a solid cultural foundation on the basis of the treasures brought back from the past of what was unquestionably a part of Africa. Ancient Egypt must play the same role in the rethinking and renewal of African culture that ancient Greece and Rome served for western culture.

Providing a bridge between purely African interpretations and Africanist interpretations obviously presupposes the recognition of the difference of these two fields of interpretation, resulting from the fact that the two perspectives are not completely congruent. Africanist perceptions, even though providing the necessary context for the emergence of more a specific African point of view, tend not to notice this new reality. But to the degree that a certain interest for the African cause exists at the heart of the Africanist endeavor, Africanist practitioners should be willing to aid this new discourse by maintaining a steadfast respect for its originality. To the degree that the specifics of such a program would be recognized clearly, the complementarity between the two approaches would be perceived in its greatest dimension and in all its implications, including the most idealist. In fact, if the fundamental goal of research is indeed not simply to take pleasure in itself but to attempt to bring solutions to life's problems, why would this not serve as the object of a coherent planning program, prescribing a role to each one of its component parts, and seeking the greatest efficiency and benefit? There is therefore a place for "African studies" undertaken in Europe and America, not only because African history constitutes a universal patrimony and forms a part of world history, but also because doing this in itself provides valuable and concrete support for historians and African historical actors.

NOTE

1. Contrary to this assertion, Boubou Hama and Ki-Zerbo (1980: 72-77) maintain that "African time is historical time." For a discussion of this, see Vansina (1978a: 18-22).

2

KNOWLEDGE AND PERCEPTIONS OF THE AFRICAN PAST

JAN VANSINA

Historical knowledge is always an interpretation of "traces" of the past, used as evidence relative to the question being investigated. The quality of the historical interpretation and its communication depends on three factors: the amount of evidence considered compared to all existing evidence; the rigor with which the rules of logical historical critique are applied; and the reader's understanding of the logical and "psychological" probability of the proposed interpretation—whether the proposed reconstruction appears "reasonable"—and in the final analysis this last factor is evaluated by one's general vision of the world.

THE HISTORICAL KNOWLEDGE OF AFRICA

These factors are critical components of all historical knowledge. The vision of Africa projected by the historians is therefore crucial in judging the "reasonableness" of the historical interpretation. But until recently the great majority of these historians were not Africans; they did not belong to the societies whose history they described, an unusual situation when compared with earlier historical practices. Modern historical method developed in Europe within a situation where the historian was a part of the society described. As written African history has emerged primarily outside of the continent, European thought has appropriated outside material and has justified this practice by reference to the universal validity of scientific thought, including that of historical critique as a form of logic. Africans with European-derived university training have accepted the European conception and techniques of historical investigation as a means of establishing an acceptable level of probability for their reconstructions, even when they question some specific European conceptions of Africa.

In other disciplines that relate to the past, such as geology, this attitude may be valid, but not in history. The object of study creates a fundamental difference between these two types of study; a schist is everywhere a schist, but human beings as objects of historical inquiry are both similar to those studying them and different, because human nature presupposes culture and this varies from community to community and from period to period. Furthermore, because in historical studies both subject and object are human beings, the researcher is engaged both emotionally and intellectually; this leads to a justification for taking stands on contemporary and practical issues. Therefore, it is important to be aware of the underlying perceptions of historical works in order to be able to distinguish between data and interpretation, and from that to be able to propose truly new interpretations.

I hope to show how a critique of these unexpressed axioms can be pursued and can open the way to new interpretations closer to the reality of the past and therefore lead to the development of new perceptions. This is necessary to the historian because history cannot be studied without vision, without stereotypes, without a global image. Becoming aware of our subjectivities is the way toward greater objectivity and the critique of perceptions of the past must provoke it, even though absolute objectivity or a total rejection of all a priori cognitive perceptions can never be attained.

Yesterday's Knowledge, Today's Knowledge

Our present perceptions of Africa and our understanding of its past are conditioned by the epistemological categories well established by 1900, and in large part derived from the observations of administrators, missionaries, and various travelers. Their perceptions were translated directly, uncritically, into their conclusions, and, once published, these have often been accepted as fact, as if they were similar to incontrovertible experimental observations on the structures of crystals.

The case of the Fang of Gabon and Cameroon is typical. From 1842, outside observers reported that a Fang migration toward the

estuary of the Gabon River and toward the coast was in process.
Wilson (1856: 302-303), one of those who reported it, portrayed a
stereotypical image of the Fang mobile hunter: noble, handsome,
virile, military in bearing, cannibalistic, egalitarian ("they have no
slaves"), iron-working, using a form of metallic money, and, probably,
he added, descendants of the Jaga, who in turn were considered
responsible for nearly destroying the Kingdom of the Kongo. Du
Chaillu (1863) built on this image and assured its wide diffusion
through his popular writings. All subsequent travelers took up the
theme of the noble warrior, the predator-cannibal in migration. In
1898, Father Trilles proposed the first hypothesis of Fang migration.
According to this the Fang had been driven from the savannahs of
Cameroon and the Central African Republic about one and one-half
centuries earlier; they penetrated into the forest areas, guided by
pygmy groups. It was clear, argued Trilles, that the Fang were not
truly adapted to life in the forest, and their language and physique
attested to their more "civilized" origins as savannah peoples.

His hypothesis became the basic paradigm for understanding Fang
history and was taken up by the authors who followed, particularly by
Avelot (1905), who incorporated it into his general view of Gabonese
migrations. The most notable work on Fang ethnography, that of
Tessman (1913), accepted the conclusions first proposed by Avelot
and Trilles; thereafter there were only embellishments on the general
paradigm. In the end the entire group to which the Fang belong was
incorporated into the same large migratory process, which became
the accepted historical paradigm both in Fang country from at
least 1948 and in academe, where Alexandre (1965) published the
"final" version, now qualified as a "provisional synthesis." This
"orthodox" version quickly found its way into the manuals of the area
(Deschamps, 1970: I, 363; II, 209-214; Birmingham, 1976: 259) and
subsequently Gabonese and Cameroonian authors accepted the
views of Avelot and of Trilles without diverging in the least detail from
the opinion of their European colleagues (Bekombo Priso, 1981: 585-
586). Fernandez (1982: 29-48, 51) is the most recent to take up this
version, despite the fact that he himself discusses the development of
the literary image of the Fang. But from 1978 Chamberlin had already
begun to remark on the factitious elements in this explanation of Fang
history, noting that there are no internal data affirming a Fang migration from the savannah area, no migration before the nineteenth
century, no tie with the migrations of other people of the larger
linguistic group to which the Fang belong. And his revision clearly

conforms more closely to the data than the earlier hypotheses (Chamberlin, 1978).

The image sketched out by Trilles has nonetheless held pride of place in the field for eighty years and will undoubtedly not disappear overnight. The more fluid and more general portrayal proposed by Wilson derives from much older perceptions developed in Europe prior to 1600 and applied to the forest areas (Miller, 1973). It is only with Metegue N'nah (1979) that the nineteenth-century image of the "savage warrior," with all its associated traits, begins to be brought into question. This illustrates the tenacity of a plausible perception-become-axiom, where the "plausibility" conforms to received images (such as the Jaga) on a larger scale, and in part conforms to the facts (such as the real Fang migration after about 1840). In such a case presuppositions prevail over any subsequent examination of the data.

The relationship of one written report to others is a point of some controversy today. But perhaps this phenomenon is less well understood when it is a question of the relationship among intellectual models, not of straightforward specific affirmations. No historian yet has systematically examined the relation of the ethnographic questionnaires and their by-product, the ethnographic monograph. Such questionnaires were utilized by all colonial powers and the ethnographic descriptions of the day betray such a relation by their organization, the divisions and phraseology retained, and their successive development. The proliferation of questionnaires was partly stimulated by practical objectives: for jurisprudence, administrative needs, and general information. But the paradigm developed for these objectives has been carried over to scholarly studies, with different objectives and methods. The interdependence of questionnaires and scholarly schools is clear, as are the influences of specific models going from one discipline to another. A basic historical form such as "the trade and politics of the X," which was so common before 1975, for example, easily betrays its dependence on the assumptions, perceptions, and anthropological models of the earlier period. The works thus produced are neither "wrong" nor useless; their data are often valuable and their specific interpretations often interesting. But they also often convey prejudice, set purpose, and specific objectives; the underlying intellectual paradigms are often predetermined.

Knowledge and the Outsider

The unknown misleads us just as the exotic charms us. The outsider remains incomprehensible because foreign to our experience.

What cannot be tied to something known cannot be understood. Therefore the unknown must be assimilated, for better or for worse, to a series of preconceived images and concepts in the collective memory. And often one "assimilates" through oppositions. An example of this is shown in the European idea of the tropical forest. From a superficial similarity—"forest"—this idea developed by opposition to known experience and by about 1900 the legend of this milieu was already in place. This was a uniform environment throughout: monotonous, terrifying, implacable, wildly prolific and fertile, impenetrable, murderous, and somber as night.

The typical inhabitants of this milieu were the pygmies, fascinating beings on the very edge of humanity: Unchanged from the time of the Pharaohs, living fossils, they were defined either by their stature (representing the "infancy of humanity") or as humans who had degenerated within the forest environment. These happy but lazy pygmies harvested the gifts of nature just as they were seen to do in the Greek mosaics of North Africa; they found their way guided by miraculous senses not given to "normal" people; they traveled through "impassable" regions, as monkeys leaping from branch to branch or by swinging from vines.[1] In their egalitarian society, the pygmies were anarchic, nomadic, and quarrelsome. They had no history because they obviously had achieved no "progress" from the beginning of humanity.

Other forest peoples shared more or less similar types of characterization. Mountmorres write of one group: "natives who, like all the forest peoples, are of a backward and feeble race, easily driven out by more intelligent and resistant peoples" (Montmorres, 1906: 36). They too were nomads and anarchic peoples, egalitarian, ignorant of any groups more complex than the family, isolated deep in the forest, but unlike the pygmies they were not masters of their environment, they were only mediocre agriculturalists, continually losing the struggle with the invading forest. They were not morally innocent like the pygmies, but cruel, vicious, cannibalistic, and superstitious. They too were without history, or almost: Instead of being autochthonous "pure" forest peoples or invading conquerors like the Fang, they were degenerate, driven into the forest because of their weaknesses. Everything in these portrayals is false and almost everything is the opposite of familiar situations known and understood by Europeans: an open ecology "humanized" by the labor of men and women; a complex society with its exchange of goods, ideas, and people; a man attached to his land, the rough but simple peasant. The qualities portrayed are the opposites of such European moral classifications as stability, constancy, work, submission, inventiveness, and civilization (especially reflected in urbanization).

Little by little this popular perception of the ecosystem of the forest was corrected by botanical studies, and clichés of the "virgin forest" type have nearly disappeared from academic writings.[2] Nonetheless, the stereotypes concerning the people of the forest remain alive. The pygmies are still "the roots of human culture" and because of this they attract the attention of scholars as well as that of young adventurers (Plisnier-Ladame, 1970; Liniger-Goumas, 1968; Francesci, 1977). We have not yet understood the real complexity of these inegalitarian societies, nor the privileged role of specialized technological knowledge among the inhabitants who knew how to exploit their environment in a consummate fashion. Except for the true forest kingdoms, or the towns and trade along the great rivers, the past of the peoples of the forest has hardly been studied. The perceptions of this "world without a past" have discouraged those historians working in forest areas who extricate themselves only with difficulty from their preconceived notions and often simply continue with atemporal descriptions of the "ethnographic present" or with studies of external relations such as migration or the slave trade. The strength of the paradigm created in Europe prevents them from reexamining the entire question from a fresh perspective.

Useful Knowledge

With only a few rare exceptions, missionaries and administrators preceded the scholars into the field and thus established the foundations for our vision of Africa. But missionaries and administrators pursue their own well-defined objectives and their perceptions are often molded by such objectives. Thus around 1950 a district commissioner in Kasai carried out an inquiry on the existence of a former Kuba national council, and subsequently convened the territorial chiefs and the king once a year at the capital. Although no consultative council of this type formerly existed, he may well have sought to create such a past to facilitate his administration of the Kuba. The "tradition"—based on his own inquiry—was a justification for this action. I would not be surprised if today, after thirty years, many Kuba were persuaded that there had been a council of chiefs in the precolonial period.

For the same reasons, the administration sought the former structures on which to build the colonial order. From the beginning the legal fiction was that of maintaining the local institutions even while abolishing the customs considered "contrary to public order": no more cannibalism, poison oracle, slave trade, slavery, pawning persons, forming a clientele by the gift of women, multiple marriage forms, such as by simulated kidnapping and so on.[3] The administrator thought of "chiefdoms" as administrative units. But the case of noncentralized societies, at least in Belgian and British Africa, required the construction of a hierarchy of command and its justification. Referring to sociological theories on the role of the family—as developed by the first anthropologists from about 1868, based on then-current juridical theories dealing with natural law—the administrator turned to the "lineage" model. Africans, as perpetual "children," lived in families. The head of the family, the father or maternal uncle, commands, and the eldest, in terms of primogeniture, is the patriarch. Only bloodlines are valid legitimation of authority. The anarchic society is therefore composed of lineages, each encapsulated within another following a master genealogy that forms the constitutive framework (Vansina, 1980).

For the Congo Free State the principal theoretician was de Calonne Beaufaict, an engineer familiar with the theories of Durkheim. The result of his research on the Boa was elevated to the status of a principle and was found in administrative circulars, in questionnaires, and subsequent elaborations of *droit coutumier*. In the north of the country the administrative personnel were fully expected to identify the structure of segmentary lineages if they hoped to advance their careers. Belgian rule then constructed lineage societies. By suppressing all sovereignty, all inequality, and all rights based on residence, the Belgians transformed noncentralized societies into segmentary lineage systems. Thus when the anthropologists of the 1950s came into the field, they "discovered" segmentary lineage systems there (Wolfe, 1961; de Heusch, 1954; see also Meillassoux, 1964, for another society "created" by colonial authorities).

This phenomenon affected the construction of all colonial societies. Rwanda and Burundi were transformed into "feudal societies" by the will of the German and Belgian administrators. The work carried out by the first residents, especially Kandt in Rwanda, was of considerable importance in this regard. The kingdom was unified and bureaucraticized, and relationships of clientship were conserved and ossified, to provide the framework of the bureaucracy necessary to modern administration. In Burundi these processes occurred more slowly, but the Belgians tried to copy the Rwandan model after 1916 and succeeded up to a certain point (Chrétien, 1982b; Kandt, 1905).

The work of jurists is often underestimated in this field; they were responsible for codifying "traditional law," using the axioms of their own legal systems (the Napoleonic code or British juridical principles, as the case may be) as their points of departure, providing the essential juridical assumptions. The legal institution of marriage, for example, could consist of only a single form. Other forms must be considered either as illegal concubinage or as "trial marriages." On this particular point the missionaries, mindful of canon law, could only agree. Even such admirable work as that of Hulstaert on Nkundo marriage (1937) recognized only a single form of valid marriage, although describing five or six forms of "matrimonial unions." Obviously, in the long term juridical precepts were reflected in our rulings and these became the norm; in this way bridewealth marriage became the only form that survived among the Nkundo. Once again the model became reality.

In the religious sphere it was the needs of the missionaries, especially their desire to base their message on a single "natural" traditional religion, that created misunderstandings of this type. The case of *Imaana* in Rwanda is typical. Formerly, this concept was tied to the context of divining, and was related to concepts of fate, fortune, or luck. After some hesitation the Catholic missionaries accepted it as meaning "God" and this notion became current and exclusive in Rwanda with Christianization. The proliferation of personal names with reference to the concept of Imaana can be traced to this process until even such a knowledgeable specialist as Kagame came to deny the existence of any other meaning of the term, even in the past (d'Hertefelt and Coupez, 1964: 420, 460-461; contra Pauwels, 1958; Kagame, 1956). Once again, the model had become the reality.

In practice, a critique will always verify if a projected image serves the purposes of those who propose it. If so, then it must be asked if this vision in fact truly guided or legitimized colonial activities, and to what degree this image corresponds to (or contradicts) earlier local realities. The argument that the people involved now assert that the custom was always thus is of no value, at least not without confirmation from concrete cases; normative declarations ("the rule was that . . .") long ago aligned themselves with the practices of colonial societies.

Knowledge and the Conception of the World

A vision of the world cannot simply be reduced to a justification for a program of action. It goes far beyond that, because intellectual paradigms tend to be integrated to other forms of knowledge to form a coherent conception of the world and of "true" reality beyond simple appearances. Every vision of Africa ties itself to larger visions of the world, or at least of the society (real or utopian) that the observers perceive as their own. Thus there is nothing surprising in the fact that in 1866 Holden thought that the "Kaffir" race had emigrated out of "the great center of human life" between the Tigris and Euphrates at the time of the Tower of Babel (Holden, 1866). Bantu migrations thus were made part of the larger migration schema that included all of humanity and were thus brought into line with the teachings of the Bible as understood at the time. This provides an exact parallel with the migration traditions of the Fang, Komo, or Kuba, all of which postulate a single point of departure, the presumed cradle of humanity (Chamberlin, 1977; de Mahieu, 1975; Vansina, 1978).

The fundamental vision of reality is as powerful today as in the past, and, at least as far as Africa is concerned, the images are embedded in the European traditions. Democratic nationalists underscore the institutions of collective decision making and overestimate the earlier sentiments of nationality. Structuralists, convinced that all reality is always hidden, find symbols everywhere. Materialists create a *deus ex machina* from technologies. Marxists find strata or classes in dialectical conflict. The important question, of course, is not who is right and who is wrong, but simply whether or not an author's particular approach has led the interpretation astray in one way or another beyond what the data will support. That is for the critic to verify. Once the elements of the fundamental vision of the author are known, either by the author's own declaration or, more frequently, by deducing these elements from an examination of the social and cultural milieu from which the author derives, the critic can proceed to the reconstruction obtained from these data. If the correspondence is too perfect the critic will be uneasy.

Thus Brausch, a former Belgian administrator, portrays the Nkutshu society of Kasai (Belgian Congo) in terms of the development of specialist corporations that allow for inequality and a democratic form of government, because certain corporations performed "ruling" functions (Brausch, 1945, 1953). Where does this conception come from? Brausch cites Durkheim, but he is the only person to have interpreted Durkheim in this manner. His work was intended to be both a scholarly work (leading to a doctorate in anthropology) and an investigation with a practical purpose (the administration of the region within colonial structures). From the beginning there is the troubling term "corporatism," which carries a certain fascist odor, rather than the term "association," which was in current use at the time (1940s). But the fascist path leads nowhere. First the author stresses the democratic characters of this society. Then he explains that the term is derived from the Anglophone sociological vocabulary of the period; "corporatism," in his eyes, is simply a more "learned" term than "association" and more correct than "secret society." We need to look elsewhere for Brausch's model.

Brausch defended his thesis at the Université Libre de Bruxelles and later was part of the cabinet of the first Liberal minister of colonies, G. Buisseret. There is no doubt that Brausch was a Liberal (that is, of conservative political tendencies). His image of inegalitarian democracy based on association in a type of free "social market" accords very well with the ideals of this party. But there remain other influences. Brausch's views existed in embryo before him. His predecessor, L. Liégeois, who was also his superior, had already offered analogous propositions from 1936 (Liégeois, 1941). Brausch altered Liégeois's "associations" to "corporations" and extended this concept in a systematic manner to all levels of Nkutshu society, in a manner similar to that in which others had earlier used the concept of kinship. The comparison between the two authors demonstrates that Brausch's Liberal emphasis comes from Liégeois.

Finally, how does one judge how close this perception approximates Nkutshu reality at that time? The corpus of documents dealing with the Nkutshu, written by different persons at different times and with different perspectives of the world (but not including any Nkutshu), indicates that the raw data are probably reliable, that generalizations without raw data are not reliable, that the democratic aspects of the process are overemphasized, and that neither the negation of fundamental inequalities nor the systematization of the entire society as simply a collection of corporations is valid. This example illustrates the ties that exist between the views on a given subject and the social and cultural background of the author who offers them. The critic must take account of such broader elements in his analysis just as the observer, to understand fully the photograph of a detail of a larger scene, must have an idea of the larger scene as a whole.

Knowledge as the Derivative of Time

Obviously, the principles of interpretation of the African past and the images of this continent have varied over time. But often these changes in perception result less from the accumulation of new data or new analytic techniques than from social changes within European societies. The changing interpretations on the Bantu expansion provide an example of this (for an extended consideration, see Vansina, 1980). Around 1850 W. Bleek coined the term "Bantu" and postulated that all the Bantu languages derived from a single "Protobantu" language of a single community of origin and a single geographical region, exactly as had happened for the Indo-European language groups. Because language, race, and culture were indissoluble concepts at this period, it followed that a point of origin needed to be identified and the migrations traced from there to cover eventually the entire expanse where Bantu languages were spoken.

The first speculations were based on Biblical interpretations. We have already cited Holden's opinion; others referred to the descendants of Ismail or of Kush, the son of Ham, thus giving rise to the Hamitic myth that justified the inferiority of certain "races." For all, the Middle East was the ultimate cradle; for the majority the Valley of the Nile was the route by which these Protobantu arrived in the region of the Great Lakes, where their dispersion began. These points of view remained dominant until around 1920; a Sumerian hypothesis survived into the 1930s.

The common thread from ancient Egypt was proposed by Homburger, who was herself following in an earlier current: the tendency to tie anything relating to Africa ultimately to Egyptian origins. This hypothesis, elaborated especially from 1912, still finds some defenders today among the early West African nationalists such as Sheikh Anta Diop and T. Obenga, both following a straight line of intellectual filiation from Blyden (Obenga, 1978). These theories, dominant before 1920, generally assumed racial superiority—Hamitic compared to Paleonigritic—to explain the success of the diffusion of the languages and a conquest by the immigrants. Between 1920 and 1940, however, Meinhof, a meticulous linguist whose work proved the unity of the Bantu languages (for which he reconstructed an ancestral grammar), developed more precise views: The Bantu were a *Herrenvolk,* united under a genial *Führer* who established a *Reich* by subjugating the aborigines. The imperialist racism of the beginning of the century had become fascism.

From 1920 most speculations of this sort were blocked by the work of Johnston, a former British consul who had been obsessed by this question from the 1880s and produced his conclusions in two volumes in 1919-1920. Johnston stuck by a conquest theory but rejected a tie-in between language and race from 1903, only to argue from 1911 that a part of the Protobantu must have been Caucasian, of Caucasian race and from Caucasia. The tiny proportion of white blood in their veins and their knowledge of iron-working (for arms) assured them of superiority over all other autochthones. Thus it was that right up until World War II and beyond, the colonialist view, a profoundly racist view of Bantu migrations, endured even in the heart of a discipline as exacting as linguistics. The occasional discordant voice was heard but found no echo in the general discipline. Even when Greenberg proved in 1949 that the Bantu homeland was in the Cameroon-Nigerian border region, there was only negative response, and little enough of that, because the question was no longer of any interest to linguists or to others. It was only with decolonization that the speculations were revived.

The first new theory was that of Murdock, who tried to place the migrations in a more general explanation of cultural history dealing with all of Africa. According to this presentation, the Bantu speakers underwent a population expansion due to agricultural innovations, and consequently had to disperse; they moved into the forest areas because they finally had developed a technology appropriate to this hostile environment. By stressing the role of ecological and biological processes on the one hand and that of technological know-how on the other, Murdock's work thus incorporated two of the fundamental bases of postwar western explanatory frameworks; the proliferation of hypotheses to follow generally reflected these premises. Gradually the stress on conquest, and hence the importance of superior arms, was abandoned and historians came to refer simply to Bantu expansion, making this expansion analagous to that of a bacillus in a favorable milieu. Even the revolution in linguistic approaches after 1973 changed nothing. With the principal role now falling to technological factors, the importance of archaeological data has grown continually, today even taking priority over linguistic documentation itself, despite the truism that ultimately the Bantu community can be defined only linguistically. But the archaeologists still accept Murdock's fundamental explanatory framework.

This overview shows that in fact only three visions have dominated research for more than a century: the Biblical vision, the racist/

colonialist vision, and the biological/technological vision. All are tied to the dominant tendencies of western thought, which went through their most important rupture not after 1914, as might have been thought, but around the period 1940-1945, although the new ideas were not applied to Africa in any systematic way before decolonization. A study of the major tendencies of African historiography will lead to the same conclusions, although they would be tied more narrowly to changes in political status and economic conditions. In large part, changes external to Africa or affecting the entire world explain changes in the point of view of the researchers working within the continent. It is precisely because the fundamental visions change with the times, affecting the interpretations of all—sometimes entirely—that critics must carefully account for the dates of writing and of publication, to examine each study in its temporal field, exactly as they must localize the epicenters where these views are elaborated—European epicenters until 1945 and American after that date, at least until about 1970.

CONCLUSION

Reflection on these particular themes has led me to touch on several attributes of all knowledge in the social sciences: the use of stereotypes, fundamental images, underlying assumptions, and un-proven prejudices. The object is not to deny all value to the more detailed analyses that are an essential part of the historian's craft; it is simply to note that the visions of Africa often derive from Europe and come still predominantly from the Western world. Our perception of the African past has always been a European perception, whether for Europeans or Africans or others, because we have all been trained in the same school of European tradition. Thus there truly exists an alienation, an expropriation of African material relative to the very African societies from which this material derives.

The object of this chapter, however, is more positive. How do we identify these perceptions, these distortions in interpretation? In each section I have tried to indicate how a critique must be applied to gauge the role of the elements foreign to the raw data. In applying such a critique it may be necessary to refer to the entire corpus of work accumulated over a century or more. The rules of the historical method are logical and systematic. They permit one to apply them even though they themselves in their own application are products of the same intellectual processes and hence the same sort of "distortions" that they attempt to uncover in others. The rules of critique should be applied automatically, for each question, each assertion, each document. The results are well worth the effort, because it is only by this route that one can account for the epistemology surrounding the subject. It is thus that knowledge renews itself and that historical understanding advances, to the degree that the role of unfounded opinion is diminished bit by bit. It is thus also that more mature reflection can finally lead this history toward its natural public, that of which the ancestors were actors in the play narrated. Obviously the visions of the past will remain subjective even in the future, but the subjectivity itself can become more likely to the mind of the reader.

NOTES

1. Trilles's (1932) work is for the most part fiction; see Piskaty (1957). Among others see Mountmorres (1906) for a description of pygmies in trees, speaking the "language" of the monkeys; on that basis he claimed he did not know if they were in fact humans or chimpanzees. His description likely derives in large part from what he had picked up during his trip through the Ituri forest to observe the most "primitive" pygmies one might meet. His narrative is simply a summary of the gossip of the day, drawn from both Europeans and African agriculturalists.

2. They continue to persist in the popular press and in literary presentations, however: See the Atlas du Cameroun, du Gabon, du Congo. For a less exotic view, and for new myths of an ecologist type, see White (1983).

3. Mountmorres (1906: 79-81) gives the text of a circular from the colonial administrative headquarters at Boma, dated April 17, 1904, dealing with chiefdoms. Almost all is relevant here, text and commentary. Such phrases as "as long as the customs are not contrary to the demands of public order" and "if they [the 'customs'] were to go against our ideas of humanity and of the civilizing mission of the [colonial] state" abound.

3

EPISTEMOLOGICAL ETHNOCENTRISM IN AFRICAN STUDIES

WYATT MacGAFFEY

The institutions of European society (religion, education, government, law, economy, family—the list is simply that of the typical buildings of a European town) provide the categories of Western (or European) social science and the vocabulary of its chronic debates. But when they apply these categories to African (or other) societies, scholars discover that they do not fit. The expected church, town hall, and market are missing, so the response of scholars has been to declare such societies institutionally undifferentiated or "primitive."

> Our very vocabulary of functions in the West—"economic," "political," etc.—necessarily reflects the particular Western institutional clusterings of structure and function. It is not so much that our political institutions are unifunctionally political as it is that the meaning we give to the term "political" in our folk usage is one that reflects what certain of our institutions do [Kopytoff, 1979: 65].

Because observation shows that institutions in other societies are in fact differentiated to some extent, although not according to the functional distribution characteristic of Western society, adherents of evolutionary theory have declared them to be in the process of dif-

Author's Note: This chapter is a much altered and abbreviated version of W. MacGaffey, "African Ideology and Belief: A Survey," *African Studies Review,* Vol. 24, Nos. 2-3, pp. 227-274. Used by permission.

ferentiation and of modernization; that is, of increasing conformity to the European model. Thus anthropologists have been on the lookout for the emergence of true religion, the state, and the market, and political scientists expect that recognizable political parties and nationalism will replace religious movements.

The derogatory assessment of religion and belief implicit in the evolutionary assumption in modern thought originates with Francis Bacon. It is a function of scientism or the myth of the scientific method. The common counterattack—namely, that there are in culture and human experience truths inaccessible to science—takes scientism too seriously and commits us to the perpetuation of a debate that is at once futile and fundamental to the structure of modern European ideology.[1] Furthermore, it has shaped the study of religion in general, including African religion. One aspect of the evolution of industrial capitalism since the seventeenth century, that known as secularization, has had the effect of setting religion apart and contrasting it with politics, economics, and other institutions such as art. The effect has been to create a unique and pejorative sense of what constitutes religion (Dumont, 1971).

Thus we call other cultures into question, although we excuse our own, a situation that Africans today much resent. Another possibility is that we distort the field of data under examination by excluding our own beliefs. As Pouillon (1979: 43) puts it:

> The believer does not believe himself to be such; it is the unbeliever who believes that the believer believes in the existence of God. . . . There is even a tendency to suppose that the extent and significance of the supernatural world are much more important for "primitives" than for "moderns."

Religion has become an affliction that *other* people have, a bizarre form of discourse for which, as Lévi-Strauss (1963: 103) points out, only bizarre explanations come to hand:

> The humane sciences can only work effectively with ideas that are clear, or which they try to make so. If it is maintained that religion constitutes an autonomous order, requiring a special kind of investigation, it has to be removed from the common fate of objects of science. Religion having thus been defined by contrast, it will inevitably appear, in the eyes of science, to be distinguished as no more than a sphere of confused ideas.

To define religion by belief in spiritual beings, as Tylor (1871: chap. 1) did, is simply to identify it with a particular complex of thought that modern positivism has consciously rejected. Since Durkheim (1915), there has been a recognition of the inadequacies for universal use of a definition thus arrived at through the back door. Reviewing such definitions, Goody (1961: 17) nevertheless decided that the Tylorian definition was the best available: "Religious beliefs are present when non-human agencies are propitiated on the human model."

Several students of African religion have expressed dissatisfaction with Goody's deliberately ethnocentric solution to the definitional problem. Douglas (1966: 28), for instance, has noted, "We shall not expect to understand religion if we confine ourselves to considering belief in spiritual beings, however the formula may be refined. . . . Rather than stopping to chop definitions, we should try to compare people's view about man's destiny and place in the universe." Eickelman (1976: 195), writing on Moroccan Islam, cites Runciman (1970: 61) as follows:

> Whatever else religion might entail, it is a set of beliefs, more often implicit than explicit, that are understood by members of a society against the background of tacit, shared assumptions about the nature and conduct of everyday life. Religious ideologies may not be entirely derivative from these commonsense assumptions, especially in the case of such "universal" religions as Islam and Christianity, but they are necessarily understood in their context.

It is not necessary to suppose that all members of a society agree on their positive statements about the universe; typically, they agree most on what to disagree about, structuring their discourse as a system of differences. As Durkheim wrote (1915: 232):

> Even the most elementary mythological constructions are secondary products which cover over a system of beliefs, at once simpler and more obscure, vaguer and more essential, which form the solid foundations upon which the religious systems are built.

It is upon such vague but essential preconceptions that all social action and all model building depends. All knowledge requires a metaphysical point of departure, given that it is selective and the principles of selection are logically prior to it (Pouillon, 1978: 11). It is therefore the case not only that cosmologies need not be excluded from the study of religion because they are true, but that any institutionalized cosmology is "true" because it effectively guides action and creates experience in the society to which it belongs. Dumont concludes (1971: 33):

> What ought to be compared is not religion but the general configuration of values, which in all cases but one is coterminous with religion. I mean that the widest framework for comparison is afforded by this configuration, and that within it the modern example, with its relative downgrading and segregation of religion, can be seen as a particular, if exceptional, case.

THE TRANSLATION OF CULTURE

Van Binsbergen (1977: 107), in an essay on the Lumpa rising in Zambia, uses the term "cultural superstructure" to refer to the general configuration of values. This approach presents two difficulties, one having to do with the identity of the superstructural phenomenon and the other with the perspective from which it is described. A common objection to van Binsbergen's approach is that it confounds religion and culture. To know how to respond to this objection one would have to know what was meant by "culture," a notoriously elusive concept, but beyond this the point of the objection seems to be that we need to set apart a discrete type of activity as "religious." Curiously enough, the segregation of politics and economics from culture seems to be taken for granted. As we have seen, however, religion, politics, and economy, inescapable though they may be, are folk categories only awkwardly applicable to non-European societies. To be applicable at all they must refer to analytically distinguishable aspects of social action, not discrete activities. Thus any social action or institution is, to some degree, simultaneously religious, political, and economic. In practice, social scientists select data for their accessibility, richness, or salience with respect to a theoretically defined issue.

The second difficulty is the question of perspective. Fernandez (1978: 214), noting van Binsbergen's astute reconciliation of idealist and materialist values, expresses reservations nonetheless:

> It is entirely possible that conceptualizations which are ingrained in a Western intellectual tradition may not capture [the imaginations of

the peoples who are the subjects of study]. In particular, the Western
penchant for slicing life up into society and culture, infrastructure and
superstructure, could appear quite obtuse or arbitrary.

Fernandez assumes that the anthropologist or other scholar concep-
tualizing African life should try to do so in terms that coincide with the
self-representation of the people studied; yet the use of such European categories as society, culture, ideology, or belief seems to render
the task impossible. This tension between insider and outsider points
of view is one that Harris (1978: 1) mentions as especially problematic
for studies of religion. Is the translation of culture feasible? Can the
representations of human experience that satisfy members of one
society be rendered acceptable to members of another?

Despite the considerable efforts of philosophers, theologians, and
anthropologists, no clear theoretical answers to these questions exist.
Much of the difficulty here lies in the sense given to "translation." We
focus our attention mostly on accurate representation of the significance, to indigenous users, of linguistic expressions, kinship relations, symbols, religious values, and the like, and pay little heed to the
fact that the grounds for selecting which representations to translate,
and the questions to which the translations then serve as answers, are
usually alien to the original context of use.

All this is familiar material, as is the inevitably ensuing debate
about relativism. It does not follow, however, from the cultural em-
beddedness of a representation, and thus its untranslatability, that it is
false. On this Mannheim (1936: 80) remarked long ago that although
human thought is rooted in a definite social milieu, "we need not
regard it as a source of error that all thought is so rooted." Thought
should be judged according to criteria appropriate to it in the context
of its use, including those that relate to its moral and political functions and consequences, and the demands of theory (see also Lukes,
1973).[2]

Nugent (1982: 524), commenting on the way "facts" seem to come
and go depending on the theory applied to them, says that each
paradigm is a manifestation of group consciousness. The relativism to
which this observation apparently commits us, he says, is a function
of the isolation of academics both from the people they study and from
their own real lives in the society that supports them. Here he seems
to exaggerate; although we may deplore a particular political stance,
we usually do so in order to promote another, and it is precisely the

political context of social science that gives it its value, or at least earns it its keep. But Nugent (1982: 526) correctly argues:

> Only by including the anthropologist and the anthropological community in our understanding of society can we avoid the "intellectual imperialism" which currently marks our profession by implicitly separating us from social processes generally. That is, a viable "theory of practice" cannot emerge until anthropologists "rethink" the epistemological and ontological underpinnings of their own work.

Without implying that African studies are thereby rendered invalid, it is reasonable to assume that the political history of the continent conditions, though it does not determine, the course and content of African studies. This historical perspective breaks down two mythical figures: that of the pure scientist engaged in accumulating politically irrelevant knowledge, and what Ajayi (1969) calls the mythical African, located uncertainly anywhere in the continent and nowhere in time. Societies, and subgroups within them, emerge and change in the course of history as audiences with particular ideological demands. They support leaders, including scholars and often religious figures, who meet those demands by formulating theories and programs of a social scientific character.

In the colonial period Europeans represented the African continent either as essentially undifferentiated, the homeland of all that was primitive, or as the irreducible confusion of many tribes, each peculiar in its customs. The hypotheses in vogue often merely articulated popular European cosmology founded on a series of binary oppositions that contrasted the supposed virtues of European civilization with their supposed absence from Africa. Colonies constituted as states with a more or less modern, capitalist, bureaucratic institutional structure included within their boundaries a number, often a large number, of very different institutional complexes, commonly called "traditional" societies. Observers participated in the institutions of the bureaucratic sectors of these colonies (that is, in the modern societies—church, university, hospital, political party), in which they also eventually found their audiences. Thus these sectors of the situations being studied were transparent to the observers; it was to the other, the traditional sector, that they posed their questions: Is this activity religious or political, instrumental or expressive? No similar questions were seriously addressed to the modern sector, where the rationality, religiosity, or progressive character of activities was accepted at the natives' own evaluation. "Pluralism" refers to institutional heterogeneity, not to cultural or ethnic heterogeneity per se; it is a condition created and maintained by political means, not a function of differential progress in some evolutionary sense. Traditional societies are by no means autonomous, given that the states to which they belong determine the conditions of their existence. (Nonetheless, it would be incorrect to describe them as simple creations of colonial and postcolonial policy. The developments that occur in them sometimes defy or are anticipated by the policy of the state; Kuper and Smith, 1969; Morrison and Stevenson, 1980.) The word "traditional" itself conceals the fact that societies so described are entirely contemporary; they are not anachronisms or survivals.

African scholars, especially philosophers and theologians, are actively engaged in efforts to overcome cultural dichotomies, but they address an audience that is predominantly European (including American), not only geographically—because that is where both the largest book markets and the source of powerful opinions that Africans want to influence are located—but also institutionally, because the languages and conceptual categories in which the audience must be addressed are those of the modern university. In the postcolonial period, this apparent extraversion or alienation of African intellectual production has been a matter of concern and sometimes of reproach. Although several writers have proposed that African scholars abandon European languages in favor of African ones, the problem is deeper than that: It is unlikely that radical differences and a distinctively African content will appear until a social transformation occurs.

NOTES

1. In addition, scientism imposes a complementary distortion on science itself and particularly on social science, which, as Mudimbe (1973: 14) remarks (in the most extensive treatise to be devoted to the epistemology of science by an African), so notably fails to be scientific.

2. Here anthropologists tend to fall into the trap that Richard Bernstein (1980: 763), discussing foundationalism and "the problem of representation" in philosophy, calls "the Cartesian Anxiety, the grand Either/Or: either there is some basic foundational constraint or we are confronted with intellectual and moral chaos."

PART II

THE HISTORIOGRAPHY OF
ORAL DISCOURSE

4

PROFILE OF A HISTORIOGRAPHY
Oral Tradition and
Historical Research in Africa

HENRI MONIOT

In academic history the use of oral sources relating to the African past dates only from the end of the 1950s; the few historians to have used them earlier had, with rare exceptions, done so without analytic rigor. Anthropologists, on the other hand, were very interested in materials of this sort gathered in the field, but generally speaking they did not consider them historical documents. The historiography of oral sources is therefore very young, and over the last 25 years it has gone through a considerable process of change, reorientation, and maturation, a process that for the purposes of this brief overview can be divided into two phases.

During the first phase, professionally trained historians finally turned their attention to the African past in a way that combined a strong interest in empirical research in the field with methodological reflection. Supported by certain anthropologists and publicly engaging in intellectual confrontation with other historians, they assured for oral data the dignity—and reality—of true historical sources. International conferences in London (1957, 1961), Salisbury (1960), and Dakar (1961) brought together those with common interests in the field and were important in underpinning the emerging orientations to historical research. More important, new publications began to appear that provided systematic elaboration of these new forms of analyses and assured their diffusion beyond a small circle of specialists; these included the *Journal of African History* (from 1960) and Vansina's landmark *De la tradition orale* (1961).

An assessment of this early period, running more or less through the 1960s, can be organized around certain important themes. The first element was the establishment of a three-tiered critical framework focusing on the textual, social, and cultural dimensions of these oral sources (though these are at best only approximate and suggestive terms for such complex phenomena). Textual analysis and criticism essentially considered oral documents from a linguistic and literary perspective, focusing on such issues as the language used in these sources, their aesthetic qualities, and the limitations associated with their oral nature, their mnemonics, and their social performance. Such criticism sought also to determine the integrity of the transmission of traditions and the validity of the data. On the one hand, this required the identification of the minimal units of testimony and the comparison of both the variants of a single tradition and the constituent elements of a single corpus of data; on the other hand, it required a familiarity with the forms of learning, transmitting, and reciting the traditions: It was the oldest and most faithful original variant that was sought (Vansina, 1961, 1971a). Much of this effort was applied specifically to traditions I will refer to as "structured" traditions, those with a socially determined (even if only partial) shaping or molding in their content and sometimes in their form. But even if such forms of criticism were resolutely adapted to the oral nature of these sources, they were still strongly influenced by the model of critical apparatus as applied to written sources.

The social critique of oral traditions tries to account for the essential fact that social determinants, which influence the development of all historical evidence, are especially important and continually brought to bear on oral data throughout their duration. These influences act both in their retention and in their use, and even in their creation after the event: Traditions are conserved in the heads of people living fully in society; even when apparently fulfilling disinterested roles, oral testimony often serves more immediate interests. This form of critique therefore studies the social functions performed by a given tradition, and the possible implications of those functions on its accumulated content, within the unique context specific to each concrete case. This approach thus retains and expresses the skepticism that anthropologists bring to all "social charters," but for historians the anthropologists' refusal to consider them as valid historical sources is only a possibility to be explored, not a starting point of the analysis, since the complex interplay of narratives and their functions is conditioned by the events in such a subtle manner (Lewis, 1962). Such an approach clarifies the nature and the potential historical value of these data by accounting for the social status of those who narrate the traditions. Many authors have noted the coexistence of two types of oral traditions, one public and official, structured and ideological, the other internal to the group: more discrete, realistic, unpolished and private (Meillassoux, 1963; Perrot, 1982).

The cultural critique of oral tradition evaluates the testimonies relative to the cultural code in which they have been expressed, that is, by reference to the total system of preexistent values and of the categories which mold them. This approach seeks to identify the representations of history and the forms of historical consciousness in the society, including the status and meaning of the past in the culture, its view of the flow of time, and the concepts of causality found therein. It also considers the manner in which references to the past are used in social discourse and action; whether, for example, history is used as a depository of examples or as the source of rights and precedents which select, organize, mold, and idealize certain forms of testimony (Vansina, 1961, 1971a, 1972).

With greater professionalism in assessing the historical value of oral data there has been a gradual abandonment of the rather casual manner which had previously characterized the procedures of the recording, referencing, and publishing of such data. New standards have been established (Curtin, 1968). It has become increasingly important to acknowledge sources, precisely and individually; to situate such references in temporal and cultural terms and faithfully to reproduce the "texts" concerned; to distinguish, where required, between variants; and to separate the texts clearly from the commentary and hypotheses of the researcher.

Although not exclusively interested in chronologies, historians must try nonetheless to provide some form of dating for the materials they work with. Since oral traditions do not include reliable dates on internal grounds, the provision of a chronological framework was an important challenge for historians in this young field. Attempts to date information drawn from oral sources and thus to construct a chronology for African history have been carried out along two lines of analysis. One is the search for tie-ins with dates (or otherwise datable) sources. The other, and very important, approach is through the internal methods where recurrent elements of social organization appear in the traditions: genealogies, lists of office holders, age classes. This presupposes the establishment of a precise series (such as the succession of generations or of sovereigns) and their analysis for chronological estimates (such as the determination of average generation-lengths or reign-lengths—and their likely changes in the past; Person, 1962; Izard, 1970).

Analytic techniques based on these principles during the 1960s served as the foundation for a truly new domain of historical practice. We are now more aware of the existence of structured traditions with various degrees of freedom in their content and form, traditions often classified into types specific to the society in question. We are also aware of the roles of the more or less specialized and favored holders of such traditions and the social domains covered by this knowledge. And beyond these relatively structured traditions, we have become sensitive to more diffuse forms of knowledge, moving freely within the society, often of more recent origin and more individual in expression. Thus a paradox emerges: If social knowledge of the past (even if not entirely inherited) and social knowledge inherited from the past (even if not entirely a witness of the past) appear more accessible, the limitations of this form of communication are also more apparent, partly because of our sharp awareness of the continual erosion of these data. One other trait is worth mentioning: Historians constantly refer to different forms of temporality found in oral sources; sometimes these are associated with different periods referred to in the traditions—recent data are sometimes associated with realistic chronological references, the earliest historical periods or the period of origins with a more condensed form of presentation, and the hiatus between these two periods can each be expressed in cyclic, linear or structural terms—but often without any clear differentiation among these distinct forms of temporality.

But with the passage of time, both the tone of the approach and the substantive interests have changed. The first decade was one of conquering heroics: optimistic, sometimes triumphant, necessarily militant before skeptical colleagues. Although respecting the work of the anthropologists, their true predecessors in this field, the historians distinguished themselves from the anthropologists and sought to reassess their earlier functionalist and symbolic analyses, taking account of the historical relativity of the sources and conscious of applying their own questions and issues to the sources. During the

1970s these approaches became more tempered, more careful, and more thoughtful, though with sometimes a touch of hypercriticism or skepticism; renewed and more respectful attention has now been bestowed on attitudes known as "anthropological" (Miller, 1980).

This is all quite normal; hypercriticism is often seen as a passing sign of the growing maturity of a field. But it is also worth noting that this new tone, so apparent among authors publishing in the United States, is only scarcely apparent in France, where the development of African studies has followed a different path. In the early years, French Africanist historians using oral sources were extremely tentative, with the notable exception of Person's "one man show." Historical studies were first undertaken by anthropologists, including those interested in structural anthropology, and even today anthropologists continue to contribute significantly to French Africanist historiography. Partly because of its recent development and lack of disciplinary confrontation, the discourse on oral sources in France is not characterized by the attitude of turning back on itself or by abrupt swings, as occurs elsewhere.

Beyond these national differences, however, a clear reassessment of earlier conceptual frameworks and undertakings is now underway; Vansina's reconsideration of Kuba history (1978a), drawing on newly developed analytic tools and benefiting from a greater depth of thought and reflection, is one sign of this. It is not too difficult to see in this trend the emergence of a second period of Africanist historiography. The principal characteristics of this new age of Africanist historical study show sometimes the deepening and development of elements previously present but formerly only superficially analyzed, and sometimes a clear change in approach.

The special attention given from the beginning to structured traditions, more or less fixed in form, has recently been pared down to give greater room for all forms of knowledge held in the memory, including marginal but fixed forms of traditions, popular knowledge communicated in irregular and informal forms, and individual knowledge not part of the larger corpus of social knowledge. Historians have drawn on two techniques to gain access to these memories. One was the questionnaire, which produced knowledge by the historian's own efforts, knowledge which without that effort to articulate it would have remained only implicit, either because those who held it considered it as obvious and of no particular interest or because they would not otherwise have had the chance or the stimulus to speak to the issue in this form. The second technique consists primarily of listening to and observing concrete social situations that elicit references to the past, references whose unfolding in the context of the social organization, whose association of ideas, whose content and expression are all in the control of those consulted (Olivier de Sardan, 1976; Vidal, 1971). The first approach does not demand less familiarity with the society studied, but handles it with greater facility (Vansina, 1973). The interest brought to structured traditions has been extended to analogous social contexts such as enthronement ceremonies and agricultural rituals, which relate social reality to the spoken word (Perrot, 1982). Family histories and individual biographies have been drawn on as well for the singular contribution of each. When assembled in sufficient quantity, they can provide insight to the general patterns otherwise neglected; they can also be used for their serial effect (Tubiana, 1981; Ranger, 1975; Vidal, 1971).

Another observation on the nature of oral sources was present from the beginning but in a supplementary role; with a clearer awareness of its implications, however, historians have made this a central feature of Africanist historical analyses: The knowledge retained by oral societies has been strongly, and at times quite early on, modified, altered, and remodeled by its juxtaposition with written forms of knowledge, by the presence of representatives of Muslim or Western literate cultures, and by the introduction of new values. At a broader level, the new social and political contexts associated with colonialism have generated African strategies which interact with representations of the past. Some of the most important alterations occurred in the early period of colonial rule with the freezing of rights and positions in society brought on by colonial structures, and even earlier in the nineteenth century with the vigorous missionary enterprises and the expansion and intensification of exchange. But the process of such alterations was continuous, and the precolonial periods themselves are susceptible to a sort of "archaeology" of the corpus of traditions, at least in terms of the meeting of distinct cultural stocks (Henige, 1982b; Délivré, 1974; Chrétien, 1981). This critical approach does not carry with it ultimately a negative effect: It compounds, enriches, and redirects the critical work and the significance of the sources.

On chronological matters, however, these considerations (and others to be mentioned below) have led some authors to very pessimistic conclusions (Henige, 1974a). This approach focuses on the

influence of written culture and of colonial administration (which
have often lent political and moral weight to assumptions that these
traditions are of great antiquity), and the social mechanisms which at
some times shorten and at other times fallaciously lengthen the lists of
office holders or of genealogies. Although retaining the general premises of Henige's critique and certain of his conclusions, his colleagues
have generally preferred to scrutinize each case individually. On the
other hand, there is widespread awareness of the fact that genealogies
are often only images of reality or that many traditions are only
personifications of a wider social group and therefore cannot serve for
purposes of dating (Miller, 1976); the canons and rigor of analysis have
clearly shifted.

   The attention focused on local representations has greatly increased over the past few years. There has been a significant refinement in the appreciation of the impact on oral sources of cosmologies
and systems of thought, or conceptual frameworks molded by a
certain "world view," or concepts of causality. Certain earlier interpretations therefore appear as too literal, particularly those relating
to origin traditions which express fundamental cosmological values in
terms of population movements or of descent categories without any
empirical relation to the history of migration and settlement (MacGaffey, 1978; Vansina, 1978b; Miller, 1980). Yet more subtle still has been
the dissection of those forms of traditions that the historian interprets
as both historical and mythical (Feierman, 1974; Spear, 1978; Willis,
1981). Above all there have appeared precise works on the diverse and
unique forms of indigenous representations of history, on the means of
defining historical units and on the organization of time concepts, the
key concepts which organize and structure official memory, the patterns and resiliency of collective memory and of the social experience
of the past, to the point where in certain works there has been a
salutary shift: Social memory was formerly considered the key to the
critical use of sources, that is, used for "technical" reasons, as an
analytic tool; it has now become an *object* of social-historical study in
itself, at the very heart of understanding the problem of documentation (Délivré, 1974; Echard, 1975; Vidal, 1974; Perrot, 1982).

   One of the most important and widespread characteristics of this
new analytic approach is the attention which historians have given to
the conditions within which such traditions are learned, and to the
transmission of testimonies. The formal instruction of traditions, or
their mechanical word-by-word memorization in oral societies are

now seen as restricted to a very few cases. Basing himself on the successive transcriptions of a single myth and on a general study of just what orality and writing mean, and what they allow for, in social life, Goody (1977a) has shown that the ideal of transmitting an "exact copy" of a tradition is both difficult and not sought for in oral societies—it is considered irrelevant to the meaning of a tradition. What is important in these narrations is their constructive rememorization, rather than a mechanical memorization. The concepts of constancy and fidelity were tied to other issues and to forms other than simple textual repetition. In this fashion the narrative was reworked according to the particular demands which had called it forth and stimulated its recitation. There is a feeling in all of this of a shift in the objective sought; no longer do historians entertain the hope of reconstructing the oldest and most faithful forms of testimonies, modeled on the analysis of manuscripts. The "documentary analogy" (Miller, 1976) evaporates after having played the useful role of general service vehicle for the development of a critical apparatus, and even the term "tradition" must now be developed only with the precaution of removing the images which might evoke the intellectual "tradition" as it is thought of and used in written cultures (Hobsbawm and Ranger, 1983).

Because the process of transmission is now recognized as also a process of re-creation, the focus of study is now on the manner in which oral documents and recitations are produced. Two major works have shed light on this crucial point. In the introduction to a valuable collection of case studies on the analysis of oral traditions, Miller (1980) has outlined the essential elements of this creative aspect of narrative recitation: the use of clichés which are the very heart of the significant and the memorable, and the important role of "episodes" by which such core concepts are elaborated in various ways to suit the circumstances. He then considers the mental processes that arrange, organize, and form these narratives, by reference to concepts of causality, time, and the selection of facts. Bazin (1979) has also pleaded for the study of the conditions in which historical traditions are expressed. If viewed simply as "historical," a narrative might seem to be self-explanatory, its very raison d'être and its meaning explained by its "historical" functions. But whether it hides them or declares them, the narrative also carries other lessons (on politics or ethics, for example) at other levels as well. The meaning of the narrative elements included relates to the earlier themes and interests, and therefore to the historical processes which originally engendered the narrative, to the conditions which were present at its selection and at its memorization. Studied thus as narrative products, and not simply as sources, these recitations serve as doubly instructive, appearing as layered history themselves as well as narrating history, containing history as well as talking about history.

Anthropologists and sociologists today are bringing about a major reassessment in our appreciation of these types of local expression, something that needs to be accounted for before formal interrogations are undertaken, or before historians begin to wrestle with oral sources. After the giddiness produced by sophisticated structuralist analyses of myth, the observations on the reasoning behind such sources or on the practical uses of a text in its social context cause one to become aware of what is involved in putting the variants of a narrative onto cards and into written form; the various narratives within a corpus provide the scholar with the opportunity of seeing the corpus as a whole, or assembling statements that are never formulated and mastered at the same moment, or combining in material form the successive individualized formulations, opportunities that never exist for members of an oral culture dealing with these materials. Socially practiced knowledge has been hidden from historians by the creation of a text-object with scholarly commentaries just as it has been hidden from others seeking to reduce a mental universe to written form: "Structural analysis is congruent with a complete negation of the actual conditions of 'la pensée indigène'" (Bazin and Bensa, 1979: 20).

5

THE PAST IN THE PRESENT
Notes on Oral Archaeology

JEAN BAZIN

> Scripta manent, verba volant. . . . Plût au ciel que les écrits restas-
> sent, comme c'est plutôt le cas des paroles: car de celles—ci la dette
> ineffaçable du moins féconde nos actes par ses transferts [Lacan,
> 1966: 27].

Two closely interconnected concepts relate to the reconstruction
of the African past: oral tradition and traditional society. To try to
clarify these two terms as they are used in African historical anthropology, we must first consider the different ways in which the past
is related to the present. Whatever form a given element of the past
may take—whether an event, an institution, or a set of social
relations—it is represented in the present, in the observable world,
either because people refer consciously to the event, or because
something is found in another form which derives from it—where
there remains some kind of residue, anything which retains a trace of
what was, in what is. This conservation of the past can itself operate
in several ways: either because of the relative inertia of certain
materials; or by repetition through time, by explicitly copying and
recopying an earlier model; or by reproduction, that is, when an
earlier situation, having irremediably disappeared in its original form,
returns to the present in new guise.

The past can be found in what we hear, simply as a referent:
something spoken about, something remembered, something narrated. This is a form of the past that is absent even in its presence; it is
not present in itself, but only by the mediation of what is said of it here

and now, or what is agreed to be appropriate to say of it on a given occasion, under the pressure of present-day concerns. In this sense, the past can be said to be contemporaneous to the events that come after it. On the other hand, the past can be found as a trace, a vestige perhaps scarcely discernible, a mere fragment susceptible to divergent interpretations, but a witness, nonetheless, in itself and by itself, of its own earlier existence.

It is important to distinguish between a trace and a reference, because if historical writing in general is found well to the side of these different forms of discourse on the past, forms which are not necessarily all of a scholarly form, it is with the specific requirement to be "knowledge by traces," as expressed by François Simiand; it aspires to the status of empirical knowledge that furnishes documentary proof. History may perhaps be nothing more than a story (Ricoeur, 1983), but it is not just any story.

The demonstrative force of a document, whether text or stone, is tied to its nature as a trace—not to its truth (for it can be either untrue or without significance), but rather to its authenticity. Once recognized by the scholarly community the document exists independent of its use: an obstacle for some, an argument for others, but permanent all the same. It is because of this relative material resistance that a history can be reconstructed, not certainly as a unique and definitive truth but as a finite collection of possible interpretations—all those contradicted by a document established as authentic become null and void by that fact alone. The more limited this corpus of documents, the easier it is to establish it as evidence, but the more the number of potential hypotheses grows also. On the other hand, with an abundance of documents, there is a narrower range of possibilities but the application of a critique becomes greatly extended.[1]

In this respect the history of Africa holds a special interest. In the oral narratives that we record and from which we draw our essential information, the trace of the past disappears in the reference, what was said formerly in what is taken up today, so that we are perhaps more rich than others in one sense but with a wealth which in itself cannot be cashed in on. We have recourse to only a single discourse, that of the present, and to a single personage, that who is opposite us, both author and intermediary, historian and document. Therefore the notion of the "oral source" implies a misleading parallelism, because when they cite their sources, historians try to distinguish between their own statements and those furnished by others and taken as evidence; but in the case of Africa, the distinction between the voices of two different ages is never immediately apparent in the unitary chorus that we hear.

In accounting for these differences our care for critique should not be confused with systematic doubt which denies the historical consciousness of the African peoples. This does not mean that the truth is simply out there someplace, well hidden but already known, and that it is sufficient to obtain its revelation by producing a kind of super-tradition which would be both the sum and the truth of all other traditions. Historians are searching for another type of knowledge altogether, neither worse nor better, neither more useful nor more respectable. The very basis of our work is of a different nature; for historians are bound to reject the argument of authority on which all tradition, oral or not, is legitimated. Our essential requirement therefore is not fidelity but verification.[2] Yet oral sources appear powerless to help us in this regard. To be sure, increasing the number of steps between data of diverse origins and independent transmission may in itself appear to impart an increased level of probability. But it is worth noting all the same that before our colleagues or our skeptical readers, we often have no defense other than recourse to the apparently absolute confirmation provided by nonoral data. In this regard, each of us disposes of exemplary cases in which, thanks to some archaeological or textual discovery, a suspect oral tradition is finally demonstrated to be either true or "not all that wrong."[3]

How then is historical narrative—or any form of systematic verbal performance—perpetuated? Before being transcribed or recorded the spoken word has no existence outside the relation of subject (who enunciates it) to audience or recipient (who receives it and, one hopes, understands it). So are there in fact oral documents or not? Without confirmation, without a stone or parchment that retains its trace, such a tradition lacks the relative inertia that would maintain its form and meaning independent of this particular and ephemeral exchange, and thus enable it to serve the historians of the future. Under certain conditions and within certain limits, however, I believe that a given oral statement can be faithfully reproduced from generation to generation, as in certain artisan traditions that preserve a single model of the object or tool that may be copied and reproduced indefinitely.

Since we are products of literate training—if we sometimes learn and recite material "by heart" it is usually from a written text—we admit only with difficulty that a mere *flatus vocis* can be exactly

maintained, word for word, in passing from mouth to ear: Consider
the children's game where a given sentence is passed rapidly to one's
neighbour and becomes unrecognizable in the end. Similarly for
rumor: The very anonymity of the message and its "underground"
circulation encourage its distortion (*Le Genre Humain*, 1982). However, even in the context of a public religious ceremony, the conservation of a given statement is not a foregone conclusion. Goody (1977a)
has shown how the recitation of even a short invocation in a society
without writing can contain many differences from one speaker to
another, differences which in the absence of a common reference
point are not seen as mistakes. Without any body of experts, nor any
kind of centralized authority on these matters, anyone is free to
develop their own version and retain it as the best text.

There are, however, situations where it can be presumed that the
probability of distortion is very low, particularly in esoteric formulas
which require exact repetition so as not to invalidate the ritual. Even if
the accompanying ritual is no longer performed, even if the individual
no longer has the historical knowledge which would enable us to
understand its meaning and estimate its age, these formulas are
nonetheless part of a patrimony which is not easily abandoned; a
belief in the power of the words themselves is a sufficient condition of
their perpetuation.

One day in Sama, a little above Ségu and one of the oldest sites on
the left bank of the Niger, my questions set off a lively debate between
the Sogore lineage, which claimed to be among the oldest population
segments in the area, and several others probably derived from the
warrior-captives installed by the kings of Ségu and still retaining the
village chiefship today. Once provoked by the assertions of their
opponents—for propriety had required prudent silence in my
presence—and holding it imperative that their rights be recognized by
this outside researcher, the Sogore, short of argument, had to provide
proof. They produced from among their family heirlooms an old spear
thought to have formed part of the regalia of the local sovereigns, then
they led me to an ancient and sacred pot the associated rites for which
were unanimously recognized as being their monopoly, and finally the
lineage elder recited a list of twelve mysterious names—very likely
the former kings of the town—that had formerly only been mentioned
secretly, during certain purification rituals; he asserted that to be their
first public recitation. These words were full of the same kind of
authority as that of relics whose exposition acquires the force of law.

These then were documents that acquired greater historical value, perhaps, since they were associated with a present-day quarrel, and showed themselves to be effective in these circumstances: Sometime later the chiefship changed hands. This type of "object-narrative" or "fetish words" can only be preserved for as long as it is retained in the memory, as a trunk in an attic, without being integrated into the experience of the subject, both retained and forgotten in the margins of the conscious mind. But it remains symbolically operative as a key formula or magic phrase, as a performative sentence not limited to "saying something" but drawn on "to do something." Therefore it is not judged by criteria of truth or falsehood, but by success or failure, according to whether the rules that apply to its recitation have been respected and carried out.

The difficulty is not found in the oral character of the transmission but rather in the opposition provoked outside the situation where it is considered effective—what Austin (1962) would call its "misapplication." One of these contexts is when the recitation becomes for the researcher simply a documentary curiosity, the material of our knowledge and no longer an act of power. In my opinion the whole problem of the historical significance of genealogies in African studies must be seen in this light. We are faced with two possibilities. One is that we obtain, often only with great difficulty, a list of names which has a performative value associated with the very recitation of the list— such as that which the legitimate authority must enunciate during a given village or lineage ritual—that provides a document which is very likely to be authentic but from which it is very difficult if not impossible to extract genealogical information. The other form is that by which we obtain access to genealogical knowledge already constituted, but having as its function the legitimation of an acquired situation, more relevant perhaps to present-day tensions than to the facts of the past, and thus functioning like myths of origin.

Yet another form of oral document is reproduced almost automatically in a similar fashion: the old refrains and popular songs that weave a sort of continuous verbal cloth across generations, wherein specific events are often noted. These are not just any events, but only that type of event sometimes referred to as a "happening." It is clear that the perception of what makes a happening varies not only from one society to another but also according to the position of a given observer within the social structure. The most important lessons derived from our oral sources are less in what they say, perhaps, than

in the fact that these things are said at all. They are indications of the
criteria of selection of what is considered worthy of being mentioned
and retained at any given moment, of the criteria of distinguishing
between the "events" of the past and other dimensions of the past; as
Paul Veyne notes: "The non-événementielle simply consists of
events which are not yet recognized as such, . . . of history which we
are not yet conscious of as such" (Veyne, 1971: 131). However, in
order for the historian truly to define freely the field of events he must
first dispose of a complete recording of the present, a work of some
absolute chronicler. Without this we need to depend on what the
available sources tell of the earlier means of separating the memorable from the insignificant. From this point of view some societies may
appear to be lacking history because nothing is given the form of
"historical event" there and the absence of archives impedes our
attempts to catalogue the daily round of deaths and births, marriages
and local conflicts, and so to reconstruct a form of *histoire non-
événementielle*. But what conditions underlie the recognition of a
given fact as a historical event? I believe that among these are oppositions between public time-space and the private domain (however
defined), and similarly, the establishment of a "historical theater" or
"historical drama" by which certain people are promoted to the status
of "actors" whose behavior is observed, commented on and appreciated by others. In a warrior state as was Ségu, combat appears as
the historical event par excellence because the reproduction of the
social system is played out there in a decisive fashion (Bazin, 1982).
The relations of dependence between the king (both as an organizer
and symbol of the collective power) and his warriors resulted from
military victory and the booty it permitted. It is by their bravery or
skill in battle that the warriors gained the respect of their peers; only
their "name" *(togo)* or reputation lifts them above the undifferentiated masses of near-captives in a state whose social structure was
not based on aristocratic status ascribed by birth. The king *(faama)*
with his "luck," his power *(fanga),* and his shrewdness on the one
hand, and his lieutenants (with their bravery), all condemned to
pitiless rivalry amongst themselves on the other, hold the principal
roles in this system. Their deeds are, to be sure, the subject of oral
accounts produced for and repeated at a variety of ceremonial circumstances by professional narrators, mostly men of a given caste
and tied to positions of power. But aside from the narrative itself and
the political representations mediated therein, the action also finds its
more immediate sanction in what we would call "public opinion": the

public gossip of the beer-halls and the songs spread from street to street, more or less anonymous or spontaneous compositions but which in any case reveal more of the heated commentary or the affective effect than occurs when these events are recounted in narrative form. These are not descriptive declarations; they praise or dispraise, they make reputations and dash them; they are associated only with their effect, or their political impact.

In his journal, Soleillet (1887) narrates the birth of one of these songs in Ségu at the time of the Futaka ("Toucouleurs"). In the beginning of January 1879, Amadu's soldiers recovered the cannons seized by the Bambara partisans; but on their return the convoy was attacked. Very quickly many stories circulated; some versions minimized, others elaborated on the incident. Soleillet tried to form an impartial opinion. But simultaneously there spread a song that ridiculed the head of the convoy, Mahmoud, the commander of one of the companies of slave-soldiers *(sofa)*. According to Soleillet it was the young Bambara girls of the town who made up and spread this song, and already it was heard everywhere, scarcely two or three days after the return of the column.

> Mahmoud is a make-believe soldier.
> He leads armed troops.
> Look, in the bush, he is handsome and proud,
> as long as he is alone with his troops.
> The enemy comes, and the guns are brought out.
> Mahmoud is afraid and wishes to hide.
> Who cares for a chicken?
> An old woman hides the handsome warrior
> under her dirty clothes.
> Such was the hiding place of Mahmoud,
> The hiding place of Mahmoud, a make-believe soldier.

The song tells us practically nothing of substance. To hide in the skirts of an old lady is a stereotype of satirical songs. The only tie to the events themselves is the name of the chief. Fifteen years later, if it were still sung then, we would no longer know who this Mahmoud was. The entire effect is pragmatic, not descriptive: A military leader, a favorite of the king, becomes the object of derision; his reputation is impugned. Hence the reaction of the person in question:

> Mahmoud has complained to the emir, and the emir has promised that those who continue to mock his captive would be whipped, which

didn't affect them in the least. It seems, moreover, that Ahmadou did not dare to carry out his threat, since Ségu had always upheld the liberty of the singer [Soleillet, 1887: 451].

When there is no inheritance of status, all honor derives from those who attribute your exploits to you. Hence the power of public opinion, "the freedom of song," from which the king may occasionally benefit (when, that is, he is not the victim of it).

On the one side historical actors, on the other, singers and women (*gada,* Soleillet's "young girls") or the servants and concubines of the Ségu population, the female common people well informed and bantering, a sort of tragicomic chorus responsible for a permanent commentary on the actions of the heroes. Confronted with this merciless jury—the daily market place of glory—the actors can anticipate these popular reactions by anticipating public commentary as a form of challenge; the opposite of sanction is provocation. Thus there emerges a constant dialogue of deeds and song between the two parties, the actors and the commentators.

Several years later, when the Futaka still controlled Ségu, a conflict broke out on the left bank, on the Bambara side, between Karamoko, the successor to former kings, and one of the lower-level chiefs, Nto Jara. A well-known warrior, Boliba from Sama, avowed that he would take Nto alive within three days. Three months later, forced to raise the ante by his own bragging, he swore that "If I do not take Nto, let me grow a tail!" All for naught. And so inevitably the young women of the opposition group began to sing:

> Boli from Sama has sworn
> to take the son of Shiyaba alive![4]
> Draw in your tail, Boli, or we will pull it off!
> To take the son of Shiyaba alive
> Is not an easy thing to do!

But the singers on the other side of this game are at work as well. As Nto remains entrenched in his capital, Marakabugu, a situation scarcely more glorious than Boliba's powerlessness, they are singing:

> Nto, do you have scabies on your hind-side?
> Nto, do you have scabies on your hind-side?
> Nto from Marakabugu, do you have scabies on your hind-side?
> The hind-side of a no-good is no good in the saddle.

Finally Boliba betrays his master and passes over to serve Nto. On his capture he is punished with a terrible fate: his head is cooked and fed to the dogs. The drama ends on this refrain:

> Boliba yo!
> For your betrayal, you have merited . . .
> Boliba yo!
> to have your head torn to bits.[5]

Thus the event is constantly reflected in a verbal mirror, and conforms completely to its verbal image. In public opinion it obtains a sort of resonance which both abolishes it and conserves it, in the sense that where it happens there remains only a song. The challenges of the old troopers, the bragging of the drunkards, the slander and gossip of the day are eminently effective, to the point of being one of the bases of action—but, by their capacity to be transformed eventually into old refrains, they can be invested with a temporal duration which serves as the basis for the emergence of a tradition.

This relates to the concept of oral documents: words directly produced by a past event but still present as its trace and capable of serving as proof of the event. To take an example drawn from an earlier period: Around 1845 Kirango-Ben, the king of Ségu, decided to go on the offensive against the Muslim state of the Fula of Massina. He sent an army to take Jaramana, a Minyanka village more or less under the protection of the Fula and near to one of their fortresses. After so many years of failures or of truce the Ségu action is celebrated in song and sung by the trumpeters *(burufyèlaw)* of the army:

> Go tell Balobo that Ségu is at Haramana . . .
> Go tell Amadu Seku that Ségu is at Jaramana . . .[6]

This sort of song of glory is a response to the deploring songs put out on the war drums which had marked the defeat of the famous Sologo, the chief of Shanro, against these same Fula troops:

> He has come with deception
> The Fula war has come with deception
> The war of Amadu the Fula has come with deception . . .
> > [Ba and Daget, 1962: 149].

The first of these songs has a documentary value: It attests that there was in fact a battle at Jaramana between the troops of Ségu and those of Hamdallahi, of which the Massina traditions apparently say nothing. In addition it allows for an approximate dating: It was in March 1845 that Amadu Seku succeeded to his father while his cousin Balobo (Ba Lobbo) became the general-in-chief of the army. However, the song provides only a trace reference, not a description, of what happened at Jaramana. It does not provide the chance to mediate between different versions. Was the place taken despite the intervention of Balobo, or, as the present inhabitants of the village relate, did the besieging army disperse because of the intervention of the Fula cavalry? The second song tells us even less. It only takes on meaning in the narrative context provided by Hampate Ba; the narrative of a tactical trick with which one day the Fula chief Amiru Mangal would be served in one of his many combats against Salogo allows a decoding of the song which serves more as illustration here than as a document.

It is possible that a song of weak narrative content is perpetuated in the collective memory even when the precise event which provided the original stimulus for the song has been forgotten. Soleillet (1887: 404), for example, recounts the following scene. On October 3, 1878 he was received in Amadu's court. To the sovereign's greeting he responded that he was not the first white to have arrived here at Ségu, alone and unarmed. Mungo Park had done the same 82 years earlier: "Surely he should be remembered here at Ségu," Soleillet suggested. Immediately everyone began to consult each other; finally he notes that "the griots have preserved songs on this traveler who had a large beard and a hat." In fact, it is very likely that no one at the court of Amadu had heard the passage of Mungo Park in front of Ségu in July 1796 mentioned; but the knowledge provided by Soleillet (which he owed to the written transmission of Mungo Park's narrative) allowed some of the griots' songs to be interpreted in this fashion, songs for which they had most likely forgotten the precise event which had brought them into being in the first place. Probably certain details (such as the beard and the hat) allowed this identification to occur. Moreover, we learn from Mungo Park himself that his pitiable allure constantly gave rise to songs. He cites one made up on the spot for him by a sympathetic woman spinning cotton:

> The winds roared, and the rains fell.
> The poor white man, faint and weary, came and
>   sat under our tree.
> He has no mother to bring him milk, no wife
>   to grind his corn.
> [Chorus by other women in reply]
> Let us pity the white man.
> No mother has he, [etc.] [Park, 1979: 198].

In this way in a society strongly affected by its oral culture, one can be entirely surrounded by the past without ever knowing it, because there still circulate fantasy-narratives derived from another age but without explicit or explicable references to the events which generated them. Except for linguistic archaisms or loan words from a population now disappeared, the words themselves do not carry the mark of time. Hence the researcher finds himself in a difficult position: He does not even know what can be indicative—even if it is true that the more research progresses, the better we can perceive what ought to be researched. On the other hand, aside from formal structures which facilitate memorization (including literary devices such as meter, alliteration, symmetry, and so on), this removal of the reference is undoubtedly the decisive condition of its reproduction, because it is no longer known to what the story refers; a message is best transmitted when those who do so ignore the content.

This is why Bloch's (1954: 61) observation on the "unconscious witnesses" to the past in the present is so valuable. Formulas and refrains can be classified in the same way as other aspects of the language (proverbs, slogans, formal testimony, toponyms, and so forth) along with many other vestiges of the past associated with archaeological or ethnological findings: all that leave a trace without having been handed down as conscious souvenir; anything, that is, of a historical value only for us and not in itself. In this context the form of cultural and institutional conservatism which designates certain societies as "traditional" is also significant, for there the past remains as a framework of present action without the need to make reference directly to it. In the region of Ségu, for example, the distinction always present in the social space of the village between the quarters of the original inhabitants and those of warrior-captives of the kings allows one to have an idea of the progressive growth of the state. In the same way Cohen has shown (1980: 208-209) how an analysis of matrimonial alliances—perpetuated not only by the tendency to reinforce them over time but also by the obligations which derive from them for those who are products of them—allows an approach to the past which owes nothing to "narrative historical tradition." These are documents that can be said to be relatively "unconscious" because they remain on the margins of "those mental compartments from which and by which the past is perceived, understood and presented in the form of conscious history."

Up to this point, I have stressed what I have termed "repetition" to distinguish it from what I refer to as "reproduction." Whatever the importance—the growing importance—of data drawn from other sources, it is still true that African historiography is primarily based on elements drawn from oral narratives. I would argue, both on theoretical grounds and from a slightly risky form of induction, that an oral performance is more likely to be reproduced over time when it is less narrative, but inversely, that a narrative is never truly "reproduced" but only repeated. I mean by this that there is no original account continued to the present through a series of successive and identical copies reproduced over time. Each performance is to be considered as a singular act determined by its own context; an earlier narration can be found taken up there again, remade, replayed but in an essentially revised form, even where the narrated event appears to be the same. An earlier narration can return today in deeds which it inspires, as in new performances which draw from it, but under another mask, under multiple guises, in a relation not of imitation but of parody (Deleuze, 1968). It is in this sense that a scene from one's infancy can recur in unrecognizable form in adult symptoms or fantasies, by what Freud calls the "constraint of repetition," or in the sense in which Marx observes that the French revolutionaries repeated elements of Republican Rome but at another level entirely, either tragic or grotesque.

It was for a long time assumed that an oral tradition was transmitted over time, from narrator to narrator, from an "initial testimony" and that our task as historians was to examine this testimony in the usual way (and to determine the changes that could have affected its transmission). This supposed analogy with written documents was of tactical utility when Vansina first presented it (Vansina, 1961), but now it appears misleading. Today we see that we are dealing not with the mere transmission of narrative but with its production, and that one must examine "how oral historians construct their narratives" (Miller, 1980: 4). However, I am not certain that one can easily distinguish the "clichés" from the "episodes," in Miller's terms,[7] that is, the inherited and memorized content from its arrangements, for that implies assuming again that a constant element has been passed on for generations, like the baton in a relay race.

Of course, our informants state that they are telling us what they themselves were told, and that is why we accept them as repositories of a "tradition." But this principle covers highly diverse situations. I will attempt to classify them into three categories, though these are hardly exhaustive.

(1) Of one or several accounts only fragments remain, which our informant gives us as they are, without trying to order them into a new narration: This is the most favorable archaeological situation. However, such reminiscences are usually not made spontaneously—they are evoked by our questions; the account which we are trying to draw up from other sources renders them significant. We tend to consider them reliable because they seem to confirm *our* view of events, although they are issued from a concept of which the meaning is lost.

(2) From one or more prior accounts elements have been extracted to form a new account: These may consist of events, revealed by names of people or places, or of stereotyped plots ("clichés"). This is the most unfavorable archaeological situation: One has built new churches with the stones of old temples, and the plan of the latter may be forever obliterated. This is the case, I believe, for most of the narratives given by professional story-tellers (such as, in West Africa, the *griots*). The final result is a patchwork of disparate data that has been put together for esthetic or moral reasons—however, this does not preclude a certain "truth" in the portrayal of customs and social relationships.

(3) The account we hear narrates an earlier account. Even supposing that the second narrator attempts to reproduce the tale exactly as heard, it cannot be the *same* account, because the situation in which it

is given is different; it is most unlikely, for example, that our demand
for "truth" be without effect on the content (leading, for example, to
self-censorship, to imposed conformity to an ideal of objectivity, and
so on). However, at least the earlier narrator can eventually be
identified, socially and chronologically situated. But he may be only
the nth narrator—the final account is thus a result of a whole series of
situations in which the "same" event has been recalled.

In all three cases an initial account is repeated, that is, given a
new meaning, consciously or unconsciously. This is an inevitable
aspect of the "narrative phase"—as Danto (1965) analyzes it—and
not a weakness of oral transmission specifically. Except for all direct
verbal traces of an event and excluding the hypothesis of an "Ideal
Chronicler capable of giving an instantaneous transcription of
events" (Ricoeur, 1983: 206), all accounts of historical events are
presented in the light of later events. Thus every narration
presupposes at least three different levels of understanding: that of the
narration itself, that of the event narrated, and that which has affected
the narration. One should not be surprised, and still less be indignant,
at such a limitation to our knowledge: Is this not the underside of all
historicity? This permanent presence of the past in the present, this
constant transformation of its meaning, is it not the condition of all
historical action?

The difficulty specific to oral history is that one generally does not
dispose of a series of distinct versions that can be situated chronologically, so that the successive perspectives by which the same event is
viewed usually merge in a single account. That does not mean denying its documentary value; it means, rather, seeing under what conditions it can have such a value, due to what analytical methods.
Because the history of the Ségu kingdom (*circa* 1720-1861) is almost
exclusively oral, I can perhaps bring a special rigor to reflection on
this matter.

I propose that a narrative becomes historical evidence insofar as
we accord more importance to what it *is* than to what it *says*. A
narrative is primarily a document of the situation in which it is told.
Our request for knowledge leads to data of a special kind: to embar-
rassed silences, to putting off the moment of giving an answer, and so
on. The account one eventually obtains is a reaction to a situation
determined by a whole network of social interactions that is not
immediately comprehensible; as outsiders we do not know what
practical effect on the participants our request for information may

have. From this point of view, the narration is a document in itself, and must be deciphered as such: Who speaks, who listens, who intervenes? Why is what is said said, and why is it said in this way, at this particular time? We must never forget that we are not the sole listeners to this narration: Groups confront each other, identities are defined in subtle ways and, perhaps, as much by what is omitted as by what is said. From my experience in Ségu and in the surrounding villages I tend to conclude that one learns more in this manner, by examining the narration as a mirror of social relationships, than by studying the tale itself. In short, it is impossible to separate the anthropology of the present from research into the past.

But a narrative can also be a historical document insofar as it repeats an earlier tale and retains traces of the way in which it was told. In this case interpretation is a delicate exercise (Bazin, 1979) for one must have access to a variety of versions and inquire about their differences. Here too the point is less to identify the event narrated, and to select the most plausible version or versions, as to identify the different ways in which the account is rendered and what they reveal of the situations in which they were narrated. It is not unimportant that a body of historical information should have been built up gradually, as was the case in Ségu, in such occasions as the official account of events that professional narrators presented to kings, as funeral celebrations in which the major events of the last reign were related, in the oratorical "work" *(baara)* the "word experts" *(kumatigi)* effected the night before a battle, to incite the warriors to bravery by recalling the heroism of their predecessors, and so on. The more we know of the way in which a society produces narratives, of the cultural and socio-historical aspects of this production, the more revealing these documents are, not because a direct testimony is transmitted but because they are "witnesses unaware" of the conditions that led to their elaboration.

NOTES

1. Hence the observation of Charles Péguy: "For the ancient world, history is possible because there are no documents; for the modern world, it is not done because there are documents."

2. I say verification, not proof; what is important is to formulate hypotheses that a "document" may or may not disqualify. I nevertheless believe that, as Bateson puts it, "science probes; it does not prove."

3. Thus, for example, the mystery of a raid led by an obscure hero against the Ashanti capital is "explained" when an allusion to the event is found in the Dutch archives (Perrot, 1982: 57ff.) or the age of the town of Jenne, for which oral accounts recorded around 1650 indicated a foundation in the eighth century, is no longer considered "legendary" with the archaeological work of R. J. McIntosh and S. K. McIntosh.

4. Shiyaba was the name of Nto's mother.

5. These songs were narrated by Sumahila Fane at Ségu, August 15, 1970.

6. This song derives from another narrative of Sumahila Fane (Teserela), July 26, 1970. The descendant of a family of blacksmiths for the kings of Ségu and literate in Arabic, Sumahila Fane is careful to establish his facts in a critical manner.

7. "Episodes are the narrative stories that oral historians develop to explain historical clichés in the present" (Miller, 1980:6f.); see also Vansina (1972) for examples.

6

CONFRONTING THE UNEQUAL EXCHANGE
OF THE ORAL AND THE WRITTEN

JEAN-PIERRE CHRÉTIEN

For at least a century all of black Africa has been confronted with the issue of the strategies of scripture, implying a simultaneous cultural and political remodeling and often associated with the crystallization of new power relationships.[1] The relationship of the oral to the written has often been remarked on, but more often in a philosophical than a historical vein. The initially foreign character of written communication in these societies has been especially neglected. In fact, the dialectic interaction between these two forms of communication unfolds only as part of the history of external contact and conquest.

Research in the social sciences in Africa has developed along with the maturing of a new historical consciousness, called on to meet the challenges of the modern world: issues of nation-building, the stagnation of the rural areas, and the pressures brought to bear by the West or the East. But cultural contradictions have had to be untangled on the spot, even where they intertwined the successive discourses of colonizers and "decolonizers" with the emergent cultural forms focused around the complex of missionary schools, administrative offices and commercial storerooms. African historians have thus been faced with two types of dominant views of the past of their peoples. One of those derives from the Africanist "laboratories" abroad, along with those of the large international news media. But in addition there exists a new African written tradition, which includes the "cultural traditions" and "customs" classified and codified by the first literate Africans in the same reductionist terms of the day as their western mentors. Over a very long period these cultures have retained intellectual traces of the original magical effect conjured up by the "power of the written word."

This intellectual struggle forms the core of the analysis presented here, drawing on examples from East to Central Africa. After considering the manner in which European observers have dealt with the oral cultures of the region we will be able to reflect on the stages of cooptation of this heritage by African intellectuals themselves. It is obvious that political trends and ideological preoccupations are important factors in the formation and presentation of such written traditions. But the role of historians, whether self-taught or, increasingly, professionally trained, appears sufficiently significant to merit particular attention.

ORAL TRADITIONS IN WESTERN PERCEPTION: FROM THE REVELATIONS OF THE ANCESTORS TO THE CRITICISM OF THE DISBELIEVERS

European attitudes toward different cultures have not shown linear development. From the mid-nineteenth century the discovery of African "literature" and the sympathy with which African forms of oral expression were received were all part of the twin currents of expanding linguistic research and reinvigorated evangelistic projects. Just as the Grimm brothers revived popular Germanic culture, so too the missionaries, both Catholic and Protestant, rapidly set about learning the languages and transcribing them, establishing lexicons and grammars, and finally publishing texts noted down from the peoples among whom they had settled. Joined by ethnographers and linguists, they published proverbs, tales, and narratives in the local languages with parallel translations in English, French, or German (Finnegan, 1970: 26-47; Gorog-Karady, 1981).

This appreciation of oral forms of literature was associated with a conviction of the fundamental universality of ideas and sentiments, as well as of the equality of peoples no matter what their color. In the preface to an anthology of Kanuri literature, for example, Sigismund Koelle (1854: vii) remarked that

> specimens like the following "Native Literature" show that the Ne-
> groes actually have thought to express, that they reflect and reason
> about things just as other men. Considered from such a point of view,

these specimens [the collected texts] may go a long way towards refuting the old-fashioned doctrine of the essential inequality of Negroes with the rest of mankind.

Such assertions provide striking contrast to the dominant ethnological discourse of the early twentieth century.

Accompanying the rise of colonial imperialisms, racial concepts dominated the theoretical paradigms of the day, revealed in the intense discussions of evolutionism, diffusionism, and functionalism; in each case "primitive" societies were judged inferior to the West, whether on temporal, spatial, or structural grounds. In such a context oral sources could only be seen as the traces of a bygone past, or as the form of expression of those societies left aside by "history." Such a lack of respect for oral testimony is shown by the absence of published texts in almost all scholarly works appearing between 1890 and 1950. Quotes were diminished to summaries or hidden in the analysis. In the end, it was the foreign observers themselves who were quoted, as if they were the authors and witnesses of an entire culture. When confronted with the written words of European visitors the spoken words of African actors were effaced.

The imposition of this screen on all speech emanating from African societies could not but result in the negation of Africa's own sense of historical dimension. The American ethnologist Robert Lowie (1917: 161) epitomized this view, noting that he "could not attach to oral tradition any historical value whatsoever under any circumstances whatsoever." In 1938 Sir Reginald Coupland (1938: 14) affirmed that "on nearly all, though not quite all, its pages, the history of East Africa is only the history of its invaders." Again in the early 1960s European historians could only view with pity those of their colleagues who wasted their time with "tribal" oddities; as Trevor-Roper (1963) averred, there was no history of Africa but "only the history of Europeans in Africa." "The rest is darkness," he added, and "darkness is not the subject of history."

In fact, however, a type of historical interest in some African societies had been apparent from the beginning of their contacts with Europeans. The system of so-called indirect administration was particularly propitious for this type of applied research to the degree to which European authorities sought to analyse as closely as possible power relationships and social cleavages in order to manipulate them, the better to serve their interests in providing some sort of enlightened legitimacy to colonial administration. The best examples of this process relate to the Great Lakes region, where a series of works by missionaries, administrators, and travelers provides an overview of this political history.

The popularity of such works provided these writers with an authority far in excess of the audience their informants could hope to reach outside of their particular locales. Under these circumstances, the witnesses interrogated, whether simple narrators or traditional experts, went unmentioned or were simply relegated to the category of "tribal elders." Sir Harry Johnston (1902), for example, based his reconstruction of the general history of the kingdoms incorporated with the Uganda Protectorate on "native legends"; he quotes only European authors, and carefully selected ones at that. The same attitude toward sources is found in Father Julien Gorju's (1920) synthesis; for Bunyoro, for example, he refers to the traditions published in Fischer's work ten years earlier (Fischer, 1910). Although some authors show greater rigor in their description of sources, identification of informants, or analysis of lines of transmission and variants within traditions (Rehse, 1910; Césard, 1931), in general the unequal treatment of oral and written sources is clear, with the latter playing a role analogous to advertising in pushing shoddy industrial goods to the detriment of local handicrafts.

Sometimes a form of technico-political alchemy promoted the self-taught, often of distinctly mediocre abilities, to the full rank of "historians." In 1904, for instance, two livestock traders went to Rwanda, then under German control; thirty years later one of them, the Boer Philipp Pretorius, published his memoirs (1948 [1934]) wherein he described "traditional" Rwandan society according to information provided by chief "Semahari," whom he described as his "guide and philosopher." Seventy years after this visit, in an article of March 31, 1974, *Le Monde's* "special correspondent" in Rwanda remarked that the observations of such a "simple ivory trader of South African origins" as Major Pretorius carried greater weight in understanding the social structures of Rwanda than the scholarly accounts of ethnologists, "who often contradict each other anyway." So here is testimony twice confirmed by the written word: the publication (and French translation) of a book, the authority of which is then confirmed by a prestigious international daily. Yet a perusal of the dossiers of the trial of this trader shows that the *mutware* (chief) Semihali was among the victims of these livestock raids: Pretorius had even held the latter hostage in order to ensure his docility![2] The references to an "informant" consulted after first having been physically detained surely represents an extreme case, yet this anecdote causes one to reflect on just what might have been entailed in handling "oral tradition" by "authorized observers" tied to the colonial presence.

No real changes in this situation occurred until the end of the 1950s, with the emergence of a school of African history worthy of the name, conscious of reconstructing the precolonial African past by taking oral sources into consideration as completely as possible. Along with the growth of this new respect for ancestral traditions (sometimes, to be sure, characterized by excessive enthusiasm and unconditional reverence in the context of the political reawakening of black Africa), there has also been an exploration of the forms of critique of these sources. Although judged as nothing short of blasphemous by those for whom oral tradition is pure revelation, the development of these critical canons has been part of a larger debate over the last twenty years on the potentiality of such data as historical sources (see the chapter by Moniot, above).

As early as 1962 Vansina had called into question the linear perception of the formation of the Rwandan state as portrayed in the dynastic traditions. His analysis distinguished between the various stages in the territorial and institutional structuring of this kingdom, showing in broad strokes the difficulties encountered in any historical reconstruction which tried to account for conflicts and setbacks, whereby a ruling group confronted with colonial domination seeks to base its legitimacy on the image of an unbroken continuity and perfect cohesion in the past. Henige (1974b) reinforced the skeptics and provoked strong reactions on the part of certain practitioners of oral enquiries in emphasizing the chronological distortions introduced to the sources by the functioning of collective memory, by the mechanisms for transmitting oral literature, and by the impact of written cultures on oral traditions.

The application of more clearly defined analytic frameworks also raised new questions. Thus, from a Marxist perspective, the reliability of oral sources in socioeconomic matters is called into question by the extent to which these, like all other forms of cultural expression, are determined by power relationships at the time they are transmitted (Vidal, 1976). Structuralist interpretations too deny the historical contribution of these sources in order to retain the message only at the mythic level, the permanent dimension of a culture (de Heusch, 1972; 1982). Thus, at just the time when oral sources have started to be accepted into the mainstream of the historical discipline, including that of the European past, extreme criticisms risk plunging the African past anew into the inaccessible regions of the "dark ages."

Our objective here is not to discuss the methodology of oral traditions, but rather to assess their authority in current Africanist historiography. In doing so, we will need to comment on the approach distinguishing between "official" (court) sources and private "lineage" or "clan" traditions (Buchanan, 1974). Classifying traditions in this manner, although appealing in its very simplicity, does not do justice to the complexity and diversity of oral cultures, and denies both the interaction between the two genres and the confrontation between the oral and the written—even after several decades of foreign colonization; it avoids any consideration of the formation of new conceptual configurations in the so-called traditional or indigenous worlds—societies at once encapsulated and marginalized (Chrétien, 1978; Henige, 1974a, 1982).

FROM TRADITIONALISTS TO CLERKS: ORAL LITERATURE TRANSCRIBED AND INTERPRETED BY THE FIRST LITERATE GENERATION

Writing penetrated East and Central Africa from the coast, and arrived in the region of the Great Lakes only toward the end of the nineteenth century. But the influence of writing was greater and more rapidly extended than one might think if they were to judge solely on the low level of education that characterized the colonial period. In fact written culture, an intellectual practice of European or Arab origin in these areas, is often very quickly absorbed in the ruling circles; from there it spreads, by oral transmission as well as by other means, to other sectors of the population. Christian schools and missions and administrative outposts, as well as the courts of "customary chiefs," are all centers of diffusion of a mixed culture. The role of "culture brokers," those participating in distinct social milieux and serving as transmitters of new ways of thought, new practices and new ideas, has been particularly noteworthy in the African colonial context, where it implies contact with a conquering foreign culture, but where it was also a necessary element in assuring foreign domination. The first literate generation in the Great Lakes region, trained in the period 1870-1890, appears to have been of fundamental importance in the historiographical development of the different kingdoms; many of these prominent persons are considered the first "historians" of their respective countries.

Among them, the foremost and most famous was undoubtedly Apolo Kagwa. This young Muganda noble came into contact with the royal court at a time of contending Moslem, Catholic, and Protestant influences. Converted around 1885, he became, at little more than age 20, the leader of the Protestant faction of Ganda politics, and later, with the assent of the British, "prime minister" or *katikiro* of Buganda, a post he retained from 1886 to 1926.

In 1901 he published *Basekabaka be Buganda (The Kings of Buganda)* in Luganda, in 1905 a second book on "traditions and customs," and in 1908 a third on "clans." The influence of his first book was enormous: he could claim to be at one and the same time the heir of the best Ganda traditions, an eyewitness of the civil wars of 1880-1890, a representative of the first Christianized generation, and a co-signer with the British of the "Uganda Agreement" of 1900. He was thus the spokesman for his clan, for a political-religious group, for the court aristocracy and a collaborator of Europeans. Therefore, he was the embodiment of the image of a "traditional" society with which the elite of the late nineteenth century so wished to identify, and as the British willingly imagined it as well. But Kagwa's work is also the result of contacts with ethnographer-missionaries: It was John Roscoe who had led Kagwa to take up writing; they even undertook parallel enquiries, referring to practically the same informants (Kagwa, 1971: preface, by M.S.M. Kiwanuka). Although the chronology appearing in his 1905 book was modeled on Mullin's work of 1904, for the rest Kagwa remained secretive about his oral sources; it was not until the 1918 and 1927 editions of this work that he provided lists of informants. Nonetheless, given the administrative and "civilizing" role entrusted to the Baganda by the British throughout the Protectorate called "Uganda," his work had an impact far beyond his native land alone (Wrigley, 1974; Twaddle, 1974).

Echoing this history, which had become a basic cultural reference and source of political legitimacy in Buganda, educated members of other kingdoms incorporated into the Protectorate set out to do similar work in their own areas and the same ambiguities may be found in their publications. In Bunyoro for example John Nyakatura,

originally from Buyaga (a Nyoro province transferred to Buganda by
the British) followed an analogous career. Educated in missionary
schools (first Protestant, then Catholic), he became an assistant to the
colonial administration, first as a "clerk" in 1912 and then from 1928 on
as a "customary chief." Throughout his life he remained a militant
irredentist over the question of the restitution of the "Lost Counties"
(ceded by the British to Buganda) to Bunyoro; both hostile to the
Baganda and fascinated by their success, he dreamed of matching
Kagwa's work. Motivated by these political preoccupations and
drawing on the recollections and memories passed on by his father,
who had served in the court of kings Kamurasi and Kabarega, he
wrote from 1938 a history of the kings of "Bunyoro-Kitara" published
only in 1947 under the title of *Abakama ba Bunyoro-Kitara,* with the
support of a Catholic priest (Nyakatura, 1973 [1947]).

Similarly in 1955 in Nkore, two "clerks," Katate and Kamugungunu, published a history of their country, *Abagabe b'Ankole (The
Kings of Ankole)* in Runyankore. The acculturated aspect of this
work is suggested simply in the name of the country as it appears in
the title—Ankole, the form adopted by the British to refer to the larger
administrative district which included the kingdom of Nkore. The
idea for the book originated with "Prime Minister" Mbaguta,
Kamugungunu's father-in-law, with the dual objectives of glorifying a
small country confronted by strong Ganda rivalry and of affirming the
status of the emergent elite (Karugire, 1979: 2-3).[3]

The majority of oral traditions known and drawn on by the scholarly world have been passed through such supposedly accurate transcriptions of these first literate persons. Referring simply to local
"oral tradition," as is often done in ethnohistorical studies, provides
the appearance of basing a work on the testimony of wise old men
sprung from the soil, those sometimes referred to as "elders" (a
much-misused term). The intermediary role of these "clerks" is neglected, as if they had been but simple pencil-pushers.

The implications of this "inculturation" are most evident in three
forms: in sociopolitical definitions, in chronologies, and in hypotheses on origins. In his history of Bunyoro, Nyakatura (1973: 17, 27),
assuming that the Cwezi were either Portuguese, Egyptians, or
Ethiopians, sought to glorify the first king of this mythical dynasty, the
famous Ndahura, by bestowing a more "civilized" status on him. He
thus attributes to him a decisive role in the diffusion of coffee as a cash
crop and even with the introduction of Egyptian cotton. The heroic

hunter-warrior of the traditions is thus presented in the form of a British governor or, even more to the point, of an innovative colonial chief. Similarly, when the Ganda aristocrats who negotiated with the British in 1900 brought into effect a feudal concept of property law and thereby transformed themselves into virtual landlords, they misportrayed the entire social fabric of their country. In such circumstances customs and tradition are no more than pretexts called on for a specific purpose; it was not the oral sources themselves that were the deforming elements but rather their written formulation and manipulation to serve particular purposes.

In 1935 the king of Bunyoro, Tito Winyi, published in the *Uganda Journal* a history that would allow his kingdom to match Buganda's previously published chronological span (K. W., 1935, 1936, 1937). To do this he felt the need to extend the king-list, and as a result, although he had acceded to power under the dynastic name of Winyi II, he subsequently became, "in a trice," Winyi IV (Henige, 1974a, 1974b: 106-115). Once again the policies of expediency and conscious calculation, in conjunction with the utilization of existing written sources, have extinguished any hint of critical oral inquiry worthy of the name.

Traditions of origins and genealogies, in spite of—or because of—their great importance, have not escaped the influences discussed here. The "scientific" dimension supposedly associated with literate cultures has intervened equally at this level, reinterpreting traditions and conferring new honors on them by combining them with anthropological, linguistic, and biblical hypotheses of the day. And such introduced distortions do not exist independent of oral cultures but have in turn fed back into it, as illustrated in the case of Burundi (Chrétien, 1981). The most widely known Rundi traditions of origin, those of the Nkoma cycle, have been obscured by other variants with a very limited expanse in both numerical and geographical terms, those of the Kanyaru cycle, which basically concur with some a priori schema associating royalty with a Tutsi conquest from the north. The replacement of one set of widely spread traditions with another of more limited diffusion required the combined authority of a bishop (Mgr. Julien Gorju), the most important "customary" chief of the period (Pierre Baranyanka), as well as of selected and selectively interpreted Rwandan traditions; the resulting thesis became entrenched in Gorju's edited work (1938). It was not until the 1970s that the country's oral sources resurfaced, after forty years of systematic diffusion of this official version in the seminaries and schools.

This last example shows how diffusion through the colonial/
missionary school network led to international scholarly recognition.
But what interests us here is its diffusion within the African milieu,
assuring for these written syntheses on the "customary" world an
audience drawn from the newly educated strata of the countries
involved. In the case of Burundi, the "Rundi historian" referred to by
Gorju and other missionaries in search of origin traditions was none
other than the chief Baranyanka (Chrétien, 1981: 16). By joining the
history of Burundi to that of Rwanda, considered older and more
prestigious, Baranyanka thus played on the attention of the Belgian
administration, his status within the circle of chiefs, and his sentiments associated with an emergent nationalism. As in Uganda, the
merging of earlier entities within new colonial state structures (such
as "Ruanda-Urundi") led the dynasties to reconsider and to adapt
their traditions. Even though firmly within the new channels of circulation of written work, Baranyanka, who until then had played the
role of the great "informant" (the Rundi had nicknamed him
musemyi, the interpreter!) knew very well how to use the established
networks of oral communication, whether in private conversations,
meetings of local traditionalists at his residence in Rabiro, or in
official speeches at the capital, Gitega, during meetings with other
chiefs (Chrétien, 1984).

   In Rwanda a similar function was performed by the priest Alexis
Kagame, though with a completely different scholarly and personal
dimension. Sometimes (though inaccurately) presumed to be the
member of an *Abiru* lineage (ritualists in charge of esoteric royal
knowledge) Kagame in fact assumed the role of great interpreter,
midway between two intellectual universes, that of his country's
aristocratic traditions and that of Christian Europe. Kagame the
Rwandan aristocrat, and Alexis, the Catholic priest, form very much
an integrated intellectual entity, something much more complex than
the simple "resonant echo" of a bygone culture which he was sometimes considered to be. His intellectual activity was based both on his
family roots and the protection of *Mwami* Mutara Rudahigwa, who
allowed him access to the dynastic esoteric codes, and on his formal
education and the encouragement provided by the Catholic missionaries. In the early 1940s he wrote an epic poem in Kinyarwanda
on the evangelization of Rwanda, *Isoko y' Amajyambere (The Source
of Progress),* culminating with the baptism of king Mutara in 1943, and
the first volume of the dynastic history *Inganji Kalinga* ("That

Kalinga, the royal drum, might triumph!"). Both works glorify the Tutsi dynasty of the Nyiginya, who were portrayed as having built the country in the distant timeless past before leading it toward "civilization." His reinterpretation of Rwandan history is built around the primordial role of the Tutsi, in Kagame's view a synonym for Hamites. The Kigwa narrative, for example, conforming precisely to the Hamitic ideology enunciated in missionary and colonial writings for the previous half-century, is represented as the founding myth of Tutsi penetration. But variants show this to be not a founding myth applying to the dynasty alone, but rather on a larger scale, applying to the entire multiform culture wherein pastoralism (a symbol of Tutsi culture) plays no particular role separate from the larger culture. Furthermore, if these accounts recorded from the beginning of the twentieth century also enhance the status of the Tutsi Ega lineages allied to the dynasty, this is undoubtedly to be viewed in the context of the preeminent political influence wielded by the Ega from the end of the nineteenth century, exceeding that, to some degree, of the Nyiginya line itself.

This example allows us to assess the impact of the transition to writing within Rwandan culture; the 1943 transcriptions of these traditions freeze their form and their significance at the time by endowing them with a timeless quality. Specifically, "Tutsi" classifications in these writings correspond implicitly to the Tutsi role within the colonial context—the concept of a "caste" holding a monopoly of power based on its supposed "racial" specificity is projected onto the entire national past; the written documents thus provide an aura of antiquity to the ideology. In other words the prejudices and outright misconceptions associated with "indirect administration" in Rwanda appear to be confirmed in these "traditions," whereas in fact these versions are heavily influenced by the calculations of the particular Tutsi aristocracy of the era (in their turn, informed of the intellectual currents of the day). When, in the 1950s, prominent persons from the royal court reaffirmed the absolute primacy of the Tutsi, they based their arguments on the text of *Inganji Kalinga* (Nkundabagenzi, 1962: 35); written sources had truly achieved preeminence in the matter of traditions!

The external origin of written culture thus confers on the first generation of African historians or chroniclers a particularly ambiguous position. The mediations of external influences were numerous, even in the more remote area where unprinted words and new ideas circulate rapidly, even if by word of mouth: "The moment a word leaves the lips it passes over the mountains," says a Rundi proverb. The lips of the literate are no exception to this rule; information drawn from literate sources, even those of foreign origin, is quickly absorbed as part of collective knowledge: Contemporary researchers in East Africa have come across references to *Misri* (Egypt) or to *Bisinya* (Abyssinia) in clan genealogies (Were, 1967: 62-64); in Burundi an old man takes his genealogy back to Kamu, the son of Nohu; another attributes a Palestinian origin to the Tutsi.

But the most effective as well as the most insidious infiltration of African traditions by foreign perceptions was undoubtedly through material published in the vernacular languages, notably in the missionary press. Newspapers such as *Munno* in Uganda and later *Rusizira Amarembe* or *Ndongozi* in Burundi, and *Kinyamateka* in Rwanda had all the more influence because a single issue could reach many readers and many more listeners for whom they were read aloud. In particular a series of historical articles published in 1943-1944 in *Rusizira Amarembe* under the title "Ingoma y'i Burundi" ("The Drum of Burundi"), probably inspired by Baranyanka, demonstrated the extraordinary cultural syncretism from both Burundi and Rwanda and combined it with much larger themes, including an allusion to Kami, the "father of all blacks" who (etymologically) was believed to be the ancestor of the *bami* (kings). Having already appeared (but relating to an Nkore clan) in Gorju's book of 1920, this pious philology integrated "pagan traditions" within a sort of local "holy" history (Gorju, 1920: 34; Chrétien, 1981: 19-20).

This improvised indigenization of foreign elements that appears in early African historiography calls into question the epistemological disagreement such as that proposed by Goody (Goody and Watt, 1963), on the leap from a "mythical" universe to one tied to scripture: "Historical consciousness can barely begin to function without permanent written archives." But without reviewing all the arguments supporting the critical use of oral sources and providing indications of their reliability, it is worth noting that these African examples also argue for a return to oral sources closest to the soil, so as to demystify the results forged under the cover of colonial schools.

In referring to ancient Greece, Detienne (1981) proposes a more subtle view of the intellectual effects of the transition to writing, arguing that the opposition between the fantastic and the rational, between *muthos* and *logos,* is not automatically achieved by the technical transformation from oral to written transmission. For a long time "noters of tales" (logographs) or "narrators of the past" (archeologues, those rationalizing or explaining the past) could simply compile traditions. It was only with the reflections of a political scientist like Thucydides or a philosopher like Plato that more refined concepts developed. Moreover, if we understand "mythology" as the application of a vision of the world seeking to account for origins and endings, one must seek it less within the diversity of innumerable local traditions as within written works: "Before having been thought, before having been spoken, the Greek 'myth' was written" (Detienne, 1981: 153-154). It is in the conjunction of oral traditions and scripture that occurs the crystallization of a mythology.

But is this not a process that recurs in Africa at the end of the nineteenth century? Doesn't this recall the work of Alexis Kagame, that "logograph" communicating from within a tradition experienced fully yet also endowing it with the "subtle markings of verisimilitude" (Detienne, 1981: 153) and at the same time molding it to the politics of his time? In a culturally colonized Africa "the pen of the logograph" is firmly held from the start and persistently controlled later on by foreign hands; mythology there is the result of a radically unequal exchange of the written and oral, or a written civilization denying to another its historicity. Twaddle (1974) cites the example of an article in *Munno,* where the Catholic Prince Gomotoka, commenting on the traditions of origin of Buganda, brushes aside "the fables and the jokes" of the account of Kintu (in this case, the intervention of a serpent and a tortoise) to fall back on the supposedly more "rational" hypothesis of a civilizing "Clovis." A foreign mythology is thus expressed in the writings of African intellectuals as if they were blinded to the logic and symbols of their own culture. In this situation, far from opening onto an "enlightened" historical horizon, writing retains its dependence on new religious, political and racial fetishism.

THE NEW AFRICAN HISTORY:
THE "HISTORIAN'S CRAFT" IN THE
SERVICE OF A CULTURAL CRITIQUE

A new stage was reached in the years 1960-1970. The development of university centers and the training of historians willing to master the rules of the "profession" coincided with the political watershed of African independence. These two realities in and of themselves

would justify a break between the new and the old generations of
literate Africans, but ethnic, linguistic and cultural continuities seem
to have made respectable ancestors of the first generation of African
intellectuals. Without wishing to deny all scholarly interest in the
works achieved during the colonial era, a more critical, even iconoc-
lastic approach would have been more appropriate, given the
methods and ideological orientations discussed above. How does one
return to rigorous historical research without bringing into question
the syntheses erected at the conjunction of two cultures and research,
even if the implications of this reality have remained till now poorly
understood?

The importance given to oral sources and the return of researchers
sharing a common tongue with their terrain but concerned also with
linguistic rigor and semantic precision, has resulted in access to richer
sources, clarifying terms literally repressed by or deformed by colonial remodeling; more important, it permits an oral culture to redis-
cover itself as its own primary audience. We are beginning to understand the significance of changing concepts of power in the African
past in studies on how political unity evolved from a variety of
supralineage cults (Kimambo, 1969), how power was wielded over
relatively wide areas without modern administrative tools (Mworoha,
1977), and on the history of early small-scale politics subsequently
subsumed within larger state systems (Nahimana, 1981). Recourse to
a historical method worthy of the name also allows the identification
of the articulations, contradictions, and evolution of differing social
phenomena within a given space and leads to a reexamination of fixed
ethnic stereotypes and frontiers previously judged eternal and
"natural." In his examination of the internal structure of Nkore from
the eighteenth century, accounting particularly for the evolution of
sociopolitical relationships between Hima and Iru, Karugire (1971)
reevaluated the earlier view of Nkore in the literature. Similarly
Bishikwabo's thesis (1982), tracing the nineteenth and twentieth century history of the small Shi kingdom of Kaziba, wherein trade along
the Kivu-Tanganyika axis assumed such great importance, helped
provide a realistic perspective to large-scale colonial divisions
("Kivu" as a whole, or "the Bashi" as a single ethnic group), divisions
previously accepted as the fundamental units of study.

Field observation, in the monographic method, and the concern for
restoring the manner in which the historical actors themselves envisaged their management of space, work, and social relations all lead

toward a reequilibrium of oral culture confronting an academism based on the cult of the foreign written word.

A comprehensive historical critique of colonial regimes is also needed, one examining the systems of forced labor, labor migration, expropriation, and taxes (Bashizi, 1980). Such work need also account for administrative manipulations, the degradation of former institutions and the promotion of chiefs assuming a pseudo-customary role (Gahama, 1983). Another dimension to such a field of study is the intellectual and cultural alienation produced by the colonial administrative apparatus, mission activities, and Western educational structures. African perspectives on these different features including the perspectives of both researchers and peasants, men and women, will provide a new assessment of colonial dependence, focusing on the historical dynamics of the situation and a greater appreciation of both the forms of oppression and the response of the colonized, not only in intermittent or open resistance but also in the passive attitudes and the opportunistic adaptations which allowed them to avoid open catastrophes. As Mudimbe (1973) emphasized in his critical work on ethnology, we need to abandon "museum" descriptions of African societies whereby Africans were but "informants" in order to better situate these people in real time and space; that is, not enclosed and not immobile, but characterized all the same by a century of dominant infiltration by the industrial world.

A renewed exchange between intellectuals and the past of their own peoples is called for in recapturing their own history. What is important in this regard is the relationship between peasant culture and a dominant industrial culture—a recognition of the issues involved in the exchange between the oral and the written in a period when more than ever they have become unequal. Neither change in intellectual careers nor the political transformations associated with the birth of new states could have been decisive in themselves without a real epistemological conversion. Reestablishing some sort of equilibrium between the oral and written dimensions of historical consciousness cannot be reduced to the simple technical task of handling "oral traditions" as concrete items. Instead it also implies a detailed analysis of the many cultural forms of dependence so as to avoid the pitfalls of Eurocentrism, or "Euromorphism," reducing Africa to a single compartment of colonial history or reformulating its past in terms of western historiography.

NOTES

1. Françoise Raison (1977, and other works) has provided a penetrating analysis of this process for nineteenth century Madagascar. Her work has influenced my own perception of the phenomenon, as reflected in the title of this chapter.

2. Tanzania National Archives, Dar es Salaam; German files; G21/123. Obergericht Dar es Salaam, case Schindelar-Pretorious (verdict of 10.12.1906).

3. Other less well-known authors have left only unpublished papers or articles in the vernacular press, but they have played no less a decisive role as key "informants" for European authors. Alphonse Aliwaali conducted inquiries throughout Buganda for Julien Gorju, and thereafter published numerous historical articles in the Catholic journal Munno. In Kiziba, Francisco Lwamgira, a follower of King Mutahangarwa, who had acceded to power with German help in 1896 and who subsequently became an important interpreter for the German Resident von Stuemer before becoming advisor to the British for Native Administration, organized the collection of court traditions which later served as the basis for Father Otto Mors's "History of the Bahaya" and other articles. An English version (translated by E. R. Kamuhangire) is found at Makerere University library and has since served as the basis for more recent interpretations of the region.

7

AFRICAN HISTORY
AND THE RULE OF EVIDENCE
Is Declaring Victory Enough?

DAVID HENIGE

I

> All that history has is "the evidence"; outside this lies nothing at all
> [Oakeshott, 1983: 107-108].

All scholarly, indeed, all mental, activity bases itself either on
experience or on evidence, which is regarded as experience *in absentia*. Historians have been among the foremost in applying the
methods of their discipline with respect to evidence, while exhibiting
growing sophistication in its generation and treatment. They have
decided that the most important tests for evidence are those based on
contemporaneity, propinquity, and faithful transmission. In practice,
they have demonstrated this by linking evidence with argument and
by trying to reduce historical practice to a set of guidelines. In all this,
the care that historians have taken in verifying their statements has
distinguished them from others interested in the past.

Even so, the esteem of historians for their evidence has from time
to time undergone periods of eclipse. We now seem to be in a time
when in many quarters evidence is devalued, no longer seen to be the

Author's Note: I acknowledge with thanks the criticisms of David Newbury, Jan Vansina, and Donald Wright on earlier versions of this chapter.

crux of historical method. Oral historiography today is a product of
these shifting values, an outgrowth of the view that theory should
determine the use of evidence rather than that each should inform the
other. In turn this is a by-product of the otherwise welcome tendency
to view competition for epistemological domains and objects of study
as inseparable from the advance of knowledge. Together with the
peculiar difficulties that are discussed below, this has resulted in
practices that may be indefensible and are seldom defended beyond
the occasional plea for special concessionary rules of evidence that
spring from the misguided notion that there can properly be differing
operational and interpretative standards for employing oral data. This
chapter begins with a review of the rules of evidence as historians
have generally understood them. A discussion of how orally derived
data resist the application of these rules follows, and the chapter
concludes with a few observations about currently fashionable approaches to the past that prefer to operate under entirely different sets
of rules.

I begin, though, with a brief consideration of the concepts of
"proof" as these relate to the handling of evidence, given that the
term has a habit of turning up in the most inappropriate circumstances. Extended discussion of the matter has been left largely
to philosophers; although philosophers tend to take a dim view of the
matter, historians should feel obliged to recognize and deal with their
arguments, if only as salutary devil's advocacy (see History and
Theory, 1981). A fair representation of the strict view was recently
expressed by Goldstein, who argues:

> What we come to believe about the human past can never be con-
> firmed by observation—can never be known by acquaintance—and
> so can never be put to the test of observation, the method of confir-
> mation that is virtually the only one that is explicitly recognized by
> science and philosophy [Goldstein, 1976: xii].

This must seem rather uncongenial, but compare it with the statement
of another philosopher, who wondered "whether we have sufficient
ground to accept any statement about the past, whether we are even
justified in our belief that there has been a past" (Ayer, 1965: 167).

Historians can hardly embrace these views and remain in business,
but an awareness of them can strengthen their defense of the scholarly
study of the past, in which five types of proof are distinguishable:

philosophical, mathematical, scientific, legal, and historical. Philosophical "proofs" are governed or "confirmed" by logic rather than experience or observation *(pace* Goldstein), perhaps explaining why there are so few universally accepted truths among philosophers. Mathematical proof, on the other hand—at least in the lower reaches of the field—is easily enough achieved because the tests are infinitely replicable and widely understood. Within the physical sciences proof is rather less absolute, as the number of hypotheses that have risen only to fall testifies (Agassi, 1975). Scientists do generally agree that a hypothesis has been "proved" when it can be verified a sufficient number of times under the same circumstances and in a given state of knowledge, always subject to advances in knowledge or experimental technique that might overturn them. In law an argument is "confirmed" by corroborative physical or personal evidence, with the former being accorded the greater weight.

In the best of times—which are among the rarest of times— historical "proof" (and here the quotes are obligatory) is less certain than legal proof because it ordinarily relies less on incontrovertible physical evidence than on humans' observations and interpretations of their own experience and that of others. Historical evidence, then, never provides more than reasonable certainty because the past cannot be repeated. Furthermore there is often no agreement over what in fact is to be proved, because historians are interested in the "why" and the significance of human activity at least as much as in questions of "what," "where," "when"—in explanatory frameworks at least as much as in empirical reality. In fact there are many cases in which there is neither adequate evidence nor any intrinsic likelihood that a given set of events occurred. Unfortunately, many of these fall squarely within the domain covered by oral tradition.

II

> The evidence we have does not guarantee us the truth, even though our only access to the truth is through the evidence [Atkinson, 1978: 11].

The starting point of all historical inquiry should be a body of evidence that occasions the need to explain it. What then is evidence? While historians generally agree that historical evidence can accurately (if unhelpfully) be characterized as traces of (and from?) the past, there is substantially less agreement as to what these traces ought to encompass. Historians reject the restrictive definitions of the philosophers, who like to argue (as in Goldstein's "human past") that only physical traces of human activity can constitute valid evidence, in favor of uncovering and exploiting any datum that might throw light on some part of the past.

Historians first divide their evidence into "primary" status, "secondary" status, and so on, but even at this level categories are neither hard nor fast. They usually hold that primary evidence must derive from close (but how close?) to that to which it is held to testify. But what is acceptable in this regard necessarily varies with the aim of individual historians and the questions they ask.[1] Accordingly, evidence generated by a single source, even about a single event, will be primary in some contexts and secondary or worse in others. There are also distinctions with genres of evidence. We distinguish among clearly objective evidence (or "evidence in spite of itself"), possibly or potentially objective evidence, and clearly subjective evidence.[2] Artifactual evidence, while most likely to fall within the evidence-in-spite-of-itself category, is also likely to survive for entirely different reasons than other forms of relevant evidence and thereby is frequently disconnected from them. Consequently, while valuable for its objectivity, physical evidence can be exceedingly refractory because of its lack of intelligible context.

Finally, there is the apparent contradiction of no evidence as evidence, that is, the faintly notorious argument from silence (Lange, 1966; Law, 1984: 195-211; Robertson, 1978). Normally, of course, it is both bad manners and bad policy to regard the lack of evidence against a hypothesis to be evidence in favor of it. This is nowhere more true than in the study of oral data, where the past has too many silences. Yet even here in some circumstances silence can be eloquent. The issue of kingship in Elmina illustrates this point: We cannot categorically affirm that Elmina kingship was an eighteenth-century development, but the weight of earlier testimony that does not allude to its prior existence allows us to hypothesize this (Henige, 1974c). On the other hand, if Samuel Pepys had failed to mention the London fire in his diaries, we would be justified only in questioning his reliability as an observer. So, again, the argument from silence must be tempered by other evidence and by a knowledge of the sources that provide the silence (for instance, silence in archaeology seldom means very much). At any rate, when historians adopt some variation of the argument from silence they must take care to do it explicitly.

The question of potential evidence must also be considered, partly as an aspect of the argument from silence, but also on its own terms. The body of oral historical data is still not very great and there is as yet little aggregation of evidence about particular times and places. Rather perversely, this very exiguousness has contributed to an impression that such data are somehow less susceptible to direct refutation. Yet, new data appear to contradict present understandings of what happened as often as they reinforce or supplement it: Witness the study of the Bantu expansion (ex-Bantu conquest and ex-Bantu migration). This is hardly to propose that contradictory evidence be ignored, and even less to suggest that the search for new evidence be relaxed for a moment for fear of an embarrassment of riches. It is, rather, to emphasize that the interplay between evidence and interpretation is likely to be more or less intricate in proportion to the amount of deployable evidence. It is clearly the *nature* of evidence that creates this seeming paradox. This is emphatically true for oral data, which embody individualized and fragmented memories, selected and sanitized slices from a larger experience that are elicited only by belated and isolated inquiry.

III

As for orall Traditions, what certaintie can there be in them? What foundation of truth can be layd upon the breath of man? How doe they multiply in their passage, and either grow, or dye upon hazards [Hall, 1628: 167]?

Hall's queries, though some might deplore his views on his fellows' capacity for truth, capture a dilemma that continues to bedevil the use of oral tradition: Is it evidence from the past about that same past, from the past about a different past, from the present about the past, or from the present about the present? Oral historiography's current vogue, while not unprecedented, is the first serious and widespread use of oral sources by professional historians since the rise to supremacy of text-oriented historical criticism some two centuries ago. In the matter of evidence, it has often developed fitfully and tangentially, as we can see from a definition of history more than a century old that, while very much on the rigorous side, would still find many adherents:

Historical evidence, like judicial evidence, is founded on the testimony of credible witnesses. Unless these witnesses had personal

and immediate perception of the facts which they report, unless they
saw or heard what they undertake to relate as having happened, their
evidence is not entitled to credit. As all original witnesses must be
contemporary with the events which they attest, it is a necessary
condition for the credibility of a witness that he be a contemporary;
though a contemporary is not necessarily a credible witness [Lewis,
1855, 1: 16].

Can oral historians possibly accept this austere conception of
historical evidence, one that allows but a single act of transmission,
from observer's mind to paper? Hardly, for historians who use oral
tradition cannot accept the notion that *demonstrated* contemporaneity is a *sine qua non* of reliable evidence. Equally, those who
adopt such a view can scarcely regard oral tradition as a useful tool for
divining the past. What then are oral historians seeking to reconstitute
the past to do in order to reconcile this apparently irreconcilable
difference of opinion? Should they adopt their own definition of
evidence, one tailored to be used with oral sources? Or dare they
argue that their sources actually fit Lewis's (and others') strict
criteria? Or should they recognize that their task cannot be to reconstruct the past, but only to interpret a small, and perhaps inconse-
quential, snippet of it on the basis of extant sources of indeterminable
pedigree, realizing that they will necessarily, if unwittingly, bring into
operation some part of the intervening period as this has been absorbed into their sources? In short, should oral historians believe that
the past should be exhumed, resurrected, or reincarnated? Since
attitudes about evidence—no more and no less—underlie these approaches, it is worth discussing each of them.

To some extent, of course, each historian rightfully determines
how he or she wishes to define his or her evidence, taking principle
and expediency into account in varying degrees. It might then be
possible to reject Lewis on the grounds that his characterization is too
exclusive, too unattainable, too tipped in favor of the written word.
Adopting this strategy would require the dissenting historian to justify
his or her charges by demonstrating that sources that are neither
contemporary nor known to be derived from contemporary sources
can still be reliable. The difficulty can hardly be met by the penchant
for ignoring the issue of evidence entirely. Though this often succeeds
in the short run, it permits the historian to proceed only by virtue of a
definition that makes nonsense of his or her reconstruction or one that

supports the reconstruction only at the cost of being indefensible
itself.

A second reaction might be to assert—or to presume without
asserting—that oral data can emulate written or artifactual evidence
in their ability to resist change over time.[3] It is no longer quite so
fashionable to proclaim the equivalence of oral and written data in this
respect. But the idea, albeit muted, still persists and residual out-
breaks of bravado may occasionally be encountered. Just as the
ancients admired Alexander's cutting of the Gordian Knot (not realizing that much of the traditional account was politically inspired propaganda), so might some moderns find such appreciations of oral
evidence appealing. Yet not even the historian most firmly wedded to
the documentary tradition would vouchsafe to defend his or her
sources against all comers simply on the grounds that they were his or
her own special sources; reasonable certainty in this regard can come
only from the operation of a critical mind.

Only the last alternative then is legitimately available to historians
using oral sources. Like the sinner entering hell, they must abandon
all hope—in this case, of reconstituting the past, in Ranke's famous
dictum, "as it really happened." They may take solace in realizing
that in this they will be following the example of most historians today,
who have accepted that much of the past is, and will continue to be,
impenetrable. There are, after all, two intermediaries between historians and any part of the past they have not experienced personally.
The first is the evidence; the second is that through which the evidence has passed or has been passed, whether humans' minds or a
series of physical environments.

For oral tradition, or any form of data that is subject to indetermi-
nate change, it is virtually impossible to distinguish one intermediary
from the other, even while historians must bear in mind the distinction
between evidence of what happened and evidence of what people
subsequently thought had happened. The data base of oral tradition is
substantially closed to rigorous testing and verification procedures.
Compare this with written sources. True, the ability to understand
such a source tends to diminish as time passes—as it is wrenched from
its context, as its language(s) fall into disuse and even oblivion, as its
physical condition deteriorates.[4] Yet whatever remains, remains unchanged, a replica of some moment in the past, not necessarily to be
accepted as true, but at least to be accepted as a true fossil. There is
no certainty in this regard—no inflexible grammatical rules, no ink on

paper, no chisel on stone—for oral sources. In their place is only human nature, that most adaptable and inscrutable of conductors.

Accepting these constraints entails realizing that no historians who use oral evidence can reasonably expect to engage in large-scale exercises in historical reclamation. Nor should they feel obliged to abandon the attempt to determine the most probable course of events and the causal relationships among them by industriously gathering, carefully sifting and weighing, and conscientiously interpreting the evidence, and above all by respecting it for what it can tell them as distinct from what they want to know. This is much to be preferred to the tempting alternative of using theory to bolster flaccid data. Of late this democratically derived tyranny of theory has made inroads into the African historiographical domain; it is to this the discussion now turns.

IV

True reality [*sic*] is never the most obvious reality; . . . its nature is already apparent in the care it takes to conceal itself [Lévi-Strauss, 1955: 50].

Writing about and understanding the past has never been, should not be, and cannot be devoid of theoretical underpinning. Wisely, if not always wittingly, historians have seldom permitted the "facts" to speak for themselves. Even the most exiguous annals and the most ostentatiously objective works have gone beyond the mere accumulation of detail. The Assyrian records were so austere in form that they could find room only for Assyrian successes. Medieval monastic chroniclers saw a ubiquitous hand of God in both past and present and interpreted and arrayed their data accordingly. Ranke's notorious past "as it really was" was no more than the past he regarded as important. Unrecognized in their time, because they were more orthodoxy than theory, these vagaries are now appreciated by historians where their own work requires using these sources and others like them. Contemporary historiography is infinitely more diverse, if less infinitely open-minded, and so less prone to operate within orthodoxies.

Even so, some historians have expressed concern that generalizing on the basis of carefully digested evidence is in danger of being superseded by the mechanical application of theoretical models as the principal means for exploring, understanding, and explaining the past. Their concern is not entirely inapropos. We do seem to be in the midst of an enthusiasm of styles of doing history and of looking at whatever evidence the past has thrown up on its fitful journey forward.

These new approaches vary widely, ranging from quantification to historical materialism to psychohistory to structuralism, even to semiotics. But however much they differ, and despite the diversity of the tools they employ, each shares with the others some degree of derogation of the traditional handling of evidence. Not incidentally, each promises to lift us to more satisfying levels of understanding than we have been accustomed to, in large part by offering to replace doubt with certainty. In each of them intuition (usually labeled "theory," but really macro-theory) is elevated to supreme explanatory status.

In large measure this assurance stems from the belief of many practitioners that they can aspire to, and attain, the full status of a "science" by being "objective" and universal in their conclusions. Given that only theory can be so, they say, each advertises itself as ultimately capable, if correctly applied, of explaining a particular past, not on the basis of accumulating and testing evidence, but on the grounds that their particular theoretical approach overcomes, indeed transcends, the very need for such procedures, in effect precluding the need for context as a prerequisite of explanation.[5]

While neither cliometrics nor psychohistory has as yet made much of an impact on oral historiography (Runyan, 1981), neo-Marxists and structuralists have already staked out strong claims. Given that they have much in common in their attitudes toward the value of evidence, we can allow one, in this case structuralism, to stand surrogate for the other. (For bibliographies on structuralism, see Lapointe, 1977; Miller 1981). In doing so, let me emphasize that all "isms" come in many shades and what follows is less about ideas than about the unacceptably one-sided application of them, the way they are misused rather than used. Still, those who are able to practice isms in moderation are likely to be viewed with impatience by their more uncompromising fellows. More to the point, by the logical imperatives of their premises, moderates run the risk of being seduced to ever more doctrinaire stances. The concern here is with those theoretical imperialists who claim to be able to domesticate their particular worlds completely.

Structuralists frequently claim just this—to be able to uncover "systemic principles operating in empirical cultural data" (Rossi, 1982: 58). They achieve this breakthrough, it seems, by discovering the "true meaning" and "deep structure" of such data by applying a set of principles largely borrowed from linguistics, where the approach is also a matter of controversy (Kronenfeld and Decker, 1979). Structuralists do occasionally claim to rely on ethnographic and historical data but it is admittedly of little concern to them to gather these disinterestedly or to evaluate them contextually. To engage evidence directly and with deference would be to descend to "empiricism," a term of both heavyhearted opprobrium and kindly commiseration in the structuralist lexicon. Oddly enough, then, it must seem to many, structuralists succumb to the gravitational pull of authority instead, with the writings of certain figures acquiring virtually oracular status. It might seem paradoxical that, while believing themselves to be scientific in method and effect, in exposition and argument structuralists' activities often resemble nothing quite so much as an expression of abiding faith by a community of believers.

For most structuralists, of course, the central figure is Claude Lévi-Strauss. Determined structuralists prefer Lévi-Strauss's appropriately Delphic pronouncements to the results of their own infrequent encounters with the evidence to determine the way they argue.[6] Untutored empiricists are apt to be taken aback by this unabashedly genuflexive posture and some are certain to share Korn's perplexity "to account for the renown of a theoretician who is unimpressive as an analyst and whose theories . . . are regularly refuted by the facts" (Korn, 1965: 145; see also Thomas et al., 1976; Dee, 1978/79; Nugent, 1982; Vansina, 1983). In effect, structuralists abandon the will-o'-the-wisp of history "as it really happened" (something that historians have long since accomplished) in favor of the *ignis fatuus* of history "as it must have happened."

For structuralists, then, "empiricism" and "literalism," as they choose to define these terms, are anathema. In this attitude they forget that literalism and structuralism are merely two kinds of intellectual straitjackets, the one imposed by data, the other by self-inflicted theory. In common with other schools of thought, structuralism presupposes an underlying universal psychic unity, and seeks to demonstrate it by an equally universal mechanism of selective emphasis; for instance, by sniffing out opposing pairs where most would see only differences, and recurring universals where others would see only coincidence. This done, structuralists have little alternative but to find, or to presume the existence of, data that can be fitted neatly into their imposed categorical abstractions. Such a broken-field approach can result only in an unacceptable degree of selectivity, practiced quite casually and almost entirely without awareness, explanation, or apology.

It is not hard to fault structuralism for this unedifying hubris alone. It is important, however, to realize that its antihistorical character comes less from this Manichaean stance than from the dismissal of historical and ethnographic evidence. Structuralism's claim to explain all by theory and its propensity to ignore alternative possibilities can emanate only from this disregard. By their work and their arguments structuralists implicitly grant that a great deal of evidence is not only unnecessary but downright unwelcome, a true embarrassment of riches. Although any theoretical approach must account for the evidence at hand as well as anticipate ("predict") new data, most theory is unable to contend with large and inhibiting bodies of evidence.

Perhaps this antipathy toward evidence underlies the *odium scholasticum* that so characterizes today's schools of theory. While faithful, in the spirit of coterie scholarship, to the teachings of particular masters, ideological theorists find it difficult to agree with each other. Instead, they often seem to resemble impotent basilisks, arguing incessantly, and perhaps quite appropriately, about what this or that master "really" meant. Only a newfound respect for evidence can control the growth of these congeries of self-proclaimed orthodoxists, too often united only in their determination to master theories and mimic masters, and in their penchant for evading the bane of data. As long as history is seen to provide exemplification rather than evidence, it is difficult to see how dogmatically applied lines of thought can lead to historically profitable conclusions. *Ex cathedra* pronouncement seldom approaches the truths to which all scholarship presumably aspires. It is not the historian's business to ask, "Will (or would) X approve?" Rather, he or she should ask, "Is my interpretation the best explanation of the evidence as I have it, and have I made every reasonable effort to uncover all the relevant evidence?" In short, apart from the binding force of sources, the historian knows no authority.

V

The moment a person forms a theory, his imagination sees in every
object only the traits which favor that theory [Jefferson, 1955: 12, 159].

Yet this binding is more in the nature of a tethering, which permits
the historian to explore and exploit evidential surroundings without
breaking loose from them. Consciously or unconsciously most historians have faced the dilemma expressed by archaeologist Lewis
Binford (1981: 21): "How do we carve out knowledge from ignorance,
. . . keep[ing] our feet on the 'empirical' ground and our heads in the
'theoretical' sky?" Historians realize that advances in knowledge are
seldom made without the exercise of some boldness and license and
that, while they must follow the lead of their sources, they must also
ask many questions that these sources never did. But the search for
new understanding intimately involves a concomitant search for new
evidence—the two activities are quintessentially symbiotic.
    Proponents of the supremacy of theory are right to point out that
the empirical approach to evidence is subjective, even if they are
wrong to imply that most empiricists think otherwise or that their own
methods are any less so. Historians generally concede that their own
biases and predispositions, whether of training or temperament, affect the ways they go about collecting and interpreting data. Most
would find little to quarrel with in Carl Becker's (1955: 327) observation that "the historical fact is in someone's mind, or it is nowhere."
In short, they accept that facts are themselves interpretations and
realize that there is no event in the historical record that does not
admit of more than one explanation. It is in accepting the ineluctabil-
ity of these ambiguities that "empiricist" historians distinguish themselves from those who would consciously eschew granting evidence
both its complexity and its indisputable centrality.
    With the study of oral historical sources the issue is rather more
complicated. Here even the most dedicated empiricist must occasionally have misgivings and many historians might be prompted to
abandon the exercise. Yet this is often neither the best nor the only
way to proceed. Oral historians have already recognized the need to
jettison the unduly narrow conventional notions of evidence by drawing on the widest possible range of sources, including those from
"exotic" fields such as botany, epidemiology, and meteorology. Doing
this involves the risk of carrying too little knowledge from one field

just a little too far in another. But failing to reach out ever more widely for evidence hobbles the historical enterprise quite unnecessarily.

Above all, oral historians must resist becoming infatuated with the impossible by unwarranted credulity, by the transformation of evidence, by making fetishes of their generations' particular paradigms, by abandoning their right to an open mind, by embracing the a priori. The besetting sin in the study of historical evidence today is an inability to abide ambiguity, a lack of discipline sufficient to avoid misleading ourselves into believing that we can go far beyond the evidence without losing our moorings entirely—in short, a reluctance to admit failure.

These aspects of current historical practice suggest a possible answer to Korn's implied question: The urge to find answers is always more powerful than the desire to demonstrate the impossibility of finding them. This is, of course, just as it should be—that is, until the desire for instant gratification completely stifles the sense of constraint.[7] Isms, like religious cults, thrive because they promise "answers" as well as an intensified degree of camaraderie. In this sense structuralism and other macro-theories are really no more than over-the-counter nostrums for the dread disease of doubt, the fear of the irregular and the unpredictable. We have learned that immediate "cures" are all too often only transitory and carry with them latent and harmful long-range side effects. For those historians who fail to recognize the need to treat evidence with the greatest respect, the most likely of these is an eventual disregard of their conclusions on the grounds that, by failing to give evidence a decisive role in their work, they have acquiesced too readily in their own arguments.

NOTES

1. Let us examine a recurrent discussion in American historiography about the Hamilton-Burr duel. To understand why Alexander Hamilton unexpectedly chose to accept Aaron Burr's challenge, we prefer to rely on Hamilton's own words, and not on the opinions of contemporaries, however well informed. But the historian interested in details of the duel itself can consider the testimony of observers (as well as contemporary prints, weather records, and so on) to be primary evidence, although not of equivalent value. In lieu of Hamilton's testimony about his *actions* that day, it is reasonable to rely on the views of others, whereas for his *motives* we can only do so *faute de mieux*.

2. Hamilton's and Burr's weapons would fall into the class of "clearly objective evidence," and in fact the pistols used offer a fascinating example of how new

evidence provides both answers and further questions. When the pistols, supplied by Hamilton, were recently examined after being privately owned since the time of the duel, they were discovered to have secret hairpin triggers. Whether this was known to Hamilton we do not know, but it certainly could not have been known to Burr. The evidence of the pistols severely damages interpretations that Hamilton deliberately fired prematurely for either humanitarian or suicidal reasons (Lindsay, 1976).

3. For artifacts, a *regular* change (such as the half-life of Carbon-14) is important evidence, but the belief that this was entirely uniform over time and space is now known to be erroneous. There may of course be other changes as yet unaccounted for.

4. Historians and philologists frequently attempt to restore lost portions on grammatical, paleographical, or comparative grounds. When they do, they scrupulously indicate any interpolations by brackets to indicate the lesser value of these portions as historical evidence (Porter, 1980).

5. Clearly excluded from this observation are such historians as E. P. Thompson, who explicitly consider the relationship between their evidence and their argument. For a discussion of Thompson in this regard, see McLennan (1982).

6. Actually, Lévi-Strauss (1966: 120) once referred to doubt as "the philosophical attitude *par excellence*," but it is precisely the sense of the tentative that is so absent from most structural analysis.

7. In this regard it is impossible not to think of the recent increased incidence (or at least detection) of scientific fraud. For a recent, though somewhat tendentious, account of this phenomenon, see Broad and Wade (1982).

8

AFTERTHOUGHTS ON THE
HISTORIOGRAPHY OF
ORAL TRADITION

JAN VANSINA

During the last generation, oral traditions have been used as evidence for the past in African history to a much greater extent than ever before, and interest in the theoretical and methodological aspects of traditions as sources for history has kept up with that pace. Practitioners tend to find the same difficulties over and over again, whether they work in Africa or not, but also—and many theoreticians forget this—the same advantages: a coherent view of the past over the century or centuries preceding the recording of narrative traditions, and an inside view of the historical development of the groups studied.

The methodological concerns in this field touch on so many topics that when preparing a new edition of *Oral Tradition* (1961) I found it impossible merely to revise it but had to rewrite it entirely.[1] The concept of oral tradition seems to have been reduced to narratives consciously intended to convey historical information; I shall call these *historical accounts*. These accounts usually stress the role of performance and the creativity of performers, although they usually relate to the performance of tales rather than to the narration of historical accounts (Scheub, 1975).[2] The dynamics of tradition have attracted attention, but only the dynamics of narrative accounts. These are seen as belonging to three successive types: flamboyant stories of origin, sparse notations (after a hiatus) that become more detailed for a middle period, and very richly detailed accounts for the most recent period. Some have even attached special notions of time to each of these stages and claimed different social roles for them. Origin stories are mythical charters and timeless, the middle period moves in cyclical time and represents the ideal (present) society, the recent period portrays events in linear time and shows the actual disorder that exists when the society functions (Willis, 1976; Spear, 1981). Causality is perceived only at this last level. This is too functional to be correct, and the three stages do not hold up to the same extent everywhere.

An enormous amount of attention has been given to "clichés" or "myths." By "cliché" some authors understand only stereotypes that recur, others add to this any image of anything "that is unacceptable as it stands," anything that *must* be reinterpreted.[3] This is simply the continuation of the debate about the meaning of myth, a debate that was old already by 1800. Less attention has been given to the implications of collective memory and the notion of a corpus of data. Several authors have underlined the problems of chronology, feedback, lack of access to sources and other aspects that limit the value of tradition as evidence (for example, Henige, 1982).

On the whole there has clearly been a gain in the sophistication with which one reasons about traditions, even if few authors really follow the whole methodological literature carefully (or even the literature on Africa alone), and even if progress seems to occur only sporadically.[4] There is no consensus on these matters, however, and disputes still pit historians against anthropologists and, even more, the adherents of various social science doctrines against unconverted historians insisting on "evidence." Yet all have accepted now that oral traditions are not like written documents and that the documentary analogy is a fallacy. The consequences that result from this realization vary enormously. Many use it to deny the criteria of evidence altogether. Others use it to insist that traditions never can be evidence. Every position in between is represented, without regard for different types of traditions.

But the stance of authors on this question is linked to their stance on other questions. A major dispute in the 1960s and 1970s opposed social anthropologists to historians. It involved the interpretation of traditional accounts (other traditions were not considered) as instruments of present day organization and expressions of current values and ideologies, as opposed to their character as testimonies about the past. For over a decade now, the extreme positions have been abandoned by most analysts and traditions are generally seen as expressions of both past and present. Nevertheless there are those who continue to hold that homeostasis operates ruthlessly, so that in effect traditions describe the present (Goody, 1977a), while others still hold that they are oral archives, untouched by the vagaries of later history (Webster, 1979: 1-37, 1983).

This dispute seems on the wane, but the various positions taken in connection with the interpretation of traditions of origin, traditions about culture heroes, stereotypes, obvious imagery, and the like tend to multiply. At present the following major groups can be distinguished. A few historians reject practically all oral tradition as evidence, because different traditions from the same society are interdependent and because the chronology is too approximate to be reliable. For them traditions are useful primarily as starting points to provide a focus for further research that will deny or confirm them. Their greatest virtue is to stimulate research (Henige, 1974b; Irwin, 1981). At the other end of the spectrum are those who hold that traditions should be taken literally (Webster, 1974, 1983); that without concrete proof to the contrary traditions should be believed, the chronology provided by genealogies or other internal data accepted, and historical reconstruction should proceed from there, based on the traditions as they stand. Suspicions about their truth and questions about their value should not be entertained if proof is lacking. When traditions seem to contradict one another compromises should be found that are compatible with all sides.

Between these two positions come those who want to interpret all traditions—especially traditions of origin. One structuralist group claims that all narratives are products of the mind when it idles. They want to show how the mind works, to show that the meaning of such narratives always has to do in hidden ways with the grand problems of human existence, the questions that are raised by human self-consciousness (de Heusch, 1972, 1982). Others reject these premises but hold that such traditions can be "decoded." Many hold that the decoding must first be sociological. The narratives are a social ideology of the present, an ideology expressed in roles, changing statuses and the like, often within the frame of a rite of passage type of action. Once this task has been done, there then remain details that are irrelevant to present-day ideology; those portions reflect valid history (see Feierman, 1974, for the earliest and most elegant of these studies). Another set of scholars holds that symbolic images were consciously construed by the creators of historical accounts to preserve the memory of complex events and situations too difficult to remember in their historical detail. Images are easier to remember and change very little over long periods of time; hence symbolism was a technological solution to problems of memorization (Miller, 1980: 7-8; Scheub, 1975).

But these positions are not rigid; it is a fallacy to think that scholars who adhere to one view may not later adopt another. Since no two scholars think exactly alike on these questions, I feel justified in presenting my own present position. To a historian *evidence* is crucial. We need to test traditions of any type or genre as evidence, either as traces of the past or as interpretations of the past. Hence we must be concerned with the analysis of performance in natural settings and the circumstances in which oral material is recorded, and today that is often no longer in performance but via informants reciting material to be recorded. We need to reflect on the relation between performance and tradition, and that between recording and performance—and their differences, for these types of relationships are not at all close.

While I remain skeptical about the special modes of thought attributed to oral societies (we all think logically and analogically), I am convinced that we still have much to learn about the dynamics of oral tradition over time. These vary according to types. Some traditions (often poetry or formulae) are memorized, even in the absence of an external unvarying standard against which they can be measured. Some (tales, proverbs) are held to be fictive and their dynamics are marked by continual innovation in performance. Thus tales, like epic, have no single author; every performer is an author. Tales have no beginning—they were never "composed"—and they have no end. They begin by taking material from the available store of tale motifs, episodes, and the like, and they "disappear" simply as material for later tales. Epics are different in that their various parts definitely require a first composition, but in their later elaborations they can vary almost as much as tales. Genealogies are sources of a different kind. They have to be added to continually, and they may well continue by regular reappraisal between those who need them for practical purposes, or simply as products of gossip. Lists are not normal in oral societies, but they nevertheless exist, especially lists of office; usually these are accompanied by mnemotechnic devices.

The different genres therefore have different dynamics. What most historians refer to as oral traditions, the accounts, begin as reminiscence or personal history or as historical gossip that can become accounts adopted by groups (Cohen, 1977). When this happens they change.[5] Stereotypes and imagery are then included which make such accounts part of a known corpus and provide meaning to them. In time it is the stereotypes and imagery which tend to remain, while the "details" vanish. Lastly there are the traditions of origin whose sources are speculation about the world and which incorporate only a few inputs from old group accounts. There may be more borrowing from the speculations of others than from their own group accounts.

The dynamics of accounts show the effects of the dynamics of memory and remembering, which are universal. What structuralists ascribe to the mind "idling" is really the product of memory at work.

It follows from the above that no interpretation of clichés can be satisfactory if it does not address the question of how they come to be. I hold, from the rare empirical evidence that exists in this realm, that imagery is produced for aesthetic reasons, to heighten emotions. Stereotypes—often in imagery as well—are adduced to give meaning and to integrate an account both within itself and into a corpus. The whole process is the product of mnemonic streamlining (making items more "logical" by discarding irregularities) and simplifying (keeping the essentials, or what seems essential at the moment of performance). The process is largely guided by contemporary interests and concerns, including contemporary world views.

Moreover narrative accounts, or narratives that consciously transmit history, are not just sources but a historiology (one can hardly speak of historiography in this case!). They are the fruit of reflection by local collectivities, who interpret their past on the basis of information heard from a preceding generation. At their best, such traditions are more like a historian's book than like the primary sources used by the historian; they are in reality the same sort of thing written down by Herodotus or the Greek logographers. It is crucial to realize that all traditions are collective. They come from a collective memory in a community; with the exception of esoteric material all can hear performances, all can perform them. Therefore different traditions held in the same collective memory cannot be "independent", and an examination of the corpus of any given type—historical accounts, for instance—held by a given community clearly shows mutual influences under the effect of the continuing dynamic of memorization.

In all of this the limitations and the advantages of oral traditions must never be forgotten. They cannot be independent, so as evidence they remain tentative. Usually their chronology for anything beyond 100 to 150 years is vague and unreliable.[6] The data are continually reselected and hence biased; therefore any direct use of them will yield a highly ethnocentric view. Finally, very detailed data cannot be kept alive in memory for long—one should not expect "oral archives." On the other hand traditions are internal to a society. They provide the necessary starting point for research, precisely because they are the products of local thought about the past. They allow the researcher to formulate hypotheses to be tested, hypotheses that are realistic and conform to local sociocultural realities. This is essential—and usually overlooked. But insofar as historians deal with specific processes and not with general forces over time, this capacity to be specific is essential. And lastly, most of the severe problems of reliability are concerned with a minority of all traditions: traditions of origin and some of those that have survived for well over a century before they were recorded.

In the future the debate about myth will continue and, I fear, remain as fruitless as in the days of solar/lunar explanations. More historians will insist on greater accessibility to the data and be concerned with data storage. The practitioner need not fear absolutely unexpected difficulties, nor hope for unforeseen shortcuts. Still our awareness of oral traditions as an intellectual and empirical phenomenon will certainly be developed by different disciplines in different directions. Social scientists will discover in practice how useful they are in the study of the present. Traditions may well become standard operating tools among anthropologists. Folklorists and students of word art know that much still remains to be discovered about the form and content of such forms of communication. And gradually the field will attract more psychologists and general students of the mind. The phenomenon of "oral tradition" is far from analyzed yet. Traditions are a marvel. They exist in the mind only, except for brief moments when they are performed. We would expect them not to be recognizably identical over a long time, and yet they are. For this, if for no other reason, they will continue to fascinate both those who use them and those who study them.

NOTES

1. *Oral Tradition as History;* Madison (University of Wisconsin Press) 1985.

2. H. Scheub (1975) was the first scholar to develop this.

3. This is the candid rendering of R. Firth (1961: 164). He goes on: "But what are to be the principles of such interpretation?" and confesses that he sees no way in which they can be decided upon.

4. The bibliography in Henige (1982b) contains 502 entries and is only partial. Most essays cite not more than two dozen or so references.

5. The crucial article here is Eggan (1967). This was a case of the reminiscences of eyewitnesses followed by a group account forty years later.

6. Even here there are exceptions. Liptako (Irwin, 1981) happens to have quite a good chronology from c. 1800 and Sereer Saluum is supposed to have a corrected chronology from c. 1450!

PART III

AFRICA FROM THE OUTSIDE
From Imperial Historiography, to Africanist Historiography, and Beyond

9

THE IDEA OF PROGRESS
IN THE REVISION OF
AFRICAN HISTORY, 1960-1970

CAROLINE NEALE

> Political independence could only have meaning if it was accompanied by *historical independence* [Ogot, 1976: 1].

In the decade following political decolonization in Africa, the mainspring of new historical writing was a desire to achieve intellectual decolonization through a revision of African history. The coming of independence was not seen as any ordinary change of government. It was to entail a fundamental change in the relationship of black nations to white nations, and of black to white in Africa, and it called for a new representation of the relationship that had obtained up to that point. There had been a political statement that black and white were to be treated as equals; now there was needed a cultural demonstration that such a thing was possible. The new version produced in the 1960s did provide a basis for pride in past achievements, but the idea that it was, thereby, helping Africans to throw off the domination of European ideas was illusory. "Achievements" were still defined in Western terms, in the context of an evolution from more primitive political forms toward the modern nation-state, which was seen as the culmination of mankind's progress to date. The creation of African self-respect was felt to rest upon repeated demonstrations that Afri-

---

Author's Note: The frustration of reading so brief a piece on so large a subject can be exceeded only by the frustration of writing it; for an elaboration of the points raised here, as well as others, see Neale (1981).

cans, too, had participated in and contributed to this development. Where colonial writing had tried to show that Africans stood outside this mainstream, postindependence writing sought to portray them as active within it. The mainstream, however, is a Western idea, and one which scarcely anyone thought to question.[1] The result was a decade of historical writing which focused on the triumph of African nationalism in a Western mold, and on those aspects of the African past which were seen as contributing to its evolution.

For historians writing in the colonial period, civilization, with its seeds in the Near East and its early bloom in the Mediterranean, had taken root in Western Europe and flourished there. Civilization meant the domestication of agriculture and animal husbandry, urbanization, the growth of trade and production, the creation of a leisured class, the accumulation of wealth and its sponsorship of art, music, and architecture, the skill of writing and the cultivation of learning, and the pursuit of scientific knowledge building on the recorded discoveries of the past. That these things had developed and continued to develop in Europe was indisputable, and it was firmly believed that they were good. That they had developed to a much lesser extent in Africa was not disputed either: What evidence there was, in the accounts of visitors to Africa and captured artifacts, was felt to be trivial or dismissed as the result of early influences from the Mediterranean. Africans did not have the wheel; except in Ethiopia, they did not have the plough. In the colonial image of Africa, people built only in mud and straw (the stone buildings at Zimbabwe were passed off as relics of some long forgotten foreign visitation); they had crafts, not arts; they did not write, so discoveries could not be recorded and scientific progress could only be of the slowest; and their wealth was barely exploited by the Africans themselves. They were not organized for civilization because they were not capable of starting the ball rolling by themselves. And once Europeans had done it for them, they still had several hundred years of social evolution to make up without being temperamentally suited to it; not a great deal could be expected all at once. The path of progress proceeded by stages, as exemplified by the European past and all that it contained. The African past, by contrast, was nothing more than the "unrewarding gyrations of barbarous tribes in picturesque but irrelevant corners of the globe," to quote (as every Africanist did) Trevor-Roper's memorable phrase (1963: 871). "History," he continued, "is essentially a form of movement, and purposive movement too. . . . Perhaps, in the

future, there will be some African history . . . but at present there is none:
there is only the history of the Europeans in Africa."

It was this picture of failure, then, that African historians had to
deal with when, in the 1960s, the political position of Africans was
reversed and colonial history, which had rationalized their subjection,
was rejected. The new nations needed a new history, and it must
refute the old, because the old was both wrong and damaging to
African pride.

> If there (are) aspects of Africa's past which deserve to be described as
> savage, these aspects are already fairly extensively documented. It
> now becomes important that the mere accumulation of extra informa-
> tion does not perpetuate the Trevor-Roper myth. Only a process of
> counter-selection can correct this, and African historians have to
> concentrate on those aspects which were ignored by the disparaging
> mythologies. So commitment to the correction of human error in this
> case might involve purposive discrimination in terms of what is em-
> phasised and what is augmented in the pool of human information.
> And yet to correct error is as respectable an aim as to increase
> knowledge [Mazrui, 1970: 123].

The error Mazrui referred to was not the idea that there are low and
high places in human development (the low places exemplified by
small-scale organization and simple arrangements for production and
exchange, the high by industrial capitalist societies), nor the idea that
the latter have a right to hold the former in contempt. The error was in
supposing that the course of African history tended more toward the
first situation than the second. The idea of social and political evolution went unchallenged, as did the idea that it was meritorious to
evolve as quickly and directly as possible (an idea which does *not*
attach to biological evolution) and that a people should be proud if
they had, and ashamed if they had not, been in the forefront of this
movement.

What was challenged, instead, was the picture of stagnation in
precolonial Africa, and of subsequent African lack of initiative. Historians set out to show, not that whatever Africa had had was somehow humanly worthwhile, but that Africans deserved the respect of
others, and could respect themselves, because they had had in their
past the things that *Europeans* valued! Their development was
presented as just as good as Europe's because it was the same, and
also because it was (sometimes) contemporaneous. This is important

because evolutionary history is competitive: "As there is but one path of human development, history can be looked upon as an intersocietal race for progress" (Chanock, 1972: 431). This point of view is exemplified by Sanders (1967: 531):

> [Historians] began to discover that Africa was not a *tabula rasa,* but that it had a past, a history which could be reconstructed; that it was a continent which knew empire builders at a time when large areas of Europe stagnated in the Dark Ages; that it knew art and commerce.

The British past had seen a move from local communities with relatively little internal differentiation to feudalism with an ever more centralized focus of power, and later to monarchies that broadened into empire, until at last power devolved upon parliaments, which ruled nations of mixed peoples under one law, one economic system, and one allegiance. All right then, we were told, the African past was like that too.

In some ways, in some places, so it was. But what is interesting is the way in which historians went overboard for those ways, those places. They took the great variety of ways of living and thinking which exist and have existed side by side in Africa, where herders have drifted through the capitals of kings for hundreds of years and are camping now on the pavements of cities, and assigned each one to its place in the different phases of man's development laid down by the scheme of western history, so that some belonged to the past and some to the future, with which the present was identified; for example Ogot (1968: 127) notes "The intrusion of the Bantu into East Africa . . . marked the transition from the hunting to the cultivating stage of civilization."

The key to understanding the model with which historians approached this phasing of African history is the idea of nationalism, for it was the success of nationalism which called forth the revision of history. History, said Davidson (1977: 39), should provide "a meaningful approach to the largest cultural phenomenon of twentieth century Africa—the advent and advance, one may even say the overwhelming victory, of nationalism and all its implications." That this is the "largest cultural phenomenon" is an extraordinary assertion, but even scholars who would not go that far gave it great importance in Africa's history because it was particularly important to them, bringing African countries into line with others as it did. As the successful management of nation-states was seen as the test of equality with whites, it seemed important to establish that this form of government was not a wholly alien one, handed down by the imperial powers, but in some sense the natural culmination of indigenous development. Hence the idea that there was a natural course of African history which would have produced something like the modern nations all by itself, even if their growth had not been forced and their particular forms determined by colonial rule: "The natural course of African history was savagely halted by European conquest and the centuries of the slave trade" (Pollock, 1970: 5). It is in this sense that Davidson (1977: 46) refers to "the restarting of the processes of African history after the long episode of colonial alienation," as if African history were some independent force which had spent the colonial period behind bars, restrained, but biding its time.

That African nationalism has been for many a moving and courageous struggle is in no way disputed; what is of interest here is the reason for scholars situating its origins as far back into the past as possible, and the distorting effect this had on the representation of African history (see, for example, Temu, 1969). As a political movement, nationalism took its force from the colonial situation; but as a historical idea, it derived its mysterious domination over centuries of African history from the evolutionism that placed Europeans and their political works at the pinnacle of human development. Historians constructed a sort of "Whig interpretation" of African history, taking the triumph of nationalism as the culmination of Africa's sociopolitical development. Each period had its focus: some aspect which could be seen, in retrospect, to contribute towards this end, and its progress would be charted, its contribution assessed.

The major themes of the period before European contact were perceived as "centralization" (the strengthening of a single political authority) and "enlargement of scale" (territorial expansion, usually by conquest). Efforts that increased centralization were presented almost invariably in a positive light with little regard for their significance in their own time and place, as it was the direction, more than the process, of change which was important. Oliver, for example (1963: 190), applauded the strengthening of the Ganda monarchy, remembered in oral tradition as a time of "bad and bloody tyran(ny)," because "Without doubt . . . strong government was an aid to expansion . . . (enabling Buganda to move) from a feudal to a bureaucratic system." An air of disappointment, by contrast, surrounds those communities which missed their chance, like Ogot's "stateless societies," the Dinka and the Nuer, who "have lived more or less in

one region for several centuries, and yet they have not evolved even a
Rwotship"(Ogot, 1964: 300). Stateless societies received little attention, and small chiefdoms were studied principally as forerunners of
larger ones. Kingdoms and empires occupied the latter end of a
continuum along which polities moved, or ought to have done. Reaching back to the earliest times we can reconstruct, then, the
"mainstream" for historians was occupied by societies that grew
into states, and the heroes were the rulers who pushed or pulled them
into shape.

In the period of trade with Europeans, before the conquest, the
heroes of this version were those who succeeded in using the trade to
their advantage, whose kingdoms did not become impoverished or
did not disintegrate under pressures of the slave trade. Indeed at one
point Fage (1969: 402) characterized the slave trade as "purposive"
because, while it "tended . . . to weaken or destroy more segmentary
societies" it speeded up the process of centralization in the stronger
kingdoms.[2] Next came the conquest, and who were the heroes then?
Not the leaders of the "romantic, reactionary struggles against the
facts, the passionate protest of societies which were shocked by the
new age of change and would not be comforted" (Robinson and
Gallagher, 1962: 639-640). No, the heroes were the "new men," those,
again, who made a "successful adaptation"—like Oliver's Baganda
whose "readiness to respond to . . . challenge . . . (would) be the
secret of Buganda's triumphant adaptation to the coming of Europe in
the late nineteenth century" (Oliver, 1963: 190).

Once European rule was consolidated, the leaders of resistance
became the forces of progress, as long as the sort of resistance they led
looked "forward"—to nationalism—not "back"—to tribalism; as
long as they

> were thinking in modern terms—not in terms of a reversion to tribal
> beliefs and tribal organisations, but in terms of Christian churches
> under African leadership, . . . and of African successor states based
> on the existing colonial territories and governed along western rather
> than traditional African lines [Oliver and Atmore, 1967: 158].

Resistance of any sort contested sovereignty, of course but to get on
the side of progress it had to contain features that were developed by
later nationalist movements into successful techniques. Looking at a
wide range of efforts involved in religious resistance movements—
spirit possession, oracles, prophecy, bullets-to-water magic, cattle

killing, witchcraft eradication; all equally plausible to participants in
the sense that all of them relied upon supernatural aid—historians
dismissed those which did nothing to undermine colonial domination
as escapes into fantasy, and wrote up the others as aspects of organization or propaganda.[3] The distinction was a western one, and the
opportunity to understand what people in such movements thought
they were doing was lost or postponed until such time as the preoccupation with nationalism weakened.

For more recent history, the focus was the nationalist struggle, the
leadership, platform, and organization of political parties, and the
form of government with which each nation embarked on independence. In the selection of material, therefore, and in the differing
emphasis placed upon events, nationalism and the evolutionist ideas
behind it dominated the writing of African history from independence
until well into the seventies. This produced three main kinds of
distortions. First, a historicism was introduced, assigning various
communities to stages of development, thus obscuring their role in
their own time and place. Second, and related to this, the subject was
narrowed to the evolutionary areas of focus, and to those aspects of
them which historians saw as functioning to propel or retard the
progress of the designated craft down the mainstream. Where historians found evidence of forms of organization which resembled those
of the European past, they extrapolated firm evolutionary trends,
treating the rest as peripheral to history. Material that might have
given a truer picture of the time was presented as extraneous or
anomalous, or did not appear at all. Third, values were allowed very
much to dictate what could appear in the new history books and how it
would be represented.

In the face of the needs of new nations in Africa, objectivity looked
like cynicism. The role of sheer embarrassment in the revision of
African history should not be underestimated. It is honest of Mazrui
to articulate the danger that the "mere accumulation of extra information (might) perpetuate the Trevor-Roper myth." Many historians,
however, did not announce their intentions in this way but simply
dropped from their agendas material which was felt to reflect badly on
African societies, or transformed it, so that internal slavery became a
family affair; conquest, an offer of law, order, and wider markets;
cannibalism, a form of social cement; and authoritarian terror, a
means of introducing new grounds of loyalty to the state. One example must suffice, but it is one that reveals a good deal about the new
historians' understanding of their role in rerepresenting material.

With the new writing on Shaka's wars it is evident how the goal of history was allowed to dominate the contemporary reality. Whatever horrors they might have involved at the time and for whatever reason they might have been undertaken, we were urged to regard wars of conquest as "positive" because of their effects on the enlargement of scale. Marks (1967: 90-91), for example, wrote that although

> it was the destructive aspects of the *Mfecane* which were most im-mediately felt, . . . out of this maelstrom new peoples, even new nations, were being born. . . . Shaka's achievement in welding a multi-tribal nation out of the numerous tribes of Nguniland in the short span of twelve years, a nation which has long outlasted the military power on which its greatness was based, was in itself out-standing. . . . And farther north, in the Transvaal, Zambia, and Tanzania, previously disorganised people were also to profit from the Nguni example. It was often those people who were either Nguni offshoots or who had responded positively to the Nguni challenge, who were able to withstand the vicissitudes of the nineteenth century and to resist new invaders—whether Voortrekkers, Arab slave trad-ers or even the colonial regimes at the turn of the century.

Omer-Cooper (1966: 173), too, found the *Mfecane* encouraging, as a type of "multitribal nation-building":

> One of the most striking features of the *Mfecane* is indeed the very general success which attended the numerous and different attempts at forming political units out of originally separate peoples. It suggests that the task of instilling a sense of political unity into peoples of different language and culture in a limited time, the task which faces every political leader in the newly independent coun-tries, is not so difficult as pessimists tend to maintain.

Here was a clear statement of what the new history had to offer, and to whom. Occasionally, this kind of writing still comes off the presses, particularly in historical surveys and textbooks which at-tempt to capture an audience assumed to be prejudiced to some degree and to present them with a synthesis of the historiographical Story So Far. For many historians, however, both from the genera-tion which produced it and from the more critical one that followed, the decade of nationalism now represents a phase which a "mature" African history has left behind (Lonsdale, 1981; Temu and Swai, 1981). To some it now seems regrettable, both from a political point of view in that it served the interests of new regimes which in hindsight were not what historians hoped they would be, and from an intellectual point of view, in that historians concentrated on narrowly political themes at the expense of social and economic ones. To others, it seems to have been a necessary phase, in that the racism against which nationalist history reacted was crippling to proper endeavors in any direction. Only when the ghost of colonialist history had been laid to rest was it possible, in this view, to proceed with a history in which some Africans, as well as Europeans, would be seen as exploiters, oppressors, collaborators, or even, simply, people who make mistakes.

The chief thrust of this new history has come from people applying Marxist ideas more or less systematically, and the debates of recent years have either been largely between these and unlikeminded scholars or carried out among Marxists who feel that other Marxists are not Marxist enough. From these debates one gets the impression that while nationalist history was a phase, political economy is the truth; the clouds of mystification have been broken through, and now real light can illuminate the field. But it is as well to remember that it was precisely in this way that nationalist historians once viewed their own endeavors. Each intellectual generation has seen what the times called for, believed that they called for the truth, and has gone out to look for it. The key historiographical question, therefore, is how a historian sees the times. In the 1960s, the times were Independence; in the seventies, they were Continuing Poverty (Ranger, 1976a). Both were features of both decades, of course, so the times must be in the mind of the historian, and this is where an intellectual history of African history must focus.

In the past two decades African history has moved, on the face of it, from a position of supporting new elites which slotted into an imperial system of capitalist appropriation from the Third World, both in terms of their class position and in terms of their model of future development, to supporting the poor of Africa by exposing the workings of that system with the tools of political economy. If, however, we try to see in the broadest terms what the two positions have in common and where they differ, at least three observations can be made. Both are characterized by a view of history that is evolutionary, unilineal, unidirectional, and assumes a progressive option to be available. Whether nationalist or Marxist, this is a cultural view, not a universal truth, and in this respect Marxism continues the domination of Western ideas over African history. The models of both schools of thought are Western ones, their adoption by African academics notwithstanding. Second, both points of view have been experienced, in their time, as support for the underdog. Finally, many of the same people have supported both points of view.

They are different models, to be sure, and in terms of the new one the heroes of the previous model ought never to have been seen as underdogs at all. They were protagonists in a different contest, one which occupies only a minor arena in the present analysis of oppositions. And it would be easy to suppose that the shift in analysis is a case of scales falling from eyes, were it not for the embarrassment that still occurs when fresh regimes, even self-consciously socialist ones forged in the experience of wars of liberation, separate themselves from the interests of their poor on attaining office.

A thread of continuity is therefore discernible through the last two decades of historical writing, as Western scholars go into the study of Africa with certain principled expectations of Africans derived from their views of Western history, and it is disappointment with their performance in terms of these expectations which opens the way for changes in historical analysis. There can be no doubt that many historians who emerged in the countries of origin of colonial Africa's ruling class felt that they *were* doing something radical in offering the new nations an anticolonial history, paying the new leadership the compliment of identifying its interests with that of the "country as a whole." The challenge of Marxist history, and the scholarly climate in which it was welcomed, grew out of the growing recognition of the disparity of interests that had been obscured, for a time, by the popularity, and the promise, of nationalism. Many historians were disappointed both by the cynicism of African leadership and by the success of neocolonialism. "Westernization" had been misunderstood by historians, and the evolutionary model could not explain the anomalies: the persistence of magic in politics, religious solutions to social ills, tribal organization, and official terror. The experience of independence revealed the weakness of a model of history in which Europe and America led the world in a common progression. An important change in perspective was found in "development of underdevelopment" theory according to which the West did not so much lead as gain an unmatchable advantage by taking from the colonized world the means to progress. These, being economic, were not restored with political independence. This model provides an alternative to the strategy of the 1960s, when historians picked out Africa's historical similarities with Europe as a basis for confidence in its future, and made it possible to look at Africa as part of the Third World, sharing the disadvantages imposed by its historical relationship with Europe, and needing a new strategy. It was, moreover, a theory in which Marxist and nationalist ideas could be (if uneasily) combined, and as such it provided a transition to the large body of writing in the tradition of political economy that followed.

NOTES

1. Two writers who did were Wrigley (1971) and Chanock (1972).

2. The use of "purposive" here can only be understood to imply that there is a purpose from which the historian is working backwards, not onwards, in time.

3. For descriptions of some of these movements, see Wilson (1969: 256-260), Andersson (1958), Young (1965: 281-288), Ranger (1975), Neale (1981: Chap. 3).

10

DECOLONIZATION IN AFRICA
A New British Historiographical Debate?

MICHAEL TWADDLE

                                                  A new historio-graphical debate? In the presently somewhat tired and emotional state of historical writing on the European scramble out of Africa since the Second World War, it might be thought that what is needed now is a period of quiet reflection and steady sifting of the evidence starting to tumble out of the Public Record Office and other archives under the terms of the thirty-year rule. But this, surely, cannot be so. If we are ever to make sense of the steadily mounting mass of archival material about the ending of European empires in Africa, we must have a theory, preferably several of them. The purpose of this chapter is to review existing explanations of the European scramble out of Africa, and to consider the possibility of constructing an alternative paradigm built around something which is presently either grossly *under*estimated in currently dominant paradigms of decolonization in Africa or woefully *over*estimated as regards its actual importance in the ending of European empires: anti-colonial nationalism.[1]

    The four basic paradigms to emerge from this debate are what I shall refer to as the "Commonwealth tradition," the "political economy" framework, the "British world system" approach, and the "romantic nationalist" paradigm. Although some historians do take rival paradigms seriously, the debate on decolonization in Britain has more frequently been conducted within the strict parameters of particular paradigms than between them, resulting in a sad "dialogue of the deaf."

THE OLD COMMONWEALTH PARADIGM

The first approach was built around the British custom of devolv-
ing power peacefully to former colonies during the nineteenth and
early twentieth centuries within the Commonwealth tradition:
Canada, Australia, New Zealand, and South Africa before World
War II, India, Pakistan and Ceylon very shortly afterward (Madden
and Fieldhouse, 1982). That created "a pervasive conviction . . . that
the representatives of British democracy would not . . . persist in a
policy of repression" where the continuance of British colonial rule
was seriously threatened by local opposition (Robinson, 1972: 129).
This tradition of granting Dominion status at least made it easier to
concede territorial independence more easily, and with less loss of
metropolitan face. Indeed, there are still distinguished historians in
Britain nowadays who stress the prime importance of the Commonwealth tradition of devolution of power from London for African
decolonization, especially after Indian and Pakistani independence in
1947 brought *colonies d'exploitation* within the tradition as well as
earlier *colonies du peuplement* such as Canada or Australia (Low,
1982). Others have even argued that subsequent African decolonization was *planned* from within the British government shortly after
World War II by Sir Andrew Cohen (R. Robinson, 1978, 1980; Pearce,
1982). (This particular argument suffers somewhat, however, from the
revelation that Cohen's memorandum on political development was
quietly put under wraps by Cohen himself immediately after opposition arose from British colonial governors in Africa itself [Cell, 1980]).
Within the Commonwealth paradigm, the principal arguments are
almost always over personalities and timing, because the basic
framework of devolution of power within the Commonwealth tradition makes long-term decolonization itself unproblematic. Flint
(1983) has suggested that planning for African decolonization within
the Colonial Office effectively began even before World War II, while
Robinson's writings on Sir Andrew Cohen suggest that planning for
postwar reconstruction in Britain's African colonies, through staged
devolution of power and economic development, was enormously
and unexpectedly speeded up by British overreaction to the Accra
riots of 1948. The subsequent acceleration of the decolonization process in East and Central Africa in 1959-1961 is also a prime concern for
this particular paradigm, with most attention currently focusing on
ministers such as Harold Macmillan, Iain Macleod, and "Rab" Butler

(Horowitz, 1970; Goldsworthy, 1970, 1971: 361-372; Gifford, 1982). Nonetheless, there are those who argue that "speeding-up seems . . . to have been primarily dictated, as elsewhere, by *events* to which Macleod and Butler and local colonial governments had to react, the principal event being the transfer of a radical nationalist sentiment from West to East and Central Africa. There is no strong evidence for schemes of reform in the sense of a prescient, preemptive policy in London" (Austin, 1980: 25).

This "radical nationalist sentiment" first became apparent in British-ruled Africa in the activities of Kwame Nkrumah and his allies. Although the Accra riots of 1948 were not especially noteworthy in themselves, the onset of the Cold War and Nkrumah's appeals for outside help combined to force British constitutional concessions.

> But the riots did provide a clear warning that, unless the British broadened the basis of their rule in West Africa, sooner or later they would be faced with something worse. . . . The British Cabinet, now convinced "that in the present state of political development in the Gold Coast no system would be workable which did not provide for a very considerable degree of African participation in the control of policy," approved the apparently far-reaching Coussey proposals [Hargreaves, 1982: 136-137].

Why, in retrospect, did the Accra riots of 1948 prove so significant for the subsequent independence of Ghana? Was it principally personal British miscalculation locally (Hargreaves, 1982: 135-136) or overreaction to Whitehall (R. Robinson, 1980: 65-66) that caused them to get out of hand, or was it the relentless work of a "radical nationalist sentiment" (Austin, 1980: 25)? And, if it was at least in part the latter, precisely wherein lay the springs of anticolonial action? In addressing these issues one observer has examined the radical nationalist movement in some detail (Rathbone, 1983). He begins by noting that many scholars who have recently studied Ghanaian nationalist politics (Crook, 1978; Staniland, 1977; Dunn and Robertson, 1973; Jeffries, 1978; Bechman, 1976) "have been unhappy about assuming the imperative of 'political liberation' " to explain why so many Ghanaians became engaged in nationalist politics after 1945. But "why did those groups who became active do so while others, no less oppressed, remain less involved?" Rathbone eschews as too simplistic arguments that an emergent petty bourgeoisie consti-

tuted the core and backbone of anticolonial nationalism because it
alone "bore the brunt of colonial restriction, shared few of the limited
privileges brought by colonialism and, at the same time, through their
limited literacy and location in 'modern' occupational strata, were
most likely to be receptive to the sophisticated ideological and organizational creations of nationalist leaders." The reality was that there
was not just one dynamic anticolonial movement in Ghana but two:
Far from dismissing the National Liberation Movement as simply
backward-looking and tribalistic, Rathbone maintains that it was
composed of an "entirely new generation of (business) aspirants, no
different in many respects from their counterparts in the Convention
People's Party five or six years previously," and a new generation of
businessmen, moreover, which "found such support for the NLM
their only means of entering the gainful sectors of the economy"
(Rathbone, 1973). Now, ten years later, Rathbone (1983: 152) under-
lines his essential arguments that

> in the terminal colonial period . . . the rapidity of change, especially
> in the social and political repercussions of a boom economy, consti-
> tuted a very significant shift in Ghanaian society. So powerful were
> these transformations that they led not only to fierce economic com-
> petition but also to a real struggle for political power. Second, al-
> though the colonial authorities and, later, scholars have given a politi-
> cal coherence to an aggregation they called the Gold Coast and later
> Ghana, it was an area in which rates of development and change
> occurred at dramatically different rates; that reality is not faced by
> stressing *ethnic* diversity which simply draws attention away from the
> differentials of regional history. Lastly, the acceptance without con-
> ceding the variety of regional historical experience leads to talk of
> national classes. The periodization of the process of class formation
> in Ghana and the regionalization of that process make, to my mind,
> the notion of *national* class a major obstacle to an understanding of
> the politics of the 1950s [Rathbone, 1983: 152].

His work also serves as a bridge between the Commonwealth
paradigm of decolonization and the political economy approach by
noting "the 'referee function' of both the British government and
public opinion" relating to the peculiarity of political competition in
Ghana during the 1950s; he thus at least hints at the importance of the
often neglected dialectical relationships between British colonial au-

thorities and anti-colonial nationalisms in the terminal colonial period.

THE POLITICAL ECONOMY PARADIGM[2]

At the heart of most demands for independence from colonial rule as studied within the political economy paradigm lies the question: Independence for whom? It was a question rarely posed during the actual struggles for independence because at the time the answer appeared so obvious, and nowhere more so than in colonial Kenya. There, in the early decades of this century, white settlers on the temperate western highlands had established farms whose affluence contrasted starkly with black squalor. After independence many of these farms were taken over by local people, bulldozers were sent into the shanty towns, and Kenya as a whole enjoyed a rate of economic development unmatched by its immediate neighbors in East Africa.

But of course independence from Britain did not benefit all Kenyans equally; Colin Leys in particular was concerned to attack earlier analyses of African independence movements which concentrated upon issues of national integration and development as perceived by ruling elites rather than upon the difficulties experienced by oppressed and exploited groups. In particular, earlier analyses were taken to task for exhibiting "extraordinary resistance to the idea that there are classes and class struggles in Africa, let alone that they may be of central importance" (Leys, 1975). Leys's argument concentrated upon the successive stages by which Kenya was incorporated into the expanding world capitalist economy during the period of formal empire, and upon how certain social strata ("comprador elements") were brought into existence whose presence would ultimately make direct rule by the metropolitan power unnecessary. The book also had interesting things to say about the peripheral capitalism of postcolonial Kenya: Economic cleavages existed within both the capitalist and peasant sectors of the economy but did not solidify into cohesive classes, and government survived by relying upon force and playing populist tricks with ethnic rhetoric.

Much of this argument, informed as it was by some of the earlier perspectives of underdevelopment theory, has subsequently been repudiated by its author (Leys, 1982) in the light of more recent research into the evolution of a national petty bourgeoisie in colonial Kenya (Cowen, 1972, 1979, 1982; Kitching, 1980; Swainson, 1980).

But the stress upon the farsightedness of metropolitan decision makers at the time of independence which characterizes the earlier political economy literature, even by the more intelligent writers, would strike even the most Anglocentric of Commonwealth historians as both excessive and ahistorical nowadays:

> Once having sensed the initial stirrings of discontent the colonial government characteristically began to evolve a *strategy of decolonization* on the basis of which it began to bargain with an African group eager to agree to marriages of convenience all along the line. The resultant successor-state, as Fanon stressed, could represent merely a change in the colour of those in positions of authority, while maintaining its internal socio-economic structure and major links with the outside world more or less intact [Saul, 1972: 66; italics in original].

But as Jeffries (1983: 1179) remarks,

> a transfer of power which might seem certain and well calculated in retrospect was uncertain, indeed muddled, at the time; . . . the model of "comprador" regimes emerging from this process is a vast oversimplification, underestimating the autonomy of the state in postcolonial economies and the different relationships with foreign capital and domestic forces which the new regimes assumed or pursued.

Nowhere does the picture currently appear more muddled and uncertain than in late colonial Kenya. Current research into the Mau Mau emergency and its background presents a complex picture of disparate social movements, sometimes overlapping one another, at other times going off in different directions: a squatters' revolt, resistance against enforced agricultural improvement schemes, a cultural revival, an internal civil war, and an anticolonial movement echoing earlier primary resistance against the initial imposition of British colonial rule (Buijtenhuijs, 1982; Lonsdale, 1982; see also Throup, 1982, 1983). But to my knowledge no one has yet taken up Buijtenhuijs's challenge to study the cultural aspects of it apart from general sympathy (outside Kikuyuland) for Ogot's view that "because of their exclusiveness, the (Mau Mau songs) cannot be regarded as the national freedom songs which every Kenyan youth can sing with pride and conviction" (Ogot, 1977: 286). However that may be, most recent British writing stresses political action during Mau Mau as an epiphenomenon of economic change rather than the other way round. That surely places it within the political economy paradigm for the most part.

Hopkins's *An Economic History of West Africa* must also be considered within this paradigm for reasons other than its title. For, quite apart from producing an enormously exciting overview of the whole range of west African economic history, its later chapters courageously offer "an economic interpretation of the rise of African nationalism that also runs counter to some well known, if simplistic, beliefs" (Hopkins, 1973: 289). The principal targets here are evidently both the old Commonwealth and the romantic nationalist paradigm of decolonization:

> Opposition to colonialism was based on an imperfect alliance of three
> major interest groups of farmers, traders and wage-earners, all of
> whom shared a degree of commitment to the exchange economy
> which distinguished them from the bulk of the population. . . . By
> taking a disaggregated view of what is often regarded simply as
> "African" opposition to colonialism, it becomes possible to relate the
> evolution of nationalism to the performance of the open economy.
> . . . Nationalism, in its modern forms, had its origins in the period
> 1930-1945, when a serious downturn in real and anticipated living
> standards occurred, following a phase of sustained, if modest, ad-
> vance [Hopkins, 1973: 291].

The argument is nicely put, but it remains as disdainful of politics as any *dependentista* account of decolonization. It also neatly sidesteps the crucial question why opposition to colonialism by such disparate interests took the form of "radical *nationalist* sentiment" (my italics).

THE BRITISH WORLD SYSTEM PARADIGM

If Hopkins's "economic interpretation" was concerned to counter both perceived Commonwealth and African nationalist simplicities, the Cambridge architects of the "British world system" approach were initially more irritated by Commonwealth ideology at Oxford.

> Hitherto empire had been analysed to a remarkable extent on un-
> sophisticated *a priori* assumptions where rulers had no subjects, and
> Europe's pursuit of profit and power was made in a world untrammel-
> led by external forces. And a great deal of imperial history had been
> written teleologically as moral force moving the rest of the world

progressively into the Civitas Dei of a self-governing, multi-racial commonwealth. . . . (Our) inquiry had to be extended beyond the areas painted red on imperial maps to include the informal empire of influence; and local circumstance in indigenous societies, whether the success of collaboration or the crises of resistance, had to be brought into play [Robinson and Seal, 1981: 120-121].

Ronald Robinson also tells us that he found his period of work in the Colonial Office immediately after World War II suggestive as regards the onset of colonialism in general, "witnessing the new terms of African collaboration in the transition from 'indirect rule' to 'Democratisation'; while local crises detonated in colony after colony" (Robinson and Seal, 1981: 122). It was perhaps only to be expected that, after his work with Gallagher on the "imperialism of free trade" and *Africa and the Victorians* (1961) had been published, they should move on from studying the beginnings of colonialism in Africa to studying its demise.

Robinson himself published a suggestive "sketch for a theory of imperialism," embracing decolonization as well as colonization, where he argued that "at every stage from external imperialism to decolonization, the working of imperialism was determined by the indigenous collaborative systems connecting its European and Afro-Asian components" (Robinson, 1972). He further suggested, on the basis of both his own and other students' work, that

when the colonial rulers had run out of indigenous collaborators, they either chose to leave or were compelled to go. Their nationalist opponents in the modern elite sooner or later succeeded in detaching the indigenous political elements from the colonial regime until they eventually formed a united front of non-collaboration against it. Hence the inversion of collaboration into non-cooperation largely determined the timing of decolonization [Robinson, 1972: 147].

This negative model of anticolonial nationalism has proved popular with a number of students of decolonization in Britain in recent years. But it fell to Gallagher and *his* students to work out the theory of anticolonial nationalism as "a ramshackle coalition" mirroring the structures and defects of British colonialism and eventually overcoming it in the context of Indian history (Robinson and Seal, 1981: 123-124), whence it has returned to African history as "the Indian model."

If the resulting image of British colonialism in Africa is thus scarcely heroic, the picture of anticolonial nationalism presented by the Cambridge School is hardly very flattering either. Among most British imperial historians concerned with Africa it has proved especially popular. For instance, of four essays on decolonization in a Festschrift for Frederick Madden (Holland and Rizvi, 1984), three follow the ramshackle line[3] and only Kenneth Robinson retains a respectful attitude towards the corrosive role of African nationalism as a much more dynamic force in British and French Africa as well as the stress upon "habits of mind" more characteristic of the older Commonwealth tradition.

The popularity of the ramshackle view of African nationalism has not been weakened by the shortage of funds in Mrs. Thatcher's Britain for historical research in Africa itself, nor undermined by the ever-increasing amounts of archival information about British policy in the terminal colonial period now starting to reach the middle 1950s. Viewed from some poorly-lit corner under this veritable mountain of metropolitan records, British policy on decolonization does appear to be more easily and persuasively understood in terms of either justificatory rhetoric regarding the importance of individual British cabinet ministers in decision making, or as a desperate quest by the British power elite to retain whatever world power was possible through NATO, the nuclear deterrent and informal influence, now that formal empire again seemed on the way out. The case for serious reappraisal of the role of anticolonial nationalism in undermining European empires in Africa therefore increasingly goes by default among British imperial historians, especially when their colleagues in economic history of both Marxist and non-Marxist sympathies write disparagingly about it. In the present economic circumstances it seems highly unlikely that the local intricacies of anticolonial nationalism in the terminal colonial period will be intensively studied by African historians themselves, and hence the disparagement of anticolonial movements is likely to remain unchallenged from within Africa, except by the romantic nationalist interpretations of history so favored by African governments and taught as official orthodoxies in schools and universities. The lack of any critical approach will only entrench the prevailing "ramshackle" view the more.

Gallagher's posthumously published Ford lectures perhaps demonstrate this disdain for African nationalism at its deepest within the British world system paradigm:

In West Africa, just as in India before it, mass parties were the sum of a series of local political situations converted by government machinery into the apparent expression of nationalist demands. In a word, goverment needed economic growth in West Africa. It suspected that this would have to be paid for by political concession. And so it turned out. . . . But where in all this are the freedom fighters? Not in West Africa, that is clear, for there was nothing to fight over except a time table. But the places to look for them are in East and Central Africa. And there they were the white settlers [Gallagher, 1982: 148].

But the disdain may well be more apparent than real, for just a few pages later Gallagher writes (1982: 153): "In practice, political developments in the colonies tended to take the game out of the croupier's hands. These colonial political developments are the one constant factor in decolonization.[4]

For what *was* anticolonial nationalism in Britain's African colonies if it was not principally a matter of "colonial political developments" from both points of view? Here, surely, is a black box left behind by Gallagher.[5] What we need now is a new historiographical paradigm within which the complexities of African nationalism may be studied as closely as the struggles to retain their respective "world systems" by the British, the French and the Portuguese, and (most importantly of all within a new paradigm) the dialectical relationships over time between the various constituent elements of these nationalist movements among themselves and with their respective colonial rulers.

A REJUVENATED NATIONALIST PARADIGM?

Certainly the existing romantic paradigm of African nationalist activity as developed by much Africanist historiography in the 1960s can no longer be accepted. It is not so much "that African nationalism was not simply a spontaneous, mass movement of the downtrodden, directed against sun-helmeted, exploiting masters and led by men whose readiness for self-sacrifice was matched only by their determination to survive long enough to improve the living standards of their fellow countrymen" (Hopkins, 1973: 291). The irony of the second part of his comment is understandable, but surely misleading: West Africa was not the first part of the world where political crusaders very quickly became mere spoilsmen upon actually attaining power. But in East Africa nationalist agitators could not have aroused widespread opposition to British colonial rule had they already been spoilsmen (Twaddle, 1976). More seriously, the first part of the comment may also be wrong, in the sense that there *does* seem to have been "a spontaneous, mass movement of the downtrodden" associated with the massive urbanization in several parts of black Africa as a result of World War II and its aftermath, a movement to which Davidson (1957) drew our attention over 25 years ago and on which more recently Iliffe has also had something to say (Iliffe, 1979: 381-404, 537-552; 1983). This urbanization does seem to have introduced new elements of uncertainty into the African political game, in the shape of mass involvement in politics from which certainly some African nationalist leaders benefited. But, even more seriously, Hopkins and most other proponents of the political economy approach are surely wrong in treating African anticolonialism as simplistically reducible to economic interest without reference to political context.

And that, let it be admitted, was not something that the pioneers of African nationalist historiography wholly ignored. At the start of his seminal study on nationalism in colonial Africa, for example, Hodgkin (1956) included a separate section on the "Policies of the [colonial] Powers," because he considered them to have been important factors affecting African nationalism. (In this his opinion contrasts with the post-Fanon fashion within the romantic nationalist paradigm of treating the more violent kinds of nationalist movement as morally superior to earlier consensual decolonization attempts regardless of crucial differences in metropolitan policies towards colonies.) As Shepperson (1961: 317) remarked,

All nationalism is the product of a reaction against external forces. But in Africa, whose partition and introduction to the apparatus of the modern state came at a time when Europe was throwing up chaotically those processes for which the terms "nationalism," "imperialism," "racialism," and "socialism" are inadequate but necessary labels, external labels have a peculiar force.

Subsequently, historical study of African nationalism, particularly in East and Central Africa, concentrated upon the African side of this story, stressing the origins of nationalism and protonationalism, debating the comparative importance of elite leadership and mass support, and the connections between primary resistance movements in the early colonial period and later political parties (Ranger, 1968a, 1969). In retrospect it is perhaps hardly surprising that subsequent scholars, disillusioned on discovering that many nationalist leaders had not behaved as their earlier rhetoric promised they would, "unmasked" anticolonial nationalism as in fact economic interest in political disguise. But this reductionist (and anachronistic) mistake would not have been made so frequently if the fascination with the genealogy of African nationalism on the part of a Hodgkin or a Shepperson had been developed with a counterbalancing interest in the dialectical political relationships over time between nationalist movements and differing European colonial powers, particularly during the period after World War II, when a "second colonial occupation" was clearly occurring in parts of East and Central Africa (Low and Lonsdale, 1976). With the current difficulties of research within Africa combined with the ongoing process of accessibility to new materials at the Public Records Office (in a few years, for instance, everything on Ghanaian independence will be available), there is likely to be an increasing bias of evidence in favor of paradigms stressing constitutional conferences within the Commonwealth tradition, attempts to retain world power through strategy and informal empire in preference to more expensive formal colonialism, and any number of hardnosed briefing papers for the British Treasury of the sort already tantalizingly abstracted by Morgan (1980). Anticolonial nationalism, on the other hand, is likely to go by default as a really serious contributor to the processes of decolonization (other than as its beneficiary or victim, depending on your point of view) unless a conscious effort is made by historians to allow for it when undertaking archival study in Europe.

Fortunately, in this we may well be helped by postcolonial developments, some of them intellectual influences emanating from outside Africa, others very much events happening within Africa itself since independence. When the first nationalist leaders of independent African countries were overthrown by military coups in the 1960s and 1970s, it seemed as if many earlier political parties (like the CPP and NLM in Ghana, and the UPC and DP in Uganda) simply vanished into the tropical night. Armies, not political parties, seemed the crucial political institutions to study. Now that military governments themselves have sometimes been replaced by civilian regimes, political parties may well enjoy a revival of scholarly interest. In Ghana contemporary political alignments reveal an uncanny similarity with earlier party competition (Jeffries, 1982). In Uganda I myself was surprised by the political survival of the Democratic Party as well as the Uganda People's Congress in 1981 and suggested "a return . . . to political research [which was] even academically old-fashioned as early as the 1950s" (Twaddle, 1976: 160-161). Cliffe (1983: 125-126) too has called for greater "understanding of the regional base for party loyalties that are now the pattern" in Zimbabwe, involving "the interplay between social groups—ethnic as well as those of class—defined in material terms (including language, culture and political power as well as relations of production), and the realms of ideology and consciousness."

How is this to be done? Cliffe (1983: 125-127) suggests that Zimbabwe, "with three-quarters [of the population] having a common language and culture and a 'minority' making up the rest, might best be analysed in terms of 'nationalities' rather than 'tribes'," and that much more research is needed into the critical moments during the last 30 or 40 years; these "critical moments" sound very comparable to the "events" of Austin (1964). But other kinds of study are suggested by two very stimulating studies of anticolonialist nationalism more generally. One is a by-product of the wider ferment concerned with the "Break-up of Britain" (Nairn, 1977), regionalism in other European countries, Solidarity in Poland, and the wars between Vietnam, Cambodia and China. These later developments serve as the starting point for a seminal study of how, first in Europe and the Americas, and more recently in Asia and Africa

> under the impact of economic change, 'discoveries' (social and scientific), and the development of increasingly rapid communications . . .
> a harsh wedge (was driven) between cosmology and history. No surprise then that the search was on, so to speak, for a new way of linking fraternity, power and time meaningfully together. Nothing perhaps more precipitated this search, nor made it more fruitful, than print-capitalism, which made it possible for rapidly growing numbers of people to think about themselves, and to relate themselves to others, in profoundly new ways [Anderson, 1983: 40].

This search, which ultimately led to the nation being imagined in colonial Africa as well as in other parts of the world, of course lies at the heart of many studies of the transition from oral to literary and part-literary cultures undertaken by historians of Africa. But before nationalism, however "imagined" in newly literate circles, could become *politically* important, another transition had to take place. Here the work of Breuilly (1982) seems extremely helpful, being the first to stress "the way in which the political and institutional structure of the state against which individual nationalisms react conditions their form and ultimate possibility of success" (Woolf, 1982: 1281). Nationalism becomes politically important when it attempts to seize political power by forming a social movement. Ideology is therefore important, but only in a secondary sense, as a means by which a nationalist leadership seeks to obtain mass support, not as a guide to what it is actually doing.

> Why nationalism should have been more effective than other ideologies in obtaining such support is explained by its ability to transform sentiments or practices habitually accepted as belonging to the "private sphere" (family, community, solidarity, etc.) into public values, as symbols and ceremonies particularly fitted to the situation and social groups for which they are intended.

There is a clear overlap here with Anderson's suggestive analysis of the impact of "print-capitalism" upon differing oral cultures outside Europe. Evidently an enormous amount of research is still to be done in this field.

Here, too, is a chance to further open up the game regarding the colonial political developments identified by Gallagher as "the one constant factor in decolonization" within the British world system paradigm. Here also is a framework for studying nationalist ideology and nationalist movements, not as a guide to what happened but as the means by which nationalist leadership seeks to gain mass support.

> Nationalism only becomes significant when it shifts its basis away from cultural identity (by intellectual sleight-of-hand, as Breuilly puts it) into a deliberate attempt to gain the support of social groups hitherto ignored or excluded from the political community. Nationalism arises among the elites of the political community in opposition to the growth of demands of the modern state. It requires the support of many different elites, but more habitually needs to mobilize broader groups among the population [Woolf, 1982: 1281].

In one of the most celebrated passages in African studies, Laura Bohannan (1952: 315) refers to how Tiv genealogies were manipulated to reveal not the past as it really was, but the past as it appeared in the light of subsequent power relations among Tiv families: "a charter" she declared, that was "at once a validation and a mnemonic device for present social relationships." This insight has been since developed (some might say overdeveloped) to make the oral and near-oral historiography of precolonial and early colonial Africa one of the most intricate crafts within the whole historical profession today.

After studying as an undergraduate under Ronald Robinson at Cambridge and attending lectures on "the extension of Europe" by Jack Gallagher in the early 1960s I went off to East Africa to work for a while before returning to be initiated into the mysteries of oral and near-oral historiography at London University and later at Makerere. But whenever I returned to earlier Cambridge pastures I felt that I was studying matters of "parish pump" concern, while *they* were tackling a "vast field" with the help of "large ideas" (Robinson and Seal, 1981: 122). Now I am not so sure. Perhaps it is time to apply Bohannan's wise observation on the Tiv to the contrasting genealogies of the vast field of decolonization in Africa as well. And when we have done this and assessed carefully each of these contrasting genealogical sets,[6] it becomes clear that the time has now come for a new paradigm within which to organize future research on the ending of European empires in Africa. I suggest that we get away from existing paradigms—old Commonwealth, economistic, "world system," or romantic nationalist—because they have become too effective at encapsulating our thought, rather than "opening up the game"; within each there is far too little eagerness to look at alternative viewpoints with any seriousness, and far too much concern to continue along existing, increasingly ramshackle lines of inquiry. I suggest instead that we pursue a more dialectic form of inquiry.

NOTES

1. This is an extremely complex phenomenon. What I shall have to say about it will be brief; most of my remarks will be restricted to what has been written in Britain over the last 10-15 years. My deepest debts are to Ronald Robinson and my colleagues at the Institute of Commonwealth Studies, which under successive directors has proved a stimulating environment for reflection on this subject.

2. Although influential with both Marxist and non-Marxist scholars, the political economy paradigm has been strengthened by the mushrooming of southern African studies around scholars like Shula Marks and Stanley Trapido. But until very recently these scholars were less concerned with decolonization than with initial colonization and its interconnections with differing modes of production and mining capital; hence their work does not for the most part relate directly to the problems discussed here.

3. Robinson (1984: 50) now writes that "the attempts to democratize colonial governments gradually from below swiftly manufactured popular national movements" but does not say why they were national; Holland (1984: 175) says: "It was African nationalists much more than colonial authorities, who feared populist dis-

turbances, since such an out-spilling of politics would reveal their own organizations as the ramshackle affairs they so frequently were"; Darwin (1984: 206) stresses that "nothing stimulated political mobilization in the British colonies more than London's efforts to encourage economic development."

4. Hargreaves (1983: 728) may well be unfair therefore when he asserts: "In *Africa and the Victorians* nationalist crises on the African continent were held largely responsible for bringing imperialists into Africa; but in his later work on decolonization Gallagher assigns them a lesser role in accelerating the end of empire."

5. I heard Gallagher argue almost the opposite case in lectures, namely that decolonization was inevitable once African nationalists got fully mobilized. But that was before the fall of Nkrumah.

6. In this chapter, I have referred to these "contrasting genealogical sets" as "paradigms," in the Kuhnian sense; or, as Gallagher would have phrased it, "large ideas, simply but powerfully stated," without which "there could be little significant advance in so vast a field" (Robinson and Seal, 1981: 122).

11

AFRICANIST HISTORIOGRAPHY
IN FRANCE AND BELGIUM
Traditions and Trends

CATHERINE COQUERY-VIDROVITCH
BOGUMIL JEWSIEWICKI

As elsewhere in Europe, it was not until the late 1950s that African history became recognized in France and Belgium as an academic field distinct from imperial history (Stengers, 1979b: 585). Not that there had been a total void before that time, but until then interest in Africa had remained restricted to those personally involved and most familiar with the area: military personnel, missionaries, and administrative agents. In terms of scholarly work, black Africa remained the domain of the anthropologists; the few isolated works of any historical interest (such as Deschamps's 1938 thesis) only underscored the historians' general indifference to Africa.

In France the first two French chairs in the history of black Africa were established (through the personal efforts of Charles-André Julien) at the Sorbonne in 1960, one year after the Ecole Pratique des Hautes Etudes en Sciences Sociales (now Ecole des Hautes Etudes en Sciences Sociales - VIe section) had initiated a study program in this field. At the same time, the Congo began to receive some attention in Belgium, but only through imperial and religious history programs. The situation was not much better at the Institut Fondamental d'Afrique Noire (IFAN) and the Institut de Recherche Scientifique en Afrique Centrale (IRSAC), the principal colonial research institutes of the two powers; despite some historical work, anthropologists outnumbered historians by about 10 to 1.

The crucial role of introducing African history to the French public fell to Suret-Canale, who published the first important guide to the African past in French (1958). Other works followed at the turn of the 1960s, as liberal historians participated actively in the renewed debates on imperialism. Intensified by the debate on underdevelopment, this focus was central to French historiography right through to the 1980s. Especially important were the contributions of Stengers (1957, 1963) and Brunschwig (1957, 1960, 1965), both in research and in training a new generation of students including C. Coquery-Vidrovitch, D. Bouche, E. M'bokolo, and M. Michel. Since then historical inquiry has been accepted as an essential component to the understanding of Africa, although there were obstacles: In both France and Belgium historical studies in general were strongly marked by nationalist ethnocentrism; more importantly, since their analytic techniques were specialized for dealing with the European cultural context, most historians showed a distrust of and disdain for people without writing and thus were biased against African cultures. Only with the "discovery" of oral tradition as a historical source (Tubiana, 1961; Vansina, 1961), and with the work of others who resisted the prevailing tendencies to marginalize precolonial studies in the autonomous field of "ethnohistory" (Brunschwig, 1965), did precolonial African history begin to receive the attention it merited. Defying such epistemological considerations, the historiography of precolonial African societies has more recently slipped back into a sort of autonomy from mainstream historiography, distinguished from other fields of inquiry by the nature of its sources.

In general the separation between historical and anthropological studies was more marked in Belgium and France than in Great Britain. After Vansina's departure for the United States, Belgian anthropology (with a few exceptions, notably M. d'Hertefelt) was dominated first by issues relating to imperial and missionary history and later by structural anthropology. The decline of African studies there after 1960 was dramatic: The journal *Zaïre* ceased publication in 1961 and a new Third World-oriented journal, *Cultures et Développement,* was launched only in 1968; in the interim many Belgian Africanists had left the country. In France most of the first Africanists were former agents of the colonial administration whose analytic interests focused primarily on the reconstruction of the events of the past. This only underscored the differences between historians and anthropologists, a gap widened still further by the growing influence of structuralist and later structural-Marxist analysis (such as that undertaken by Godelier).

Three initiatives were important in overcoming the opposition between history and the social sciences in France. Balandier (1963, 1967, 1971a) stressed the importance of the dynamic character of sociological and anthropological inquiry: The realities of the African world could be understood only by reference to historical factors, thus reincorporating historical analysis into the very heart of anthropological inquiry. At the same time, the growing influence of the Annales School in historical studies brought greater attention to the various structural levels of the understanding of historical dynamics, thus both enriching historical studies and allowing historians to reach out to assume new roles in other disciplines (see on this orientation Veit-Brause, 1981).

Through a series of crises focusing especially on the connections between the epistemological foundations of anthropological inquiry with the larger structures of colonial rule (Leclerq, 1972; Copans, 1975; Moniot, 1976a), African studies in France (including African historical studies) became gradually more sensitive to the realities of African societies. Finally the growing accommodation between history and other social science disciplines from the mid-1960s was most clearly illustrated in France by the growth of economic anthropology (Moniot, 1976b), the elaboration of the concepts of modes of production, and their articulation within a context of unequal exchange at the global level. The conjunction of these various developments for a time brought French Africanist studies into the vanguard of the field.

Since the 1960s Marxism (used in the widest sense of the term) has constituted an important source of inspiration of French historical research on Africa. This was a phenomenon hardly specific to Africanists, however: "A good part of the liveliness of the French historical school seems to me to have been more or less a product of what came out of Marxist studies, either by reacting to it or by falling into line with it" (Duby and Lardreau, 1980: 118). Either working through or arguing against dependency paradigms, Marxist influence renewed the debates on imperialism (Marseille, 1984), on the impact of colonialism, and on the dynamics of the socioeconomic structures of African societies and their specificity (*Cahiers d'Etudes Africaines,* 1976). The enduring nature of this theoretical debate, and the place accorded it in historical discourse right up to the end of the 1970s, penetrated French historiography deeply and reinforced its

integration with the social sciences. More recently a mild reaction has
surfaced (one not restricted to historians alone: Amselle, 1985; Copans, 1977, 1982; Terray, 1984b). As Devisse (1981: 645) notes

> Marxist historians are more careful to account for the relations of
> force, social tensions resulting from even slow economic evolution;
> "specifist" historians probably place greater emphasis on ideological
> questions and aspects of conceptual structures; however, neither
> group today would take the risk of neglecting the domain of the other;
> in this regard, the division of methods and fields of research if it ever
> existed for the historians, has ceased to carry political significance.
> Moreover, in the end, all groups concur that studying the history of
> Africa requires the use of a specific methodological approach, even if
> the elements constituted must not remain irreducible from all others.

It became firmly accepted that a historical perspective was essential
to understanding African social formations (Terray, 1983) even
though historians were no longer always the principal proponents and
practitioners of this view. As one leading geographer noted about
his field: "Everyone seeks to situate contemporary changes in a
longer time span and occasionally within the very long span" (Raison,
1978: 7).

Beyond the quarrels between various schools of analysis,
specialists in African studies often share more fully than other disciplines in the human sciences. The Ecole des Hautes Etudes en
Sciences Sociales has played an important role in this regard, mainly
through the influence of people such as Balandier (1971a) and Sautter
(*Etudes Rurales,* 1970) from within and Meillassoux (1975a, 1975b)
from outside. The research of many anthropologists from either
Marxist or structuralist persuasions became increasingly empirical,
more preoccupied with ideology and symbolism, and more historical,
as was the case of Dupré, Terray, Bazin, Augé, Izard, and Tardits
among others. At the same time historians (Chrétien, Perrot, Raison,
Jourde) established a new relation to anthropology and linguistics.
Drawing on the analysis of oral and ethnographic data as well as
written and archaeological documents, they undertook the reconstruction of the past as a dynamic creation of local agents placed between
local forces and the growing world capitalist system. Partly through
Wallerstein's work (1974), but also in more direct ways, Braudel's
(1969) influence on these historians was also important.

A great effort was made in the 1970s to integrate African history
fully within the mainstream of French historiography; in 1974 the

most prestigious collection of university handbooks, "Nouvelle Clio," published a volume on African history (Coquery-Vidrovitch and Moniot, 1984). From 1981 African history was included on an optional basis as a subject in French secondary schools and by then had become widely recognized by other French historians. This has been essential since in France there is no African studies association or annual conference of Africanists; as in the case of Brunschwig, however, many leading French historians of Africa are fully integrated into the mainstream of the Nouvelle Histoire (Le Goff, 1978; Coutau-Begarie, 1983). But what will probably be determinant in the desired renewal of concepts, methodology, and research structures in the future is the recognition by the Centre National de Recherche Scientifique of the laboratory "Third World/Africa: Societies in Their History and Environment," uniting Africanist historians from the Université de Paris I with researchers from the Université de Paris VII participating in the multidisciplinary program "Understanding the Third World" (and therefore not necessarily Africanists).

A certain number of French historians and anthropologists (whether interested in metropolitan France or in non-Western societies) have been working in the field of historical anthropology, focusing on the reconstruction of the total context of the social life of the group considered. Such research requires reference to both traditional types of sources and material sources such as industrial archeology, iconography, and especially oral testimonies relating to material and cultural life. Initiated in the 1970s through the conjunction of the Paris and Aix-en-Provence centers of historical research, the field of French oral history has developed rapidly in the 1980s (Joutard, 1983). African historiographical contributions have played an important pioneering role in the development of this genre. Some of the earliest indications of African contributions to French historical methodology are found in Bloch's (1941) writings; more recently they appear in the opening pages of Duby and Lardreau's (1980) celebrated work. An important outlet for diffusing recent Africanist scholarship has been the prestigious journal *Annales E.S.C.,* which publishes articles on African history on a regular basis; moreover, the *Annales* influence on African history is much wider than simply the French-speaking world alone (Clarence-Smith, 1977; Vansina, 1978b, 1984b; Thornton, 1983a).

Such collaboration between Western and Africanist scholarship demonstrates that African history, while original in substance, is not an analytic field specific to itself, encapsulated in its own methodological requirements; in its analytic goals and basic methodological assumptions, Africanist historical scholarship is analogous to that of every other part of the world. One example is found in the manner by which certain French anthropological and historical studies have brought into question the validity of the concept of ethnicity (Mercier, 1968; Verdeaux, 1981; Dozon, 1977; Chrétien, 1981; Copans, 1982, Amselle and M'bokolo, 1985) and shown that ethnicity is first and foremost a historical construction.

The complementary approaches of the social sciences and history contribute to the emergence of a new crossdisciplinary, dynamic approach to African societies. In Belgium, with some important exceptions (notably Vellut and Verhaegen) African historical studies in the 1970s were oriented predominantly to the political and economic history of Belgians in Central Africa (Huybrechts, 1970; Stengers, 1974). This research produced a new and very rich picture of the creation and expansion of the capitalist market and material flow as well as a new understanding of the political and economic forces leading toward decolonization (Peemans, 1970, 1975a, 1975b). The creation in the 1970s of the Centre d'Étude et de Documentation Africaines (CEDAF), oriented primarily toward the period from the 1950s, and of the Institut des Pays en Voie de Développement and the Centre d'Histoire Africaine, both at the Université Catholique de Louvain, offered a new base for the study of African societies of former Belgian Central Africa. The Flemish Katholieke Universiteit at Leuven tried unsuccessfully in 1974 to create a center of African precolonial history with the collaboration of Vansina; as Stengers (1979a: 170) remarked, its demise "was a sign, to some extent, of the loss of interest in Central Africa among certain Belgian circles" (see also Coupez, 1983: 17).

In spite of the past and continuing potential of human resources, the originality of personal research and a very large base in social sciences, particularly economic history, demography, and geography (Coupez, 1983) from the end of the 1940s through the 1970s, African historical study in Belgium remains to some extent a personal affair, based on the dedication of a few high-quality students. Although more historians from the former Belgian areas of Central Africa studied for their Ph.D.s in France rather than in Belgium, nevertheless by the beginning of the 1980s there were signs of a new start: the collaboration established between CEDAF and the Université de Paris VII, some important recent works (Bezy, Peemans, and Wautelet, 1981; Vanderlinden, 1981; ARSOM, 1983; Raymaekers and Desroche, 1983) and the small but valuable annual publication edited by Vellut,

Etudes et Documents d'Histoire Africaine (from 1976). With increasing distance from the political and social trauma of the Congo's precipitate decolonization (Stengers, 1978), Belgian society may be now ready (see Eynikel, 1984, published for a general reader in both French and Flemish) to learn about Zairean societies for their own value. Meanwhile in France and Belgium archeological research has extended its traditional field of study to include more recent periods (seventeenth to the nineteenth centuries) and now draws more fully on written or oral sources to complement the conventional archeological data (Devisse, 1981; Van Noten, 1981). Such an expansion of interests and increasing collaboration tends to dissolve earlier disciplinary boundaries separating historians and archeologists, with one result being that most history departments of the Francophone universities of Africa include archaeologists.

Along with economic anthropology, twentieth-century socioeconomic history has become one of the strongest fields of French Africanist studies. Until recently this field of research has remained under a sort of taboo, in part because of nationalist sensitivities in the decolonization period. A wide variety of analytic techniques are called on to account for the profound internal social transformations produced by the colonial experience and to probe the history of work, the policies of public health and demography, the interaction of town and countryside, deculturation, the distortion, deconstruction, and deformation of earlier forms of political power, and similar topics. Until now the analysis has concentrated on the major turning points of domination and dependence, such as the impact of the Great Depression and the state in Africa *(Revue Française d'Histoire d'Outre Mer,* 1981, Coquery-Vidrovitch, 1976b).

Studies have also been undertaken on long-term changes, the imposition of forms of dependence and the distortions of peripheral capitalism, both through theoretical analyses of the process as a whole (Coquery-Vidrovitch, 1976b), and by pursuing the history of colonial enterprises and entrepreneurs in Africa over the last two centuries (Laboratoire "Connaissance du Tiers-Monde", 1983; Peemans and Lefevre, 1980). Particular interest has focused on the interdependent processes of urbanization and the creation of a proletarian work force over the course of this century (Lakroum, 1983; Vellut, 1981) as well as on the ideological and linguistic dimension to the formation of a bourgeoisie (Raison-Jourde, 1985).

But if history has recently assumed an important place in French Africanist anthropology, the contribution of anthropologists remains crucial to the construction of global social history. During the colonial

period, anthropologists—for all the deficiencies of the prevailing anthropological paradigms—were virtually alone in sustaining scholarly
interest in non-Western societies. Although anthropological work in
general was overshadowed by the rush of other disciplines into the
field at the time of decolonization, more recently French Marxist
anthropologists have had a major impact on our understanding of the
internal social structures tied to the forces of production in African
rural societies, on the analysis of social relations of production (including the control over land, crafts, or trade), and especially on
identifying the interactions between economic domination and political power. This research has prompted a renewal of interest in questions relating to internal "domestic slavery," the political uses to
which it was put, and the expansion and evolution of the forms of
social control associated with it—approaches which form a clear
break from earlier work (Meillassoux, 1975, forthcoming). All the
while, important studies continue to appear on the trade in slaves and
on contacts with the Atlantic world (*Revue Française d'Histoire
d'Outre Mer,* 1975; Mettas, 1978, 1984).

In questions relating to more contemporary history, research by
both historians and geographers (Raison, 1981) has begun to consider
problems of work, focusing particularly on the imposition of structures of proletarianization but extending these to account for the close
linkages between the formation of an urban work force and the
development of new work patterns in rural areas. Similarly the complexity of the "informal" or "autonomous" sector, studied in France
and Belgium by economists and anthropologists (*Tiers-Monde,* 1980;
Deblé and Hugon, 1982; Comeliau and Leclerq, 1978), is clearly one
of the determinant social forces in Africa today—and an issue of great
significance for the future.

Some of the most compelling and longstanding debates in France
and Belgium involving economists and political scientists as well as
historians relate to the origins of underdevelopment, the factors of
contemporary underdevelopment, and the place of black Africa in the
Third World. Though more often argued on a theoretical or ideological plane than in historical terms, these issues essentially compare the
theories of economic take-off to those of the development of underdevelopment based on the historical phenomenon of unequal exchange between center and periphery. Much of this work seeks to
reassess the theoretical advances of the 1970s, to provide a periodization of political and economic dependence of the African continent
from the earliest contacts to the present, and to probe the forms and

processes of peripheral capitalism. Some of the most valuable contributions of this approach have been to provide a long-term historical perspective to the work of development economists (Coquery-Vidrovitch, 1978b, 1985).

Despite the dynamism of French Africanist studies which has transformed both our historical understanding of Africa as well as our approaches to historical inquiry in general, there are nonetheless severe restrictions to this work. One of the most obvious relates to geographical and cultural scope. Both French and (even more) Belgian historical studies of Africa are predominantly limited to former political or administrative dependencies; more than 90% of Ph.D. theses presented up to 1980 in France concerned former French Africa (Devisse, 1981: 640). Comparative studies (such as the seminars on popular resistance in central Africa organized in 1984 by Columbia University and the Université de Paris VII) remain rare, and specialized research outside these regions is exceptional. One notable attempt to surmount this obstacle is found in the international seminars organized by the Maison des Sciences de l'Homme: the Franco-German seminar on historical anthropology and the Franco-British seminars, which focused in 1982 on elite formation in colonial empires, in 1983 on Islamic leaders in tropical Africa; in 1982 as well, the *Past and Present* Annual Conference on peasant unrest was organized with French collaboration.

Finally, perhaps the most serious limitations of all relate to structural and financial factors. In some ways French Africanist research is only marking time after a promising beginning in the 1960s and productive reassessment of conceptual frameworks during the 1970s. Since then, primarily for lack of funds and position openings, research personnel have scarcely even been replaced: We are all growing old together, without being able to offer to young French researchers positions which correspond to their skills and potential. The only compensating factor—though one of considerable importance—is in providing training to African researchers (Devisse, 1981: 640-641, notes that up to 1980 about 75% of Doctorats d'Etat and Doctorats de Troisième Cycle in African history were awarded to Africans); they may well transform the nature of historical understanding of Africa, despite the hegemony that French universities have till recently exercised over African university structures.

What then are the characteristics of recent French historiography of Africa? During the 1960s and 1970s the principal strength of African studies in France was in the field of analytic and conceptual advances, with an anti-imperialist orientation and a conceptualization of the process of transition to capitalism in Africa. This emergent commitment tended to undermine and weaken precolonial history and especially social history, two (by no means exclusive) fields that found themselves relatively marginalized because isolated from the dominant conceptual paradigms of the day. However, the empiricist tradition was by no means dead (Person, 1968-1975; Michel, 1982; Perrot, 1982). The reaction of the 1980s led principally to a new approach to social history (Chrétien; Raison-Jourde; Coquery-Vidrovitch; Lakroum; M'bokolo); at the same time the integration of a historical dimension was reinforced throughout the social sciences in general, but in African studies this integration was particularly evident in anthropology (Terray, 1984a) and in political science (Bayart, 1983a).

This large and often noisy conceptual debate is nearly forgotten (is this a testimony to the trendy character of the issues of that day?); almost no one speaks of modes of production any longer, few mention social classes, and even the underdevelopment paradigm is worn. Must one conclude that all conceptual debate is dead and that social history (or anthropological history) is a harbinger of the return of narrative empiricism—the general approach of Anglosaxon Africanist history of the 1960s and 1970s? It would not seem so: The debates continue among those strongly influenced by the *Annales* tradition; much of this debate focuses on the vocabulary and the fundamental perceptions which guide our understanding of African societies.

A different debate begins to emerge along two other lines. One relates to the utility of Marxism in comprehending the true relation between base and superstructure by seeking ways of integrating ideological and political dimensions within a single analytic structure, in a way which does not relegate these dimensions to the category of epiphenomena (Godelier, 1984); this quest has led to the discovery of the work of Bourdieu by certain structuro-Marxists (Le Pape and Vidal, 1982). The second line is marked by the reintegration of historical analysis (of the type of Vovelle and de Certeau) into the work of political scientists, as most clearly developed in contributions to the journal *Politique Africaine*. This reflects the most important characteristic of Africanist historiography in France: that it is as much a part of French historiography as of Africanist social science (Jewsiewicki and Létourneau, 1985).

Such integration relates to another characteristic of recent French historiography: that of institutional structures. Research and teaching in France are carried out within state-run structures; hence the lack of professional associations dealing with a given field, which are only beginning to emerge, slowly, in Francophone Africa. The concentration of specialized research and teaching is another notable trait: the field is dominated by four preeminent institutions, three of which are in Paris (the Universities of Paris I and Paris VII, the Ecole des Hautes Etudes en Sciences Sociales, and the University of Aix-Marseille). At the Centre National de la Recherche Scientifique in Paris, African studies are largely dominated, with few exceptions (such as Chrétien) by anthropologists. Even if the Doctorat d'Etat has just been dropped, its effects in great part dominate the French Africanist world. Research is oriented to monumental projects, undertaken over a very long term, and within which the conceptual frameworks and methodologies of particular *maîtres* are reproduced through their students. Furthermore, the system is dominated by certain personalities which often are projected through the scholar-clients who depend on them. It is no accident that in the 1970s the most intensive discussions and most fruitful innovations have come from the EHESS, independent of the structure of the Thèse d'Etat. Each of the three other universities involved has its own geographical and/or chronological fields of specialization as well as its particular methodological approach tied to a clearly defined political ideology. Thus at Aix-Marseille 50% of the theses presented relate to the Maghreb and the Indian Ocean areas, and 90% deal with the colonial period; Paris VII covers especially Central Africa and the Gulf of Benin (65% of theses), and the nineteenth and twentieth centuries account for 90% of these theses; and although Paris I, with two chairs in African history, covers geographically all areas of former French Africa, two-thirds of the theses relate to the precolonial period (Devisse, 1981: 640-641). Each university also has developed its own ideological stance and associated methods: Aix-Marseille is dominated by a sort of legalistic positivism, Paris I is socialist and generally works along the lines of the New History, and Paris VII is of more Marxist tendencies and oriented to socioeconomic subjects.

The Thèse d'Etat imposes a weight and slowing in the diffusion of the results of research which makes of it merely oral information passed by word of mouth, rarely published quickly; its time has often passed at the moment when the monument finally appears. The Thèse de Troisième Cycle and especially the Thèse d'Etat must be presented unpublished, and thus its publication—even of partial results—in article form is compromised; it is worth noting that France has no journal specializing in African history. Because of their length and because they rarely provide any economic return, these theses are published more or less in dribs and drabs. Thus in France—one of the few countries where works on history become popular best-sellers—the paradox emerges that Africanist production is heavily polarized between theses (for all practical purposes restricted to the few colleagues specialized in the field) and political or ideological pamphlets whose circulation is scarcely any greater.

Even if attenuated over the last few years, there is no doubt that the elitist orientation and mandarin structure of the French university has greatly affected African studies (Clark, 1967, 1973; Amselle, 1977; Alexandre, 1977) just as heavily as the explosion of autonomous institutions competing for the few state resources essential to their survival in the university system. In addition, the last several years have seen a rapid growth in the numbers of African universities offering courses in African studies, but these programs often terminate on the completion of two or three years of study, just at the threshold of research. Still, the degree to which francophone African universities today reflect conformity to the French university model—even to the point of caricature, as if the shock waves of 1968 had never occurred—is striking. The system is heavily hierarchialized: Although African francophone historians with a Doctorat d'Etat are still quite rare, this is still taken as a necessary criterion for access to positions of responsibility.

In such a system there is a risk of ending up with, instead of the necessary renewal of a young discipline in full growth, a simple blind reproduction of outdated structures and inherited rigidities, poorly adapted to the African context. Often the very model drawn on is itself archaic, outdated even in France. But fortunately there is a strong current of autonomy making itself felt today, especially among the younger generation. The importance of this cannot be overstated: It is absolutely essential, even if the strength of the reaction against the model means new problems arise, such as militant nationalism and intense internal political cliques. But this is another story, and in any case does not argue for preserving outdated structures.

12

AFRICANIST HISTORICAL STUDIES IN THE UNITED STATES

Metamorphosis or Metastasis?

DAVID NEWBURY

The growth of
African historical studies had its greatest impact, aside from African
countries themselves, in the United States. Most European countries
had had a long tradition of such studies (albeit on a small scale), with
established research centers, clearly defined lines of analysis, and (in
some cases) ties to African universities. But in the United States,
African studies broke onto the scene virtually as a new discipline, a
new field of interest, at a time of thorough-going and broadly based
transformations in Western approaches to Africa. Academic disciplines appeared to be fundamentally changed in that period; placing
Africa at the center of inquiry required the accumulation of new
research techniques, the utilization of new types of sources, and,
most important, the development of new analytic techniques based
on perceptions of historical process radically different from those
that dominated U.S. scholarly analyses of the postwar period.

From a popular and political point of view, this evolution in perceptions and approaches may prove to have been only ephemeral. There
are currently many signs of a strong backwash, and older forms of
portrayals have recently inserted themselves in the popular press, in
literary circles, and apparently as the basis for the formulation of
governmental policy toward Africa and the Third World in general.[1]
African studies have clearly failed in one of their most important

functions: that of providing the general public with a richer, fuller understanding of non-Western cultures. This gives cause to inquire into the true foundations of Africanist studies—was this development simply a product of changing United States/European perceptions and needs, or did it truly relate to the realities of Africa? And if the latter, then what accounts for the recent eclipse of the field? For the conditions against which the African people struggled in the 1950s and 1960s—in whose name this new field of study was developed—have if anything intensified.

Despite the crisis of contemporary Africanist studies, in their methodology and conceptualization of the field—the way one thinks of the Third World relative to other areas—academic disciplines have been fundamentally transformed over the past 20 years. The earlier broad liberal consensus in the United States was that Africanists could serve both the U.S. public and the African people, that there was ultimately a convergence of interest between the two. What was needed, it was assumed, was a sharpening of technique, more rigorous analysis, and more broadly based data sources. But that approach has raised new questions. Broader data and increasing emphasis on analytic aspects has brought the need for new conceptual frameworks. Simultaneously the widening gap between popular images and academic analyses seems to be symptomatic of an abrupt shift in political orientation and agenda in the United States. As political and scholarly perceptions diverge, Africanists have had to face some hard decisions as to where their principal responsibilities lay, rather than taking it for granted that they could serve different audiences and different purposes simultaneously. The choice, of course, is not simply between the United States and Africa, nor even determining "Which Africa?" Instead the issue is that of how Africanist historians perceive fundamental processes of societal change and how they identify the significant historical issues which impinge on Africa's present and future.

The present crisis of African studies lies not in its lack of vitality and productivity per se; in fact, simple productivity for its own sake, without an awareness of deeper issues of understanding—the simple reinforcement of earlier conceptual models—may be part of the problem, not a sign of its passing. The more fundamental questions facing Africanist studies in the United States relate to the direction or meaning of these efforts. What are the fundamental issues we seek to address? There is a need to focus on the epistemological basis of

Africanist studies in the United States and to account for the structural components that underlie our understanding.

In the 1960s several factors combined to create an explosion of Africanist interest and infrastructure in the United States. One precondition of course was that the United States had not been directly identified with formal colonial structures in Africa, and thus was well placed to capitalize on the Third World movement toward clearer self-definition and the search for new relations with former metropolitan powers which accompanied the process of decolonization. Many Americans supported the Africans' struggle for independence; in the intellectual sphere this was reflected in support for "decolonizing" African history, and working toward a truly "African" history.

Decolonization was one factor, and an important one, to be sure, in the emergence of African studies programs, but it was not the only one. Three other factors combined to restructure earlier perceptions. The growing economic hegemony of the United States in the postwar period both created a perceived need for "experts" abroad and provided the financial foundations for the considerable expansion of the university system that occurred during the 1960s. The Civil Rights movement in the United States (often with leadership ties to black populations outside the United States) was another important factor, creating an interest in the African origins of this population sector and generating political demands for the establishment of African and Afro-American studies programs in the universities.[2] At the same time the emergence of a new educational climate in the United States, bolstered by postwar intellectual influences from Europe, led to a remarkable growth in interest in a whole host of new conceptual and methodological approaches: the systematic analysis of oral tradition, a heightened appreciation of ethnographic and cultural materials as historical sources, various types of structuralist studies, a variety of *Annaliste* approaches, diverse theories of underdevelopment and a growing interest in Marxist paradigms; all found direct application to Africa, the newest field of scholarly historical analysis. The conjunction of these four factors promoted interest in the field among the public at large, generated funds for research, and attracted large numbers of students: African studies in the United States flourished.

But dramatic shifts in this intellectual climate of the 1960s were to occur during the 1970s. To some, the newer analytic frameworks seemed "to go too far" (a commonly heard complaint) and the changing economic and political climate seemed to favor backing off from such intellectual exploration. Proper independence for African countries was viewed within an extremely narrow range of acceptable political alternatives; in no way was "independence" as perceived in the United States intended to challenge "dependence"; still less, the status quo. These unspoken assumptions, combined with growing dependence of the United States on Third World areas in some regards (not only for raw materials, but also as outlets for bank loans and as strategic U.N. votes), the setbacks to the rising curve of postwar U.S. hegemony from the least expected quarters in the Third World, and the threat to Western economic and financial structures that emerged in the 1970s (in the form of pricing policy or defaults on debt repayments) all contributed to these abrupt shifts in the intellectual climate.

In many domains, in short, there was under way a process of increasing peripheralization of African studies, and this perceived isolation led to many setbacks for African studies programs at the time of university retrenchments of the 1970s. With popular perceptions transformed and job retrenchment in full swing, enrollment in graduate programs fell dramatically. Although undergraduate enrollments in Third World courses often remained high and the contributions of African methodological innovations became increasingly incorporated into more mainstream analyses, these arguments could not hold against the strong conceptual bases of action on the part of administrators and departmental power brokers when it came to decisions affecting African studies. Straightforward ignorance played a role, to be sure, but there were many ways in which such programs brought themselves into question, either by not sufficiently reaching out to other areas (within the larger discipline or with other disciplines) or by becoming involved in other types of programs without strong institutional foundations. The return to the late nineteenth century pedagogical concepts associated with the "back to basics" movement did not always allow room for cross-cultural study.

There have also been significant structural transformations within the field over the last ten years. African studies had been a part of the curriculum in certain predominantly black colleges from early in this century, but significant expansion awaited the 1950s, when African studies were built up rapidly around a few individuals interested in the field. Where these pioneer figures found themselves at major institutions at the moment when vast increases in financial support were made available, the early centers flourished, and there developed a relatively few dominant locations where specialized training in African studies was available: principally, Northwestern University, Boston University, the University of California—Los Angeles, Indiana University, and the University of Wisconsin—Madison. The subsequent expansion of the field saw the establishment of specialized Africanists at a whole host of other institutions that have sought to include at least some representation of African history in their course offerings. The decade from the mid-1960s to the mid-1970s, then, witnessed the proliferation of sites where African studies were carried out, as the former centers lost some of their funding and as the students of an earlier era (grouped in a few centers) dispersed to jobs in a variety of institutions. In important respects such a dispersal of the field was itself an indication of the very success of the early centers in assuring for African history an important place in the perceptions of world history as well as turning it into an important field of study in itself. But such dispersal also threatened dilution of research energies.

At the same time that African history was achieving a degree of recognition at the academic and intellectual level, financial constraints from the mid-1970s exerted even more severe influence in the development of the field, eventually affecting conceptual and intellectual spheres as well as institutional developments. These new constraints were perhaps first reflected most directly in the increasing difficulty of conducting fieldwork. For North American students, research in Africa has become prohibitively expensive in some cases, and difficult in many other ways as well—in receptivity of African scholars to their Africanist colleagues, in access to archives, in support systems. The result has been that one of the essential characteristics of U.S. Africanist training, the fieldwork experience in Africa, has been less accessible and in some cases impossible to pursue. This has been a critical blow to Africanist scholarship in a country lacking the substantial archival collections found in former European colonial powers, where fieldwork has generally been less significant an aspect of training or where it takes different forms (often consisting of associate status with African university teaching staffs).[3]

During the 1960s students often spent a short period in Africa, usually on a twelve-month research grant, and returned to North America to write it up. The pace was breathtaking, and the results sometimes showed it: In many ways the research was superficial, particularly in the conceptualization of historical problems. With important intellectual influences exerted by a relatively few centers, the short research period accorded most students, and the need for immediate results primarily oriented toward filling in the "historical map" rather than pursuing intellectual approaches and paradigms fully relevant to the particular historical issues being addressed, certain models of what was acceptable in the presentation of African history became firmly entrenched. For a field in rapid development this was perhaps inevitable, even beneficial; but in a period of retrenchment, revision and reevaluation have been more difficult to achieve because of the relatively narrow range of acceptable intellectual alternatives available on which to draw.[4] At a time when Africanist historians might be reaching out to really new challenges there emerged a general sense of closure of the field, of clinging to past models or arguing past battles, of slow decline rather than opening out and exploration, and, critically, of the loss of personal contact with the current realities structuring the lives of African peoples. Hence Africanist writing, for better or for worse, lost some of the excitement and sense of purpose of the earlier years.

In seeking new lines of development, archival sources have not been exploited in U.S. Africanist historiography with any of the sense of renewed vigor or urgency as has occurred elsewhere, theoretical exploration has in general been timid, and the encouragement of new scholars or the intensified training of African scholars has been notably withdrawn. There have been some exceptions, to be sure, and there have been some thoughtful, reflective contributions by both older and younger scholars.[5] But in general, following a period of enormous methodological interest and change, research in African history has been slow in developing new theoretical approaches and new types of analysis to meet the changing circumstances of the field.

Three factors have contributed to this retard. Although surely a positive element in itself, the diffusion of African studies among many institutions has been combined with severe loss of financial support and the loss of the intellectual influence of the older centers. This has led increasingly to a lack of focus, an absence of a "critical mass" of scholarly energy. It is possible that the effectiveness of younger scholars in dispersed areas is compromised by the obvious decline in the intellectual approaches—a situation of regional proliferation without intellectual change; a replication and profusion of earlier models without the circulation of vital new ideas: metastasis rather than metamorphosis.

This would be less a problem were not practicing Africanist scholars also isolated, by changes in the general intellectual environment, from other departmental colleagues. Thus a second and complementary factor relates to the sheer size of the U.S. university system, a system so massive as to generate largely its own intellectual dynamics independent of other (European or African) intellectual universes. In the postwar period U.S. academics in general have tended to be slow in reaching out to or building on intellectual currents in Europe, and those who have tried to do so have not always received the support or encouragement of their older colleagues because of the overwhelming predominance of U.S. intellectual paradigms within this country.

Structural factors affecting the place of the individual within the university system in most U.S. institutions have also played a part. The relatively narrow categories which define university departmental organization in the United States sometimes oppose history to other fields in an artificial manner. Despite verbal deference to the value of interdisciplinary studies, critical decisions are often based on more narrow criteria of departmental autonomy—an autonomy often jealously defended in a time of retrenchment. In such a context African studies is often perceived by others as severed from mainstream developments in the discipline: An Africanist historian is not "really" a historian but an anthropologist; oral sources are not "really" hard historical data but "folklore" or "perception"; Africa is not "really" historical because it is not intimately tied to the "centers" of modern history. Such (often implicit) characterizations result partly from the ties of African history to nontraditional structures (such as Black studies or area studies programs); partly from the inability of young Africanist scholars to communicate effectively with older scholars and to illustrate the important methodological, intellectual, and theoretical contributions which the study of African history can make to (and indeed draw from) the study of other areas; partly from the dramatic decline of available publishing outlets (or rather a shift to marketing criteria over intellectual criteria on the part of university presses) to provide the imprimatur of respectability; and partly from the divisiveness resulting from a field very much in transition and the lack of support which young Africanist scholars have been able to generate for each other's work.[6] Indeed, so deep is the crisis that not a few Africanist scholars—even those with jobs—are voluntarily moving into new areas of non-African research.

One example of the power of the U.S. intellectual climate over Africanist historians is reflected in the time it has taken to recognize the essential banality of the concept of studying African history "from

the African point of view." As a conceptual category in opposition to
European ethnocentricity, at best it refers to a nationalist approach.
Beyond that it signifies nothing at all of a theoretical nature; it begs the
question of which African point of view and, by accepting the basic
categories of European/African oppositions, it simply replicates the
racist overtones of the very paradigms it was intended to refute. But
as surrogate theory it carries no explanatory power, no analytic
strategy for determining relevant data and significant patterns in the
historical record.

While the original stimulus for adopting such a framework is obvious, the reasons for its continued persistence are more complex.
Thirty years ago there may have been greater consensus on historical
theory and hence less recognition of the need to articulate that
framework. For more recent periods, however, the general lack of
receptivity to conceptual frameworks is often explained by the empty
assertion of "letting the Africans speak for themselves." Surely it is
necessary that Africans of all classes participate directly in formulating a vision of their own past, but that simple assertion is not enough;
it avoids the question of analytic approach. While it may indeed be
true that "the Africans" may not have seen their history through a
framework that was explicitly *Annaliste,* Substantivist, Marxist,
Structuralist, Formalist, or whatever, insofar as historians apply any
analytic framework to their work, this is derived from "outside" the
data. It is not the provenance of the conceptual framework that is in
question here but its relevance in illuminating the basic historical
issues involved and the skill and intelligence with which it is handled:
how comprehensive and convincing an explanation results, and how
relevant it is in identifying historically significant problems. Certainly
the Khoikhoi didn't see their history as it appears in *Kraal and Castle*
or the Imbangala theirs as in *Kings and Kinsmen* any more than the
Kenya coastal societies of the Baule saw theirs as presented in *From
Slaves to Squatters* or *Baule Resistance.*[7] Similarly Semboja,
Womunafu, Mapondera, Mekatalili and others might have been surprised to have seen the variety of forces acting to mold their worlds.[8]
While all historical works employ a theoretical framework of some
sort, the critical issue is that some frameworks are more relevant to
identifying important issues than others: Hence the need to consider
them openly as part of the historian's task, not as a substitute for or in
opposition to "empirical" data, but so that we can identify with
greater clarity the nature of our own intellectual parameters—and
their limitations.[9]

The most comprehensive attempt to consider such parameters on any large scale is found in the recent initiative by the Joint Committee on African Studies of the American Council of Learned Societies and the Social Science Research Council to commission a series of papers, each to address one of the basic intellectual issues facing the Africanist community in the United States—issues that are "continually reemerging in new constellations requiring renewed definitions of conceptual tools and methods best suited to deal with them" (Janzen, 1983: v). These papers seek to identify and assess the analytic paradigms commonly encountered and to explore the possibility of alternative conceptual frameworks. In doing so they have also served as a critical review—not perhaps exhaustive in all cases, but certainly very extensive—of the recent literature and a focal point for identifying the elements which need be accounted for in any theoretical revision and development.[10]

In general the papers divide into two categories: those that seek an overview of work in a given field, and those organized around an argument addressing the issues. Within the latter group Lonsdale's work is particularly noteworthy, proposing new lines of analysis, identifying emergent debates, and even (to a degree) producing a new vocabulary to accommodate the analytic perspectives on "the state and social processes," perspectives sometimes quite different from those of other recent analysts. Cooper's tour de force on "Africa and the World Economy," however, is both review and argument, and written on a different plane entirely from most other essays in this series. Not that the debate on world systems has ceased, but there seems to be a pause, a shift in paradigms as earlier empiricist, *dependiste,* and Marxist paradigms yield to other forms of analysis not yet fully articulated. Cooper argues for an informed comprehensive Marxist framework flexible enough to accommodate to the demands of precise historical specificity and dynamic political process, rather than relying on universal static categories. By its argument, at once lucid and comprehensive, Cooper's work transcends the "overview" format and provides instead an elegant framework within which to situate the debates of the future.

The three-stage shift from a focus on research technique to critical analysis to an exploration of broader theoretical interests has been characterized by two related developments: a vast expansion in the range of interests pursued by historians, and the corresponding disintegration of earlier categories through which history was understood. With new fields to explore (including epidemiology, forms of labor control, ecology, transformations in agricultural systems, the social relations of work patterns, varieties and changes in marriage systems, forms of women's organization) and new questions to ask, the former structures simply could not be sustained; broadening the range of inquiry forced a reconsideration of the epistemological basis of historical understanding: a process still in its very formative stages, and one that threatens to open the gap between professional historians and popular concepts—even with traditional scholarship—still wider. And as this occurs, of course, it will also threaten to divide Africanist historians among themselves all the more.

There is a good deal of evidence of this type of shift on the part of the "middle" generation of historians—the principal formulators of the new paradigms of the 1970s. Many went through a relatively quiescent period after their initial publications, but conference papers, articles, and books indicate that their more recent work is significantly different in both tone and approach from their earlier work. In many cases they are on the way to working out important new paradigms: Feierman (1979, 1984) continues to work on the social aspects of health and medicine; Wright (1975, 1982, 1983) is undertaking studies on gender relations within the political economy of colonialism; Alpers (1983) is conducting research into Somali urban and economic history; Cohen (1977, 1983) continues to work on comparative strategies of settlement and alliance in the Great Lakes region; Cooper (1984) has turned to urban history and the history of work in Kenya; Miller (1980, 1983) is pursuing work on the impact of ecology and disease environments on changes in the forms of slavery and the slave trade in West Central Africa; and Crummey (1980, forthcoming) has analysed issues related to social banditry and modes of production.

There has been a similar shift in approach and fields among the younger scholars whose current work diverges sometimes markedly from their earlier dissertation research—whose earlier work in fact sometimes showed the ambiguities of the transition period within which their research was carried out. To take but a few examples, Brantley is following up her first work on resistance (1983) with research on the impact of colonial rule on food and nutrition; Packard (1981) has shifted his focus from precolonial eastern Zaire to aspects of epidemiological history in southern Africa; Northrup has turned from early trade in southeastern Nigeria (1978) to problems of labor recruitment in northeastern Zaire; Berger has shifted from precolonial work on religion and resistance in the Interlacustrine area (1981) to women and labor organizations in South Africa (1983); after early studies on Kongo (1983a), Thornton has concentrated on demographic problems (1977; 1983b).[11]

Despite the salutary advances, there are nonetheless certain dangers. One is that of losing sight of individuals in their historical specificity, of the fact that historical structures are articulated and expressed through—they only exist in—the actions and words of individuals. But if individuals are important, then conceptual structures as well as material structures are also important, and we restrict the openings to such understanding at our own risk; perhaps the reactions among historians against all types of structuralist approaches has been too intense, too relentless, too inclusive. To be sure structuralists—and here for the sake of argument I focus on the single field of structural anthropology—sometimes bring on such reactions, by their recourse to extreme idealist examples and by their rejection outright of all oral data as historical sources. But when handled with sensitivity to historically and culturally specific contexts—that is, when they account for the empirical groundings of historical scholarship—these approaches can carry us far beyond more conventional narrative styles. The time may have come to moderate the acrimony; we need to be able to draw on structuralist insights without being captive to structuralist dogma, to distinguish between *Totemism* and *Mythologiques,* for example, or between *Le Rwanda et la région Interlacustre* and *Rois nés d'un coeur de vache* (to stay with the anthropological examples). Finally, and most important, there appears to be a growing new orthodoxy against oral tradition. If we seek to retain the value of "history from within," even while also drawing on outside records, we must remain sensitive and aware of the importance of oral data and the techniques of oral analysis (as well as being sensitive to its limitations). Many factors at present militate against this: Research conditions are lamentable, resources are scarce, the training and simply the work that goes into careful analysis are demanding, too demanding perhaps to accommodate the time structures within which many scholars work today; but worse, those who do undertake such work are often castigated for their effort, even (or especially) by those who have never undertaken work of this type. This is not, of course, to deny the essential value of archival work, but only to note that in many ways archival work can beneficially be complemented by oral research—by informed work from within. In addition the personal ties between U.S. institutions and Africa seem to be diminishing, especially in terms of African scholars with access to U.S. institutions; in an important way, the vitality of the field depends on continued intense interaction, dialogue, and the realization that colleagueship is a product of practice, not of status.

Despite the movement over the past decade or so, scholarly traditions die hard. There is excellent work being done in some corners of U.S. Africana—probing and informed, and seeking to identify the issues and the particular type of question to which African historical experience most directly speaks. But despite this, there is a general sense of timidity, of resting with the old intellectual habits, even of active resistance to new initiatives, and such attitudes seem to find support and validation in the general public disinterest in Third World issues. Structural issues facing Africanist scholars are also important: The older pioneers are retiring, the middle generation overburdened, and the younger scholars unemployed. The dispersion of Africanists facing the relative decline in the influence of earlier centers, earlier focal points for discussion; the heterogeneity of the ASA; and the obstacles to effective intellectual dialogue with scholars in other fields—all reduce the intensity of Africanist research. Although in part a product of early successes, such a diffusion has not resulted in the development of intellectual paradigms that better address the issues that confront Africa today; in some ways they have impeded such a development.

However, three aspects tentatively militate for a return to more active exploration in the future, and a more clear-cut break with past Africanist paradigms. The SSRC/ACLS papers collectively form an extremely valuable, and timely, foundation for discussion, reflection and regeneration. The work of individual scholars shows that important research and thinking continues among an influential if small group of historians, and serves as testimony to the accumulated expertise and resources available. And most important, but not a factor to celebrate, the reality that most Africans continue to live out their lives in perpetual crisis demands that those who are concerned continue to explore the meaning of this reality, seeking more powerful ways of understanding the past, the better to explain the present. Progress towards this larger goal is by no means assured; perhaps that alone calls for greater effort and commitment. At the very least it calls for a reassessment not only of African history but of the Africanist paradigms—and the historical conditions which produced them—that have generated historical understanding in the past.

NOTES

1. To take but a single example (but not an isolated one), an article on the Sudan which appeared in the *Christian Science Monitor* of July 6, 1984 begins: "Deep in Sudan's Great Sudd Swamp—at this time of year a Florida-sized sea of papyrus, ferns, reeds, crocodiles, and rotting ooze—a rebellion is taking root." It continued: "In the 1970s the south's Dinkas—purple-black, often 7 feet tall, thin as rails, with long skinny necks and small heads but huge grins—lived in a sort of happy anarchy tending their big herds of cows. Their world in the swampland was malaria-infested and swarming with flies and mosquitos but one could not help but be impressed with the tribesmen's pride, humor, liveliness, their drumming and dancing" and later referred to "these human relics of neolithic times."

2. In fact the simultaneous rise of African and Afro-American studies led to a confusion between the two in the minds of many—despite profound differences in the two fields of study.

3. While I would agree with much of what Henige has to say on the importance of the role of "evidence" elsewhere in this volume, I would demur from his conclusion that too much attention has been paid to theoretical concerns. Instead I believe that not enough has been paid to such matters, since even a proper critique, to be complete and intellectually powerful, need be undertaken "from within," that is, fully informed with the theoretical assumptions and premises on which the object of critique is based. Indeed a strong theoretical basis seems indispensable to evaluating or even defining the "evidence."

4. The work of such scholars as Richard Roberts, John Thornton, and Leroy Vail, among historians, provides exceptions to this general rule, but it is to be noted that each of these scholars has been working for much of the time without academic security.

5. Most notably in Jan Vansina's *The Children of Woot* (1978) and David Cohen's *Womunafu's Bunafu* (1977).

6. In addition surely one of the reasons for the disrepute which has attached to African history in the United States was tied to the frantic pace of publication during the 1970s. Some historians seem to have forgotten that good writing is a central feature of the historian's craft; for the historian, who is also an interpreter and mediator between the present and our understanding of the past, effective communication is essential. Especially relating to theoretical discourse, clarity of exposition is vital; some writers apparently assume that theoretical discussions are an excuse not to write well.

7. The references here are to Elphick (1974), Miller (1973), and Cooper (1981a).

8. Semboja: Feierman (1974); Womunafu: Cohen (1977); Mapondera: Isaacman (1976); Mekatalili: Brantley (1983).

9. I want to stress here that I in no way see "theory" and "data" as opposed categories; only that U.S. paradigms have generally been slow to see them as mutually important, and that an "African point of view" is not a substitute for a comprehensive theory. Nor am I arguing that one should decide between one or another existing theoretical paradigm; one can draw from several or indeed formulate one's own, but the exercise should be part of a conscious process.

10. To date these papers include Berry (1983b), Cooper (1981b), Feierman (1984), Freund (1983), Lonsdale (1981), Mac Gaffey (1981), Mudimbe (1984), Richards (1983), Scheub (1984).

11. The scholars noted in the two paragraphs above, of course, in no way constitute a definitive list.

13

THE HISTORIOGRAPHY
OF SOUTH AFRICA
Recent Developments

SHULA MARKS

Since the late
1960s, there has been a burgeoning of historical research on South
Africa by a number of scholars who have questioned many of the
basic assumptions of the earlier writing on South Africa's past.[1] Of
great significance was the presence at that time of a number of South
African historians and social scientists studying in the United Kingdom and coming into contact with a far more varied intellectual and
political diet: the new African history; American writing on slavery
and race; the *Annales* school; British and European Marxist traditions (preeminently Althusser, Poulantzas, Gramsci and Haber-
mas); the Latin American underdevelopment debate; British social
and socialist history; and especially, from the mid-1970s, the History
Workshop movement. Initially based almost entirely in the United
Kingdom, since the late 1970s a great deal of new work has been
inspired from within the Republic, and the new insights have begun to
gain currency in accounts of South African history designed for a
popular audience, black and white.[2] Today, the research of the 1970s

Author's Note: This essay began as a shortened version of a previous article published in
Samuel (1981). It has since been transformed in the reworking, though there are certain
sections in common. I am grateful to Richard Rathbone, Stanley Trapido, Ian Goldin, and
Mary Rayner for perceptive comments on the manuscript.

is not only transforming the historiography of southern Africa itself
but is beginning to make a wider impact, both on African history and
more generally, as American historians and social scientists in particular are coming to realize the significance of the South African case
from a comparative vantage point (Greenberg, 1980; Frederickson,
1981; Lamar and Thompson, 1982; Cell, 1982; Denoon, 1983; Foner,
1983).

As the research of the past fifteen years reaches our bookshelves,
what is impressive is its diversity and richness. Far from being the
monolithic product of a single revisionist school, the work varies in its
scope, methodology, approach and subject matter. Clearly there are
as profound disagreements and as lively a debate between the so-
called "revisionist" authors as between the so-called left and right or
the radical and liberal traditions of South African history.[3] What they
do share is a sense of the importance of history and its excitement; a
common acceptance that history "not only enables one to understand
the past, but also offers the best critical vantage point from which to
view the present" *(History Workshop,* 1976: 2). Insofar as the new
work is concerned both with the structures of oppression and domination in South Africa, and with groups that have been "hidden from
history" (the phrase is inspired by Rowbotham, 1976) and with their
cultures of survival, opposition, resistance and revolution, it begins to
present "an alternative conception of history" in South Africa (Bozzoli, 1981). At its best, it not only challenges the stranglehold of ruling
class orthodoxies and mythologies but is also "capable of shaping
people's understanding of themselves and the society in which they
live" *(History Workshop,* 1976: 2).

Quite how recent these developments have been can be witnessed
both from the nature of Wilson's and Thompson's (1969, 1971) edited
synthesis of South African history and the reviews which greeted it.
At that time there were good grounds for deploring the extent to
which South African historical research had fallen behind not only
that of the rest of the white Commonwealth and other industrial
countries, but of other African countries as well (Gray, 1972: 84). For
historians of South Africa, Wilson's and Thompson's synthesis
marked a watershed. In many ways, it represented the apogee of the
liberal and positivist tradition in South African historiography of the
1950s and 1960s.[4] In attempting to do for South African history what
had been done for African history in the 1960s, it was a bold and
challenging endeavor. But in South Africa, the history of blacks was
still poorly served by the ancillary evidence from archaeology, oral
tradition, and historical linguistics, and it was grafted onto a strong

English-speaking academic liberal tradition, which led to a concentration on the process of "interaction" and "cooperation" between white and black. There was little appreciation of the changing nature of precolonial African societies or of the independent development of very different social formations in large parts of South Africa until the mineral discoveries in the last third of the nineteenth century; virtually no attention was paid to the uneven impact of capitalism and colonialism on African and Afrikaner precapitalist or noncapitalist modes of production and the resultant subordination of both, or on their differential class formation and class conflict.

In part, then, the limitations of the Wilson and Thomson *Oxford History* in the new context of the early 1970s spurred reassessment. On the one hand, there was a widespread dissatisfaction with the conception of the volumes at a general organizational and intellectual level. Eminent practitioners in the disciplines of archaeology, anthropology, economics and political science were called on to make their contributions, while historians were left to get on with the political narrative. On the other hand, at a more profound level perhaps, it was the nature of the questions which remained buried under the welter of "facts," the failure to see and explain hidden historical structures and relationships, which was more worrying at a time when, to the north of the Zambezi, the first flush of enthusiasm with the nationalist revolution had swung into disillusion with the realities of African poverty and neocolonialism.

Thus a number of scholars, some of whom had left South Africa for political reasons during the previous decade, began to ask new kinds of questions. In this there was decided resonance with what was also beginning to develop to the north, with the increasing awareness that independence in the political sphere had in many African countries resolved relatively few economic inequalities, and had not solved—despite the euphoria of the 1960s—the problems of development. With this change in focus, the South African example became of relevance elsewhere, as the Republic came to be seen as one of the few peripheral countries to have successfully industrialized—albeit at the expense of the majority of its inhabitants.

Probably at the center of the transformation of South African historiography was a shift away from explaining contemporary South African society in terms of the manifest salience in daily life of race and racism. A key moment in this change came with an essay by Legassick in 1972, which not only provided an illuminating analysis of the role of the frontier in the past, but also seriously questioned the metaphoric use to which the notion of the frontier had been put; it suggested that racism could not simply be explained in its own terms, as something somehow carried over intact from the eighteenth century frontier, but had in some way to be related to the changing material base of society. While not denying the presence of racism in seventeenth and eighteenth century South African society or the relative autonomy of ideology, he pointed to ways in which American historians (Lamar and Thompson, 1982) were beginning to contextualize racism and to urge that the specific forms it had taken in South Africa in different historical epochs be distinguished.

Four other researchers in the early 1970s assisted in what has in some sense been a shift in paradigm in South African studies: Johnstone (1970), Trapido (1971), Wolpe (1972), and Bundy (1972)— the latter's pioneering article much influenced by the Latin American debate on underdevelopment. It is not possible here even to summarize their arguments adequately. What is important for our purposes however is that while liberal writers of the 1950s and 1960s, heavily influenced by neoclassical economists, had been content to accept capitalism in South Africa as given, essentially neutral and somehow extraneous to the shaping of its racist society, the new work, together with Legassick's (1974a, 1974b, 1975) later articles, pointed precisely to the significance of South Africa's capitalist development in accounting for its peculiarities. In particular, the role of the deep-level gold mining on the Witwatersrand, with its huge demand for labor and vast sums of international investment, was emphasized as crucial in the transformation of South African society in the nineteenth century. Thus, it was in the policies of the Chamber of Mines with its drive to cut labor costs that the origins of many of the critical constituents of contemporary apartheid were found: the migrant labor system based on pass laws and compounds; the policy of setting aside "reserves" in which the African population could reproduce itself and thus reduce the welfare costs to be borne by industry; the division of the working class into white skilled and highly paid labor, and black unskilled and super-exploited labor.[5]

Far from being inimical to growth, the interventions of the state and the establishment of a racially hierarchical division of labor in South Africa, they argued, were crucial in South Africa's successful industrialization. In addition Bundy (1972, 1979) showed how, from the nineteenth century, African cultivators had taken advantage of the new markets in South Africa, with considerable success, until the demand for a mass unskilled black proletariat on the one hand, and discriminatory state assistance to white farmers on the other, undermined the prosperous black peasantry. Contesting the notion of a dual economy, a white, "modern" capitalist sector and a "backward" black agrarian sector, Bundy maintained that the two were intrinsically related; so-called black backwardness or underdevelopment was not a natural state but had resulted directly from the development of South Africa's industrial economy.

Collectively these articles challenged the conventional wisdom, accepted almost as much by the left (for example, Davidson, 1952; Simons and Simons, 1969) as by liberal economists (Houghton, 1964; Horowitz, 1967) in the 1950s and 1960s, which held that the processes of capitalist development in South Africa demanded a rationalization of color attitudes, and that the forces of economic growth would in and of themselves break down apartheid, a view which accords well with the interests of those who call for increased overseas investment in South Africa. This vision drew on what was supposed to have happened during the English industrial revolution: in some versions a Whig interpretation (in which the British ruling class benevolently expanded the franchise to include the working class and increased their wages), in other versions, a Rostowian interpretation (embodying an extraordinary economic determinism, based on the inevitable political developments which flow from different stages of economic growth; O'Dowd, 1974 is typical). By breaking with the notion that racism was simply an atavistic carryover from the eighteenth century, and by recognizing the complex paths which different societies have followed to industrialization, the revisionists exploded these comforting myths as applied to South Africa.

More importantly, perhaps, their work broke the hold of the dominant pluralist models of race relations in South African history, and not only for the twentieth century: Their demand for a return to a materialist analysis of class and race had implications for the whole of South African history, from the first contacts between the Stone Age hunter-gatherers and Iron Age farmers to the present. I do not intend to tackle these earlier epochs here, except to point out that few of these implications have been teased out as yet, a reflection of the greater emphasis given to work on the nineteenth and twentieth centuries.[6] Yet even work on the seventeenth and eighteenth centuries not using a materialist framework has been influenced by the questions posed by Legassick's earlier work (see Eliphick and Giliomee, 1979).

If much of the first stage of the revisionist history concentrated on the importance of the mineral discoveries in the last third of the nineteenth century, there was always a parallel stream of work on preindustrial South Africa, which was increasingly informed by the renewed debate on the effects of mining capital, and the demand for a materialist analysis.[7] From the mid-1970s this was joined by a growing

body of research on the twentieth century, focusing on the nature of
the South African state and capital accumulation, especially in mining
and agriculture (Davies, 1979; Kaplan, 1977; Morris, 1976 and 1980;
Innes, 1984). This work, following that of Legassick and Wolpe and
informed by the writings of such French structuralists as Althusser
and Poulantzas, addressed central and urgent questions, and has
expanded our understanding of twentieth-century South Africa;
nevertheless it is not unfair to suggest that it was more concerned with
the structures of oppression than with the struggles of the oppressed,
with conflicts between "fractions of capital" than with the struggles
for survival and modes of resistance among blacks; where the working class entered the arena, it was, by and large, the white working
class. Blacks on the land, especially on the African reserves, were
largely left out of account, despite the attention paid to the capitaliza-
tion of agriculture (Morris, 1980; Keegan, 1981). Outside the Poulantzian framework, although still largely concerned with ruling class
politics, major studies were produced on Afrikaner nationalism and
the ideology of English-speaking South Africans (Bozzoli, 1981;
O'Meara, 1982).

The silence of much of this writing on the nature of black political
consciousness—not necessarily class consciousness—was not, I
think, accidental; nor was it simply a function of the greater intracta-
bility of sources. It was in large measure a reflection of the silenced
political struggle in the late 1960s and early 1970s, the ambivalence of
the white student towards the black consciousness movement of the
period, and the continued absence of an African contribution to this
historiography. As we shall see, the reawakening of the African
working class in the 1970s brought to the forefront some of the
limitations of the work on the twentieth century, although discriminatory education and the alienated versions of history taught to
black schoolchildren have continued to deprive us of a black voice in
South African academic historiography. And this is to be deplored,
not because I believe in any simple sense that only blacks can write
black history but because until they do a crucial dimension is going to
be missing from that historiography.

By its emphasis on the stucture of the white state and the processes
of proletarianization and impoverishment, this structuralist work underlined the crucial power of international capital and settler agencies
in the control of black destiny in South Africa; clearly both are central
to South Africa's historical and contemporary predicament. To write
social history without an analysis of these determinants is to imagine
you can have flowers without roots or trunk. In the South African
case, it is perhaps more difficult than elsewhere to ignore the realities

of power and domination.[8] Nevertheless, in order to understand the
specificities of capitalism and form of the state in South Africa, no less
than to understand the possibilities for and constraints on change, it is
as important to understand the history of the dominated classes.

The contemporary work on preindustrial South Africa was
perhaps more sensitive to African history than to the imperatives of
capitalist accumulation, but was nonetheless concerned with a materialist interpretation of the past. This attempted to explore South
Africa's precapitalist social formations and the ways in which these
were first affected by mercantile capital, then conquered by imperial
armies and finally transformed by industrialization. Although the
monographs are only now beginning to appear, some of this work
originated in the approaches to African history developed elsewhere
during the 1960s; by the mid-1970s it was transformed by the revisionist debates about twentieth-century South Africa and was profoundly influenced by the revival of peasant studies, and French
Marxist and other anthropology (Hedges, 1978; Bonner, 1983; Guy,
1979, Marks and Atmore, 1980; Peires, 1981; Beinart, 1982; Delius,
1983). The authors were historians rather than social scientists, and
their preoccupations and methodology inevitably differed from that of
the structuralists; moreover, despite a common concern with the
nature and shape of contemporary South Africa and an awareness of
the longer-term political significance of their work, both by occupation and preoccupation, they were less insistently driven by the
immediacy of the present.

Again, it is impossible to do justice to what is a considerable and
varied body of work, tackling different subjects and with diverse
sources of inspiration. It is united in its attempt to show African
people not simply as victims but as active agents in the making of their
own history, and to understand the dynamic of that history. While it
breaks down any notion of Africans living in a static entity labeled
"traditional" on the one hand, it contests romantic notions of a
classless and conflictless African past on the other. Thus, while
attempting to come to terms with the mode of production in precolonial southern Africa, these works are also concerned with process and
change, and as a result, despite their apparently narrow regional
focus, are beginning to illuminate a much wider canvas (Bozzoli,
1981).

As a result, our understanding of the impact of colonial society on
African peoples in the nineteenth century and of the origins of migrant
labor has been transformed. Although Trapido's (1978, 1980, 1984;
Trapido and Delius, 1982) work on the Transvaal political economy
was virtually alone in its exploration of settler society in the interior

and its agrarian mode of production, when taken together with these studies of African peoples on the high veld it suggests that settler society was never as monolithic in its attitudes to people of color as the textbooks imply; nor was it able simply to dominate the African groups it encountered. The random terror that characterized Boer-African relations in the nineteenth century was a sign of the weakness of the trekker state and not its strength. In the interior before the mineral discoveries, what is striking is the uneasy coexistence of social formations whose power was at many levels relatively evenly matched (Atmore and Marks, 1974). And even when the British intervened and forcibly conquered the remaining independent African societies in the wake of the mineral discoveries, neither they nor the increasingly dominant mining capitalists were able to impose their will on African societies in immediate accordance with their needs (Marks and Rathbone, 1982).

Thus the local and regional studies not only suggest the inadequacy of an imperial historiography which stresses the humanitarianism of the British; they also reveal the limitations of the early revisionist writing which sought the origins of migrant labor simply in the imperative of mining capital. What the recent historiography has shown is that while the demand for labor was the result of the expansion in South Africa of capitalist forces of production, that the response took the form of labor migrancy was related to the complex struggles between the black and white ruling classes and even within homesteads over the disposal of the labor power of young men. Power relationships within African societies acted as forcefully on the actions and consciousness of migrants as any pull of market forces, growth of new wants, or voluntarist choice on the one hand, or the "determining role of the South African state" acting on behalf of capital on the other (Marks and Rathbone, 1982).

This revisionism, based on a careful study of African society in the rural areas, has further implications for our understanding of twentieth-century South Africa. As scholars like Beinart, Bundy and Delius, who first worked on subsistence and peasant societies in nineteenth-century South Africa, have more recently turned their attention to twentieth-century South Africa, what is becoming clearer is the far more complex nature of the South African state when seen from this perspective. In the 1970s much of the radical writing tended to portray the South African state in instrumental and monolithic terms, perhaps as a reflection of the instrumental and monolithic image that the state itself projected in the 1960s and early 1970s; at the same time policies of segregation and apartheid were seen in somewhat simplistic fashion as the response of the state to the changing demands of accumulation. Thus while Legassick (1971), for example, argued that segregation consisted of a set of policies specifically devised to cope with the strains of rapid industrialization, Wolpe (1972) maintained that apartheid policies were the state's response to the undermining of the migrant labor system which resulted from the rapid expansion of secondary industry and the disintegration of the reserve economy. More recently, detailed attention to political developments in the rural reserves and to the nature of African political consciousness has suggested that neither sets of policies can be understood simply as impositions from above. Undoubtedly framed to meet the strains of class formation and to defuse class conflict, segregationist policies crystallized as they did in South Africa because they took up and reworked elements in African, especially rural, popular consciousness. Thus in the reserves, policies that recognized communal land tenure and bolstered the powers of chiefs coincided with and in turn reinforced a powerful communal separatism, which a focus on the nationalism of the urban intelligentsia obscures (Marks, forthcoming; Beinart, 1982; Beinart and Bundy, 1984).

It is perhaps no coincidence that this reexamination of the complex nature of state policies and of the role played by the dominated classes in its shaping should be so marked a feature of the historiography of the 1980s. Just as in the mid-1970s the reawakening of the African working class brought to a head the limitations in the existing literature which ignored African agency (O'Meara, 1975 is an exception), so in the 1980s it is the disarray of the South African ruling class which has in part forced this reexamination. The historians of the first half-century have had their counterpart in political scientists concerned with the current attempts of the South African state to grapple through reformism and a new ideological discourse with the multiple challenges of the transformed geopolitical situation, the demands of an economy increasingly dominated by monopoly capital, the collapse of the intricate network of labor controls established in the 1960s, and the resurgence of African nationalism within (Saul and Gelb, 1981; Marks and Trapido, forthcoming). Consideration of the material realities created by the social engineering of the past two decades has similarly impelled an understanding not simply of African "initiative" and resistance, but of the more profound ambiguities and contradictions at the heart of many of these struggles by men and women against their oppression and of the ways in which they "have become accomplices in their own subjection" (Samuel, 1975: XIX).

Other work has also confronted the heavy structuralism of the earlier research on the political economy which left so little space for

political action, ideology and consciousness, or the meaning of South
Africa's industrial revolution for the men and women who experienced it so traumatically throughout this century. Although focused
on the mining industry in southern Rhodesia, van Onselen's early
work (1976) opened the way to rethinking southern African labor
history more generally, providing an escape from the heavily institutionalized history of trade unions available hitherto. The publication of the *South African Labour Bulletin* in Johannesburg and the
symposium on labor history organized at the University of
Witwatersrand was the first indication of the impact of the strikes of
1972-1973 on academic endeavor. It was in the wake of this work that a
workshop was established in London to look at "the making of the
African working class." A further inspiration to the London workshop were van Onselen's (1982) graphic essays on the social history of
Johannesburg between 1890 and 1914, work which, like Thompson's
classic relating to a different time and place, set out to recover the
place of the working people of the Rand from "the enormous conde-
scension of posterity" (Thompson, 1970 [1963]: 13). Subsequent work
which he and Bozzoli are currently directing in South Africa itself,
together with studies by Willan (1979) and Hemson (1979), tackle
some of these "silences" in methodologically exciting ways and are
beginning to provide nuance and texture to our understanding of the
ambiguities and contradictions of twentieth-century South Africa.

This essay began by suggesting that the past few years had seen a
major transformation in the nature and amount of historical research
being done on South Africa in the United Kingdom. It has not
attempted to take account of developments elsewhere; in particular it
has not adequately considered the remarkable work now being undertaken in South Africa itself, now feeding back into the research
undertaken elsewhere. Inevitably, academic history there is still almost entirely the prerogative of white students and academics: The
major exceptions are the achievements of the Johannesburg History
Workshop, with its ambitions not simply to popularize but to return
their history to ordinary people;[9] the oral history project at the African Studies Institute at University of the Witwatersrand, where black
social historians are being trained and are carrying out their own
research (Matsetela, 1980; Nkadimeng and Relly, 1982); and more
limited work in Durban and Cape Town.

What is striking in the development of the historiography of the last
decade is the dialectical relationship between the work of the historians and the world in which we live and act. This is only upsetting to
those who see it as a burden rather than a challenge (Wright, 1977) and

who believe that there can be and should be a value-free social science. This relationship does not mean that one can write history simply "as a weapon in political struggle." As Burke (1981: 8) has pointed out, to do so is counterproductive, for one comes to believe one's own propaganda, to overdramatize the past, and hence to forget the real complexity of issues at any one time.

Yet in South Africa, where history has an acute relevance to the present, and political passions are so intensely engaged, it is perhaps not surprising that the clashes between liberal and radical historians have been sharp. But that is not all: Over the past half dozen years there have been as fierce divisions between social historians and structuralists—as much a part of the debate about South Africa as they have been in the broader field of British and European historiography (Thompson, 1978b; Johnson, 1978; McClelland, 1979; Williams, 1979; Anderson, 1981). Undoubtedly on both sides there are dangers and pitfalls, as social historians pursue the richer moments of individual idiosyncracy oblivious to the constraints on human agency posed by structure, and as structuralists ignore the complexities of human consciousness and individual variation in the interests of overarching theory. Yet if we are to move forward, it is necessary to bring together structure and meaning, process and consciousness, to engage in a constant dialogue with empirical data and theory, and to use the former to refine and modify the latter (Abrams, 1982).

Needless to say, much remains to be done. We are still a long way from a materialist reinterpretation of South African history. Nor can there be any agreement about what the outcome of such a materialist project might be. Major areas remain unexplored: The histories of women and the family, for example, whether black or white, are still in their infancy (*Journal of Southern African Studies,* 1983; *Journal of African History,* 1983); there has been virtually no exploration of the history of ethnic minorities; there is only now a welcome return to rethinking the history of nationalism and rural resistance (Beinart and Bundy, 1984). Even such major episodes in conventional South African historiography as the Great Trek or the coming of Union in 1910 cry out for reinterpretation. If the work of historians and social scientists working on South Africa is to retain the vitality of the 1970s, it is more important than ever to sustain the mutually enriching debate between scholars in different disciplines in a constant process of rebuilding, refinement and reconceptualization, as we take up the work of our predecessors, in constantly changing social and political contexts.

NOTES

1. Much of the earlier debate was published in the collected seminar papers on the societies of southern Africa in the nineteenth and twentieth centuries, produced annually from 1970 by the Institute of Commonwealth Studies, University of London. Some of these, together with additional articles, are included in Marks and Atmore (1980) and Marks and Rathbone (1982).

2. See, for example, Callinicos (1980), a model of popular exposition. Many of the new insights have been embodied also in the popular history published by SACED in the South African newspapers as part of their black adult literacy campaign. Ravan Press has published several historical monographs in reasonably priced and attractively packaged paperback editions. The Johannesburg History Workshop is discussed below.

3. The labels appended fail to do justice to the diversity of either "tradition," and do a disservice to both. I use them in what follows with reluctance and a sense of their inadequacy.

4. As Lonsdale (1983) points out, one should discriminate those "liberal" historians of the 1920s and 1930s like Macmillan and de Kiewiet, whose work can still provide inspiration for younger researchers, who were concerned with the traumatic impact of industrialization, and who were fully aware of the class conflict it engendered, from their successors who were writing after World War II under the influence of modernization theory, neoclassical economics, and the Cold War. As Macmillan was a Fabian socialist, the term "liberal" was as inadequate then as it remains today.

5. The key work was Johnstone (1976). Wolpe (1972) discusses the role of the reserves, and Davies (1979) looks at the division of the working class. Yudelman (1983) takes issue with the Poulantzian interpretation of the first thirty years of this century, but is ultimately trapped in the same paradigm. To fully explore the relationship of race and class in early industrial South Africa, it is necessary to start with the towns of the Cape and Natal and with the diamond discoveries; see Worger (1982) and Turrell (1982).

6. Recent work, however, is beginning to question much of the received wisdom about the eighteenth and early nineteenth centuries (Ross, 1983a, 1983b; Worden, 1982; and research in progress by Susan Newton-King, Mary Rayner, and Robert Shell).

7. Recent detailed research on the mining industry in the late nineteenth and early twentieth centuries has also modified and refined some of the hypotheses generated by earlier work (Worger, 1982; Turrell, 1981, 1982a, 1982b; van Helten, 1982; Richardson, 1983; Yudelman, 1983; Innes, 1984; Davies, 1979; Kaplan, 1977; Morris, 1976, 1980).

8. Much of the criticism of British and American social history in the 1970s related to its alleged ignoring of power relations; see Judt, 1979.

9. Much of this is represented in the volumes deriving from the Johannesburg History Workshops of 1979 and 1981 (Bozzoli, 1980); the third Johannesburg History Workshop was held at the University of the Witwatersrand in February 1984.

Part IV

AFRICA FROM WITHIN
National Historiographies

14

MARXIAN METHOD AND HISTORICAL PROCESS IN CONTEMPORARY ETHIOPIA

ROBERT S. LOVE

It is common for **Marxian** observers (as well as others) to account for the 1974 coup in Ethiopia in terms of feudalism collapsing under the strains introduced by capitalist penetration, manifested during early 1974 in the form of various popular protests (Valdelin, 1978; Sellassie, 1980; Gilkes, 1975; Ottaway, 1976). Too often, however, such approaches have paid insufficient regard to the precise use and articulation of the concepts used. Only seldom is a preliminary case made for the usefulness of Marxian concepts in historical research (Crummey and Stewart, 1981; Kelle, 1981). The consequence that has been a lack of rigor in Marxist-based Ethiopian studies in regard to both the application of terms and the analytical use of concepts and relationships. This, in turn, has served only to cloud our understanding of contemporary Ethiopia and to undermine the objectivity of analytical procedures.

Many writers have, of course, referred to the nature of class relations and political power before 1974, though this has often been in order to explain the actual events of 1974 rather than the broader pattern of later developments. But even in this context a number of problems can be readily detected. Although Halliday and Molyneux

Author's Note: An earlier version of this essay, "Marxian Method and Concept in Revolutionary Ethiopian Studies," appeared in *Northeast African Studies,* Vol. 5, No. 2, 1983. Used by permission.

(1981: 65), for instance, recognize some of the problems involved in using the term "feudalism" in an Ethiopian context, they settle rather open-endedly for the view that the Ethiopian social formation "contained social relations analogous to feudalism . . . parallel in certain of its institutions but diverging in important respects." Ottaway (1976) and Markakis (1981) also differ markedly in their analyses of the bourgeoisie, where the former emphasizes the significance of the formation of a bourgeois class during the later years of Haile Sellassie's reign, while the latter refers to the lack of development of such a class because of foreign capitalist preemption. For Halliday and Molyneux (1981), on the other hand, the small size of the bourgeois class in Ethiopia is accounted for by the dominance of precapitalist social relations. Nor is the postrevolutionary period free from confusion, as, for example, where Markakis uses the term "garrison socialism" to describe the later activities of the Provisional Military Administrative Council. Beyond the confusion in the terms used, a more serious problem still is the number of important aspects of Ethiopian society that have not been sufficiently considered.

FEUDALISM AND CAPITALISM

Although the importance of the *rist* land rights of the peasant farmer in the north of the country is usually recognized, the nature of the presumed similarity of Ethiopian structures to European feudalism is seldom discussed in sufficient detail to allow the important differences to be given due weight in subsequent analysis; Crummey (1980) provides an exception to this general rule, though one might dispute his suggestion that Marx's Asiatic mode of production has relevance to the Ethiopian situation. Chege (1979), on the other hand, justifies the relevance of the feudal mode of production on the theoretical base of the landlords' ownership of the means of production, but ignores the question of control over the reproduction of the means and conditions of production, stressed by Hindess and Hirst (1975). A more detailed comparison of the social relations pertaining to the Ethiopian *rist* holder and the feudal vassal and serf is required, especially considering their relationships to *gult* rights, often assumed to be analogous to those of the fief in European feudalism.

Comparison with European feudalism is thus difficult and fraught with theoretical problems. On the empirical level the analysis of feudalism in Europe tends to be dominated by concern with political power and the interplay of obligations and exploitation in extracting economic surplus from a subjugated peasantry, whereas the starting point for most analyses of the peasantry in the Third World tends to be that of land right, which is often viewed as customarily inviolable and upon which a hierarchy of political control is constructed. These differences of approach make comparison difficult and lead to incomplete and confusing results. It would be more pertinent to analyse the precapitalist Ethiopian social formations in reference to contemporary theoretical debates on the conceptual basis of different modes of production and on Marxist historiography. Although often highly abstract these debates serve to heighten the empirical scholar's awareness of the real nature of the relationships that he is attempting to understand. It is not, for example, sufficient simply to describe the *gult* and *rist* systems in order to arrive at an understanding of the dynamic processes of the underlying mode of production.

To explain how and why the system sustains and reproduces itself, and why it has experienced change over the last one hundred years, it is necessary rather to probe deeper into the relationship between the *gult* and *rist* systems, to take a holistic view of the process of surplus production and expropriation, whereby different varieties of *rist* may, for instance, have been sustained by *gult* processes for this purpose.

Analysis is further complicated by the fact that the southern regions of the country conquered by the north in the nineteenth century tend also to be characterized as feudal, though with absentee landlords and peasant tenants having little security and subject to sharecropping. Usually, scant reference is made to the nature of the preconquest modes of production in these areas. Yet the somewhat uncertain allegiances of several nationalist movements in Ethiopia today must be based to some extent on the vestiges of preconquest social and economic relations. The information available on traditional formations in the south of Ethiopia does not, for example, indicate a communal or fully pastoral system, but one of petty kingdoms whose leaders managed to maintain, in the form of *balabats,* a certain influence and economic base throughout the postconquest period (Markakis, 1974; Hiwet, 1975). It is not at all clear, therefore, that in opposing Amhara dominance from Addis Ababa some southern peoples are also rejecting social relations dating from before the Amhara conquest.

This example serves to illustrate a more general point. A considerable body of research exists on Ethiopian society before 1974, mostly in orthodox anthropological and sociological terms (Levine, 1966;

Bauer, 1977; Hoben, 1973, 1975) but producing information and describing patterns of behavior that have not been effectively integrated into radical accounts either of the 1974 coup or of postcoup events. What is at issue is the precise nature of the relations of production prior to 1974, of how they have reacted to the changes introduced since then, and in particular of how they may have circumscribed the behavior of the Provisional Military Administrative Council. It becomes essential to include the detailed groundwork of social anthropologists and political historians if Marxist analysis is to be both historical and specific.

Although all postrevolutionary commentators stress its importance, the true nature and effects of capitalist influence in Ethiopia remain problematic. Halliday and Molyneux (1981: 65) provide a representative view:

> Prior to the Second World War . . . this pre-capitalist system remained almost untouched, except for Eritrea where Italian colonialism had since the 1890s been developing capitalist agriculture; and the environs of Addis Ababa where the demand for food from the urban population had expanded market relations.

Similarly, Gilkes (1975: 137) states that "both a money economy and manufacturing industry are relatively new to Ethiopia. Both are essentially post-war developments." Such statements fail to provide a satisfactory basis for analysing the effect of capitalism in Ethiopia.

Foreign enterprise and ownership of capitalist production in Ethiopia have attracted considerable attention and have been identified both as cause and effect of the small size of the Ethiopian bourgeoisie. It is not always fully appreciated, however, that especially during the postwar period, relatively small-scale, independent operators of Armenian, Greek, and Italian descent were an important source of foreign capital, many of whom had no permanent base outside Ethiopia, and to refer to them only as old established expatriate communities, as do Markakis and Ayele (1978), is to overlook their importance as a petty bourgeoisie in themselves and to forego the possibility of seeing them as a fraction of an indigenous petty bourgeoisie, thus contributing to the development of a capitalist orientation among the educated elite.[1] The role of the latter during Menelik's time together with that of the "Japanizers" of the 1930s and 1940s, is referred to in some detail by Hiwet (1975), whose work includes early reference to the notion of capitalist underdevelopment.

In accounting for the main characteristics of the Ethiopian social formation it is difficult to assess the role of the Christian Orthodox Church. Although both Islamic and Christian traditions have been important in Ethiopian life and politics, the dominant religious influence in the highland areas has been that of the Christian Orthodox Church. But despite its importance as part of the historical fabric of precoup Ethiopia the political significance of the church in the Ethiopian social formation has rarely been explored in depth (Heyer, 1982, makes a start in this direction).

THE STATE

Many authors refer to the growth of the administrative powers and bureaucracy of the imperialist state under Haile Sellassie and identify the class background of the bureaucracy as a crucial factor in explaining the role of the contemporary Ethiopian state. While many useful insights have emerged from this approach in recent years, the true character of the state in Ethiopia remains unclear. It owes little to colonial factors, and the Ethiopian case does therefore not fit readily into theories of the postcolonial state. Most accounts situate the state in an uneasy relationship between the centralized feudalism of Haile Sellassie and an incipient capitalism. This ambivalence largely reflects the failure to specify adequately the dominant relations of the mode of production of the past hundred years in Ethiopia. If the dominant mode was feudalism, then is the expanded role of the state since 1945 best accounted for as establishing the legal framework for capitalism, or as institutionalizing feudalism and thus restricting capitalism? Was it the personal instrument of Haile Sellassie created for raising revenue, legitimization, and control but ultimately growing out of control, or did it, as in an absolutist state, serve some broader function?

Although much is made of the post-1945 expansion and modernization, the earlier periods should once again not be overlooked. Tewodros's court administration was sufficiently developed to keep records of tax revenue and debts in the mid-nineteenth century (Pankhurst, 1979). It is likely, therefore, that the state grew out of the needs of the emperor to maintain central control over precapitalist social relations and especially over the conquered areas, coping only incidentally and ad hoc with capitalist requirements. Such a view is supported by those who interpreted many of the changes introduced by Haile Sellassie, both before 1935 (including the 1931 Constitution) and after (such as the gradual erosion of *gult*), as attempts by the emperor to centralize the powers of a precapitalist state in order to consolidate his own position following the turmoil of the dyarchy period. In this respect Halliday and Molyneux's (1981) dismissal of the presence of a standing army before World War II is simplistic. While the gradual expansion of the state in imperial Ethiopia can be seen to parallel the slow expansion of capitalist relations, it would be premature to leap to a quick conclusion about cause and effect. It is possible, for example, that while external modernizing influences at the technological level were putting new strains on the precapitalist modes of production, they simultaneously provided a new means of control for the traditional dominant class. The imperialist state may thus have expanded partly in response to external technological influence—principally as it affected communications and armaments—and partly to allow the armed forces to expand, thus allowing Haile Sellassie a longer period of dominance than was common among his predecessors.

This suggests that the imperial Ethiopian state should be viewed primarily as a superstructural institution of the dominant precapitalist mode of production in Ethiopia, a view also supported by Crummey's (1981: 244) review of the nineteenth century, where "the Abyssinian state, here viewed broadly as a form of class rule, revealed striking continuity and growth during the 19th century, in spite of dramatic changes in the fate of its symbolically central institution, the monarchy." To some extent the development of the Ethiopian state may also be viewed as evolving from the nineteenth century expansion southwards, which in itself was a response to Italian colonial pressures and contests in the north. This makes the situation more complex but does not make the state a capitalist one or one that has developed in response to direct capitalist penetration as usually understood.

Yet another interpretation is to view the development of the state under Haile Sellassie as the emergence of an absolutist state in the classical tradition, in response to certain problems of mature feudalism (Anderson, 1979). While appearing to preserve the dominant position of a particular Shoan dynasty, such a state also served to protect the interests of the dominant ruling class as a whole. A number of outstanding questions remain, however: Why did a tendency to absolutism emerge so successfully only in the twentieth century, and what factors of the peculiarly Ethiopian precapitalist mode of production can account for its appearance? In this view, developments of the state even in the nineteenth century and earlier were possibly of greater significance in determining the nature of the state under Haile Sellassie than were the inroads made by capitalism both before and after 1945.

A large number of questions then arise concerning the nature of highland Ethiopian power relations. Were these, for instance, basically feudal or tributary, or a combination of both? If some parts of the country are best described by lineage or tributary modes, then why did others develop as feudal, and why did the feudal come to dominate? How did the articulation of multiple precapitalist modes influence the development of the state in Ethiopia? Such questions indicate the complexity of the Ethiopian social formation and call for extensive social and historical research, which, when allied to appropriate theory, may be expected to lead to a better understanding of the growth of the state than has hitherto been the case.

The complex social relations of prerevolutionary Ethiopia, together with the role of the state, cannot fail to have influenced postrevolutionary affairs; in the author's view they form a necessary starting point for analysis of contemporary Ethiopia. A useful approach is that of Halliday and Molyneux (1981) which emphasizes the autonomy of the Ethiopian state, albeit in terms of underdeveloped precapitalist class relations and the repression of an indigenous bourgeoisie. While this provides a useful first approach I believe the question of the autonomy of the Ethiopian state goes deeper. Whether or not one views the state under Haile Sellassie as absolutist, it would seem sensible to regard any autonomy of the state as serving the interests of either Haile Sellassie and his heirs or the class which he represented, or, more likely, both. That is, relative autonomy from the direct manipulation of the dominant precapitalist class was an essential element of both the stabilization of the precapitalist mode of production and of its attempts to control the inroads of capitalism in the interests of that same class. The attempt may have failed, but the important point is that the state apparatus which emerged over the long period of Haile Sellassie's reign was one that was generic to the needs of the dominant class throughout the period, and which, rather than withering away or being otherwise transformed after the revolution, has survived in most important respects (Brietzke, 1982).

It is useful here to refer to the pre-1974 research of Hoben (1973) and Bauer (1977). It may be remembered that a major feature of this research was the observation of upward and downward mobility that was characteristic of traditional Amhara and Tigre societies, combined with problems in maintaining wealth and power from one generation to the next. But in an agricultural economy political power is based upon land right, and from a Marxist perspective this provides the key to control over the means of production and appropriation of surplus. It is not clear that the nature of the landholding system in Ethiopia could provide a secure base for longterm political power, which would therefore have to be bolstered by force as much as by ideology. Thus, in postrevolutionary Ethiopia, where the military does not even have recourse to traditional forms of land rights to consolidate its power base, the degree of insecurity felt by the revolutionary state must be considerably greater than before.

If the actions and motivations of the Provisional Military Administrative Council are best comprehended in the context of the traditional role of land as a basis for political power, it is significant that in Ethiopia the basis of this power was insecure from one generation to the next, even if it did provide a set of production relations which could be used in the consolidation of power for prolonged periods. Amhara individualism and limited communal commitment (Levine, 1966; Bauer, 1977) are associated factors. With the destruction of feudal relations of production after the 1974 revolution the military government deprived itself of even this source of power. It is therefore not surprising that the Provisional Military Administrative Council increasingly came to rely upon military strength, backed by the coercive apparatus of the inherited absolutist state, in order to maintain power. But the military has not built itself up in recent years in isolation from the social forces which affect the rest of the nation: The postrevolutionary state emerged from the peculiar network of social and production relations of the previous regime. What is needed therefore is a more historical view of the Provisional Military Administrative Council and the postrevolutionary state than is evident, say, in the writing of Markakis and Ayele (1978), Markakis (1981), and Valdelin (1978).

The autonomy of the state under Haile Sellassie has thus provided the military with a ready-made superstructure of control and repression that may serve the immediate needs of a military government, but that will require radical transformation if it is also to serve the longer-term object of transition to a mode of production alien to that which it was designed to preserve. To some extent, it may be argued that important moves in this direction have already taken place with the reforms of rural and urban committees, but the central structures of government and the organization of labor in places of work seem as yet to be relatively unaltered, and it is unclear whether these changes represent a genuine, if cautious, move toward a "path of socialist orientation" (Halliday and Molyneux, 1981), or, as is perhaps more likely in the historical context, a defensive reaction by the basically unaltered Solomonic state serving the interests of its own survival. State autonomy as inherited from Haile Sellassie thus serves at one and the same time to provide a means of consolidating military control and as a constraint on future development of a more democratically based social formation.

CONCLUSION

A proper understanding of contemporary Ethiopian affairs can be achieved only in the context of an accurate and comprehensive specification of the prerevolutionary social formation, and of recognition of continuity of prerevolutionary class relations and ideologies in the fields of production and exchange. This is not to suggest that the outcome of revolution in Ethiopia has been entirely predictable but rather to explore how "the mode of production of material life conditions the general process of social, political, and intellectual life" (Marx, 1859: Preface).

In the process of such analysis, however, the Marxian historian of Ethiopian affairs must attempt to make use of the range of historical data and analysis provided by orthodox researchers. There are clearly problems in interpreting and in evaluating the results of an orthodox corpus of resesarch that has been conducted according to the rules of a different conceptual paradigm, but in the absence of a solid tradition of Marxian research in Ethiopia there is little alternative to taking this approach.

But while solid analysis must take account of the work available, Marxian research into Ethiopian political and social relations, both past and present, must also be directed towards the development of more sophisticated theoretical approaches. In doing so, it is imperative for Marxian historians of Ethiopia to be aware of the pitfalls that are present in such analyses; this requires an appreciation of the theoretical debates on Marxist historiography and on modes of production and their articulation. The inconclusiveness of many of these debates does not justify their neglect; it is only through a properly theoretical analysis of the past in Ethiopia that a realistic understanding of the present is likely ever to be obtained.

NOTE

1. Their own position remained ambiguous, being perhaps similar to that of the merchants and craft-workers in medieval Europe. On the one hand they depended upon the patronage of the ruling feudal elite while on the other they were prepared to advance into capitalist market relations. The activities of such "foreign" capital in Ethiopia were not confined to trading but also included domestic manufacturing and servicing (such as beer, soft drinks, wine, motor repairs, restaurants, and so on).

15

NIGERIAN ACADEMIC HISTORIANS

E. J. ALAGOA

The contemporary academic community of Nigerian historians derives from a long line of ancestors in the three convergent traditions of historiography that have operated in the country. Of these traditions, the oral tradition has priority in terms of both age and geographical spread. The Islamic tradition resulting from contacts with North Africa and the Middle East comes second in age, having reached Borno by about the eleventh century A.D., but its geographical spread is more circumscribed, influential only in the Hausa-Fulani and Borno areas of northern Nigeria before the nineteenth century. The Western European tradition reached the Nigerian coast only in the late fifteenth century, but has become dominant and prestigious because of the influence of the Western-based educational system, and the dominance of the West in the contemporary world.

The Islamic and Western traditions were first introduced to Nigeria by foreigners or those associated with them, acting as traders, missionaries, travelers, explorers, or agents of governments. These people recorded both their own observations and local oral traditions in the light of their own cultural and historical traditions. Only later did Nigerians acquire the skills (and feel the need) to record accounts of their own history using the tools and techniques of the outsiders.

The Islamic tradition began to produce local historians from about the sixteenth century. In Borno, the Imam Ahmad ibn Fartuwa wrote two books about the reign and wars of the famous ruler of the Kanem-Borno empire, Mai Idris Alooma (1569-1619). Another Borno

historian, Muhammad Salih ibn Isharku, wrote an account of the
capital of the empire, Ngazargamo, in 1658. The city chronicle became a widespread form of literature among the Hausa states, the
best-known example being the Kano Chronicle. The tradition of
composition in Arabic script reached a high point during the rise of
the Sokoto Caliphate resulting from the jihad of Shehu Uthman dan
Fodio in the nineteenth century. Uthman, his brother Abdullahi dan
Fodio, and his son Muhammad Bello all wrote books recording their
views of the jihad. The man who stopped the eastward expansion of
the Sokoto Caliphate, the Shaikh Muhammad Al-Kanemi of Borno,
was also a scholar-statesman.

EARLY HISTORIANS

The earliest known works by Nigerians in the European tradition
date to the eighteenth century. The earliest surviving work by a
Nigerian is the *Diary* of the Efik trader, Antera Duke; composed in
the pidgin English used in the coastal trade, fragments of the 1787
portion of this work have been published (Forde, 1956). However, the
best-known early work by a Nigerian is the autobiography of the Igbo
ex-slave, Olaudah Equiano, published in England in 1789. Curtin
(1967) records other ex-slave authors, but the most prolific in this
category was Bishop Ajayi Crowther who came back to Nigeria as an
explorer and missionary in the nineteenth century.

The establishment of Christian missions and schools from the
middle of the nineteenth century produced a large number of local
historians able to use the new skills of literacy to record oral traditions
and history. The most successful were Samuel Johnson on the Yoruba
([1897], 1921), Jacob Egharevba on the Benin kingdom ([1934], 1956),
William Moore on the Itsekiri ([1936], 1970), and Akiga Sai on the Tiv
([1939], 1965). It may be noted that Egharevba first wrote in Edo, and
Akiga Sai in Tiv. They recorded local traditions principally to
preserve knowledge of traditional history and culture against the
threat posed by the new forces of missionary and colonial activity.
Akiga Sai, for example, hoped that the "new knowledge" would not
sweep away "the things of Tiv"; in his own words, "The old mushroom rots, another springs up, and the mushroom tribe lives on."

Another group of educated Nigerians wrote works of polemics in
direct confrontation with colonial propaganda. Political activists such
as Nnamdi Azikiwe (1937) operated in this tradition. But others, such
as the Rev. Olumide Lucas (1948, 1970), claimed that the Yoruba were
descended directly from the ancient Egyptians. This form of his-

toriography came to be incorporated into the traditions of origin of some Nigerian ethnic groups. Thus the traditions of the Hausa concerning Abuyazidu or Bayazida, the Borgu concerning Kisra, the Borno concerning Sayf ibn dhi Yazan, and Yoruba concerning Oduduwa all derive these founding ancestors from the holy places of Islam in the Middle East. In another variant of this argument Equiano and the British missionary Basden suggest Hebrew origin for the Igbo (Afigbo, 1981: 6).

The establishment of the University of Ibadan as an affiliated college of the University of London in 1948 provided the focus for a new school of academic historians. Professor K. O. Dike, first Nigerian head of the Department of History, and first president of the Historical Society of Nigeria (founded in 1955), became the leading inspiration of this school. Dike and Saburi Biobaku, also of Ibadan, exercised leadership through the influence of their pioneering publications (Dike, 1956; Biobaku, 1957). Dike was also responsible for the establishment of the National Archives of Nigeria in 1954 to take custody of all public records in Nigeria.

Dike and Biobaku's books became the models for the new historiography. In an important departure from conventional historical canons of the day, they championed the use of oral tradition, which they used in their books to a limited extent together with British documents.

Members of the first generation of Nigerian historians were concerned with proving that African history was a viable discipline. They also reinterpreted the colonial period of Nigerian history as one in which Nigerians continued to exercise a will of their own independent of the actions and policies of the colonial governors. Ade Ajayi has argued that Africans were actively engaged in the "politics of survival" and maintained a continuity of institutions throughout the colonial episode. These efforts to "decolonize" Nigerian history have been greatly extended since 1960. The objective has been to write a history mainly for Nigerians, to serve in the education of the people and in the process of nation building. Ikime (1979), for example, has called for the direct application of the work of historians to the solution of present political, economic, and social problems.

INTERDISCIPLINARY RESEARCH PROJECTS

The writing of a "decolonized" internal history of Nigeria has called for the extensive use of oral tradition and the application of interdisciplinary methods. The major impetus for the systematic

study of oral tradition came from the projects for interdisciplinary
study directed by Dike and Biobaku from 1956. Although both
scholars recognized oral tradition as the major historical document, it
was thought essential to seek evidence from other types of sources
and analytic skills from disciplines outside history for support. Indeed, research in oral tradition was conducted mainly by anthropologists rather than by professional historians in both Dike's
"Benin Scheme" and Biobaku's "Yoruba Scheme."

In the 1960s, research projects using oral traditions received considerable government support. It was accepted that historians were
engaged in activities in tune with the interests of the politicians in
promoting the slogans of negritude and the African personality.
Dike's concern with documenting the largest political system on the
Guinea coast easily commanded support. Similarly, Biobaku's implied object of relating the Yoruba to the ancient centers of civilization in the Nile Valley and the Middle East appealed to the first
Nigerian government of western Nigeria under Chief Obafemi
Awolowo. Consequently, by 1966 a Northern Nigeria Research
Scheme directed by Addullahi Smith and Thurstan Shaw and an
Eastern Nigeria History Project under Dike and Anene had also been
initiated. It became more difficult to obtain funds for new projects in
the 1970s, and funding has virtually dried up in the 1980s. The only
new project undertaken on internal funds in this period was the Rivers
State Research Scheme started by Alagoa in Ibadan in 1971; in the
same period, the historians of the University of Lagos had failed to
obtain funds for a Lagos State project.

Some research projects continue on outside funds, however; since
1974, for example, J.B. Webster has drawn on Canadian funds to
organize the Benue Valley Project, studying Kwararafa, Igala, and
Idoma, among others.

Political perceptions in the post-civil war context help explain this
difference: It was important for the government of the Rivers State to
define the identity of its peoples against the wartime propaganda of
the Biafran regime that all peoples east of the River Niger were
"Biafran" or Igbo. The government of the Cross River State, with
interests similar to those of the Rivers State, also provided funds to
Okon Uya of the University of Calabar to commission a collaborative
study of the history of the Cross River Valley in 1978. Indeed, the
creation of states from 1967 increased interest in regional and community history. In northern Nigeria, an Arewa House was created at
Kaduna under the direction of Abdullahi Smith for the collection of
documents in Arabic and Hausa. However, some of the new northern

states established their own state history bureaus, the most successful being the Sokoto History Bureau.

The Benin project resulted in a number of substantial publications by individual members on the history, ethnography and oral tradition, art history, and archaeology of Benin (Ryder, 1969; Bradbury, 1973; Dark, 1973; Connah, 1981, respectively). The Yoruba project has resulted in publications in methodology and art history (Biobaku, 1975; Williams, 1974), but appears to have been more successful in training local scholars in the techniques of collecting oral data. The project even recruited traditional historians, and some Nigerian members have begun to make contributions, especially in oral literature; the most prominent among these are Wande Abimbola and Adeboye Babalola in oral literature and I. A. Akinjogbin in history. However, the wide range of Johnson's *History of the Yorubas* appears to have discouraged any new major synthesis of Yoruba history. Yoruba historians have concentrated on particular kingdoms (Atanda, 1973) or on particular themes (Gbadamosi, 1978).

The newer projects have not yet produced syntheses or monographs of note. Connah (1981) has published his archaeological work in the Chad basin, but little else has come out of the northern project apart from project reports. For the Rivers project, a study of Ijo oral tradition of the Niger Delta (Alagoa, 1972) provided a basis for the archaeological survey since conducted; some of the results have been published in Nigerian journals, and a collaborative synthesis is in press. The eastern Nigeria project was aborted by the civil war, but one of its members continued his work at the Institute of African Studies at Ibadan. This work, combining anthropology, history, and an evaluation of the archaeological discoveries of Thurstan Shaw at Igboukwu has now been published (Onwuejeogwu, 1981). The Igboukwu bronzes have, indeed, proved attractive to Igbo scholars, who have shown great resentment at the image of statelessness. Afigbo (1981) of Nsukka has led other Igbo historians in writing about Nri and Igboukwu, the economic system of the Aro oracle, Igbo relations with the Igala and Benin kingdoms, and Igbo origins.

The early stress on the value of interdisciplinary research has been maintained and strengthened, and Nigerian historians have benefited from the stimulation of scholars from other disciplines. Anthropologists have been generous with models and explanatory theses, mainly in Yoruba history; they have also contributed to discussions of oral tradition. Archaeologists have proved most stimulating, even inspiring, in the interpretation of the artifacts from the Nok culture area, Igboukwu, and Benin. Art historians too have tried to work out relationships among Nok, Ife, Benin, and related communities. It is only recently that linguists have come strongly into the picture, and in the Rivers State project, for example, the work of Kay Williamson has become a fixed part of the historical work in the area.

THE INSTITUTIONAL BASES OF
HISTORICAL RESEARCH

The Historical Society of Nigeria has served as the forum for Nigerian historians to compare notes for creating a synthesis of the regional studies toward a unified history of Nigeria. Most of its activities have been geared to the concerns of the historians in the universities (now numbering 14), but there has also been an attempt to recruit traditional historians, schoolteachers, and graduates of history who went into government or private business. The Society supports itself, and receives only a token annual subvention from the federal government at irregular intervals.

The publications of the Society are its most effective means of reaching the public and influencing the direction of historical scholarship and education. Since 1956 the Society has issued the *Journal of the Historical Society of Nigeria,* aimed at a professional academic audience. *Tarikh* was added ten years later as a medium for communication with undergraduate students, schoolteachers, and the general lay public. The most ambitious publication so far has been the *Groundwork of Nigerian History,* issued at the celebration of the Society's Silver Jubilee in 1980.[1] The *Groundwork* provides a summary of current knowledge within the limits of the long delays in publication schedules. At the annual congresses, members present papers on their most recent work and meet with specialists from other disciplines invited to give addresses at the opening session. Since 1980 also, the Society has awarded fellowships to some of its members for scholarship, and associateships to traditional rulers and oral historians for their support of historical research. This expansion of horizons has included membership in the International Association of Historical Sciences, the invitation of historians from neighboring countries to congresses, and efforts to form a continental Association of African Historians.

The Historical Society of Nigeria depends on the practical support of the departments of history in the universities at which the annual congresses are held in rotation. In addition, most of the original research is carried out in the fourteen university departments and the three Institutes of African Studies. Accordingly, the expansion of the university system over the country since 1970 has opened new research areas previously neglected for more accessible areas. This has been the case, for example, with the region of the Jos Plateau, where the volume of work has increased enormously with the establishment of the University of Jos. Recently, the department of history has started a project for the publication of oral texts, the Jos Oral History and Literature Texts, and has also produced an interdisciplinary history of the region (Isichei, 1982). Now that government funds for major research projects have run dry in 1980s, work on local history within the undergraduate university context goes on mainly at the level of the first-degree long essay or research essay. All history departments require history majors (currently numbering about 4000) to carry out original research in the long vacation of their penultimate year, and to write essays in their final year. A large number of these essays are accounts of the oral traditions of the communities of origin of the students.

The general empiricist orientation of much current Nigerian research (discussed in the following chapter) follows a similar pattern elsewhere in Africa. The first urgent task is to assemble a reliable data base before the depositories (of whatever type—personal libraries, art objects, ethnographic features, or oral traditions) disappear. While this empirical research can continue despite increasing constraints and difficulties, there is room for branching out in new directions, especially in examining the theoretical frameworks guiding such research and in historical relations beyond the present-day political boundaries (whether at the local or national level). Some of the newer departments have indeed attempted to strike out in such new directions in their course offerings and in their research specializations. Notable among these initiatives has been that undertaken at Ahmadu Bello University, Zaria; under the leadership of Bala Usman, Zaria scholars have begun to reinterpret the history of the Sokoto jihad and of the Hausa kingdoms and emirates in Marxist terms.

Subtle differences in orientation, in subjects of research, or in methodology are reflected to some extent in the various departmental, humanities, or social science journals published at most of the fourteen federal universities. These journals have greatly increased publication outlets for the historians, in spite of the long delays and the difficulty of some journals in keeping to publishing schedules. The more successful outlets include *Odu* (Ife), *African Notes* (Ibadan), *Savannah* (Zaria), *Kano Studies* (Bayero University, Kano), *Kiabara* (Port Harcourt), *Ikenga* (Nsukka), and *Lagos Notes & Records* (University of Lagos). The difficulties experienced by local journals ensure that each institution attempts to establish its own independent outlet, and also that Nigerian historians continue to seek external outlets and keep in touch with outside currents of historical thought.

The Nigerian community of academic historians is still a developing one, and the nature of debates is not as intense as it could be. But the historians get to meet in the annual congresses of the Historical Society of Nigeria, read each other's views in the journals, and the system of external examiners keeps professors informed of new teaching programs and orientations. It is a young community, and not without its problems, but it has, all things considered, withstood the test of time and survived the political turbulence of the past 25 years as well as could be expected. The community of historians in Nigeria can draw on adequate numbers, a respectable tradition of scholarship, and current status (as much from its internal "calling" within Nigeria as from its prestige among other African—and European and North American—historians) to tackle the problems now facing it—the problems of identity among historians, development, the educational crisis in Africa, and the general transformation of the discipline. How it meets these challenges remains to be seen.

NOTE

1. It had been planned to issue an edition for schools at the same time, but the manuscript for the schools edition, entitled *History of Nigeria for Schools and Colleges,* was not submitted to the publishers until 1983.

16

NIGERIA
The Ibadan School and Its Critics

PAUL E. LOVEJOY

**The development
of the** University of Ibadan in the 1950s—first as a college of the
University of London (1948) and then as the first Nigerian university
(1952)—determined the direction of modern Nigerian historiography
well into the 1970s. The scholars associated with Ibadan, and increasingly a new generation of scholars trained there, not only have dominated the field but were also instrumental in the establishment of
history departments in the newer universities. Especially important
were those at the University of Ife (1962), the University of Lagos
(1962), and Ahmadu Bello University in Zaria (1962), which each
produced their own variants of the Ibadan tradition, resulting in a
nationalist school of historiography for all four centers (Kapteijns,
1977: Fage, 1971; Dike and Ajayi, 1968; Afigbo, 1975b). Nigerians and
expatriates alike, whether trained in the United States, Great Britain,
or Nigeria, were involved in the reconstruction of the African past in a
form which could be used to further nationalist aims.

The Ibadan school of historiography includes those scholars, particularly Nigerians, who have dominated the scholarship of Nigeria
since the mid-1950s: S. O. Biobaku, K. O. Dike, J. F. A. Ajayi, A. E.
Afigbo, E. A. Ayandele, and O. Ikime, among others. They in turn
have trained a large number of Nigerian graduate students not only at

Author's Note: I wish to thank Philip D. Curtin and Bertin Webster for their
comments on this chapter.

Ibadan but elsewhere in Nigeria (University of Ibadan, 1973). But in a
more general sense the Ibadan school is a convenient label for Nigerian scholars who were not necessarily trained at Ibadan but who
have concentrated on the range of subjects identified with the University and its offshoots (Afigbo, 1975b). Specific themes include trade
and politics (Dike, 1956), the missionary impact (Ajayi, 1965), and the
Islamic revolutions (A. Smith, 1979), but the common orientation to
all this research was the glory of the Nigerian past, especially in the
context of European expansion. Expatriate scholarship did not challenge this orientation; rather, expatriates joined in the search for the
"legitimate" past. In short, most expatriates who have taught in
Nigeria, including M. Crowder, Abdullahi Smith, J.B. Webster, R.J.
Gavin, Robert Smith, and J. D. Omer-Cooper, have been associated
in one way or another with this school and have helped to shape it.

The development of African history was a "new" field in the 1950s
and 1960s, radical by area of specialization and hence distinguishable
from more conventional historical preoccupations as they existed at
the time. Africa was not of general interest to historians; the continent
figured in historical reconstruction only in so much as it was a stage
for European imperial actors. The activities of Africans themselves
did not fit into the mainstream of historical research until a new
generation of scholars arose, critics of colonialism, sympathizers
with the plight of "Africans abroad," especially Afro-Americans in
the United States, and African nationalists. Ironically, the Ibadan
school was part of a break in the historiographical tradition of Britain,
Europe and North America, but the contribution of the Ibadan school
has stronger links with the conservative tradition of orthodox historiography than with the revisionist historiography of the past two or
three decades—it was radical in area of application rather than in its
conceptualization of historical discourse. The concern was to establish chronology and to reconstruct political and military events, not to
examine social and economic change as such. "Kings and battles"
was the order of the day; only to the extent that Africans as a
collectivity were the oppressed people of a European-dominated
world order did those other than the mighty and powerful enter into
the historical record.

This preoccupation with political and diplomatic history—the
areas on the defensive in Britain, Europe, and North America—was
understandable. A chronological framework derived largely from
political events has been necessary for historical reconstruction.
Without such a chronology the revisionism of social and economic

history, whether in the *Annales,* Marxist or neo-Beardian tradition, would not be possible. Elsewhere the revisionists reacted against the mainstream; in Africa, and especially at Ibadan, the reaction was against the absence of a mainstream.

The first two decades of this historical work in Nigeria were partly concerned with the confinement of British and American academic influence, which was often perceived as a perpetuation of colonialism. Although individuals could study abroad and expatriots could conduct research in Nigeria, usually in friendly circumstances, there was a general feeling at Ibadan that London and Birmingham in the United Kingdom and Boston and Madison in the United States were centers of academic imperialism. At this state in the development of Nigerian historiography, the serious rift was between Nigerian-based historians and those from abroad. Some scholars even boycotted the *Journal of African History* in order to promote the *Journal of the Historical Society of Nigeria*. There was a strong sense of pride in the rapid accomplishments of the Ibadan school.

The achievements of the Ibadan school are considerable, most especially in the study of European expansion and the African reaction. Although detailed studies of political history continue, the broad outline of Nigerian history is now clear. Biobaku and Dike, in setting the direction of the field in the mid-1950s, did not study trade as economic history but as an important component of political history in the context of European commercial expansion. John Flint's study of the Royal Niger Company reflects a similar development in scholarship; while Flint concentrated on the European factor rather than the African, his approach was as balanced as Dike's and Biobaku's. Missionary activity has also received excellent treatment. In exploring the extension of Christianity to Nigeria, Ajayi and Ayandele placed their studies in the context of political and diplomatic history; Webster's work on the independent African churches again highlights the compatibility of expatriate and Nigerian scholarship. Invariably all of these studies uncovered important material on social and economic topics, but the thrust of the work was still political. Afigbo and others who analysed the colonial period continued this orientation. They added the African dimension to history, but it was mainly political history. The establishment of Ahmadu Bello University promoted the study of the Islamic component—the "neglected theme" of political history in the north.

The first wave of historiography was nationalistic, whether or not the scholars were Nigerian. Nigeria had a history, and that history

would be important in the evolution of a modern, independent Nigerian state. Wrigley (1971) was certainly correct in identifying the
dangers in this trend as historicism—letting the dreams of the present
shape the understanding of the past rather than undertaking a reconstruction of the past on the basis of sound historical methodology.
Even some in the Ibadan school, such as T. N. Tamuno, were critical
of glorifying past leaders and events.

> The Nigerian past, as I see it, contains a lot of unpleasant things
> which need frank analysis. . . . I see no virtue in glorifying the past if
> the known record points in the opposite direction [cited in Afigbo,
> 1975: 718].

E. A. Ayandele (1969: 19-35), too, voiced reservations about a history
focusing on "the cream of society rather than the people," and called
for a broader perspective avoiding the exclusive concentration of the
"traditional patricians," the western-educated elite in the south and
the "Islamized aristrocracy" in the north. Yet in their own researches
Tamuno has concerned himself with the evolution of the Nigerian
state, an orthodox subject to say the least, and Ayandele's work has
been well within the Ibadan framework. Wrigley's criticism should
not be taken too far: The perception was that historical study also had
to be relevant to the new nation, as Ajayi made clear in a number of
early discussions. Despite the search for protonationalist heroes, the
methodology employed by the Ibadan historians was not shoddy.

Traditional as a concentration on political history may sound, there
were important differences in this approach from the old, European-
oriented history. First, the Ibadan school recognized the need for
additional source material. Both Biobaku and Dike—and virtually all
subsequent historians—used oral data in a critical fashion more or
less in conformity with the canons of the discipline; later historians,
notably A. E. Alagoa, must be considered particularly successful in
the collection of oral material. And virtually all scholars in the Ibadan
school work with archival holdings. Second, the Ibadan school recognized the importance of an interdisciplinary approach, primarily
because of the value of such an approach in the collection of source
material. The Institute of African Studies, founded at Ibadan in 1963,
brought together scholars from a variety of disciplines. Historians
fought long and hard to establish archaeological studies at Ibadan,
and the arrival of Thurstan Shaw and Graham Connah introduced a
new dimension to the study of history. Cooperation, in part through
departmental seminars, with such scholars as Peter Morton-

Williams, Robin Horton, Christopher Wrigley and Esien-Udom did much to maintain contact between the disciplines, and such collaboration was important in several research projects (as Alagoa notes elsewhere in this volume). Yet despite these strong interdisciplinary currents in the search for data, it bears repeating that this approach hardly affected the Ibadan analytic framework. The orientation remained fundamentally political; it continued the conventional and orthodox tradition rather than transcending this heritage (Smith, 1977).

Such a catholic approach to historical study notwithstanding, it was not surprising that journals, historical associations, and other institutions similar to those in Europe, Britain, and North America should spring up in Nigeria. The Ibadan school was responsible for the implementation of a whole set of structures necessary for the development of the discipline in Nigeria. To fill the void in Nigeria took a considerable effort, for it was necessary to evolve a curriculum for secondary schools as well as undergraduate and graduate programs. Textbooks were written and a journal for secondary schools (*Tarikh*) was launched. These projects were as important in the dissemination of nationalist historiography as the professional associations and interdisciplinary research were in promoting the reconstruction of the "legitimate" past. With the institutions of history in place, scholars and students were able to amass a remarkable quantity of data and write an ever-increasing number of books, articles, theses and papers that resulted in a truly astonishing achievement. Where once it could be charged that "Africa had no history," now it can be demonstrated that the extent of historical documentation and scholarship makes it difficult for any given historian to master the field.

By the 1970s, only two decades after the quest for the Nigerian past had begun in earnest, the focus of concern among historians began to shift from the cooperative venture of collecting data to a lively debate as to how best to interpret that data. In part this change was a result of the Nigerian civil war, which led many Nigerians to reexamine their perceptions of their country and which called forth different interpretations of the origins of the war; in part it came about because the historian's craft has matured with the increasing number of historians in Nigeria. This shift in emphasis revealed that the Ibadan school was more than a school: It was a microcosm of history itself, with its ideological schisms and its methodological divisions. Nigerian historiography too experienced what Ranger (1976) identified as "the crisis in African history"; long before, Ajayi (1961: 206) had thought

the crisis so serious that it required "radical reform." While for
Ranger the need was to come to terms with African poverty, for Ajayi
history in Nigeria needed to address such problems as "national
integration," economic and social development, and cultural development. The lessons of the Nigerian civil war had taught some
scholars that the earlier promotion of nationalist historiography had
not been strong enough.

As the Ibadan school became more closely associated with Nigerian politics, expatriates found themselves less involved in the search
for a past that could be converted into political and educational dogma
for the new nation, while the nationalist historians found themselves
divided between the established Ibadan school and a break-away
group of Islamic legitimists, largely centered at Zaria but found elsewhere in the north as well. More properly now, the Ibadan school was
identified with the Universities of Ibadan, Ife, Lagos, Port Harcourt,
Nsukka, Jos, Benin, Ilorin, and Calabar—and while the tradition was
maintained, both within Nigeria and abroad, by those scholars who
continued to focus on the established themes of political, missionary
and colonial history, there was now a challenge from within.

The Islamic legitimists emerged as a school in their own right,
despite the early connection with Ibadan, in the early 1970s. Although
R. A. Adeleye, B. O. Oloruntimehin, and others studied the history
of Islam at Ibadan and the Centre of Arabic Documentation at Ibadan
continued to promote the collection of Arabic materials, the real
focus for the study of the Islamic north shifted to Zaria, where
Murray Last, Sa'ad Abubakar, Muhammad Al-Hajj and others followed the lead of Abdullahi (H. F.C.) Smith in reconstructing the
political history of the Sokoto Caliphate. Smith, the doyen of the
legitimists, even dreamed of recreating medieval structures of Islamic
scholarship as the basis of a revived ${}^c ulema,$ and his Northern History Research Scheme in Zaria and Arewa House in Kaduna became
the libraries and research centers for the study of Arabic texts and
oral traditions. In 1975, about the time that Ranger was becrying the
"crisis" in African history, Smith (1979: 246) was challenging a conference in Sokoto to accept the need for "time-honoured ideals and
traditions of scholarship which had formed the basis of intellectual
endeavor in the Islamic world for centuries: traditions and ideals
which the ancient universities of the Islamic world had founded to
preserve." For Smith (1979: 256-257) the nationalism of the Ibadan
school was bankrupt because it drew on the "terrible corruption of
Western society"; what was needed was a reorientation of Nigerian
universities, and the field of history in general, so that they might

"embody in their traditions something of the academic ideals of the Sokoto *jihad.*"

The same criticisms of the Ibadan school are evident in the writings of Yusufu Bala Usman, Smith's most articulate student. Usman's conception of history is also strongly nationalistic; his work focuses on diplomatic and political history, especially the history of the Katsina aristocracy. As such, Usman continues the preoccupation with chronological reconstruction, the search for protonationalist heroes, and cultural revivalism that can be found in most studies by the Ibadan school. But Usman (1979: 224) contends that "African scholars must get down to creating a proper conceptual framework and not waste time trying to resurrect and revise these dying systems of value and thought" that derive from "western studies of African societies." He charges that scholars have been too willing to accept "the concepts and units in the European languages as if they represent the absolute and final categories of human existence." Usman even introduces class analysis into his comments on contemporary Nigerian society, which indicates that he may have begun to criticize his own scholarship for its failure to break with the dominant Ibadan school. Indeed he now calls for "an approach to the precolonial history of the Nigeria area which emphasizes economic, social and cultural connections between the various peoples" as a means of "correcting a distorted picture derived from an unbalanced use of the actual internal primary sources." Such a process, for Usman, amounts to "decolonizing perceptions of Nigerian history and society" (Usman, 1979: 34).

Other historians, also centered at Zaria, have carried this criticism of the dominant school of Nigerian historiography even further. Temu and Swai (1981) introduced their experiences from Dar es Salaam, where a group of neo-Marxist historians had been exploring a new problematic for Africanist history even as Ranger was calling attention to the crisis in the discipline and Smith was calling for reactionary, Islamicist scholarship. Although their call for Marxist analysis is at odds with the Islamic revival, Temu and Swai fit into the Zaria department because of its antiestablishment orientation; it remains to be seen what their impact has been. In fact throughout most of the 1970s the scholars in Zaria remained an eclectic group. The Ibadan school has been represented but not dominant: R.J. Gavin and E.J. Inikori were the most important scholars from Ibadan, but even they had moved far beyond their Ibadan background and were engaged in research that was neither political nor diplomatic. Gavin was concentrating on economic issues, while Inikori was working on statistical data relating to the slave trade. It may well be that the influence of these scholars has been more profound than that of the Marxists.

Internal criticism at Ibadan, challenges from Zaria, and the general expansion in the number of historians has not shattered the ascendency of the Ibadan school. Nigerian historiography has maintained the shape cast by its first generation of scholars—essentially nationalistic and conventional, despite the use of unorthodox source material. Sound scholarship has continued to be pursued; oral data are still gathered to supplement archival holdings. What is different in the 1980s is the existence of a rival school of Islamic legitimists and the emergence of neo-Marxist scholarship. But despite their differences, the Islamicists and the Ibadan school responded to the neo-Marxists in a similar way: Despite occasional cries that the "people" must be studied, historians in both schools have continued to concentrate on elites and political/religious institutions. What is missing in their work, as the neo-Marxists point out, is class struggle, analysis of social formation and its economic base, and critical treatment of ethnicity in the context of interethnic relations. The neo-Marxists, on the other hand, have so far only addressed the problem of class as it relates to capitalism and colonialism and have not ventured onto the more difficult terrain of internal exploitation.

Ironically, perhaps, the Ibadan school, despite its limitations, has come closest to the study of social dislocation and internal class struggle, although without the consciousness derived from theory. The early focus on missionary activity made clear a number of difficult problems in nineteenth and early twentieth-century society. Returning freed slaves eventually became part of a new, westernized elite, but the process of their transformation from ex-slaves to respectable merchants and farmers entailed struggle which can be analyzed in class terms, even though Ajayi, Ayandele and others did not do so. Nonetheless, their work revealed unrest among the slave population, attacks on indigenous customs by the freed slaves and missionaries, and the participation of these people in economic and political reforms. E. A. Oroge (1971), for example, found substantial evidence of a fugitive slave crisis, and Agiri (1972 and 1981) has pursued this theme further; but like Oroge, Agiri is approaching the subject not from a Marxist perspective but with the perspective of a historian out to destroy myths. In fact, scholars such as these may well end up challenging the dominant Ibadan tradition from yet other perspectives, influenced more by the neo-Beardian or *Annales* approaches, but the direction of their thinking is not yet clear.

By the middle of the 1970s, most Nigerian exponents of the Ibadan school, with few exceptions, had published but a single book, usually an unrevised thesis. One effect of this was that scholarship stagnated, and despite the emergence of different schools in the 1970s, the field as such suffered. Each thesis added new data and covered a neglected subject, but individual historians have not pushed themselves to reconsider their topic on the basis of the more mature perspective that can be provided by teaching and additional research (Kapteijns, 1977: 128-158). The record in the decade since the mid-1970s has been no better; the number of scholarly histories continues to grow, especially with the addition of the Ahmadu Bello University Press history series, but new books are by and large Ph.D. theses and not new works by established scholars; the rethinking and exploration of new paradigms by mature minds—and most importantly the model for this kind of reflective, critical, probing scholarship for young historians—is lacking.

The Ibadan school has its critics, but its domination of Nigerian historiography will continue, and in my opinion it should. The setting for sound historiography is the mainstream—chronological precision and political events. To the extent that the Islamic legitimists pursue these same ends, they also contribute to the mainstream. Schools of history are now associated with the northern and southern universities that reflect not only differences in historical interpretation but current politics; it is certain these schools will remain the two dominant influences, even though both are nationalistic. The impact of expatriate scholarship will serve to support one or another of the schools that already are recognized as revisionist in the Nigerian context. Although Temu and Swai would like to see the end of western influence on Nigerian historiography and a renunciation of "bourgeois" historiography within Nigeria, it is unlikely that either the Islamic reactionary school or an African-based Marxism will prevail. The Ibadan school is too strongly entrenched, perhaps to the advantage of the dialectical struggle within the discipline of history. Class struggle, the significance of ethnicity, and the impact of imperialism in the nonpolitical arena all need to be analyzed. The Ibadan school has failed to do so, but it has laid the groundwork for the further study of Nigerian history.

17

SENEGALESE HISTORIOGRAPHY
Present Practices and
Future Perspectives

MOHAMED MBODJ
MAMADOU DIOUF

Senegalese historiography has not escaped the scholarly debates that have characterized African historical studies. These debates seem to have run their course, principally because African practitioners have not taken a very active part in them; but they have at least raised some fundamental questions of historical analysis. What most marks this historiography is its strictly university character: It is almost exclusively published in scholarly journals, and is concentrated especially in the *Bulletin de l'I.F.A.N.* (the Institut Fondamental de l'Afrique Noire), published in Dakar. And although recent research has been divided more or less equally between African and foreign authors, the ratio of Senegalese authors drops markedly in the higher degrees. Most master's theses by students at the University of Dakar (of 111 titles, 88 are by Africans, 76 by Senegalese) focus on political history during the colonial period; primarily because of the available documentation, the favored fields are the Wolof areas and the Senegal River Valley. Most other scholarly work on Senegal by Africans is done at foreign, particularly Parisian, universities. These works concentrate on the period of the establishment of colonial rule (the seventeenth to the nineteenth centuries), and the colonial period (especially the twentieth century). The history of Senegal is built around the colonial phenomenon—with the focus on the Wolof areas and the valley of the Senegal River.

For this period, political and religious topics have taken precedence over economic and social perspectives. This approach is perceived as part of the effort to "decolonize African history": to show that Africa has its own history that was interrupted and deformed by the colonizers, that the decline of Senegal came essentially from external causes, and that Africans had resisted these influences but finally were forced to adapt to them. Under the pretext of providing balance to our historical understanding of the area, these works tend to present the Senegambia at the best moment of its history. The focus is essentially on political features, emphasizing the "harmony" and the "balance" of the region before colonization. Such colonial resisters as Lat Dior, Ali Bouri, and Ahmadou Bamba are seen less as defenders of their own particular privileges, and more as symbols of the values of their privileges within the existing order. These values involve a certain type of nationalism, or at least a protonationalism, highly appreciated by a generation of writers who had themselves experienced the colonial system (primarily those twenty years or over in 1960). Such an approach leads to the concept of "traditional African democracy" and stresses an unalterable African specificity. From this perspective, independence becomes a rupture of colonial domination, and an opportunity to establish some form of harmonious balance; with the return of liberty, the equilibrium can be reestablished and society can recover its own internal historical rhythm.

The argument today for social and economic history is based on the presumed universality of the dialectical method applied using historical materialism as the principal analytic tool. Senegambia is seen as a part of the global economic system, dominated from the sixteenth century on by capitalism. This approach tends to see historical evolution in global terms, and tries to account for (and favor) economic factors. It does not seem to be a simple reaction against the earlier political approaches. Such an approach, stressing global economic trends, derives less from a conflict of generations than from a sensitivity of historical discourse to the global condition. Based on the continuity of history, this second group stresses groups and conflicts of interest, even classes; precolonial Senegambia is thus portrayed simply as an ordinary region of humanity, where exploitation exists as it does everywhere else. From this point of view the colonial period is no longer a rupture of some "true" internal historical rhythm, but simply an intensification of processes that are always present and that continue to this day. Henceforth the roles of political cadres (the aristocracy, the chiefs, party leaders, or religious leaders) are seen in a less positive light: They resisted, then collaborated during the colonial period, and then became the heirs of the system of imperialist domination.

These different premises have led to equally different results. Nonetheless, there exist many points of convergence between these two broad tendencies. The least important is the fact that both types of studies privilege oral tradition as a source of documentation. Comparison of oral sources with written sources makes it possible to trace an internal portrait of the societies under consideration, and the values that form them. This method allows one to obtain quite a clear idea of the relations maintained with imperialism, and the forms of political, social, and cultural readjustments required. More important, the results show a historical tendency toward integration between the valleys of the two large rivers of the zone, the Senegal and the Gambia. This evolution, increasingly integrating the area over time, is confirmed by the obvious trend toward the formation of a single socioeconomic community of the Senegambia. Here the complementarity of the visions is notable and deserves to be welcomed.

In spite of important gaps there is nonetheless a solid historiographical tradition in Senegal. There are two distinct bodies of literature. One of these is tied to the colonial tradition of hagiography, which stresses the role of the "technicians of the French colonial empire" and the "civilizing mission" rather than the destructive aspects of colonial rule on the Senegalese societies. The other is the nationalistic historiographic tradition, which has two forms: a very ancient one associated with dynastic, village, or familial oral traditions; and another related to the nationalist struggles that led to independence. In many ways these two approaches share important methodological perspectives and objectives: Oral traditions are important, and the two approaches share a focus on the "great deeds" of history, the important personages.

The diverse and sometimes contradictory aspects of Senegalese historiography are only reflections of the nature of the sources drawn on. Becker (1982) stresses both the richness of the sources available and their limitations (and rather summary utilization). He argues that the nature of the historian's task need account for both continuity and transformation, and thus the historian need recover a wide variety of different types of sources to avoid the opposition between event-history *(histoire evenementielle),* for which oral tradition is the essential depository, and structural history, derived primarily from written testimonies. Since Senegalese historical production is primarily ori-

ented to the Wolof areas and the valley of the Senegal River, and
secondarily to the Manding states of the south, it is clear that the most
important sources are dynastic oral traditions retained by the families
of the royal griots. Such an approach overlooks familial and village-
level oral traditions, which remain poorly known but can add an
important dimension to dynastic traditions.

The most important error, however, is the absence of an internal
epistemological critique of data by the historian. Historians have a
tendency to accept descriptions of political and social structures, and
the collective representation and attitudes that follow from this,
without asking how the complex translation of reality and image is
made by social groups interested in the maintenance of the social
order. This approach has shaped the historical discourse because
historians have forgotten that oral traditions, especially dynastic
traditions, are themselves, like academic analyses, a distinct form of
historical discourse. Becker is correct in denouncing the ritual references to certain earlier authors and the failure to cross-check and
compare oral traditions and written sources. In most academic
works, but also increasingly in the diffusion of radio and television
programs, there is both a break and an interlacing of various time
periods. It is clear that the concept of time in oral traditions, stressing
continuity, duration, and the absence of any careful recording of
innovation, differs from the concept of time held by the traveler who
describes exotic phenomena, extraordinary events, and the political
reality without first mastering the logic of their happening.

The presentation of the process of Islamization and the social
consequences of the adoption of Islam have very important political
and ideological implications today. Kane (1982) has remarked that the
historiography of Islam in Senegal has been dominated by "the spirit
of the crusade"; what was needed was to recreate the history from
within. In this perspective there were two important points to consider: the need to distinguish between Islam of the court and Islam of
the masses, and the need to recognize that the Islamization of the
Wolof and Sereer dates only from the nineteenth century.

The debate today focuses not only on the processes of Islamization
but also on its political and social consequences. Sembene's 1977 film
Ceddo proposes a reading of one of the historical periods (seventeenth to the eighteenth century) in the Wolof country. He stresses the
dichotomy between court Islam and the Islam of the masses, and
especially the resistance of the masses to this religion that challenged
their ancestral values; his analysis focuses on social conflicts. This

conceptual approach has been illustrated by Barry for the Waalo (the movement of the Buur Julit; Barry, 1972) and the Futa Jalon with regard to the Hubbu movement (Barry, 1978). The fundamental difference between Barry and Sembene is that between the historian and the creative artist. Sembene does not portray Islam as a force of conflict and of questioning of the authority of traditional elites in the context of the slave period, but rather as an ideology for preserving a neocolonial system in contemporary Senegal. His argument proceeds in part on the basis of chronological telescoping. Barry, on the other hand, interested primarily in the establishment of Senegalese dependence, stresses the emergence of new social contradictions and the increasingly important political presence of the Muslim communities in the context of which the marabouts, in a dialectic of opposition/cooperation, are seen from the perspective of the destruction of traditional power.

Bathily (1974) and Barry are the two authors who have shown the political and social implications of Islamization in the eighteenth and nineteenth centuries, one in the context of the slave trade and the other in terms of military colonization. In our opinion, however, except in reference to conflicts, they have not adequately addressed the specific processes of Islamization in the Senegambia: That is, how were these Muslim communities formed, and by what means did the marabouts—originally confidants and secretaries of the kings—then break with these kings and succeed in withdrawing the masses from the rhythms of collective life and from its expression embedded in secular, social, and religious forms? Within all this, how did they adapt their ideology in order to appropriate this social, political, and religious space in order to introduce new elements to the social dynamics, and bring into question the existing social order? On this point, Schmitz's (1982) current research provides some very valuable observations and complements the work of A.B. Diop (1981). The development of the process of Islamization has not been well traced out in the writings to date, yet they mold our understanding of the relationship between the Islam of the court and the Islam of the masses. The localization of religion does not necessarily imply either a new technique of proselytization or a rupture with the traditional organizations, but indicates the parasitic relations between these two and their redefinitions, above all in the strategy of clientship. While sociologists have studied the brotherhoods and their relations with the colonial and postcolonial state, the relative lack of historical depth in these studies precludes any analysis of the different phases of

adaptation and the evolution of their relations to the successive crises
of the so-called traditional societies. In this sense, the history of Islam
can be seen only as the history of the Senegalese societies in its
broader dimensions.

It is perhaps at this level that it is necessary to reconsider the
analysis of political reality in state societies. This approach follows
the work of Daigne (1967) and Diop (1960, 1981), who have focused
above all on state institutions and the role of state power. Such an
exclusive analysis of structures almost completely ignores movement
and change, placing the accent on the notion of the specificity of
Senegalese political organizations—a specificity defined in relation to
Europe and the nation-state. It is a perspective that, although comparative, is static and organized in terms of stratification, and therefore of immutability.

In analyzing state structures, most authors assume from the beginning that these structures exist and that the roles assigned to institutions within the larger political system are necessarily carried out as
they are "supposed" to be. The emphasis has been placed on the
normative definition of institutions—the way they ought to function,
rather than the way they actually do. This orientation has provided
the foundations for affirming a basic Senegalese democracy by influencing our understanding of the evolution of Senegalese societies
not in their proper historical role but in the historical logic of the
Western world or in the mirror of the *longue durée,* where pharaonic
Egypt plays the principal role.[1] An analysis that avoids such a
simplistic conceptual framework can show that the political reality is
more complex and bring into question the assertion of some vague
"traditional African democracy."[2]

The works of Barry (1972, n.d.), Bathily (1975), Becker (1975,
1976), and Diouf (1980) open new orientations for research. For most
Senegalese societies, the emergence of the Atlantic trade initiated a
period of political and social crisis that was to deepen right up to the
colonial period. But the destruction of an existing local political
organization does not imply its automatic insertion into the world
economy (which itself creates growing inequalities between communities, groups and regions).[3] Following on this descriptive phase,
we need now consider the internal forms of systems of domination
and inequality in their own turn, accounting for internal and external
influences in the context of spatial integration. This will lead to a
better understanding of the relation and interaction between the
ideology of the system (philosophy) and its real practices, to determine the basis of power, the social layers that result, and their mate-

rial bases. It is also necessary to reexamine the nature of dependence, the symbols of subordination, and ideological representations.

This analytic framework focuses on the strategies adopted by the existing social categories as they adapt to changing socioeconomic contexts to reinforce their local power or resist its erosion. Clientship plays an important role in such strategies, and constitutes the central core of Senegalese political systems to the present. It is very difficult to understand the functioning of the postcolonial state if one does not trace out, as precisely as possible, the relations between the preexistent social and political systems and the administrative system of the colonial period. The analysis of clientship, and of these political, social, and economic developments, is still to be carried out, which means that existing studies in no way support the concept of "traditional democracy" except in attributing a reality to the simple existence of institutions and ignoring their functions and operation within the political system.

The principal historical phenomena are that of violence as a means of gaining or retaining power, and that of providing for the expansion of the social basis of political power by means of clientship institutions. The mechanisms and procedures of this development must be explained: Their omission is an important lacuna. Such an explanation is the only condition that would allow one to question the idea of political continuity up to colonial rule, both in its forms and in its significance. The idea of static history characterized by immobility and based on the acceptance of a type of historical discourse found in oral traditions is unacceptable.

We have already sketched out some possible lines of future development. Influenced in part by efforts to establish and legitimize African state structures, local historians have often pushed too far and tried to move too quickly. Priority should therefore be given once again to the local monograph, based on well-defined empirical research, considered within the framework of a regional or ethnic corpus of work where these internal data could be associated with external documents. Researchers must no longer assess their projects from the point of view of immediate utility because it is imperative to understand the situation well before such goals can be met. African historians must not allow other disciplines to dominate their self-realization through some power over their conscience: Unlike the griots who reflect the vision of the clientship network to which they belong, Senegalese historians of the present must illuminate networks that have until now often been ignored, relating them all to a single social basis that gives the whole coherence and meaning.

Local or national development projects rarely incorporate historical data because of some pretended universal rationality to economic
paradigms. But these approaches cannot hide the failure of
economics, which results in large measure from a poor understanding
of the societies concerned. We need to move beyond some sloppy
developmentalist ideology that sees indicators, norms, and stages
everywhere.

From the cultural point of view, the people are the "consumers" of
history. But this history suffers from the compartmentalization of
history between the traditionalists (epic history) and the university
historians (written "scientific" history). The Association des Historiens du Sénégal has tried to bring together these different forms of
historical discourse in Senegal, each important in its own way, but
there is considerable distance to go, with each sector fearing to lose its
soul and, less admitted, its interests and status. In the final analysis,
the historiography (similarly for oral tradition) must not simply return
to its earlier image. Using modern media and scholarly manuals, this
history must be able to respond to the questions asked by societies, on
both the origins and the objects of the themes pursued. Thus with the
cycle completed, they might be able to embark upon another path and
to rely henceforth on the dialectical characteristics present in all
history, those of change and continuity.

NOTES

1. Cheikh Anta Diop (1960, 1981) is the most influential scholar in Senegambian
precolonial studies. His works generally are based on the premise that political
domination is balanced by economic redistribution, thus assuring stability and making revolution almost impossible. Diop is also the determined defender of the theory
of the black origins of the ancient Egyptian culture and population—the matrix of all
black institutions and the initiator of all civilizations; see Diop (1981) for the most
recent statement of these theories.

2. A. B. Diop (1981) shows the existence of a dual political and social system with
different roots that interfere with each other and draw off each other and that are both
founded on domination and the principle of inequality. But although this work traces
out the characteristics of this system as a whole, there is an absence of historical
perspectives reconstructing the evolution of structures.

3. Most works produced in economic history are by foreigners and are based on
macroeconomic analyses, focusing almost exclusively on peanuts. Such an approach, based predominantly on European sources, leaves out the actual experience
of the Senegalese themselves—the people most concerned. True economic history,
focusing on significant changes over the long term and accounting for the role of
Senegalese, is a neglected field, the major exception being Curtin (1975).

18

THE DEVELOPMENT OF
SENEGALESE HISTORIOGRAPHY

MARTIN A. KLEIN

                                                **Senegal should
have been** one of the leaders in the development of the new African
history, but it was not. At independence, to be sure, Senegalese
writers had produced noteworthy works in poetry, fiction, and social
and political thought, but no significant corpus of historial writing.
This is all the more incongruous because history should have been the
logical fulfillment of Leopold Sedar Senghor's négritude philosophy.
Although two Senegalese scholars had completed doctorates in
France during the 1950s neither had made a substantial subsequent
contribution to historical scholarship. The reclamation of an African
past, which was so high on the agenda of anglophone Africa and
neighboring Guinea, had to wait a decade in Senegal.

    Senegalese intellectuals in the 1950s were faced with three tra-
ditions of historical thought. The first derived from the colonial administration's early attempts to understand African societies; in line
with this, administrator-scholars like Maurice Delafosse and Henri
Gaden published both written and oral traditions and bequeathed a
substantial corpus of documentation to subsequent generations
(Delafosse, 1912; Soh, 1913). Others, often less committed and less
proficient, dashed off an article or two on their *cercles*. But these
traditions and Delafosse's attempts at synthesis never successfully

---

Author's Note: I would like to thank Mohamed Mbodj and Abdoulaye
Bathily for their comments on an earlier version of this chapter.

joined to create a tradition of professional scholarship. Furthermore, their work was done largely during the early colonial period when France was still trying to understand a world recently conquered.

The second tradition, the work of administrators and scholars, was both academic and pedagogic, and focused not so much on Africa as on French colonization.[1] Most French academic scholarship at independence followed in this tradition, which was prevalent both in the secondary schools and at the University of Dakar; the only text on African history used in the public schools as late as 1963 devoted 17 of its 25 chapters to the French in Africa.

A third tradition was the most interesting for me when I first arrived in Senegal as a young historian in 1963. It was a tradition of schoolteachers, of Senegalese bureaucrats, of students. In almost every corner of Senegal, for almost every major family, the inquiring scholar was given the name of someone who knew the history. Most of these amateurs were totally isolated from professional historians, as were the griots who broadcast regularly on Radio Senegal. Their accounts were garbled, often heavily and uncritically influenced by nationalist ideology, and sometimes edited to glorify the collector's family. Nevertheless, the intensity of their involvement in the past foretold a rapid development of Senegalese historiography in the 1970s.

There are numerous reasons for the relatively slow Senegalese response to the new currents in African history. The University of Dakar was a French university and the French did not see the development of an African historiography as their responsibility. The dominant figure in French historical writing on Africa, Henri Brunschwig, was a fine teacher and a good scholar, but he was not moved by Africa, which he did not visit until 1963, or by African concerns (Brunschwig, 1960, 1965). He was a colonial historian, interested in what the French had done. Brunschwig influenced the best young French historians of the time, but attracted few African students. Raymond Mauny, who went from the Institut Français d'Afrique Noire (IFAN) in Dakar to the prestigious chair at the Sorbonne, also attracted few African students. A second crucial variable was the lure of politics. Elites were thin and nation-building was the most exciting game in town. Senegal's first two doctorates in history, Cheikh Anta Diop and Abdoulaye Ly, became the leaders of opposition parties. Ly published his thesis, but made no further contribution to the historiography of Africa. Diop, a man of great passion and a fine intellect, has been one of the storm centers of African intellectual

life, but his obsession with the question of Egyptian impact on Black
Africa has steered him away from concrete historical questions; it is
hard to classify his writings as history. Ly has never taught at the
university and Diop has taught there only in recent years.[2]

Probably the most important variable inhibiting the development
of a Senegalese historical community was the continued control of the
university by the French and the French degree structure. The
French *doctorat du Troisième Cycle* involves a thesis often as long as
an Anglo-Saxon Ph.D. The candidate then has at least 10 to 15 years
of work before earning his *doctorat d'état*. The double doctorat has
had several negative effects in Africa. The young scholar remains a
client, in most cases into his forties. He can publish little of his own
work, and when he finally does finish, he often has a manuscript
which is both long and highly specialized, and which therefore usually
goes unpublished or must be heavily subsidized. In Senegal, the
subsidies were often given by Senghor himself, and were a way of
keeping academics in line. Finally, the institutions remained in a
dependent position: A scholar must have the doctorate to be eligible
to supervise other doctoral theses; if a university could provide
neither juries nor thesis directors, the candidates had to fly off to Paris
to receive their degrees.

In slowing the process of Africanization, the tenacity with which
the French kept control of the university was at least as important as
was the degree structure. Formerly designed as a French university
designed to serve Africa, the University of Dakar became Senegalese
in 1961, but remained fully integrated into the French system. The
curriculum was French; even more important, hiring was done by the
French Ministry of Higher Education. With time, some Senegaliza-
tion took place, but even at present, there are two cadres within the
university, one hired and paid from Paris and the second hired locally
(Congress of Cultural Freedom, 1962). Abdoulaye Ly told me in 1963
that he would not apply to Paris for a job in his own country. Among
the locally hired faculty, a substantial cause of bitterness was the
radical difference in salaries between those hired in Dakar and those
hired in Paris, and many Senegalese were convinced that their French
predecessors had taken an unseemly time to move on. In Dakar there
seemed to be little effort to promote African scholars.

At a time when Kenneth Dike and Jacob Ajayi were establishing
an agenda for Ibadan history, Dakar did not have a single African
teaching history. French control of the university, the French curriculum, and the long period of training required, all operated to steer

bright and creative Senegalese in other directions. African history
was not a recognized subject of instruction until 1963. Yves Person,
who spent only three years in Dakar (1965-1968), turned the situation
around. A man of tremendous intellectual energy with a capacity for
detail matched by few other scholars, Person produced a thesis which
is a monument of scholarship (Person, 1968-1975). For students interested in history, the very fact that 2300 pages could be written
about a great African leader opened new vistas. If no one else read the
thesis, they did. *Samori* was also a model of what African history
could be. A synthesis of wide archival reading and 846 interviews, it
involved critical use of oral data and it made clear that a vast amount
of archival data could be available on such a subject. It also contained
buried in the detail some sections marked by lucid synthesis, including a masterful introduction on Malinke history.

The 1960s also saw an invasion of North American scholars, of
which I was a part. The most important, Philip Curtin (1969, 1975),
has been a controversial figure. While the undeniable scholarship of
his study of Senegambian economic history is respected, though
somewhat grudgingly, his analysis of the slave trade and its effects has
been the target of much Senegalese historical writing, and his relations with many Senegalese scholars have been cool. Though there
were many other North American scholars in this field, it is difficult to
say how much influence we have had. We were intensely involved in
an African agenda. We were concerned to go outside the archives and
find African sources. Victoria Bomba Coifman (1969) and Eunice
Charles (1977) collected traditions in Jolof, and James Johnson (1974)
did so in the Futa Toro. James Spiegler looked at the prehistory of
African radicalism in francophone Africa. Wesley Johnson (1971)
studied the Four Communes and the rise of Blaise Diagne. Lucie
Colvin looked at politics and diplomacy among the Wolof (1972 and
1977). Some outstanding historical work was done by social scientists, most notably by the Irish political scientist, Donal Cruise
O'Brien, on the Mourides (1971 and 1975), by his wife, Rita Cruise
O'Brien, on the French community, and by Sheldon Gellar (1976) on
colonial rule.

The problem was that once our research was completed, we left.
We wrote some good history, but we published little in French, in part
because we were busy establishing our professional credentials back
home, in some cases because we were immersed in social conflicts
that divided our home countries; the same could be said of a Nigerian
historian who has worked in Senegal, H. O. Idowu (1969, 1970). While

our theses were probably read, a new generation of French scholars had more direct contact, including Jean Boulegue (1968 and 1972) and Yves Saint-Martin (1967 and 1970) as historians and Jean Copans (1980b) and Christian Coulon (1981) among social scientists. But the most interesting among these new scholars is undoubtedly Charles Becker, who works out of a modest base in Kaolack. After collaborating for years with Victor Martin, Becker now works with a variety of Senegalese historians. He has amassed a vast village-by-village documentation on history, archeology and ethnography. More than any other contemporary French scholar, Becker has taken root in Senegal's sandy soil.

The Person years laid the basis for the development of an African community of historians. The first African historian on staff was S. M. Cissoko, hired in 1966. He was followed by Mbaye Gueye and Oumar Kane, both scholars solidly planted in their traditions, Gueye in the Wolof of Kajoor and Kane in the Tokolor of the Fuuta Toro.[3] In 1979, Cissoko became the first Dakar historian to defend his *thèse d'état*. An increasing number of *mémoires de maîtrise* were being written and the *mémoire* became the prerequisite to study abroad.[4] The 1970s saw an increasing migration of young historians to France, most of them to work with Person at the Université Paris I. If there was a strength to the history being written by the first Dakar historians, it was in Person's agenda. Person was a Breton patriot, intensely involved in the preservation of particular cultural traditions. His immersion in detail flowed from his belief that any and all should be preserved. The particular was important, not for what it could tell us about the whole, but for itself. Though a former colonial administrator, Person was in sympathy with the nation-building imperatives of the 1960s. He was concerned both to save past societies and to provide Africa with a past. This history was, like the Ibadan history, essentially political and military history. In a sense, it was the flip side of colonial history, strongly marked by its concern with nation-building imperatives, focused on the state and interested in putting African names and faces into history.

But Dakar was not isolated. Samir Amin's Institut Africain de Développement et de Planification brought a steady parade of visitors to the city and its fine archives made Dakar a center for historical research on any part of francophone Africa. Most important, Dakar was a lively marketplace of ideas, and this began to reflect itself in the variety of historical questions being asked. A major influence in these developments was Catherine Coquery-Vidrovitch of the Université

Paris VII, who since 1979 has been teaching an MA methods course at Dakar. An increasing number of students have been working with Coquery, especially since Person's death in 1982. The importance of Person and Coquery-Vidrovitch was not as creators but as midwives. Each in their own way spoke to the situation of the moment and smoothed a development that was already taking place. The flowering of the Senegalese historical community has involved African scholars in Senegal asking their own questions.

Equally important in the maturing of Dakar as a center of historical studies are two other variables. The first is a certain distance from the state. This does not mean that the state is absent. Concerned as he was with the world of letters, Senghor was undoubtedly disappointed that he had strong support neither among students nor faculty. There have been at times plainclothes policemen in classes; several able intellectuals were refused university appointments; and faculty members often complain about low salaries. At the same time, the active intervention of the state in the university has declined. Several members of the history department are involved in opposition parties, including two party leaders. Under President Abdou Diouf the university poses little threat to the state; as in the West, the university has become a sort of loyal opposition: critical, sometimes hostile, but not subversive.

Two very striking cases are Iba der Thiam and Abdoulaye Bathily. Thiam was a leader of the teacher's union when he obtained his *licence*. He was accused of the bombing of the French cultural center and imprisoned, but was permitted to take his exams under police guard. He was eventually cleared and permitted to go to France to study for the *agrégation en histoire*. He was then hired and rapidly absorbed into the establishment. In 1983 he defended a 4400-page *thèse d'état* and he is now Minister of Education. Bathily is a more interesting case because he has never been absorbed into the establishment. A student leader during a period of contestation, Bathily was imprisoned several times for opposition activities, and on one occasion, was put into the army with a group of student leaders. He was also banned, which meant that he could neither go to school in Senegal nor get a fellowship under state sponsorship. Several French scholars who were impressed with his intellect arranged a fellowship at the University of Birmingham, where he completed his Ph.D. In spite of his record, he was hired on his return to Senegal. He has since been one of the leaders of a teacher's strike and is now the secretary-general of the Ligue Démocratique, the most important Marxist party. In many other countries, he would either be in prison or in exile.

A second very important development is that we are no longer speaking of a small community. At any given moment, a large number of students are working on *mémoires de maîtrise*. Most of those working on the *maîtrise* end up in secondary school teaching, but the group is varied; the chief of the army general staff is working on a degree in military history, and in 1984, I was on the jury for a thesis defended by an administrator two years short of retirement age. Most of those who complete the *maîtrise* never go further, but a handful receive grants to go to France. The Association des Historiens du Sénégal was formed in 1980 and now publishes the *Revue Sénégalaise d'Histoire*. Dakar historians also played a key role in the Association des Historiens Africains and its journal *Afrika Zamani,* both now moribund, but, one hopes, only temporarily so.

Finally, we must ask if there is a Dakar school of history. I think there is, but we must define it in terms of certain general questions and tendencies. First, there is an older generation, which has been slow to produce, is cautious in its analysis, and traditional in its questions. All are working on intensive studies of single societies: S. M. Cissoko did his thesis on Khasso in the upper Senegal River Valley; Thierno Diallo is working on the formation and development of the Futa Jallon and Omar Kane on the Futa Toro; Mbaye Gueye is interested in Wolof resistance to the French. The second generation is more productive and has a tendency to look at broader and more comparative questions. The key person up to now has been Boubacar Barry, whose *Royaume du Waalo* is the most impressive product of the Person years. Barry transcended Person's concern for the particular and looked at Waalo not for itself, but as a case study of a state first shaped by its involvement in the Atlantic slave trade and then destroyed by an expanding French presence; his work focuses on the strengthening of a slave military sector, the increasing centralization of the state, and the growth of Islam as a countervailing force, all as responses to the Atlantic slave trade. Barry's conceptual framework and his analyses, sharpened over the years by his continuing disagreement with Curtin, are reflected in the work of many of his peers and students, most notably Bathily, Diouf and Becker.

While the internal adaptations to the slave trade are central to Barry's analyses, a second theme is Islam, but on this subject there are very different approaches within the Dakar historical community, in some ways reflecting the continuing concern over the role of Islam

in modern Senegal. Kane and Diallo are interested in the creation of
Muslim states. Here too, Barry (n.d.) takes a broader, more dialectical, more comparative and secular approach, which develops out of
his analysis of Islam's response to the slave trade; his current work
describes the way in which states forged in the jihad became more
conservative as they became more involved in long distance trade.
The discontented were then forced to go back to the ideals of the
original jihads and use them against Muslim states. In making this
argument, in debate with Cissoko, Barry (1980; Cissoko, 1980) pulls
together material from much recent historical work, most of it still
unpublished. His argument is very persuasive, though he may sometimes exaggerate the element of resistance in comparison to the
internal dynamic.

Not surprisingly, given the importance of Dakar's archival holdings, there is an increasing body of work on colonialism, but relatively
few pure administrative studies. Within this tradition, Iba der Thiam
(1983) has worked on labor and nationalism, while Babacar Fall (1984)
has done a fine thesis on forced labor in Senegal, Guinea, and Mali.
Mbodj's (1978) work, marked by the skillful use of oral sources for
economic and social history, provided an intensive study of the development of Senegal's richest cercle, Sine-Saloum; he is currently
working on an even more intensive *thèse d'état* on economic and
social changes in the area between the Gambia and Saalum rivers.

Dakar historians generally work on Senegalese subjects, in part
because the sources are there, in part because they are involved in
their own history. To the degree that they are concerned with questions of identity, that concern is neither narrowly ethnic nor
nationalistic. Their concerns are often with larger cultural zones and
there is a strong consciousness both of Africa and of ties with other
former French colonies, reflecting the cosmopolitan nature of Dakar.
Whether because of the integrating influence of Islam or the secure
predominance of Wolof culture, Dakar has been blessedly free both of
interethnic violence on the streets and the more polite forms of ethnic
warfare that have troubled the halls of academe in countries like
Nigeria and Zaire. There is also in Dakar a striking professional
integrity. The 1960s demanded heroes; where there were no professional historians to provide them, journalists and broadcasters did so.
Today, there is a willingness to call these heroes into question. In what
is the most lucid piece of historical writing to come out of Dakar,
Mamadou Diouf has tried to set the resistance leader Lat Dior into
context. A summary of his thesis in *Afrique Histoire,* a popular
journal edited by Cissoko, led to Diouf being literally convoked to a

meeting with members of Lat Dior's family, but he held firm. In an age marked by the phony charisma of beribboned saviors with large bank accounts in Switzerland, it is hard to believe in heroes.

But this represents only a part of what is being done. Dakar is striking both in the size of the historical community and the variety of subjects being explored. Yoro Fall has published a thesis on the history of cartography. Ibna Diagne is working on stone age archaeology. Samba Ka is interested in interactions between pastoralists and agriculturalists during the premodern period. Research has been done using notarial records and oral sources. Subjects studied include colonial finances, economic development, land law, slavery, crime, and key social groups. The Senegalese historical community may be all the stronger because of French resistance to rapid Africanization. Growth was slow, but it has speeded up. The department is now virtually all African and its standards are high, probably higher than when Dakar was staffed with French academics waiting for a good appointment in the *metropole*. Most of the research is unpublished, but much of it is quite fine. Given the freedom of expression and the accessibility of Dakar intellectual life, it is likely that Dakar will remain a major center of historical research.

NOTES

1. The ablest scholar in this group was Georges Hardy, a colonial educator (Hardy, 1921, 1943; see also Cultru, 1910; Sabatie, 1925; Villard, 1943). Victoria Bomba Coifman (1969) and I (Klein, 1975) were probably the first professional scholars in the postwar period to use oral traditions in a systematic manner.

2. Ly's work (1958; defended as a thesis in 1955), is a study of a French slaving company, Ly became the leader of PRA-Sénégal, and when his party merged with Senghor's UPS, he entered the government. He was dropped soon afterwards, but has not been either politically active or intellectually productive since then. Diop's well-known study (1955) is a wide-ranging and controversial exploration of links between ancient Egypt and West Africa, but it is not history; it offers no insight into the evolution of African societies during the current millenium. Diop has continued to write and do research, but has also been the leader of two opposition parties. He accepted an appointment to the History Department of the University of Dakar only in 1982.

3. Gueye's 1983 work is a published version of his 1969 thesis, but he has been working since on Wolof resistance to the French. Kane is working on the Muslim revolution in the Futa Toro.

4. To the best of my knowledge, only three mémoires were defended at Dakar in the 1960s. During the early 1970s, there were two to four a year, and in the latter part of the decade, ten or eleven were defended in some years.

19

HISTORICAL RESEARCH IN ZAIRE
Present Status and
Future Perspectives

MUMBANZA MWA BAWELE
SABAKINU KIVILU

**It is only within
the last** fifteen years or so that Zairean historians have had access to
formal training and have begun to reflect on historical problems in
Zaire. Over that time there has emerged a corpus of MA and Ph.D.
theses that, taken as a whole, forms a substantial contribution to the
development of our historical understanding of Zaire. However, as
elsewhere, those who have produced this work have scarcely given
thought to the manner in which this history is related to the needs of
the population as a whole. Often they conceive of their research
without examining the relationship of their scholarly work to popular
culture, and especially to the current politicoeconomic situation in
contemporary Zaire. In this chapter, we will sketch out the organizational structures of research in Zaire and look at some of the themes
and new orientations that have characterized recent research in Zaire,
stressing the need for a greater social praxis and a more popular
history of the country.

THE STRUCTURES OF HISTORICAL RESEARCH IN ZAIRE

The emergence of historical research in Zaire was tied to the
creation of the Department of History at Lovanium University in
Kinshasa in 1965 (Lacroix, 1972), and subsequent alterations have
been strongly associated with the alteration and development of the

department within the context of the continual transformations of the larger university structures in Zaire. Established in 1965 to respond to the postcolonial need for teaching and research in African history, the department offered an MA program (*License avec thèse*) from 1968 and a Ph.D. program from 1972; until now 9 Ph.D.s and more than 400 license degrees have been granted. The reorganization of the university structures in 1970 consolidated all history teaching formerly located at the Université Libre du Congo (Kisangani), at the Université Officielle du Congo (Lubumbashi), and at Lovanium (Ndaywel, 1976). From then on, although the Educational Colleges retained their own history departments, all university teaching and research in history focused on Lubumbashi, and there rapidly developed a Lubumbashi school whose graduates and general orientations dominated—virtually monopolized—historical thinking and research in the country. Even those historians in other locations (such as Bukavu or Kinshasa) are closely tied to the Lubumbashi intellectual milieu; there is no other network.

At the end of the 1960s the department adopted a curriculum focusing on central Africa, with a general orientation close to the Anglo-Saxon school, emphasizing local research. As defined at the first staff seminar in 1971 the research priorities included social history, socioeconomic history, demographic history (especially focusing on the urbanization process), as well as the history of art and archaeology. In the early 1970s the first two Zairean Ph.D.s in history (trained in France and the USA/Belgium) and former staff members of the Université Libre du Congo at Kisangani all joined the department, and more fields were added to the research orientations: precolonial cultural history, administrative history, and the history of education. But in all fields special emphasis was placed on social transformations (Vellut, 1974b), but for practical reasons (principally that of accessible documentation) there was a special emphasis on the colonial period. Because the unified department was located in Lubumbashi with access to archival materials in the Lubumbashi area, and because the Educational Colleges elsewhere did not initiate research programs till 1975-1976, Shaba (and to some extent the neighboring Kivu region) served as the privileged foci of research in the early years; only from 1978-1980 was a more balanced approach achieved.

Research undertaken in the Department of History was extended with the establishment of two new research-oriented structures. The first was the Centre d'Etudes et de Recherches Documentaires sur l'Afrique Centrale (CERDAC), created in 1973 in Lubumbashi following the UNESCO Conference on "The contribution of Central Africa to the general history of Africa" held in that city and strongly influenced by the presentations and orientations of T. Obenga (1973; 1980). CERDAC was intended to serve as the regional focus for historical research on Central Africa, complementing the teaching orientations of the Department of History. As part of the larger nationalist reassessment inspired by the policy of authenticity, which appeared to give a role to historical understanding in the development of policy, the Société des Historiens Zairois (SOHIZA) was created in 1974 (Ndaywel, 1974; Pilipili 1974a). One of the principal objectives of this association was the assertion of the role of Zairean historians in determining research orientations (Pilipili, 1974b), taking account of state policies and the perceived demands of nation-building in general (Stengers, 1979b).

Meanwhile the department had embarked on an ambitious series of publications intended to reach different audiences. As early as 1970 the department published *Etudes d'Histoire Africaine,* an important annual journal intended essentially for an international audience of professional Africanists. In 1973 a collective of history teachers and students of the department undertook the publication of *Likundoli: Enguêtes d'Histoire Africaine,* intended essentially as a review of departmental activities to ensure rapid diffusion of recent research to a national audience; today *Likundoli* is published by CERDAC in three series on an irregular basis. With the support of SOHIZA, the department and CERDAC jointly attempted (unsuccessfully, for lack of funds, as it turned out) to organize a national network of historical archives relating to the colonial period; the National Archives of Zaire covers only the western part of the country and has no authority over regional archival depositories. In 1980, with the strong support of SOHIZA, the first legislation concerning the preservation and conservation of historical documents was enacted.

From 1976 the staff of the Lubumbashi History Department was almost entirely Zaireanized. Because most members of the department and of CERDAC as well as many members of history departments in the Educational Colleges (with the notable exception of the Institut Pédagogique National in Kinshasa) were trained at Lubumbashi and shared a strong common interest in particular approaches and themes, especially on social history based on written documents, this Lubumbashi school dominates historical research and teaching in Zaire today. Having failed in 1972-1974 to develop a strong current of archaeological teaching and research, the department also failed to develop any strong tradition in precolonial history, at least at the level of the License (nevertheless see Ndaywel, 1972; Vellut, 1972). However, it is not a field entirely lacking: In addition to recent Ph.D.s of Zaireans (Ndua, 1978; Mumbanza, 1980; Bishikwabo, 1982), there have been about 20 recent Ph.D. dissertations (most by Americans) on various aspects of the precolonial past, and many of these researchers have subsequently been associated with local teaching and research institutions in one way or another. (In this context, it is also worth noting the growing influence of North American scholarships, at both the Ph.D. and post-doctorate level, with the closure of French ties and severe limitations on Belgian opportunities for training abroad.) But the most important weakness at the moment is the absence of a strong interest in postcolonial history (a field currently dominated by the social science faculty and the associated research centers) and of political history in general. With few exceptions nineteenth- and twentieth-century colonial history is at the center of historical research interests of the Lubumbashi orthodoxy (Verhaegen, 1977); with few new positions opening up and increasing difficulties in undertaking research projects, this situation may well remain for some time to come.

Among the regional academic centers, three are particularly important. The Centre de Recherche Interdisciplinaire pour le Développement de l'Enseignement (CRIDE, 1976) was created in Kisangani in 1972. Despite its title, the research interest of this group of scholars far transcends any narrow concept of teaching. In its work (the principal outlet for which is the *Cahiers du CRIDE*) CRIDE is primarily oriented to larger epistemological and political questions, which have played such an important role in postcolonial Zaire. Another "regional" center important for historical research is the Centre d'Etudes et Recherches Universitaires au Kivu (CERUKI) in Bukavu, with its own journal, *Antennes*. From its founding in 1976 this center has been very active, serving not only the Institut Supérieur Pédagogique but other higher educational institutions in Bukavu as well. Interdisciplinary in its approach, its work focuses primarily on the Kivu region, but it also—and in this it is unique in Zaire—includes work extending beyond the national boundaries to the Great Lakes region in general. In addition, CERUKI undertook the publication of the only general history of Zaire to date written by a Zairean (Tshimanga, 1976).

Finally, there exists a heterogeneous group of historians centered at the Institut Pédagogique National in Kinshasa whose interests and training are markedly different from those of the Lubumbashi school—and whose location in the capital provides access to the resources and political influence to retain their independence of the Lubumbashi school (Lutumba, 1972; Lumenga, 1982). Their training is disparate and their research interests diverse—although since the tragic death of Bimanyu Kamanzi in 1980, they have been mainly interested in recent political history (but adopting an approach markedly different from the Kisangani group associated with the *histoire immédiate* paradigm; see chapter 19 below). Despite the personal standing of some among them, these historians do not form an alternative "school" to that at Lubumbashi because they lack the coherence as a group and intellectual definition to characterize them as such; nevertheless the potential for forming such an identifiable "school" may be there, especially with the decentralization of the university structure now under way in Zaire.

Aside from scholarly institutions there are other organizations that share an interest in historical research. The Institut de Recherche Scientifique (IRS)—the successor to the colonial Institut de la Recherche Scientifique en Afrique Centrale (IRSAC)—has retained a Human Sciences Department composed primarily of anthropologists and linguists. But with numerous organizational changes and severe financial problems, the future of this organization is problematic. From 1976 the Office National de Recherche et Développement (ONRD) has been primarily oriented to the study of problems associated with nation-building but also has shown an interest in precolonial history. From 1968 to 1973 ONRD published *Etudes Zairoises* (formerly *Etudes Congolaises*), an important journal first established in 1961 (and still published on an occasional basis); ONRD also published for a brief time *Cultures au Zaire et en Afrique,* with issues on precolonial subjects. The Institut de Recherches Economiques et Sociales (IRES), created in 1955, was particularly oriented to research, publishing *Cahiers Economiques et Sociaux* from 1962. Finally, the Centre d'Etudes de Problèmes Sociaux et Economiques (CEPSI) has from 1946 published the *Bulletin de CEPSI,* more recently appearing occasionally as *Problèmes Sociaux Zairois.*

Journals supported by religious institutions have also been important outlets for scholarly publications on a wide range of social issues in Zaire. The Centre d'Etudes des Religions Africaines (CERA), created in 1967 at the Lovanium University in Kinshasa and which publishes the prestigious *Cahiers des Religions Africaines,* shows the clear influence of the Second Vatican Council with its emphasis on the integration of African religious values within the

Catholic Church. The Centres d'Etudes Ethnologiques de Bandundu (CEEBA), created in 1966 as a branch of the Anthropos Institute in Germany, has focused on the problems of acculturation, particularly those related to the evangelization of the population (Hochegger, 1966). In addition the tradition of local centers is represented by a group of researchers informally associated with the journal *Aequatoria* (Bamania, Equateur Région). Serving from 1939 to 1961 as one of the most important outlets for anthropological and historical articles on Zaire, the journal was resuscitated in 1980 as *Annales Aequatoria*.

But despite the multiplicity of such institutes and publishing outself, many of these organizations are plagued not only with problems of finances and material, but with rapid changes in leadership and organizational status: They often lack a clear definition of their tasks and their sense of purpose has in some cases been eroded, if not totally extinguished, faced as they are with the magnitude of the Zairean problems of underdevelopment (Tshund'olela, 1980; Gran, 1979; Jewsiewicki, 1984). Consequently, although it is important to realize that the Lubumbashi Department of History is not the only center sharing the goal of reconstructing an integrated total history of the Zairean peoples, its central institutional role in this process is enhanced by the disarray and dispersion that characterizes other such efforts.

CURRENT HISTORICAL RESEARCH IN ZAIRE

We have noted that the Lubumbashi School is distinguished from the more conventional liberal tendencies of the historians located at the Institut Pédagogique National in Kinshasa; in addition, because the general research interests of the members of the Lubumbashi department do not include the postcolonial period, they are equally distinguished from both the conventional "political science" paradigms—which in Zaire have taken a historical approach representing a fairly long temporal span (Young, 1965)—and the work of the school associated with "histoire immédiate," more clearly articulated towards present concerns, and the general utility (or nonutility) of academic study. But the Lubumbashi department nonetheless constitutes the essential structure around which historical discourse and research in Zaire is elaborated today. Therefore it is useful to examine the principal methodological character of the works produced by the members of this department.

Despite the Zaireanization of personnel in 1976, the epistemology and
research interests of the department remain largely drawn from
outside. The forms of such studies often draw simultaneously from
the *Annales* School, Anglo-Saxon, and neo-Marxist approaches,
often without clearly articulating the oppositions between them although such oppositions may form the implicit lines of future cleavage. At the analytic level, Zairean historians have adopted an attitude
intermediary between radical and liberal paradigms; the approach
favored by two of the most influential former teachers of the Lubumbashi department (Jewsiewicki, 1972, 1979; Vellut, 1974, 1977, 1980).
Most works concentrate on the history of Zaire from the late nineteenth century mercantilist penetration to the 1960s, including the
socioeconomic history of the large commercial zones (Vellut, 1972):
the integration of "traditional" economies and societies within the
larger market economy (Mumbanza, 1980); the formation of a salaried
work force (Bashizi, 1980; Tshibangu, 1980); the general evolution of
rural societies and agricultural policies within colonial state structures (Jewsiewicki, 1975; Mulambu, 1974); the restructuring of social
and economic space (Bimanyu, 1970; Tshund'olela, 1980; Sabakinu,
1981); the emergence of new social formations (Jewsiewicki, 1976);
and forms of social conflict during the colonial period—both peasant
revolts (Sikitele, forthcoming), and strikes by urban workers (Jewsiewicki, Kilola, and Vellut, 1973).

Demographic history has concentrated especially on statistics on
the colonial periods and after, and studies on urbanization have been
particularly important in tracing the reorganization of demographic
space from the precolonial period (de Saint Moulin, 1974; 1976; 1982;
1983; Verhaegen, 1975; Jewsiewicki, 1978). Research hypotheses
have been established for assessing population distribution and identifying both the causes of depopulation from the end of the nineteenth
century and the population growth rate from World War II (Sabakinu,
1981, 1984).

Cultural history has also begun to find a place in the current
historiography of Zaire, and three principal perspectives in this field
can now be distinguished. The cultural history of modern Zaire is
particularly concerned with issues of elite formation and educational
structures; missionary influence has been particularly emphasized in
the process of elite formation (Mashaury, 1983; Feltz, 1981; *Etudes
d'Histoire Africaine*, 1979; Mumbanza, 1974). Material cultural differences between different cultural traditions form a second dimension to such studies, including the internal development of new tech-

niques, as well as the integration of new techniques introduced from the outside (Mumbanza, forthcoming). A third perspective is provided in the history of art, oriented toward the inventory and analysis of Zaire's cultural patrimony formed of art objects and various material elements of African civilization (Belepe, 1982; Cornet, 1972; Neyt, 1981; Vansina, 1984).

Although not the centerpiece of new Zairean historiography, political history, the "old maid" of traditional historiography, still has an important place in the current historiography of the country (Tshimanga, 1976; Lutumba, 1972). In precolonial history, attention has been increasingly focused on the articulation of small political groupings and communities peripheral to the large political units (Ndua, 1978; Bishikwabo, 1982). Noncentralized communities (referred to in the earlier literature on Zaire as "*sociétés lignagères*") have not been omitted; they serve as the focus for studies on the broader concepts of power (Mumbanza, 1980).

Not all these methodological approaches are accompanied by real advances in the use of traditional sources. The exploitation of written sources is the strongest aspect of the Lubumbashi school; this explains the preference for the colonial period in their analyses (Vellut, 1974b). The renewed interest in these sources, especially archival documents (Jewsiewicki, 1980), results both from the new questions asked of them and from their comparison with oral data which casts new light on the relatively narrow perspectives of European documents; greater familiarity with the African cultures concerned permits their more effective utilization (Bontinck, 1976; Vansina, 1982). But in general, such sources are used with neither the frequency nor the skill that they might be. By comparing very early oral traditions recorded by colonial agents with more recent versions, historians can sometimes trace the evolution of this type of source; such changes over time in the traditions can indicate the nature of historical processes at work. Thus oral data can increasingly be utilized within a double perspective: to explain or provide the basis of critique for other types of sources, and to provide the foundation for historical reconstruction (Miller, 1980; Vansina, 1983; Newbury, 1973, 1978, 1979b).

There exist other categories that till now have not been fully exploited. With some exceptions (Vansina, 1978; Hoover, 1978b; Fabian, 1983a), linguistic data is still poorly utilized for lack of proper training among Zairean historians. Statistical data, although very abundant in colonial written sources, have been poorly used and without a properly critical assessment; the introduction of more sophisticated quantitative methods will hopefully permit better use of such data (Sabakinu, 1981; Fetter, 1983). Similarly the contribution of material culture to understanding technological and cultural change is becoming increasingly apparent. Some studies on material culture have shown the existence of diversified and complex political cultures from very remote times. But although the principal mechanisms or their organization and functioning are understood (Birmingham and Martin, 1983), the material and cultural foundations of such political constructs are not well established and need to be sought beyond purely political factors—in economic, religious, and other cultural factors which transcend the boundaries often drawn between centralized states and more supple forms of political organization. The articulation between these diverse forms of cultural space can only be ascertained by the application of more subtle forms of social and cultural analysis (de Heusch, 1972; Vansina, 1982; Hoover, 1978). Recent reassessments of the emergence of states and the different forms of social restructuring accompanying them has led to new perspectives on questions of changing ethnic and even clan identities—which until recently seemed to be of interest only to anthropologists (Mumbanza, 1974; Vellut, 1973, Newbury 1979a; Ndaywel, 1980; Jewsiewicki, 1980; Vansina, 1980). The demographic dimension of early societies—and particularly the ecological equilibrium of such societies—is also a field which despite its importance is largely neglected by Zairean historians, partly because of the methodological difficulties of such research (Boserup, 1974). There is a clear need for Zairean historians to follow the lines of ecological research recently developed in East Africa (Kjeckshus, 1980; Ford, 1971; see also Jewsiewicki, 1979) to explain, among other things, the crises of mortality that increasingly draw the attention of historians of population (Miller, 1981; Vellut, 1983; Sabakinu, 1974, 1984; Thornton, 1977, 1980).

The integration of the various political and economic spaces that came to form Zaire occurred as part of an extended process that was specific to each local cultural and geographic milieu; until now this type of analysis has been undertaken by economists (Huybrechts, 1970; Peemans, 1970). Combined with the limited historical research available on such problems, such analyses suggest the degree to which colonial policies were influenced by these economic "spaces" and these earlier sociopolitical networks. The unequal distribution of wealth and the possibilities of acquiring and dispensing it explain the early exploitation of some regions and the neglect of others (Tshund'olela, 1980; Tshibangu, 1980; Bakonzi, 1982). In addition several works have shown the important role of beliefs, particularly religious beliefs, in African responses to the Europeans and their socioeconomic system (Mumbanza, 1974; Vansina, 1971, 1973; Vansina et al. 1976; Raymaekers and Desroche, 1983), but more work of this type is needed on such themes, which are as significant as they are neglected. Religious structures often served to preserve the cultural foundations of many African societies. That is why the missionary attack on these structures helps explain both the early infatuation (and later withdrawal) of Africans from mass conversion movements, and also why the attack on these structures of social regeneration was so important in the production of new forms of social perceptions and social action conforming to the colonial reconstruction of social reality.

Urban growth from the late 1940s in Zaire is a well-known phenomenon; documentation on this point is abundant and accessible (see Vellut, 1974a for a bibliography). But the towns have not yet been adequately examined as a form of dynamic interrelationship bringing together people of all social categories and constructing from this process an urban culture both diverse and unique (Fetter, 1971; Malira, 1974; Vellut, 1981; M'bokolo, 1981). Moreover, urban transformations can only properly be considered as part of a larger reorganization of social and economic space; they can only properly be assessed relative to the rural space. Zaire is still a rural society, and the lives of most of its citizens are dominated by agriculture. Historical research on the agricultural sector, up to now superficial and lacking global perspective (Jewsiewicki, 1975; Vellut, 1977), needs to accord a prominent place to the transformations of this basic sector of society, including analyses of such factors as internal technological innovations (Jewsiewicki and Chrétien, 1984), the impact of soil deterioration on political and social relations, the development of cash crops (Mulambu, 1974), or changes in subsistence crops, and the significance of such transformations in social relations (Vellut, 1983).

The mobilization of the masses is a related theme often neglected in local historical research. This was a subject that interested political scientists from early on (Young, 1982; Demunter, 1975) and has been explored by some Zaireans studying abroad (Nzongola, 1970). But such inquiry essentially examined the subject from the point of view of the political forces which eventually led to independence; in general they were researching the roots of nationalism (Monnier, 1971; Verhaegen, 1966). It is time for national historians to reexamine this important theme, giving due weight to the important role of the rural masses in the processes of political transformations and especially with the objective of illuminating the essential dynamism of the colonized societies.

The problem of national integration is implicitly present in all national research (Kayamba, 1984; Wamba, 1984; Loko, 1979). It is within this perspective that ethnic history should be studied by anthropologists and historians. Although colonial studies on local populations were undertaken in order to administer them more effectively, they were also often related to the emergence of political consciousness and contributed to the political mobilization and awareness of ethnic groups. If today we question the criteria by which ethnic groups were identified, and can show their dynamic character (Mumbanza, 1978), that only increases the importance of understanding the forces of cultural or political mobilization that lay beneath such processes rather than relying on the extremely tenuous reconstructions of population movements on which many earlier analyses were based (Newbury, 1978). But if ethnic histories are fluid and illusory, the local features which underlie such cultural diversity as well as the broader factors which condition social perceptions and historical action must be understood as essential features of the historical patrimony of the country, necessary factors to account for in the development of modern Zaire culture. It is the historian's task to seek an understanding of the nature of these ethnic transformations in the past; for ethnic identity, even in all its contextual subjectivity, appears to be one of the key elements of mobilization which cannot be ignored in modern Zaire, and as important in the cities as in the rural areas.

Historical research in Zaire today, for all its dynamisms, however, is in crisis, as shown by the great gap that exists between historical discourse and political discourse. The present demands of society require a "history for development," a history that should be based on the preoccupations of the masses and the needs of the society as a whole. Similarly a true history in construction must be conceived not primarily from above, but as a set of relations focusing especially on the base, that is, on the interests, aspirations, and capabilities of the masses, who should be able to recognize themselves in this historical presentation, because they constitute the true historical actors of the country. But our present historical discourse is foreign to the society of which we speak; it is ignored both by the masses and by the intellectual, political, and economic elites. It is in fact history for the historians, for the specialists. And it totally lacks commitment.

PART V

WHICH WAY OUT?
Trends in the Developing
Historiographies of Africa

20

THE METHOD OF
"HISTOIRE IMMÉDIATE"
Its Application to Africa

BENOIT VERHAEGEN

> History is something far too important to be left to the historians
> [Chesneaux, 1976: 5].

From 1956 to 1966 Zaire was the scene of unprecedented political
and social disruption, which resulted in the overthrow, several times
over, of the value systems, the political and administrative institutions, forms of economic and social organization, and the composition of the dominant class. During this time Lovanium University in
Kinshasa became almost in spite of itself the principal locus for the
development of the methodology discussed here. From 1960, the
university was a focal point for powerful external ideological influences and from 1962 the first generation of African university students
to emerge from among the colonized population became researchers
and teachers. Under their influence and under the pressure of events
themselves from 1962, the foundations were laid for a new form of
understanding contemporary political culture. For them, *Histoire
Immédiate* had to become both a scientific alternative to the academic
methodologies imported from Europe and America, and a means of
actively participating in social change.

The challenge was on two fronts. Politically the country had acceded to independence in conditions of such disorder and so little
preparation that the colonizing power was taken totally by surprise.
Consequently the social upheavals associated with the process of
decolonization were actively opposed even by those who otherwise

ought to have foreseen and welcomed them: the scholars, the teachers, and especially the specialists in the human sciences that the colony had retained at great expense to help prevent these very changes or to redirect the course of the political upheavals already underway. The two words "immediate independence" (pronounced in 1958 by an obscure African clerk with no university training who was to become the first President of the country, Kasavubu) weighed heavily on the future of the country because they were more prophetic than the entire corpus of colonial pronouncements; the most perceptive and generous of these foresaw decolonization occurring in thirty years at the very earliest, and even such a prediction was ridiculed in almost all colonial milieux.

A second challenge also contributed to the elaboration of such new analytic methods and forced a revision of scholarly practices and methodological foundations. What was referred to for many years as "the Congo Crisis," that enormous acceleration of history which followed on such a long period of apparent immobility within the structural behemoth of colonial Congo, could not fail to attract young students into the politics of the day and demand their active participation. What was sought was not only to reconstruct a "science of the present" based on entirely new foundations, but also to put it into the service of those who were making history before our very eyes.

HISTOIRE IMMÉDIATE: WHAT IT IS AND WHAT IS IT NOT

Histoire Immédiate is a means of understanding, drawing simultaneously on history, sociology and anthropology. The approach borrows from history its foundation on firm documentary sources, its analytic techniques, and especially its critical approach to sources; from anthropology and sociology it borrows their living sources as well as their techniques of observation and of collecting and analyzing data. But it undertakes such analyses in a new manner. The term "Immédiate" is not used here in a chronological sense, but in an epistemological sense; the term does not apply primarily to the most recent events of the present situation, for which the term "Instant History" would be more appropriate. "Immediate" knowledge is used in the epistemological sense of the term, when two elements (the subject and the object of understanding) are brought together without intervening stages, without a third, intermediary, device. It is clear that no understanding, even that based on intuition, functions entirely

without mediation and therefore the term "immediate" must be understood in a relative sense: The "immediate" character of knowledge does not entirely avoid the need for mediating processes but
reduces these to the bare minimum and brings the researcher and the
object of research into the closest possible proximity, physically and
psychologically; at the same time it builds understanding on the
subjective and dialectic interrelationship between the two. The practice of Histoire Immédiate acknowledges that even when the historian is placed directly in contact with the informant, there always
exists a distance between the subject and object of understanding;
there are divergences—even tensions—in their perspectives and
communication. But in seeking recourse to the concepts of dialectical
exchange, the method of Histoire Immédiate presumes simply that
within the process of seeking understanding there is a means of
establishing forms of interaction and transformation between these
two partners which are truly reciprocal. Historians must recognize in
their counterparts not only a passive informant but a historical actor, a
subject, not an object, and a colleague in knowledge as well as in
action. They need to acknowledge in addition their own subjectivity
and therefore their permeability and fluidity to the other within the
context of their interaction. Once treated within the framework of a
dialectic exchange and recognized as a conscious actor in the historical process, the "informant" takes on the character of a full partner in
the process of generating knowledge, not only informing the researchers but also transforming them.

To reverse the ties between the past and the present, or to place the
present in the commanding position, is a conception of the historian's
task which goes back to the nineteenth century (Picon, 1970;
Lapeyre, 1971). The dialectical relation between the past and present
was also a theme emphasized by Bloch (1974: 14-15). Chesneaux has
even called for an explicitly regressive method, one which would
depart from the better known present to move back into the past. But
that is not all; for Chesneaux (1976: 19) it is the future which matters.
Historical understanding in which the present and past are closely
associated must have as a goal the transformation of the future; it
must "open the way to social practice, to an active and concrete
commitment." It is therefore politically committed history.

It is not the abundance of information and the proximity to the
event which characterizes Histoire Immédiate and gives it an advantage over the histories of more distant and less well-known periods; it
is preeminently the possibility of carrying out a living history and

allowing the historical actors to participate in the understanding of their own history which confers such advantage. Nevertheless, it is still true that subject and object do not form a single entity. The document, the oral information, the materials of understanding are not transparent; the specialized tasks of collecting, criticizing, and analyzing are retained but they have changed their nature because Histoire Immédiate permits, and indeed requires, the establishment of a form of dialectic relation between the object and subject of understanding. Such inquiry does not consist of a scholar on the one hand, who alone possesses the ability to understand these things independently of others, and simply amorphous facts, on the other hand, to be submitted clinically to rules of criticism and of scholarly interpretation. The facts are nothing more than significant social practices; behind them there is a historical actor who is the ultimate depository of the meaning of these practices. Histoire Immédiate tries to make of this actor a full partner in the process of understanding history.

Three conditions must be fulfilled for the method to be productive. The first relates to the historical actors and to the position in which they are situated. In class-based societies or in other systems of exploitation, it is the dominant segment which in large part controls the production of historical documents and which monopolizes historical discourse to defend its class position and to propose an ideology supportive of the established order. That is why it is useless in a society divided by oppression or class struggle to seek to determine historical truth by the simple multiplication of witnesses or of information and by research into the character of the informants. The dominant minority cannot teach the historian about the dominated majority. It can only repeat, in different ways, its own ideological version of events.

To understand the movement of history, Histoire Immédiate seeks to address itself to those who are interested in change: to the exploited and alienated populations or classes, to the social minorities, to the marginal classes, to the oppressed categories. But these social fractions are often passive and silent during periods of stability or equilibrium. It is the moments of crisis which bring about heightened political consciousness, a commitment to struggle and to change. It is during crisis situations that contradictions are entered into, that the unity of the different levels of social practices (economic, political, ideological) appears, and that political action is awakened and finalized in the consciousness of the actors. That is why Histoire Immédiate seeks to restore the importance of the *event* as an expression and catalyst of the crisis, as the moment when the conjunction of political factors and the historical actor is the clearest and the most conscious. From the point of view of Histoire Immédiate, there is in fact no opposition or epistemological rupture between the long term trends and the event, if the importance of the political domain is correctly assessed and adequately accounts for change.

The second condition, relating to the commitment of the scholar and especially of the historian, is to know how to apply the Eleventh Thesis of Marx on Feuerbach: "The philosophers have only interpreted the world in various ways; the point, however, is to transform it"—that is, how to confront the contradiction between praxis and theory. Is there such a thing as a history that is simultaneously scholarly and committed? I am convinced that historians can commit themselves to revolutionary praxis without losing their quality as specialized scholars in the production of knowledge, without becoming compromised intellectuals or simply pamphleteers. Scientific practice must be included within the more global practices of any historical subject—even that of historians themselves acting as participants and historical actors in their own cultures. Historians must consequently organize their search for understanding within the framework of this type of dialectical communication with social praxis. But dialectial relations between the scholar and the historical subject should not be conceived of in a mechanical fashion in which the roles would be distributed once and for all, wherein for one party there is scholarly reflection, for the other the function of transforming the world in a more concrete fashion and of "making" history. Histoire Immédiate seeks to place the dialectic relation between scholar and historical actor at the very heart of the process of understanding. It is the role of theoretical reflection to transcend immediate experience and to provide a historical consciousness within the on-going process of dialectical exchanges—to unmask unarticulated consciousness.

The third condition for a productive application of Histoire Immédiate is the choice of a suitable theoretical and conceptual framework, one that addresses the following questions. For a given situation who is the historical actor, the privileged focus of the researcher? What is the place of the masses in present history? What are the dominant contradictions in a crisis? How are different aspects (economic, political, ideological) of a given social formation related to each other to form a meaningful totality? How can the structural understanding of an event respond to the fundamental demands of historical explanation? Historical materialism provides guides to the theoretical answers to these questions, but these cannot be mechanically applied, nor can their usage be reserved exclusively for the professionals of an academic and elitist science. The conceptual tools of historical materialism (including concepts of structure, mode of production, contradiction, class formation, and praxis, among others) are all the more necessary to approach from the perspective of Histoire Immédiate since it addresses problems relating to ongoing processes. Interpreting such numerous events, understanding contradictions or ongoing struggles, indentifying living historical actors: all presuppose the need to refer to a preexisting theory of history, suitably complex and suitably supple to be constantly subjected to critical revision and constantly developed.

Although Histoire Immédiate appears as a history of the present, of the living, in its sources of information and analytical techniques it incorporates more conventional approaches—the consultation of archives wherever possible, the reference to other documents of the past, the use of statistical series—as well as the collection of oral narratives, autobiographies, testimonies, or first-hand observations. From the point of view of the techniques used, this is a "total" history rather than an "oral" history. But the choice of techniques and sources, their combination and their hierarchical organization, the continuing critique of the results produced, and the reorientation of these techniques as a function of this critique are not simple operations; they require methodological coherence and critical rigor, open to the active participation of the historical actor in understanding the world, and to the practical commitment of the researcher (Verhaegen, 1981).

Systematic recourse to "living" documentation produced in the course of research, an important emphasis in Histoire Immédiate, poses three concrete problems: Who should be interviewed? How is significant oral information produced? How is the transition from individual testimony, from an isolated fact or a unique event, to the collective praxis of the group as a whole, accomplished? To the first question there is a simple theoretical response: It is the true historical actors which must be allowed to speak; these include the rising classes, the popular masses in movement, the oppressed or marginal categories. But in practice a whole host of difficulties arise. History selects the survivors in reverse priority to that of the historian: Death, disease, and dissolution first strike the oppressed, especially in poor countries. And even then, the survivors are often isolated, marginalized by physical weakness and cultural handicaps; this is especially true in Africa where media outlets are presently reserved to the urban milieu and to scholarly social categories, despite the fact that the burden of colonial and postcolonial oppression and exploitation weighs most heavily on the peasant masses and the proletarian classes.

In the second place, how can we render more fruitful the exchanges between actor and researcher? How can we transform these into intersubjective relations which will produce a better and more objective understanding of history? First, all dialogue, all fruitful communication requires mutual respect and confidence between the participants, the choice of appropriate questions, the use of mutual categories of discourse shared by the two partners, and communication within a relatively nondirected interview. Second, it is essential to establish the dialectical reversal of the respective positions of researcher and actor in the course of an exchange, with each in their own turn recognizing both the extent and the limitations of the understanding of the other. It is only to the degree of this reciprocity that the experience of the historical actor can be inserted into the collective praxis of the group, and only to this degree that it is possible to understand the full significance of historical movement. The third condition implies the commitment of the two partners in a compatible political project; this constitutes a necessary prerequisite of the establishment of effective relations of exchange applicable to and significant for historical understanding.

Finally, how does one pass from the individual to the collective, from the subjective to the objective, from the practical to the theoretical? An initial response is contained implicitly in the manner by which informants are chosen. If they belong to the social category for which the situation and practice can be based on collective consciousness, the narrative of these responses transcends individual limits, so collective memory becomes relevant for historical understanding. Individuals are the despository of a corpus of information, and thus the range of memory reaches far beyond the individual's experience; it can be virtually indefinitely expanded thanks to their participation in the group; the informant's social practice rejoins the praxis of the group as a whole. It is equally true that in the course of such an intersubjective exchange, if this is well conducted on both sides, informants are able to transcend their individual level of perception and spontaneity, to approach a better understanding of the whole.

Finally, the historian disposes equally of a powerful tool to convert individual testimony into collective understanding, and the practice of the actor into theoretical understanding, by situating received information within a suitable theoretical and conceptual framework, namely, a materialist, structuralist, and dialectic theory of history. Such a theory, based on the abstract totalization of earlier practices adding context and sensitivity to the individual experience allows a "decoding" of the narrative from individual practice, to assume its full historical significance.

The Application of Histoire Immédiate in Zaire

The Congo Crisis of 1960-1965 made imperative a reassessment of colonial ideology and severely challenged Western analytic paradigms; it also provided favorable terrain for the techniques of living and popular history. This research was carried out along three lines of inquiry: the secessions of Katanga and of South Kasai (1960-1963), administrative decentralization and the formation of 21 largely autonomous political entities referred to as "provincettes" (1962-1963), and the movements of rebellion which occurred in Kwilu and in the eastern half of the country (1963-1965). The study of these three types of centrifugal movements led researchers to draw on the techniques of anthropology and history and to focus especially on the ethnic foundations of political movements as well as on the history of ethnic groups during the period of colonial domination; the role of the young Zairean researchers was decisive in this second phase, when the field of application and the principal methodological rules of the techniques of Histoire Immédiate were developed.

The setback to the centrifugal movements, and the foreign pressures, led in 1965 to the installation of a centralized and authoritarian political regime. The state was put at the service of a radical form of economic exploitation and appropriation. In this context, research was increasingly oriented toward the political mechanisms and economic bases of the new forms of power structures, and simultaneously toward the study of opposition movements. There was clearly a felt need for a theoretical framework capable of understanding the origin and strategies of the new ruling class. Consciously or not, historical materialism was adopted by an increasing number of researchers to fulfill this role.

A fourth field of application, politically less dangerous but equally as powerful, has been in the more recent analyses—still in progress—on the urban pathology and the marginalized categories during the crisis: the unemployed and the sub-proletarians, the women, the handicapped, the delinquent, and the mad. Recourse to the "living techniques" of life narratives and of observation, practiced in this field for four years and more, has shown itself a particularly productive approach, in which the analysis operates at two interrelated levels: that of the life of the individual interviewed, and that of the group of analysts.

Under the influence of the Departments of History and Sociology at the University of Lubumbashi, there has developed a fifth field of application: the history of colonization. Two lines of research have been explored for the period 1940-1960 using the techniques of research outlined above for Histoire Immédiate: colonial violence and the political rise of the social category known as the évolués. The investigation of these two subjects, seldom considered in earlier colonial documentation, has led us to utilize oral techniques intensively.

Although it is too early to try to evaluate the use of Histoire Immédiate as applied in Zaire, a few preliminary conclusions can be offered. The utilization of these techniques has altered with the succession of different fields of research and with the progress made in the development of the method as a research tool. As the framework of accumulating data and submitting them to critical analysis has been constantly improved by successive groups of researchers, oral and living techniques have assumed an increasingly important role within the methodological approach as a whole. Recourse to other sources of information (questionnaires, statistics, documentary studies) has always been combined with oral techniques, but in proportions and following sequences which vary with each subject. One strength of this method has resulted from publishing the results with a minimum of delay, so that the participants—both researchers and informants—have been able to assess and verify the use to which their information has been put. This has done much to establish strong ties of confidence and has led to further collaboration of a more spontaneous nature.

THE VALIDITY AND UTILITY
OF THE METHOD IN AFRICA

No one any longer questions that it now falls to the Africans themselves to write their own history and to develop their own methods of analysis. This is not a question of recognizing "proprietary rights" on their past, at the same level as for historical monuments or for art objects which become part of the national patrimony, but simply to notice that it is their future which is at stake and that this can only be constructed on the foundation of a certain type of relation with the past. History is an active, essential element of movement and of liberation that will break Africa's present chains. It is at this level that it belongs to Africans. The method of Histoire Immédiate offers several means to contribute directly to the development of this "other" African history, at least for the contemporary period. First, the technique postulates the preeminence of practical understanding over scholarly understanding, and bases historical understanding firmly on the dialectic which essentially reverses the conventional relationship between the historian and the historical actor. Being African or residing in Africa is less important than being committed in a revolutionary praxis with Africa as the principal point of reference.

Histoire Immédiate is also particularly useful during periods of upheaval and in crises because these mobilize social actors and make them more conscious. Therefore the method of Histoire Immédiate would appear well adapted to the situation in Africa, and particularly Zaire, has experienced over the last 25 years. As with most African societies, Zaire has undergone an exceptionally rapid and brutal rhythm of change, which has produced extremely rapid social and geographic mobility of both individuals and social groups. But colonial or neocolonial history has very little to say about (where it does not entirely neglect) the crucial moments of change and the processes associated with such changes. There is abundant documentation to describe the norm of social stability, the instruments of power and the stated intentions of the powerful, but this documentation seldom refers to the forces and ideologies of change. That is why understanding the trajectories of the lives of individuals constitutes an indispensable introduction to the history of the period. Only the "living techniques" of Histoire Immédiate adequately permit the actors or the witnesses of change to speak for themselves.

Official or private documentation on the colonial period is sullied with another weakness which severely limits its value: It is written by, or under the guidance of, the foreign colonizer. It is first and foremost an instrument of bureaucratic control and of ideological propaganda, capable of providing only the colonial version of history. Since such colonial-period documents are often abundant, well presented, and varied, it is tempting for the historian to consider this abundance and this variety as proof of the truth of what is written. But in fact this material is produced as a form of pure imitation and consists principally of repetitions of the same version of events and vision of history. Such abundance of documentation is therefore illusory. What is presented is in fact only a partial representation of reality. Often the illusion created by the abundance of colonial documentation is shattered by listening to but a single person who was colonized.

Since Histoire Immédiate is total history, it tries to account for all aspects of a social formation and the greatest possible number of explanatory factors. It therefore presupposes an interdisciplinary approach, and a collective organization of research is needed to master the great diversity of sources and to analyse their content with competence. This goal, in some ways the opposite of an academic and individualistic conception of research, has been shown in Africa and elsewhere to be very difficult to attain. But, when a group of researchers succeeds in concentrating their efforts on the same field of research over a period of several years, unexpected results are often produced. The intensity of exchanges, the mutual critique of information and interpretations, the repeated collective discussions of difficult questions, the concern of each to bring the maximum to the common research, now an indivisible objective: All these factors allow for a collective efficiency far surpassing the sum of individual efforts and possibilities. From our experience in Africa alone we cannot determine whether this productive form of scientific interplay is typically African or common to all societies in crisis, intensely preoccupied with self-awareness in order to seize control over their own destinies. We can only affirm unequivocally that it is possible in Africa.

Some Limitations and Criticisms of the Method

Based as it is on eliciting the full participation of the historical actor, the method depends on the knowledge and the degree of consciousness of such historical actors. The typical alienation resulting from colonial ideology has by no means disappeared with independence; in fact, new and even more subtle mechanisms of constraint have been established since then. In addition the lively resurgence of earlier beliefs and alliances (in material symbols of belief, and belief in ethnic unity) constitute even greater obstacles to a clear and rational perception of these realities. The historian's analysis must take account of such factors.

The living techniques of information utilized by Histoire Immédiate during periods of crisis can lead the researcher to overstress the political aspects of history and to detract attention from its principal object, which is economic reality. This requires an understanding of the development of the productive forces and objective contradictions between and at the heart of various modes of production, an understanding of the struggles between exploitative classes and the oppressed classes, and an understanding of the ultimately imperialistic determination of these factors; but all these aspects escape the perception of the individual. This is the reason such a global theory of history and its rigorous dialectic application to each stage of research is indispensable, just as is also the need to draw on quantitative techniques of information. But this brings up the persistent question of the dialectic articulation between the microscopic approach (for example, a significant witness) and the macroscopic and structural approach (such as provided by a body of statistical data).

In some respects Histoire Immédiate resembles a rather naive approach to history in that it is based on popular participation; there are real risks of the manipulation of sources of information, either from the researcher "adapting" the data to confrom to preconceived ideas, or from power considerations, as the ruling classes retain an interest in appropriating to their own benefit this ideological capital constituted by the memory of the people. In addition, the critique of oral sources is a difficult and delicate task, and their post facto validation by others is almost impossible. The collective memory of the actors and witnesses of events and spectacular changes is subjected to a certain number of systematic deformations well documented by historians and psychologists: quantitative figures may be amplified, especially for accidental or bloody phenomena; historical periods may become confused; dating is uncertain; the influence of external or magical forces may be overestimated to the detriment of the role of internal contradictions; in case of conflict, the adversaries may be stereotyped and their cohesion exaggerated—the camps are described in a Manichean manner. The absence of written information at the disposition of people capable of completing and confirming such reminiscences is thus both an advantage (because not simply reflecting the hegemony of the literate elites) and a handicap for the collective memory. But these drawbacks can be partially controlled by the sheer quantity of sources available and by establishing standardized procedures of transcription, conservation, and publication which permit other historical actors to verify the veracity of these data rapidly.

In the course of a study of the impact of World War II in Kisangani (Zaire), we have noticed that our informants, who themselves witnessed this period, portrayed it in a much more favorable light than did the colonial documents of the time. Such a systematic deformation of reality and idealization of the past can be explained by the age of the informants, the recent severe reduction in their material standard of living, and their social standing at the time of the observed activities. Membership in the social group of *évolués* tends to affect the judgment of such informants as well; if today they belong to a social level reduced to near begging, at the time of the war their situation and aspirations differentiated them from the mass and set them objectively on the side of the colonizer. Even if shortly before independence the colonial structure appeared as an obstacle to their continued upward mobility, and hence as the "class enemy," immediately after independence, when they had for the most part succeeded to the place of the former colonizer, it was normal that they would try to idealize it. This changing status in society directly affects their portrayal of the past. One obstacle of a political origin is beginning to confront the committed historian today: most African countries seem to be experiencing a period of ideological confusion and pluralism of ideas; the oligarchies and the bourgeois class have become aware of the importance of a stake in historical understanding and have begun to exercise control over the researcher in social sciences.

There remains one last difficult question, that posed by the Chinese philosopher Luxum: "For whom are we writing?" (Chesneaux, 1976: 7). One of the rules of Histoire Immédiate is to restore to the historical actors an awareness that they have co-produced historical understanding jointly with the researchers; such an objective is required not only by the canons of elementary honesty but also so that the process of critical understanding continues. The historical work is therefore destined for the people who produced the history and co-produced its proper understanding. Is it possible to attain this goal? If so, what are the political and epistemological consequences? To the first question the answer is clearly positive, to the degree that the historian renounces the conventional Western norms and objectives of the academic production of knowledge; only the future can answer the second.

21

DAR ES SALAAM AND
THE POSTNATIONALIST
HISTORIOGRAPHY OF AFRICA

HENRY SLATER

                                      **The production
of historical knowledge** is a political question. This is due to a fundamental duality in the nature of knowledge itself. Knowledge is not
only a product of contemporary social reality, and in some senses a
reflection of it, but also contributes to the molding of that same social
reality; that is to say, it represents a political intervention that
contributes to the forces determining the movement of a particular
present toward a particular future. A dialectical relationship exists
between these two processes; of reflection, on the one hand, and
intervention, on the other. Significantly different forms of historical
knowledge are produced on the basis of different methodologies.
Methodology is also, then, a political question.[1]

    This chapter discusses the methodological and practical contribu-
tion of the Department of History at the University of Dar es Salaam
in Africa to postnationalist historiography in Africa. "Postnationalist" historiography is here understood to be that historiography which has sought to move beyond the bourgeois limitations of
the Africanist historiography of the 1960s, and toward the production

Author's Note: This is a revised version of a paper first given in the Department of History Seminar at the Department of Dar es Salaam. While the
author is grateful for, and has benefited considerably from, the comments of
his Dar colleagues on this and other occasions, the chapter remains a
personal rather than an "official" Department view of the processes
described.

of a form of historical knowledge whose objective is to understand and present the processes of Africa's history from the standpoint of the workers and peasants, the oppressed classes of Africa in the present conjuncture. It is important that "postnationalist" in this sense not be misunderstood as "antinationalist."

The character, periodization, and, indeed, the very existence of this contribution has not been accidental, but needs to be understood in the context of the changing sociopolitical situation, the network of contradictions, within which the Department of History at Dar has operated since its inception in 1964. The changes in the historiographical position of the Department—in its syllabus, personnel, and publications—need to be understood in the context of the struggles arising from both the social setting within which the members of the Department of History operate, and the place that they occupy within this setting. The setting is constituted by three interlinked levels of social relations: the University of Dar Es Salaam, itself; the Tanzanian social formation; and third, the international situation within which the Tanzanian social formation exists. But the changes in the social product of the Department's work have not only reflected these various fields and levels of social struggle, they have also generated new ideological interventions in these struggles. The relationship between these two processes has been, as we have already suggested, a dialectical one.

Although the pattern since 1964 has been one of continual struggle and almost continual change, certain "crises" leading to firm "breaks" can be identified which enables a periodization to be established. Three major phases can be identified, each characterized by the hegemony of a particular historiographic tradition, understood as a specific organic combination of a particular form of historical scholarship or methodology, the historical knowledge produced by that scholarship or methodology, and the historians and others engaged in its production and dissemination. We shall attempt to classify these traditions by their fundamental class character; secondly, by their methodological position; and thirdly, by their political outlook.

The first break led to a transition from a bourgeois historiography which was essentially idealist in its methodology and colonialist in its political outlook, to one which was certainly different in its political outlook but still remained bound within the parameters of an idealist methodology. The second break saw the replacement of this "bourgeois nationalist" historiography with a tradition which was essentially petty bourgeois in character; this was transitional in both its methodological approach and sociopolitical outlook. The third break, which led to a paradigm arguably still in the process of articulation, represents an attempt to carry through a move beyond this "petty bourgeois transitional" tradition, to a historiography of Africa which is at once proletarian (in its class character), rigorously materialist (in its methodological position), and socialist (in its political outlook).

For each of these periods a key "vanguard," or type-figure, can be identified—a member of the Department who appears to have played a major role in structuring the break concerned: Terence Ranger, the late Walter Rodney, and Jacques Depelchin.[2] This is not to suggest, however, that these individuals undertook the work of structuring the changes singlehanded. Still less is it to suggest that the new forms of historical knowledge simply emerged through the power of their minds. It is to say that, for one reason or another, they were in a particularly favorable position to respond to the social contradictions bearing on the Department at the time concerned, by playing an active role in the debate which developed around the analysis of these contradictions and out of which the new form of historical knowledge took shape.

We are now in a position to offer an overall periodization, in diagrammatic form, of the Department's contribution toward the development of a postnationalist historiography of Africa (see Figure 21.1).

The remainder of this essay first discusses the characteristics of the kind of nationalist historiography which was being produced in the Department in the 1960s. Secondly, it examines the methodological and political critique of this historiography developed at Dar es Salaam. Thirdly, it proceeds to examine the characteristics of the "transitional" form of historical knowledge to which this critique initially gave birth. Fourthly, the chapter discusses the nature of the critique which, in turn, came to be leveled against this historiography. Fifthly, the struggles to try to define the methodological characteristics of a new "proletarian socialist" historiography of Africa, struggles which are still very much in process at Dar, are briefly introduced. Finally, an assessment is attempted of the extent and significance of the Dar contribution to the overall postnationalist historiography of the continent.

THE BREAK WITH BOURGEOIS
COLONIALIST HISTORY

Independence in 1961 produced a crisis in historical scholarship and history teaching in the then Tanganyika, because at this stage the

	HISTORIOGRAPHY	Crisis of Independence		Crisis of Arusha Declaration		Crisis of the Present Conjuncture		
	1955	1960	1965	1970	1975	1980	1985	1990
Theory of Knowledge				Idealism		Materialism		
Class Position	Metropolitan Bourgeois		National Bourgeois		Petty Bourgeois	Proletarian		
Politics Position	Colonialist		Nationalist		Transitional	Socialist?		
Vanguard Figure			Ranger	Rodney	Depelchin			
			First Break	Second Break		Third Break		

Figure 21.1 Main Historiographic Trend at the University of Dar Es Salaam

252

processes of the production and reproduction of historical knowledge were still dominated by the metropolitan bourgeoisie, with its colonialist outlook. It is in this context that the appointment of Terence Ranger as the first Professor of History is the new University College of Dar es Salaam in 1963 needs to be understood. Ranger already had a considerable reputation as a pioneering "nationalist" historian in what was then Southern Rhodesia, and was almost certainly brought to Dar to lead a similar assault on colonialist ideological hegemony in the field of history there.[3] The first students were admitted to the Department in 1964, by which time Ranger had been joined by Isaria Kimambo and Arnold Temu, two young Tanganyikans returned from studies in North America. Together, these three set about structuring the break which would lead the Department at Dar to become known for its militantly nationalist positions in the late 1960s.

The central theme of the new historical knowledge was taken to be the emergence of a socially undifferentiated Tanganyikan nation, with deep historical roots. This development, as indeed was the case with almost all other historical developments in Africa, was to be explained in terms of the central role being given to "local" rather than "external" initiatives (Ranger, 1968, and 1969). It was a history emphasizing politics and, with the notable exception of the celebration of long-distance trade, one that virtually neglected economic and social questions. It was a history that, its "liberal" critics suggested, had been deliberately tailored to meet the needs of a new state and of its new governing class (Denoon and Kuper, 1970; Ranger, 1971). The interpretation found its broadest, if not necessarily purest, statement in the collection of essays edited by Kimambo and Temu (1969), a volume which grew out of the Tanganyikan History Teachers' Conference of 1967. The book has served the needs of students and teachers in Tanzania for more than a decade and is only now being superseded.

THE BREAK WITH BOURGEOIS NATIONALIST HISTORY

The Kimambo and Temu volume proved to be one of the last products of the "bourgeois nationalist" phase of the Department's work, and perhaps its crowning achievement. By the time the book appeared, a new turning point had already arrived, reflecting a more general crisis in the society as a whole, a crisis produced, in its turn, by a sharpening of the social contradictions in the immediate postcolonial situation. At the national level, this led to a significant

shift to the left, heralded by the Arusha Declaration of 1967, as the
governing petty bourgeoisie sought to contain the economic and
social threat to its position. On the one hand "Ujamaa," or "African
socialism," and on the other, economic nationalism or "self-reliance"
now joined political nationalism on the official ideological agenda in
Tanzania.

At the level of the university, the bourgeois nationalist scholarship
and the social knowledge produced by its deployment, designed as
they were to meet the ideological needs of an embryonic national
bourgeoisie which had now proved to be nonexistent (or at least too
weak to spearhead a national transformation), no longer appeared
capable of meeting the demands of the situation, at least to some
radical students and teachers. The campus was plunged into a period
of fierce intellectual and political struggle, out of which a new direction, though not necessarily a new consensus, gradually began to
emerge. The History Department was deeply affected by the sharpening
contradictions and was one of the key centers of the struggle. Historians
and historical knowledge which remained bound by the parameters of
the narrow politico-nationalist interpretation now came under attack
(Shivji, 1980).

As a result of these struggles, and with the late Walter Rodney
coming quickly to fulfill the role of the new "vanguard" figure, the
historical knowledge produced by the department gradually took on a
new orientation. Rodney devoted relatively little attention to the
development of a systematic critique of existing positions, or to the
formal delineation of a new methodology, but instead plunged straight
into the task of producing a new form of knowledge. Implicit in his
seminal work (Rodney, 1972) are both a critique of existing positions
and a methodological statement; but it remained for others, for Abul
Sheriff and particularly for Bonaventure Swai (1977, 1978, 1980, 1982;
Swai and Temu, 1977; Temu and Swai, 1981), then a young lecturer in
the department, to develop a thoroughgoing critique of the existing
"bourgeois nationalist" tradition.

At one level, "bourgeois nationalist" historiography was criticized
for its concentration on politics conceived in a social vacuum, and for
its romantic emphasis upon the role of African initiative, both of
which singularly failed to provide a historical explanation of the
present condition of African economic and political powerlessness.
How then could such knowledge contribute to Africa's contemporary
struggles to overcome these conditions of powerlessness? Clearly it
could not; indeed, in its false or partial representation of the forces at
work in Africa's history, it constituted a formidable obstacle to popular mobilization in such struggles.

At another, and perhaps more fundamental level, "bourgeois nationalist" historiography was criticized for its methodological poverty: its idealism, empiricism, and rejection of theory—precisely the same set of methodological propositions as the historiographical tradition it was attempting to confront and displace. "Bourgeois nationalist" or "Africanist" history was simply the negative mirror image of "bourgeois colonialist" history (Luanda, 1979). A formal methodological statement has not appeared to complement this critique, perhaps because, as suggested by a metropolitan critic of the new position, it was not necessary (Hopkins, 1975). The methodology could be, and was, simply imported in ready-made form from outside the continent (albeit from another part of the periphery of the world capitalist system, rather than, as previously had occurred, from one of its *metropoles*).

Within the post-Arusha context of the production of historical knowledge, the "development of underdevelopment" replaced the "growth of nationalism" as the central motif, and the focus therefore shifted from the political superstructure to the economic (if not exactly the productive) base. The stress was no longer placed on the determinant role of local struggles but, despite the great courage of the African resisters, on their virtual powerlessness in the face of the penetration of local social formations by the agents of European capital. A new emphasis was placed on the colonial era, because these very colonial structures, which were glossed over in the "bourgeois nationalist" interpretation, were now seen to be instrumental in establishing the conditions for the continuing exploitation of Africans in general, and of Tanzanians in particular, by metropolitan capital after independence. By 1974, these new positions were sufficiently structured and their application to the Tanzanian case adequately worked out that they could be introduced to a wider local audience, that of the Tanzanian History Teachers' Conference held at Morogoro in June of that year. Most of the then members of the Department contributed to the Conference, the vanguard figure of the era, Walter Rodney, among them (Kaniki, 1980).

In the unevenness of this collection of papers lies a clue as to the transitional and contradictory nature of the historical knowledge which was being produced in the Department at this time. Some chapters exhibit the idealism, empiricism and neglect of theory which had been hallmarks of the earlier "bourgeois nationalist" phase of Dar historical writing. Other chapters anticipate a more rigorously materialist tradition yet to be born. The contradictions are particularly sharp at the points of transition in the book, where the authors attempt to link an understanding of the forces operative in the colonial era and which are discussed from a substantially materialist perspective, to an understanding of the forces operative in the earlier and later periods which are still discussed from a substantially idealist perspective. The nub of the problem thus appears to lie in the tension between two theories of knowledge: idealism, with its explanatory concept of ethnicity, on the one hand, and materialism, with its explanatory concept of class, on the other (Slater, 1981).

THE BREAK WITH PETTY
BOURGEOIS TRANSITIONAL HISTORY

By 1975, the outlines of a new crisis could be seen in Tanzania, the product of both internally and externally determined contradictions developing in the post-Arusha situation, and manifested particularly at the economic level. The crisis brought to the fore both a rightist and a leftist critique of the existing socioeconomic framework and political leadership, albeit much of it mounted from outside the Tanzanian social formation. The Right called for a return to the untrammeled reign of capitalist market forces, and the Left for a move beyond "African" socialism toward a full-fledged "scientific" socialism. Once more the University, and the Department of History within it, were not unaffected by these contradictions and struggles. The debates that developed within the Department at this time, and in which Jacques Depelchin played one of the leading roles, led to the beginning of the structuring of a new break. The intellectual and political difficulties of the move beyond the existing historiographic tradition have perhaps both been reflected in the preponderance of methodological and historiographic work in the Department over the past few years.

The first stage of the break has been marked by the development of a critique of the transitional "petty bourgeois" position. The progressive aspects of this tradition included its use of a materialist theory of knowledge and of a methodology rooted in such a theory, taking the economic level as the starting point of the analysis; the deployment of the notion of class struggle and of other Marxist concepts; Rodney's call for the political engagement of the historian; and the development of a critique of capitalism, and of the world capitalist system, which "bourgeois nationalist" history singularly failed to mount. Nevertheless materialism has not fully replaced idealism in providing the philosophical and methodological determination of the work. Rather, a situation of pluralism, juxtaposing the two overall orientations, has developed. Thus, for example, Rodney sees class struggle essentially as being fought out between socially undifferentiated continental, racial, or national blocs of people. The analytic concepts deployed are those of "Europe" and "Europeans" or "Britain" and "the British," on the one hand, and "Africa" and "Africans" or "Tanzania" and "Tanzanians" on the other. But this is drastically to oversimplify the patterns of social contradictions that have fueled Africa's past and that will determine the future (Mishambi, 1977; Mbwiliza, 1978; Slater, 1981).

The second stage of the articulation of the break from transitional "petty bourgeois" history, has involved a debate which has taken as its objects the clarification of the methodology to be used in the production of historical knowledge and the development of a clearer understanding of its precise relationship to the concrete realities of the contemporary African situation.

A Dar-based sociologist, Henry Bernstein, probably initiated the debate with his discussion of the relevance of Marxist methodology to the work of historians of Africa. His contribution took the form of a review of Endre Sik's *The History of Black Africa,* one of the earliest attempts to apply Marxist analysis to African history (Bernstein, 1976). While conceding the overdeterministic and Eurocentric aspects of the specific work in question, he defended the principle of applying Marxist methodology to African history and went on to outline his understanding of the essential features of that methodology. At about the same time, Depelchin (1975, 1977, 1978) began to take on a range of African historiographic targets from a rigorously materialist stance, and to become involved in the production of historical knowledge of recent and contemporary social reality which, by means of interview techniques, drew on the direct experience of workers and peasants. By the late 1970s (in what may have been a premature attempt) Bernstein and Depelchin were ready to reach out to the centers of western Africanist studies to prompt a more wide-ranging debate on conceptual issues transcending questions of analytic technique alone, a debate which remains sorely needed.

In 1978 Josiah Mlahabwa (1978) reviewed the general trend of historiographic work in the department and concluded both that the methodological basis had been laid and that the appropriate social conditions existed for the production of a "proletarian-oriented" history of Africa. Ernest Wamba (1980) was not convinced on either count, and expressed his reservations in a critique of the residual idealism of the "Althusserian Movement" in African historiography which he took to be implicit in the methodological statement of

Bernstein and Depelchin. At the same time he questioned the
possibility of producing a "proletarian history" of Africa outside of an
organized proletarian movement, which is hardly evident in most
parts of Africa at the present time and to which, in any case, few
African historians are organically linked.

But in Africa as elsewhere the production of historical knowledge
constitutes a significant element of the class struggle and should be
understood historically in this context (Slater, 1981a, 1981b, 1982a);
knowledge not only reflects social reality, present as well as past, but
also constitutes an ideological intervention designed to help produce a
particular future, whether it be a reproduction of the present or
something radically different. The general and specific methodologies
for accomplishing this ideological task do exist, can be outlined and
should be embraced (Slater, 1983), while the temptation to carry over
elements of bourgeois traditions, such as the idealist tendencies to
deal in heroes and ethnicities, should be firmly rejected (Slater,
1982b). In replying to these issues Wamba (1981) has raised questions
on the validity of a universalist (structuralist) methodology in Africa,
the extent to which dialectical materialists are engaged in "scientific"
rather than "ideological" work, and the political dangers implicit in
continued adherence to the bourgeois compartmentalization of
knowledge which the very notion of "historical knowledge" implies.

Although the debates focusing on the question of "proletarian
socialist" history have clearly had a profound impact on the orientation of the syllabus and teaching in the department in recent years, the
production and publication of new historical knowledge from this
perspective, the third stage of the articulation of the break with earlier
traditions, has only just begun.

CONCLUSION

Any review of the Dar es Salaam debates on postnationalist historiography in Africa must, at this stage at least, be regarded as an
interim report, in at least three respects. Firstly, the debates are, of
course, still continuing, and insofar as the History Department at
Dar exists in a setting of social contradictions, its work and the
positions taken up by its members on methodological as well as other
questions will necessarily continue to reflect these contradictions.
Secondly, this overview does not claim to offer a complete survey of
the work that has been produced in the department. It has concentrated on questions of methodology rather than on the new knowledge
produced in the department on the basis of these different meth-

odological positions. Finally, the chapter has only been able to convey the barest outline of the positions in the debate, and has been unable to do full justice to the range and depth of the written and verbal contributions which have been made to the debates by other teaching and student members of the department and by those now based outside it.[4] A fuller treatment of the theme must, perhaps, await publication of the work of another researcher.[5]

The impact of these debates on the total field of African historiography is extremely difficult to evaluate; here we can offer only a few tentative remarks on the question. Insofar as African and overseas historians of the continent receive their basic training and recharge their intellectual batteries in London, Paris or Los Angeles rather than in Dar es Salaam, the impact of the Dar debates on the direction of African historiography is necessarily limited. Similarly, the weakness of the publishing base in Tanzania has also limited the impact of the Dar debates, especially as few of the metropolitan centers regard the question of method (in its conceptualistic dimensions, at least) as a legitimate field of inquiry.

Despite these difficulties, however, the Dar school has made its mark on the postnationalist historiography of Africa—at the very least it has kept alive a viable historiographical alternative to the liberal postnationalist historiography elsewhere in Africa. The most notable case was Rodney's seminal work (1972), which contributed in no small measure to a fundamental change in the conception that most Africans had of the past and present relationship of their continent to that of Europe, and suggested thereby new political questions to be posed of the existing order at a territorial, continental, and world level. At an earlier stage the department attracted a core of productive and dynamic historians whose work, whatever its limitations in retrospect, was on the cutting edge of the research of the day. The department has always been oriented to more than simply producing and disseminating historical knowledge on the basis of existing paradigms and for its own sake. Its energies have also been given to exploring the means of making historical knowledge available and useful to the people who produced the history as well as to those who produce historical knowledge (Historical Society of Tanzania pamphlets, *Tanzania Zamani,* and many others). That tradition of formulating useful history (and defining the object of that utility) has continued and been strengthened in the present, and has been a very strong characteristic of the school, as exemplified most dramatically in the life and work—and death—of Walter Rodney. Today the debates that go on among the members of the department are less visible to those outside, perhaps, but they are no less intense and no less important, and they are based on the same principles as those of the earlier stages: that of liberating historical scholarship from the dominant paradigms of the day, whether colonialist, nationalist, or bourgeois, and that of making historical knowledge accessible and meaningful and useful to the people who need it, deserve it, and who made it what it is.

NOTES

1. This is not, of course, to say that historical knowledge produced in present time *determines* social reality in future time, nor to say that historians are necessarily conscious of the role their work may come to play; still less is it to suggest that the question of the quality of a historian's contribution can somehow be reduced to the question of its political perspective.

2. For a fuller consideration of Rodney's life and work, see Alpers and Fontaine (1982). Depelchin joined the Department in 1975. There is a suggestion that his departure in 1979 was not entirely of his or the Department's own choosing. He now works at the African Studies Centre of the Eduardo Mondlane University in Maputo.

3. This pioneering role had, in fact, led to his being forced to leave Salisbury, as the forces of the African nationalism which he supported were temporarily beaten under by the forces of a virulent settler nationalism.

4. This chapter does not, for example, review the important contributions of John Iliffe. Iliffe's work in the Department in the 1960s began more or less in line with the bourgeois nationalist orientation of his colleagues at the time, though it often paid much closer attention to economic and social questions than was the norm. Since leaving Dar, however, he has followed a different line of development from that of the debates within the Department itself, and now stands, with A. G. Hopkins and others, for what one might term a "pure bourgeois" historiography of Africa which, in its celebration of market forces, now stands in direct contradiction to the dominant position of the Dar school at the present time (1969, 1971, 1979, 1983).

5. Wim Bossema, of the African Studies Centre of Leiden, is working on a doctoral dissertation on the subject.

22

POPULIST POLITICAL ACTION
Historical Understanding
and Political Analysis in Africa

JEAN-FRANÇOIS BAYART

To identify
modes of people's political action in Africa, it is not sufficient to think
in simple topological terms, of the "top" and the "bottom" of a social
system. Nor should we set out to look for some "motor force of
history" or for some sort of political essence that characterizes all
popular culture; there does not exist naturally any single "popular"
manner of conceiving political order or of political action, because
politics is not something intangible and constant from one culture to
another (de Certeau, 1980a).

Popular practices cannot be treated as simply residual activity,
assigned to some undefined but impotent traditionalist sphere of
activity. To understand that African societies are like the others, to
think on their banality (or universality—their attributes common to
other societies), to grasp the essential point that their specificity
exists exclusively on a historical level: These are observations that
official Africanism has scarcely touched on, whatever the considerable mass of detail assembled in recent years. The image of Africa
projected in Africanist literature is at least as ambiguous as the image
of the Orient produced by "Orientalism" analyzed by Said (1978) or
Rodinson (1980). Western public opinion is replete with stereotypes
that often exude the racism of yesteryear. The fundamental aberra-
tion is undoubtedly that which sets up an analytic model within which
to explain the day-to-day events of the present, the global configuration of the African awareness, and the future of black societies. But

Africa is most emphatically not the continent where simplistic conceptions are applicable; it is a continent that illustrates the triumph of
diversity, whether in terms of culture, politics, economics, or history.
Simply to recall this fact is to sense already that the term "African
powers" cannot be understood in the singular and that in Africa there
have developed extremely complex networks of relations that inevitably
belie any simplistic presentation.

   Therefore, African societies need to be understood in terms of their
complexity; they need to be recognized as fully historical societies.
Their increasing underdevelopment has not in the least interrupted
this historicity; it has in fact constituted a resurgence of it. It is an
error to conceive of colonial or postcolonial dependence as simply an
external relation between African societies qualified as peripheral on
the one hand, with the Western core on the other, or alternatively as a
monolithic structure of domination by the Western world on the black
continent. It can never be overstressed that the process of colonization, far from being some sort of Manichean opposition, as it is so
often portrayed in the sources, was basically a common enterprise of
black and white actors, the former looking to manipulate the latter
within their particular strategies (and vice versa). This is still true
today for contemporary economic development which provided for
certain indigenous social groups the key to their hegemony; the
process of underdevelopment cannot therefore be reduced to a simple
dichotomous relationship between Africa on the one hand and the
West on the other.

   It must also be kept in mind that for the last several centuries
Africans have been living out a particularly traumatic existence, one
that has constantly brought into question their sovereignty, their
identity, even their survival. Even if the slave trade had much more
complex effects than is often recognized, it struck Africa "in its body
and in its consciousness," and it continues still today to affect this
consciousness, as well attested by certain contemporaneous forms of
sorcery (Rosny, 1981). Colonization was a heavy burden on Africa,
one whose human cost was very high because of both the repression
and the conscription of forced labor integral to the process; it too
severely affected the dignity of the peoples of the continent. Finally,
decolonization allowed only for symbolic independence, "flag independence" alone, as Julius Nyerere characterizes it, and it has in no
way ended Africa's status of dependence on the West. It is impossible
to exaggerate the depth of the suffering engendered by this state of
affairs; two of Africa's poignant "world records" demonstrate this

reality: the number of its "less developed countries," and the number of its refugees.

The dependent situation of most African societies is reflected primarily in their internal structures. What are the dominant groups in such societies? What became of their internal structures over the course of the slave trade and then of colonization? Have they undertaken a partial or radical redistribution of the balance sheet, and, if so, to the benefit of which social groups? What goes on today under the guise of "state institutions"? Such are the questions that should be asked, and for which there is but a single response: a step-by-step political analysis which replaces Africanist fantasies and generalizations with concrete understanding of the diverse historical realities and situations. Contemporary political and economic structures, and especially the contemporary state, can only be understood in light of this historical continuity: Yesterday's lines of cleavage have been retained into the present. The possibilities offered under colonial rule were only partial, and were offset by the reinforcement of earlier cleavages. The dominated and exploited classes of the postcolonial state tend to be the same groups as were dependent in precolonial societies: young single men, or women—the historic "dependents" par excellence—as well as slaves, low status castes, or subject ethnic groups. In the shadow of the postcolonial state these categories adopt strategies that are only new episodes in this ancient struggle that opposes them to the dominating class.

For this reason it seems relevant to tie the contemporary state, no longer to a given structure, associated with a relatively stable and unidimensional class structure, but to a hegemonic crisis provoked by a dependence syndrome; that is, a structure of classes in the making. Till now the essential lines of the debate have consisted of linking the state to a dominant class and to characterize this latter; it is thus reduced to variations on the theme of the bourgeoisie, whether perceived as nationalist, bureaucratic, agrarian, comprador, or some other type. It would be more valuable to reintroduce as the elements essential to our understanding the complex processes of interaction between various class forms different in their very nature: those related to earlier forms of social stratification, those participating increasingly in the modern state, those class forms of material accumulation increasingly dependent on the global economic system.

It is at the level of each specific case that these positions converge or contradict each other. As an example, a position of power is often a position from which to gain wealth, and it is not unusual that the titular leader might be descended from an earlier aristocrat. But that varies from one historical situation to another; not all situations are equivalent, because the insertion of African societies within the world economy and their political evolution privilege one or another among them. Village by village, region by region, the conflicts between these various positions carry over to the national level, and these conflicts result in a new system of inequality and of domination. To the degree to which the political regime molds the relationships of power between the parts, it becomes the mistress of the situation. The ultimate objective of this dynamic is the transformation into a homogeneous social class of those diverse groups seeking domination within the state apparatus and for which the state provides a locus of conjunction and of conflictual mediation. Thus, torn apart by their dependence syndrome, African political reconstructions are in the process of seeking new systems of totalizing domination which differ from one social formation to another in the type of groups and of positions which it favors. The search for internal hegemony is a relatively uncertain process, which attests to the well-known political instability of black Africa.

In such a political context the distinction between the state and the civil society is a political reality: The state is "the Other" and the opposition between the two forms of identity is seen very clearly in these terms, even if only from some sort of "architectural" point of view. This distinction between state and society dominates the social field of action, both by the latent (and sometimes active) threat of political repression that the state projects, and by the more ordinary forms of physical suffering or symbolic discrimination that it underwrites. As a concept the notion of civil society applies to a dynamic, complex, and ambivalent set of relations between the state and the society. The formation of social movements and their capacity to prevail over state forms of political power are by no means clearly established; in fact such movements are not immune to the inverse processes of fracture and dissolution so common to people's modes of political action. It is therefore not possible to inquire into some imaginary entity of "popular politics" in the way in which studies of folklore have built on stable and undifferentiated isolates. The complex dynamics of what is known as "popular culture" are formed of the processes of acquisition, of enrichment, and of reappropriation, that preclude the possibility of treating people's practices as simply residual activity, assigned to some undefined but impotent traditionalist sphere of activity. Nor can they be simply if vaguely identified with some "motor force of history."

Despite the increasing hegemony of the state, the process of constructing a dominant class and restructuring state power has constantly been attacked and opposed by subordinate social groups. Popular uprisings (such as those in Madagascar, Kenya, Cameroon, Zaïre, and Chad) projecting scenes from *The Wretched of the Earth* (Fanon, 1961) have often provided a general reshuffling of the cards within "catastrophic equilibrium" (Gramsci, 1949, 1971), but this response has failed, too, in Angola, Mozambique, or Ethiopia, where the subordinate groups appear to be progressively dispossessed of their association with the nationalist or agrarian struggles.

The social category most determined to confront the system of domination, because it has nothing to lose (either from a traditional or from a modern point of view), is composed of young people marginalized by the structure of production, living only by their wits, submitted to the meddling authority of the older generation, and representing, even if only in passing, nearly half of the total population of the continent. But such participants are also the least prepared to assume leadership roles in the changes that its actions provoke. This "class" is probably easily manipulated because of its rapid turnover, because its members are prone to abuses, and because there is seldom any unity of action and identity of interest between the young and the other social categories of the postcolonial state: The women are forced to utilize the resources of this class in the political and economic sphere to carry out strategies of individual or familial (only rarely collective) advancement, and they disapprove of the violence which so often characterizes the activism of the young; the peasantry—another much-discussed potential revolutionary force— is often weakened by internal cleavages and appears at present to be more disposed to reappropriating the fruits of the capitalist economy than to threatening them by explicitly disruptive actions. The same is true for the working classes that are, in any case, but a small minority.

But this does not mean that the dispossessed masses would always be passive or powerless. They pose a threat to the state by innumerable flexible and variable tactics even while failing to offer any firm alternative strategy (de Certeau, 1980b). Revolts, the refusal of some kinds of work, slowdowns, strikes, electoral abstentions, migrations, the increasingly frequent resort to the sacred domain (even so far as creating virtual theocratic communities outside the control of civil authority), reference to transcendent religious allegiances (messianic or revolutionary), smuggling, the burgeoning informal economic sector, the intensive circulation of information not controlled by the official media, undermining authority by ironic humor, conflictual

participation in the structures of political control: There is a long list
of people's actions which limit and reduce the field of state action, and
which thus assure a sort of revenge of civil society on state institutions.

The political evolution of different African countries is thus
marked by two contradictory processes, that of state totalitarianism
undertaken by the established power, and that of de-totalitarianism
produced by the counterinitiatives of the society at large. The nature
of the postcolonial state in black Africa, specifically its authoritarian
or even totalitarian characteristics, is best understood by accounting
for even the little that we know of the general atrophy and dependence
of the civil society that it dominates. Where state and society engage
in more balanced relations it is because of previously mentioned
alternatives to state organization.

Once this insidious or brutal task of reappropriating the postcolonial state by the society is perceived, it is no longer so obvious that the
state remains, in Africa as in Asia, "a purely imported product"
(Badie and Birnbaum, 1979). The veneer of the European origin of the
postcolonial state resting on African societies, even if proscribing a
truly autonomous social restructuring from the bottom up, has still
not prevented a continuing interaction with the state structures, one
measure (among many) of the true historicity of these political systems. The future of the continent depends in good measure on the
continued extensions of this disordered relationship of state and
society, and its eventual institutionalization, in the form of the construction of political societies of a more democratic character.

The analysis of this process must be defined first with respect to a
certain conception of the individual on the one hand, and the community on the other (see Dumont, 1966, 1977). Most of the key notions on
which political analysts rely are defective in this respect. Sometimes
they participate in a teleological vision of history (or nation, or class)
and obscure other, equally important, identifications (forms of collective consciousness such as 'asabiyya in Arabic cultures or the household in many African cultures); at other times they are literally invented as part of a process which is at least more political and
administrative than scientific, even if in the end such identities (such
as ethnic categories and Islamic brotherhoods) have often been appropriated by the very people to whom they have been applied. The
analysis need also be characterized by reference to the representation
of the stratification of power which exists in a given society. Consequently, "a large part of Western social science is simply the con-

ception that capitalism has of itself" (Sahlins, 1976). Hierarchy, status, power, authority, and legitimacy do not all fit together in the same manner, and the antagonisms that tend to focus social relations are not everywhere identical.

The analysis is further determined by the analyst's conception of wealth and its relationship to power. With the modern era there has emerged an autonomous and relatively unified category of wealth which serves as the basis of the perceived autonomy of politics and economics. In historical systems where this differentiation has been only recently and incompletely imposed within the larger process of increasing underdevelopment, political activity tends to be confused with the drive toward accumulation. It is probable that the contemporary state, integrated as it is with the world capitalist economy, is the construction of groups which control opportunities produced within the very heart of traditional societies by different mechanisms. Such processes of enrichment are often so intense that they come to absorb the state itself; the division of the fruits of power rather than the division of power itself becomes the major stakes of the social struggle.

Last but not least, political action refers to the totality of cultural representations (deeds, symbols, aesthetic forms, religious or cosmological values, and so forth) and of historical traces that provide them with significance and consistency. All these elements taken together form the dramatic texture of history, although power and forms of resistance to its exercise are not always located exactly where the observer seeks them. One is thus led to inquire into the conditions within which cultural repertoires are produced and transmitted.

Therefore, it is necessary to isolate, as a full part of clearly defined historical situations and clearly delimited social fields of action, the procedures associated with a single practice or narration, as differentiated from one actor to another. The ambivalence of the structure and the political systems would be better understood when seen in such a framework: A structure of domination and control is not only what those in power wish for but also what the people make it to be. On the other hand it is not sufficient only to perceive the "weight which encumbers history and of which those affected are unaware" (Vovelle, 1983: 93) to hold fast to the illusion of a monolithic "collective memory" all too often reduced to the negative function of resistance. Cultural capital which is spread along the entire length of the past and from which political actors draw in a more or less tentative and contradictory way, is both an original production and the result of mechanical reproduction. Historians have written of the "reinvestment" or "recycling" of such cultural capital at the same time that they have shown how "tradition" is sometimes purely and simply invented; yet they have also discerned the incidence of the particular foundation-events or the "trauma of events" on longer-term structures (Poitou, 1981). True political potential is created which structures social space, retains attitudes and representations, and provides the privileged idioms and models of action. But the meaning thus accumulated has its own coherence, formed of the political game and of the legitimate framework of understanding, the only one accepted.

23

TOWARD A RESPONSIBLE
AFRICAN HISTORIOGRAPHY

CHRISTOPHE WONDJI

Historical research today is not simply a quest for cultural or national identity; it is also a quest for reconstruction and renewal, and a fundamental requirement for the qualitative transformation of African societies. In Africa, the human and social sciences—especially history and social studies—often suffer from the general discredit applied to disciplines characterized as useless and encumbering, or even subversive. Nonetheless, it is well known that in Western societies the social sciences have often been mobilized for reconstruction and development and that in East Asia today critical recourse to a national past has favored the most audacious forms of change. Consequently, any reflection on the future of African societies is useless if not firmly based on an objective analysis and evaluation of the past.

History remains a powerful means of awakening political awareness among oppressed peoples. The importance accorded to historical studies by the leaders of the African renaissance was no accident: Sarbah, Hawford, and many others fully understood the political and social institutions of precolonial Africa. Convinced that "each nation builds its future on its past" (Dike, 1956: 221), African intellectuals have in the past thrown themselves into historical research; Diop's (1955, 1981) work was the most significant expression of the narrow tie between historiography and a growing political and national consciousness (Diagne, 1977). For the peoples and nations in struggle for their effective liberation, history provides a valuable understanding of earlier patterns of development in these societies; it thus clarifies the problems of development in the present as well as analyzing those of the past. The experience of a given society, however, would not be sufficient in itself: Attention should also be given to neighboring and contemporary societies. Comparing the experiences of their own civilizations with those of others, African historians have become more aware of the possibilities of African progress; at the same time, they have also been able to define more clearly the transformations and modifications that are required to assure this end and to enrich it continually (Wondji and Loucou, 1976).

ON THE RESPONSIBILITY
OF AFRICAN HISTORIANS

In referring to the "opening to the continent of history," Marx and Engels did not wish only to grasp the reality of mankind as "the totality of social relations" or to analyze "the process of the self-realization of man." They sought also to promote a total history in which law, political economy, and history would be reunited in "a single and unique dialectic science of the movement of the society as a totality." But this "science of praxis" is not intended simply as a melting pot of lessons and recipes. History is an explanation of the world, a method of analyzing reality and, still more, a means of transforming it. The process of regaining awareness refers to the process of reclaiming and reconstructing an African consciousness that was alienated—even destroyed—by the slave trade and imperialist colonization. For Africans, it is a question of expressing the consciousness they have from within themselves in the present situation of the work structure, and thinking deeply on questions of what they seek to become as functioning societies, as peoples, and as nations, cultures, and civilizations in the face of the challenges of the contemporary world. Africa must not posit the problems of its development in terms of accomplishing some mythical program, but in terms of overcoming and transcending a concrete historical situation, the result of secular relations between Africa and the dominant West. Development, then, consists of initiating a new historical process on the base of this heritage and reconstructing a new civilization liberated from these disequilibria and these tensions, a process whereby Africa recovers its self-mastery and control of its own destiny.

In the face of responsibilities that flow from this, African intellectuals must feel themselves committed, in Sartre's sense of the term. They must take sides in their work and in their deeds, in the social, political, and ideological struggles of their time. They are committed in the degree to which they refuse to seek refuge in the ivory tower or to undertake art for art's sake or science for the sake of science. For the African historian, it is a question of contributing to the growing consciousness of the situation of underdevelopment, to bring the clarity of the lessons of the African past to bear on the present condition of the people of Africa, so that they may accede to a better vision of the tasks that await them. This is a question of bringing scholarly illumination to these problems; that is, adopting an objective approach without complacency, and avoiding narcissistic illusions about Africa, the source of errors in understanding the real problems that Africa faces in the gigantic effort of reconstruction and development.

Considered as a lucid vision of the African future, this "conscientization" includes several aspects: first, the increased awareness of a cultural and national personality that must be recovered and enriched after the depersonalization of the colonial experience. A valid historiography would permit Africans to move beyond the inferiority complex that has infected the continent, to recover self-confidence and confidence in the destiny of their continent. But the recovery of a clearly defined personality is not in itself sufficient. The process of depersonalization took effect at two levels: dispossession and impoverishment, as shown in the uprooting and deportation of people, and the exportation and destruction or removal of works of art. Consequently, in addition to experiencing political domination, Africa has suffered a mutilation of its cultural consciousness. If, for example, the Ivoirien youth knew of the war drums of the Ebrie, which are today located in the Musée de l'Homme in Paris instead of the Musée d'Abidjan, they would have retained a different idea of this people Ebrie, who offered such intense resistance to the French colonial conquest.

The second aspect of this "conscientization" is the growing awareness of the importance of a free and active participation on the part of Africans in the present evolution of the world, following on the ravages of the economic extraversion provoked by the slave trade and the political subordination of the colonial period. Here, the historical experience of the African peoples is perfectly illuminating: Instead of fragile and disoriented economies, turned toward the former European metropolitan powers, the precolonial past offers the vision of perfectly integrated and complementary economies.

The liquidation of the great African political superstructures (centralized kingdoms, or empires that included several confederated ethnic or national groups) and the impoverishment of those that survived the colonial conquest have encouraged the belief that the only forms of political organization remaining were found at the level of the local community: lineages, clans, villages, "tribes." In such a context the present political regimes—variants of the European models of tyrannical or patrriarchal autarchies—appear in the eyes of foreign observers as elementary "tribal" games. Nonetheless, in the past, certain kingdoms and empires functioned as quasi-national units, belying the assumptions of outsiders (Wondji, 1981). Reference to this past also justifies the restoration of African solidarity at the continental level: The Sahara, for example, was never a barrier between black Africans and Arab-Berbers, but a common space across which exchanges of the most productive kind were carried out. As for the black world itself, whose unity has been so often proclaimed, might not this concept be reorganized on the basis of conscious relations of solidarity between mother Africa and the blacks of the Diaspora? Awareness of this solidarity can be reclaimed only by a new historiography, oriented toward the reaffirmation of our personality and of our unitary destiny (Dailly, forthcoming).

The third and final aspect of this heightened consciousness must include the awareness of a new form of technical and scientific efficiency. The colonial conquest in the end was the expression of the technical supremacy of Europe. Our resistance has never failed for lack of power, bravery, and initiative (as shown in strategy, tactics, and diplomacy), or for the lack of will to form a common front against imperialism. What most distinguished Africans from their adversaries were two centuries of technical scientific revolution that rendered Western civilization more efficient. This deficiency must be recognized without complacency; the universal history of sciences and techniques must permit us to evaluate with firmness and fairness the technological insufficiencies of African civilization. To assert this is not an apology for the West, nor blind admiration of the values on which Western civilization is based; is it not a sin to hide behind the romantic exaltation of our so-called spiritual civilization when faced with the urgency of development? In the applied sciences, African production has been characterized by elitism and esoteric consciousness, by the mysticism of thought and by purely artisanal technologies. The cause of this situation would obviously not reside in a supposed "African genius," a sort of racially defined essence, one specifically religious and inappropriate to a rational-scientific understanding of the world. A clear presentation must reinstate the analysis of all social formations and show just how they were propitious or not to scientific and technological innovation.

Thus is posed the double question of commitment and responsibility. Our responsibility for reconstructing our sense of identity, our ability to draw on the living forces of our past for the necessary inspiration to develop models of an original future, must reinforce our responsibility as citizens and as scholarly researchers, responsible for the future of our societies faced with the crisis of identity Africa has inherited from the colonial period. We are accountable to the ideals and methods of science as well. That is why the necessity of a committed research coincides with the necessity of objective research; that is why a consciousness continually deepened by the awareness of a historiography in the service of reconstruction and development implies rigorous respect for the principles of scientific research.

HISTORICAL RESEARCH AND THE TEACHING OF HISTORY

In terms of research, what is needed is to undertake, after having removed the myths and prejudices of the colonial period of racism, a scientific and objective analysis of the African past based on all the sources provided by both traditional cultures and universal historiography. If no one today believes in the Hegelian thesis of the ahistoricity of African societies, and no one pretends to explain Africa's situation by the insalubrity of its tropical climate and its geographical isolation in the past, it is no less true that certain prejudices have remained firmly alive (Ki-Zerbo, 1972). Thus the problem of historical sources in Africa has not yet been liberated from the fetishism of writing. Founded on a narrow definition of history in which the search for diverse, singular, and accidental facts is considered more important than the understanding of the structural determinants, this written tradition suggests that there is no history where there are no written sources. Certain Africanist scholars still echo this definition: "An eminent Africanist, after having noted the existence of African history, concludes on a fairly pessimistic note. He writes that African history is like a cloth where there are more holes than cloth" (Kaké, 1982: 20), thus evoking the lack of written documents on our history.

Instead of setting out to write the history of Africa by mobilizing all sources, even where this necessitated a preliminary overview of relatively new sources, African researchers have very often had a tendency to examine only those subjects for which there exist abundant sources. Thus African history often has been written from the point of view of the existing sources and not from the perspective of the problems that relate to the question of African consciousness. But these problems must be left behind in order to seek out and discover the sources even where they do not seem to exist, by the exploration of new lines of access to historical information, to reduce the disparity that persists in the understanding of different periods and regions. Hence the mutilation of the collective consciousness of the young nations for whom historical memory has thus been reduced to that of the groups that historiography has made emerge. Therefore, research must proceed to a global reconstruction of African history, that is, to a study of all periods and all peoples without exception, so that the history of Africa will no longer be only the history of kingdoms and empires of the past, or of the formation of colonial territories alone. This perspective is assuredly very difficult, but difficulty does not necessarily imply impossibility. It would permit us, in particular, to leave the heavily trodden paths of colonial history, for which the associated conceptual framework—rebaptized "the development of underdevelopment"—returns in the end to the study of specific cases of imperial expansion.

It would be more interesting to study precolonial history. This is the period when Africa was still master of its own destiny, a period for which reflection on the capacities of the historical initiatives of our peoples can be applied most usefully outside the colonialist control over theoretical suppositions. While colonial Africa cannot be analyzed properly without accounting for the factors of imperialism, the study of precolonial Africa, based on anthropological work, presupposes the establishment of scientific concepts and categories for which the constant evaluation constitutes a most valuable contribution to the theory of the social sciences. It is also the period of our history for which the mobilization of the essential sources of our own culture is most imperative. Oral traditions, in the sense in which this has been understood since the publication of *De la tradition orale* (Vansina, 1961), are not sufficient for these purposes; other methods must also be found and other forms of analysis explored and developed. It is in this field that the effort of reflection on and conceptualization of history demands greater originality and creativity, because new explanatory theories must be constructed.

Finally, in dealing with the precolonial period it is necessary to seize the specific idiom through which the historical consciousness of African peoples is expressed: the meaning of myths, legends, and symbols; the meaning of institutions and of customs; but above all the meaning of the type of discourse that formalizes them and makes them explicit. In other words, the comprehension of forms and of content of traditional history must allow the establishment of epistemological bases for an objective reconstruction and interpretation of the facts, to mediate—through a form of multidisciplinary collaboration—the passage from the discourse of oral history to a modern analytic form of discourse.

The establishment of a scientific history has thus become a necessity for contemporary Africa, not only because of the destruction of traditional societies under the weight of colonialism and the imposition of a capitalist mode of production, but also because the construction of new nations demands a new approach to history at a more general level. With the diffusion of writing and modern instruction, history, formerly the concern of families, clans, chiefdoms, or states, has now become the concern of peoples and nations. Public instruction has replaced the familial tutorial and initiatory schools, and new African nations need to develop a collective psyche by the entrenchment of their consciousness in the organic past of the peoples. Still, at the present stage of the precarious unitary evolution of these countries, this should not be confused with the past of a dynasty or of a particular ethnic group, no matter how brilliant these may seem; it is instead the past of these people in their diversity and in their unity, in their glorious moments and in their setbacks, that must be privileged.

African history must therefore become positive, critical, and relevant, by the establishment of demythologized facts, by the application of both internal and external critique to documents derived from oral tradition, to precolonial texts and colonial archives. It will distance itself thus from ideological history (or predominantly ideological), in the Marxist sense of mystification or of automystification, of codified illusions or of speculative chimeras, basing its discourse on real knowledge; that is, on the concrete analysis of practical problems that were posed in the past. It is thus that the passage from ideology to science (in the sense outlined by Marx and Engels) might be achieved.

But that does not signify that the African historian ought to give up all ideology or all mobilizing utopia, in the sense that Houtondji (1981) defines it; that is, of a coherent collection of ideals, of motivations, and of objective practices. As a guide for action, this ideology (or these mobilizing ideas) must promote and clarify all scientific practices, and, in terms of what is important for this analysis, incite historians to apply their science to the qualitative transformations of African societies.

As for teaching, it is not a question simply of taking the opposite point of view of colonial teaching, extraverted and Eurocentric, but also, and above all, to teach historical reflection. The discovery of the African past must enable the youth to penetrate its sociocultural milieu, to develop reflection by the consideration of evidence of larger unities in the reconstruction of events and by the search for the most pertinent articulations between historical periods. This means leaving the ghetto of "ethnologic" history so dear to colonialist practitioners, and stressing transethnic historical dynamics instead.

To take the point of view opposite to colonialist teaching, which glorified the merits and praised the good deeds of Western civilization, is to teach history from the point of view of the colonized and to implant teaching in the national-cultural patrimony of the Africans. The expansion of Europe in the world should no longer be studied as a phenomenon in itself, an object worthy of absolute interest; of greater interest is the "vision of the vanquished," the resistances and methods by which the structures of colonial oppression functioned. Forty years ago, colonial railways were studied exclusively as great works of civilization; today, historical inquiry focuses more on how these railways made possible colonial exploitation and how Africans perished from the horrible work that was imposed on them during the construction of these railways (Mémel-Foté, 1979). Further, to place Africa and Africans at the center of this teaching is to be opened up to world history on the basis of African examples. To take the case of railways: Historians cannot simply judge the effect of railways only on the classes that most benefited; they must also consider the impact of the process of railway construction on local societies. The "railway revolution" in Europe served particular interests, but railway construction there did not spare the lives of the masses in those countries whose societies this was supposed to transform; the peoples of Russian central Asia, for example, paid dearly for the construction of these works.

The development of historical reflection requires also the restitution to African history of its fundamental intelligibility. Born in the wake of ethnography, the historiography of the precolonial periods has long been a microhistory of ethnic groups, which privileged the description of migrations, of institutions, and of customs at the expense of any full understanding of historical dynamics. The indifference of the positivists to explanation or to explanatory theory justified their rejection of interpretations and of syntheses. In this fashion, teaching came to juxtapose segments of history, or even "ethnic history," instead of seeking the unity of historical processes, and the chronological articulations or underlying logic of these transformations. Bringing to bear concepts of mode of production, culture, ideology, social formation, and articulation permits the most daring historians to throw new light on the historical evolution of precolonial African societies. Considered, in fact, as an active tie to the past (Chesneaux, 1976), this type of history allows for greater clarity on problems of the present. The vision of world history from Africa is the vision of history from the perspective of the real problems in Africa. Where it used to bring its light to the construction of nations or to contribute to the restoration of cultural values, the scientific efforts of the historian must today predominate over the narcissistic vision of the past and against speculation lacking any foundation in the reality of experiences of the people.

Today, as formerly, Africa aspires to a unified consciousness. But this theme can play a negative role or a positive role. It plays a negative role if it implies a unified conscience in the old style, despite the fact that the communitarian basis of the traditional economy has collapsed, and despite the divisions that have been established. In this case, it camouflages these divisions, serving as a tool for the mystification of those who are disfavored by these divisions. On the other hand, it plays a positive role if it presupposes the recognition of these divisions, the scientific analysis of these divisions, of their consequences for the society, and the ways and means of the abolition of divisions. For all those who wish to be faithful to the past, the new unified conscience is not to be found in such an approach; it seeks not to perpetuate the divisions but to reduce them (Mémel-Foté, 1979). If our commitment assumes a vision of history that is seen as an active tie to the past, the African people in their present situation do not take great delight in the simple pleasures of remembered history, whatever its usefulness; instead, they need a history that contributes to the understanding of the problems of the present. This history must constantly open itself to the universal experience or derive from it, bringing to awareness examples and models from the transformation of other human societies.

But this vision requires our responsibility as researchers because the scientific spirit obliges us to put into action an objective and rational explanation of the facts, and thus removes us from the hasty and subjective justifications that would simply reinforce the old myths and prejudices still held by those who cling to racism and colonialism. In this way history will be able to contribute, and in part already does contribute, to the development of consciousness at both the national and African levels, to the affirmation of the spirit of responsibility, and to the formation of African citizens conscious of their place and of their role in today's society, as citizens in solidarity with all the people of the world who are undergoing the same necessities and who are influenced by the same realities.

REFERENCES

Abrams, P. (1982) Historical Sociology. Somerset: Open Press.

Académie Royalle des Sciences d'Outre Mer [ARSOM] (1983) Le Congo Belge durant la seconde guerre mondiale. Bruxelles.

Afigbo, A. E. (1975a) "Reflections on the history syllabus in Nigerian universities." Journal of the Historical Society of Nigeria 8, 1: 9-17.

———(1975b) "The flame of history blazing at Ibadan." Journal of the Historical Society of Nigeria 7, 4: 715-720.

———(1981) Ropes of Sand: Studies in Igbo History and Culture. Oxford: Oxford University Press.

Agassi, J. (1975) Sciences in Flux. Dordrecht, Netherlands: D. Reidel.

Agiri, B. A. (1972) "Kola in western Nigeria, 1850-1950: a history of the cultivation of *cola nitida* in Egba-Owade, Ijebu-Remo, Iwo, and Ota areas." Ph.D. dissertation, University of Wisconsin—Madison.

———(1981) "Slavery in Yoruba society in the nineteenth century," pp. 123-148 in P. Lovejoy (ed.) The Ideology of Slavery in Africa. Beverly Hills, CA: Sage.

Ajayi, J.F.A. (1961) "Historical education in Nigeria." Journal of the Historical Society of Nigeria 30: 206-213.

———(1965) Christian Missions in Nigeria, 1841-1891. Essex.

———(1969) "The continuity of African institutions under colonialism," pp. 189-200 in T. O. Ranger (ed.) Emerging Themes of African History. London: Heinemann.

Akiga, S. (1965) Akiga's Story: The Tiv Tribe as Seen by One of Its Members (R. East, trans.). London: Heinemann. (Originally published 1939)

Alagoa, E.J. (1972) A History of the Niger Delta: An Historical Interpretation of Ijo Oral Tradition. Ibadan.

Alexandre, P. (1965) "Protohistoire du groupe Beti-Bubu-Fang: Essai de synthèse provisoire." Cahiers d'Etudes Africaines 20: 503-560.

———(1976) "Avant propos." Cahiers d'Etudes Africaines 61-62.

———(1977) "Du haut du cocotier." Cahiers d'Etudes Africaines 68: 639-642.

Alpers, E. A. (1983) "Moquodisho in the nineteenth century: a regional perspective." Journal of African History 24, 4: 441-461.

———(1983) "Futa Benaadir: continuity and change in the traditional cotton industry of southern Somalia c. 1840-1980," in Laboratoire "Connaissance du Tiers Monde."

———and P.-M. Fontaine [eds.] (1982) Walter Rodney: Revolutionary and Scholar. Los Angeles: UCLA African Studies Center.

Amin, S. (1971) L'Afrique de l'Ouest bloquée: L'économie politique de la colonisation. Paris: Editions de Minuit.

Amselle, J. L. (1977) "L'anthropologie, ça sert à quoi?" Cahiers d'Etudes Africaines 68: 633-637.

———[ed.] (1978) Les sauvages à la mode. Paris: Le Sycomore.

———(1985) "Beyond Marxist anthropology," pp. 99-105 in B. Jewsiewicki and J. Letourneau (eds.) Mode of Production: The Challenge of Africa. Quebec: SAFI.

———and E. M'Bokolo [eds.] (1985) Au coeur de l'ethnie. Paris: La Decourverte.

Anderson, B. (1983) Imagined Communities: Reflections on the Origin and Spread of Nationalism. London: Verso/New Left.

Anderson, P. (1979) Lineages of the Absolutist State. London: Verso/New Left.

———(1981) Arguments in English Marxism. London: Verso.

Andersson, E. (1958) Messianic Popular Movements in the Lower Congo. Uppsala.

Atanda, J. A. (1973) The New Oyo Empire. Ibadan.

Atkinson, R. F. (1978) Knowledge and Explanation in History. Ithaca, NY: Cornell University Press.

Atmore, A. and S. Marks (1974) "The imperial factor in South Africa: towards a reassessment." Journal of Imperial and Commonwealth History 3, 1: 105-139.

Augé, M. (1969) Le rivage alladian: Organisation et évolution des villages alladian. Paris: ORSTOM.

———(1977) Pouvoirs de vie, pouvoirs de mort. Introduction à une anthropologie de la repression. Paris: Flammarion.

Austen, R. A. (1968) Northwest Tanzania Under German and British Rule, 1889-1939. New Haven, CT: Yale University Press.

Austin, D. (1964) Politics in Ghana, 1946-1960. London: Oxford University Press.

———(1980) "The transfer of power: why and how," pp. 3-34 in M. Morris-Jones (ed.) Decolonization and After: The British and French Experience. London: Frank Cass.

Austin, J. L. (1962) How to Do Things with Words. Oxford: Oxford University Press.

Avelot, R. (1905) "Recherches sur l'histoire des migrations dans le bassin de l'Ougoué et la région littorale adjacente." Bulletin de Géographie Historique et Descriptive 20, 3: 357-412.

Ayandele, E. A. (1966) The Missionary Impact on Modern Nigeria, 1842-1914. London.

———(1969) "How truly Nigerian is our Nigerian history?" African Notes 5, 2: 19-35.

Ayer, A. J. (1965) Philosophical Essays. London: Macmillan.

Azikiwe, N. (1937) Renascent Africa. Lagos.

Ba A. H. and J. Daget (1962) L'empire Peul du Macina. Paris: Mouton.

Babatunde, A. A. (1981) "Slavery in Yoruba society in the nineteenth century," pp. 123-148 in P. Lovejoy (ed.) The Ideology of Slavery in Africa. Beverly Hills, CA: Sage.

Badie, B. and P. Birnbaum (1979) Sociologie de l'Etat. Paris: Grasset.

Bakonzi, A. (1982) "The gold mines of Kilo-Moto in Northeastern Zaire, 1905-1960." Ph.D. dissertation, University of Wisconsin—Madison.

Balandier, G. (1963) "Sociologie dynamique et histoire à partir de faits Africains." Cahiers Internationaux de Sociologie 34: 3-12.

———(1967) Anthropologie Politique. Paris: Presses Universitaires de France.

———(1971a) Sens et puissance. Paris: Presses Universitaires de France.

————(1971b) Sociologie actuelle de l'Afrique noire. Dynamique sociale en Afrique Centrale. Paris: Presses Universitaires de France. (Originally published 1955)

Barnes, S. B. (1972) "Sociological explanation and natural science: a Kuhnian reappraisal." Archives Européennes de Sociologie 13, 2: 373-391.

Barry, B. (1972) Le royaume du Waalo: Le Senegal avant la conquête. Paris: Maspero.

————(1978) "Crise politique et importance des révoltes populaires au Futa-Djalon au XIXé siècle." Afrika Zamani 8-9: 51-61.

————(1980) "Le mouvement Omarien et le renouveau de l'Islam militant." Revue Sénégalaise d'Histoire 1, 1: 70-81.

————(n.d.) "La Sénégambie du XVème au XIXème siècles: Traite negrière, Islam, et conquête coloniale." (unpublished)

Bashizi C. (1980) "Paysannat et salariat agricole rural au Bushi (ancien Territoire de Kabare, Province du Kivu), 1920-1960." Ph.D. dissertation, Université Nationale du Zaire-Lubumbashi.

Bathily, A. (1974) "Islam and nineteenth century resistance movements in Senegambia." Presented at a conference at the University of Aberdeen.

————(1975) "Imperialism and colonial expansion in Senegal in the nineteenth century with particular reference to economic, social, and political developments in the Kingdom of Gajaaga." Ph.D. dissertation, University of Birmingham.

Bauer, D. F. (1977) Household and Society in Ethiopia. East Lansing: Michigan State University African Studies Center.

Bayart, J. F. (1979) L'Etat au Cameroun. Paris: Presses de la Foundation Nationale des Sciences Politiques.

————(1983a) "Les sociétés africaines face à l'Etat," Pouvoirs 25: 23-39.

————(1983b) "La revanche des sociétés Africaines." Politique Africaine 11: 95-127.

Bazin, J. (1979) "La production d'un récit historique." Cahiers d'Etudes Africaines 19, 1/4: 435-483.

————(1982) "Etat guerrier et guerres d'Etat," pp. 319-374 in J. Bazin and E. Terray (eds.) Guerres de Lignages et Guerres d'Etats en Afrique. Paris: Editions des Archives Contemporaines.

————and A. Bensa (1979) "Avant-Propos," pp. 7-23 in J. Goody, La raison graphique: La domestication de la pensée sauvage (translation of Goody, J., 1977a). Paris: Editions de Minuit.

Bechman, B. (1976) Organising the Farmers. Uppsala: Scandinavian Institute of African Studies.

Becker, C. (1975) "La Sénégambie à l'époque de la traite des esclaves." Revue Francaise d'Outre-Mer 235: 203-224.

————(1976) "Essai sur l'histoire du Saloum et du Rif." Bulletin de l'Institut Fondamental de l'Afrique Noire 38: 813-860.

————(1982) "La période pré-coloniale à la Sénégambie du XVe ou XVIIIe S." Presented to a conference on the history of Senegal.

————and V. Martin (1975) "Kajaar et Baal. Royaumes sénégalais et traite des esclaves au XVIIIè siècle." Revue Francaise d'Histoire d'Outre-Mer 62, 1: 270-300.

Becker, C. L. (1955) "What are historical facts?" Western Political Quarterly 8: 327-340.

Beinart, W. (1982) The Political Economy of Pondoland, 1870-1930. Cambridge: Cambridge University Press.
————and C. Bundy (1984) "Hidden struggles: Rural resistance in South Africa." Presented to the Peasants Seminar, Institute of Commonwealth Studies: London.
Bekombo Priso, M. (1981) "Essai sur le peuplement de la région cotière du Cameroun: les populations dites dwala," pp. 503-510 in C. Tardits (ed.) Contribution de la Recherche Ethnologique à l'Histoire des Civilisations du Cameroun, 1. Paris: Editions du CNRS.
Belepe Bope M'Binch (1982) "La triade des masques bwoom, mosh'amboy et ngandy a mwaawsh des Kuba du Zaire." Ph.D. dissertation, Université Catholique de Louvain.
Bellah, R. N. (1970) Beyond Belief. New York: Harper and Row.
Benveniste, E. (1974) Problèmes de linguistique générale. Paris: Gallimard.
Berger, I. (1981) Religion and Resistance: East African Kingdoms in the Precolonial Period. Tervuren: Musée Royal de l'Afrique Centrale.
————(1983) "Sources of class consciousness: South African women in recent labor struggles." International Journal of African Historical Studies 16, 1: 49-66.
Bernardi, B., C. Poni, and A. Triulzi [eds.] (1978) Fonti Orali/Oral Sources: Antropologica e storia/Anthropology and History. Milan: Franco Angali.
Bernstein, H. (1976) "Marxism and African history: Endre Sik and his critics." Kenya Historical Review 4, 1: 1-21.
————and J. Depelchin (1979/1980) "The object of African history: a materialist perspective." History in Africa 5: 4-19/6: 17-43.
Bernstein, R.J. (1980) "Philosophy in the conversation of mankind." Review of Metaphysics 33: 745-775.
Berry, S. (1983a) Fathers Work for their Sons: Accumulation, Mobility, and Class Formation in an Extended Yoruba Community. Berkeley: University of California Press.
————(1983b) "Agrarian crisis in Africa?" Presented to the ASA Annual Conference, Boston.
Berto, C. (1980) "L'invention de le Bretagne. Genèse social d'un stéreotype." Actes de la Recherche en Sciences Sociales 31: 45-72.
Bezy, F., J.-P. Peemans, and J. M. Wautelet (1981) Le Zaire: accumulation et sous-développement, 1960-1980. Louvain-la-Neuve: Presses Universitaires de Louvain.
Bimanyu, D. (1970) "A propos des premiers mouvements de resistance: cas de la révolte de l'expédition Dhanis (14 février-19 mars 1897)." Mémoire de License, Université Lovanium: Kinshasa.
Binford, L.B. (1981) Bones: Ancient Men and Modern Myths. New York: Academic.
Biobaku, S.O. (1957) The Egba and their Neighbours, 1842-1872. London.
————(1959) "Les responsabilites de l'historien africain en ce qui concerne l'Afrique." Présence Africaine (27/28) 2: 96-99.
————[ed.] (1975) Sources of Yoruba History. London.
Birmingham, D. (1976) "The forest and savanna of Central Africa," pp. 222-269 in J. Flint (ed.) The Cambridge History of Africa, 5. Cambridge: Cambridge University Press.

————and P. Martin [eds.] (1983) History of Central Africa. (2 volumes). London: Longman.

Bishikwabo, Chubaka (1982) "Histoire d'un État Shi en Afrique des Grands Lacs: Kaziba au Zaire (c. 1850-1940)." Ph. D. dissertation, Université Catholique de Louvain.

Bloch, M. (1954) The Historian's Craft. Manchester: Manchester University Press.

————(1969) "The rise of dependent cultivation and seignoral institutions," pp. 235-290 in The Cambridge Economic History of Europe, I. Cambridge: Cambridge University Press. (Originally published 1941)

————(1974) Apologie pour l'histoire ou le métier d'historien. Paris: A. Colin.

Bohannan, L. (1952) "A genealogical charter." Africa 22: 301-315.

Bonner, P. (1983) Kings, Commoners and Concessionaires: The Evolution and Dissolution of the Nineteenth Century Swazi State. Cambridge: Cambridge University Press.

Bontinck, F. (1976) "Voyageurs africains (1853-1855) en Afrique equatoriale: I. Robert Feruzi." Zaire-Afrique 107: 411-424.

Bony, J. and C. Wondji (1979) "La recherche historique et la construction et la nation africaine." Afrika Zamani 10/11: 21-25.

Boserup, E. (1974) "Environnement, population, et technologie dans les société primitives." Annales: E.S.C. XXIXs: 538-552.

Boubou, Hama and J. Ki-Zerbo (1980) "Place de l'histoire dans la société Africaine," pp. 65-76 in Histoire Générale de l'Afrique, I. Paris: UNESCO.

Bouche, D. (1968) "Autrefois notre pays s'appelait la Gaule." Cahiers d'Études Africaines VIII: 110-122.

Bouleque, J. (1968) "La Sénégambie du milieu du 15e siècle au début du 17e siècle." Ph. D. dissertation, Université de Paris-I.

————(1972) Les Luso-africains de Sénégambie au XVe-XIXe siècles. Dakar: Université de Dakar.

Bourdieu, P. (1983) "Vous avez dit populaire?" Actes de la Recherche en Sciences Sociales 46: 98-105.

Bouvier, J. C. [ed.] (1980) Tradition orale et identité culturelle. Problèmes et méthodes. Paris: Editions du CNRS.

Boy, R. (1931) "Le Sénégal d'autrefois. Etude sur le Toube papiers de Rawane Boy." B.C.E.H.S. AOF 3: 334-364.

Bozzoli, B. (1978) Labour, Townships and Protest. Johannesburg: Ravan.

————(1981) The Political Nature of the Ruling Class: Capital and Ideology in South Africa, 1980-1933. London: Routledge.

Bradbury, R. E. (1973) Benin Studies. London.

Brantley, C. (1983) The Giriama and Colonial Resistance in Kenya, 1800-1920. Berkeley: University of California Press.

Braudel, F. (1969) "Histoire et sciences sociales: la longue durée," pp. 41-83 in F. Braudel, Ecrits sur l'histoire. Paris: Flammarion.

Brausch, G. (1945) "La société Nkutshu." Bulletin des Juridictions Indigènes et du Droit Coutumier Congolais 13, 2/3: 29-89.

————(1953) "Les groupes sociaux des Ankutshu de la Haute Lokanye." Ph. D. dissertation, Université Libre de Bruxelles.

Breuilly, J. (1982) Nationalism and the State. Manchester: Manchester University Press.

Brietzke, P. (1982) Law, Development, and Ethiopian Revolution. New York: Associated University Press.

Broad, W. and N. Wade (1982) Betrayers of the Truth. New York: Simon and
Schuster.

Brooks, G. (1975) "Peanuts and colonialism: consequences of the commercialization
of peanuts in West Africa, 1830-1870." Journal of African History 16: 29-54.

Bruel, G. (1914) La France équatoriale Africaine. Le pays, les habitants, la colonisation, les pouvoirs publics. Paris: Larose.

Brunschwig, H. (1957) L'expansion allemande outre-mer du XVe siècle à nos jours.
Paris: Presses Universitaires de France.

———(1960) Mythes et réalities de l'impérialisme colonial francais, 1871-1914. Paris:
Colin.

———(1965) "Un faux problème: L'ethnohistoire." Annales: E.S.C. 20: 291-300.

Brunt, P. A. (1980) "On historical fragments and epistemes." Classical Quarterly 74:
477-494.

Buchanan, C. (1974) "The Kitara complex: the historical tradition of western
Uganda to the sixteenth century." Ph. D. dissertation, Indiana University.

Buijtenhuijs, R. (1982) Essays on Mau Mau: Contributions to Mau Mau historiography. Leiden: African Studies Centre.

Bundy, C. (1972) "The emergence and decline of a South African peasantry." African
Affairs 71: 369-387.

———(1979) The Rise and Fall of the South African Peasantry. Berkeley: University
of California Press.

———and W. Beinart (1984) "Hidden struggles: rural resistance in South Africa."
Presented to the Peasants Seminar, Institute of Commonwealth Studies,
London.

Burke, P. (1981) "People's history or total history?" in R. Samuel (ed.) People's
History and Socialist Theory. London: Routledge.

Cahiers d'Etudes Africaines 61/62 (1976) Special Issue: "Histoire Africaine: consta-
tations, contestations."

Callinicos, L. (1980) Gold and Miners. Johannesburg: Ravan.

Campbell, H. (1980/1981) "Walter Rodney: people's historian." Ufahamu 10, 1/2:
35-42.

Cell, J. W. (1980) "On the eve of decolonisation: the colonial office's plans for the
transfer of power in Africa." Journal of Imperial and Commonwealth History 8:
235-257.

———(1982) The Highest Stage of White Supremacy: The Origins of Segregation in
South Africa and the American South. Cambridge: Cambridge University Press.

Centre de Civilisation Burundaise (1981) La civilisation ancienne des peuples des
grands lacs. Paris: Karthala.

Centre méridional d'histoire sociale, des mentalités et des cultures (1981) Les inter-
médiaires culturels. Aix-en-Provence: Publications de l'Université de Provence.

Centro de Estudos Africanos (1982) "Towards a history of the national liberation
struggle in Mozambique: problematics, methodologies, analyses." London: The
History Workshop.

Centre National de Recherche Scientifique (1979) L'anthropologie en France: Situation actuelle et avenir. Paris: Editions du CNRS.

de Certeau, M. (1980a) La Culture au pluriel. Paris: Christian Bourgois.

———(1980b) L'invention du quotidien: I, Arts de faire. Paris: UGE.

Césard, E. (1931) "Histoires des rois du Kyamtwara d'après l'ensemble des traditions des familles regnantes." Anthropos 26: 533-543.

du Chaillu, P. (1863) Voyages et aventures dans l'Afrique équatoriale. Paris: M. Levy Frères.

Chamberlin, C. (1977) "Competition and conflict: the development of the bulk export trade in central Gabon during the nineteenth century." Ph.D. dissertation, Stanford University.

———(1978) "The migration of the Fang into central Gabon during the nineteenth century: a new interpretation." International Journal of African Historical Studies 11, 3: 429-456.

Chanock, M. (1972) "Development and change in the history of Malawi," pp. 429-446 in B. Pachai (ed.) The Early History of Malawi. London: Longman.

Charles, E. (1977) Precolonial Senegal: The Jolof Kingdom, 1800-1890. Boston: Boston University African Studies Center.

Chege, M. (1979) "The revolution betrayed: Ethiopia, 1974-1979." Journal of Modern African Studies 17, 3: 539-560.

Chesneaux, J. (1976) Du passé, faisons table rase? Paris: Maspero.

Chrétien, J.-P. (1970) "Une révolte au Burundi en 1934." Annales: E.S.C. 25, 6: 1678-1717.

———(1978) Review of Henige 1974b, in Revue Française d'Histoire d'Outre-Mer 65, 239: 262-263.

———(1979) "Anthropologie et histoire dans les sociétés non-européennes de tradition orale," pp. 155-161, 176 in Centre Nationale de la Recherche Scientifique.

———(1981) "Du hirsute au Hamite: les variations du cycle de Ruhatsi, fondateur du royaume du Burundi." History in Africa 8: 3-41.

———(1982a) "Intervention à la commission," pp. 480-481 in 15è Congres international des sciences historiques (Bucarest, août 1980), Actes IV, 1: Problèmes et méthodes de l'histoire orale. Bucarest.

———(1982b) "Féodalité ou féodalisation du Burundi sous le mandat belge," pp. 367-382 in Etudes africaines offerts à H. Brunschwig. Paris: E.H.E.S.S.

———(1984) "Nouvelles hypothèses sur les origines du Burundi: les traditions du Nord," pp. 11-53 in L. Ndoricimpa et C. Guillet (eds.) L'arbre-memoire: Traditions orales du Burundi. Paris: Karthala.

Cissoko, S.M. (1979) "Contribution à l'histoire politique des royaumes du Khasso dans le Haut-Fleuve Senegal des origines à la conquete française (XVIIe S.-1890)." Ph.D. dissertation, Université de Paris-I.

———(1980) "El Hadji Omar Tall et le mouvement du Jihad dans le Soudan occidental." Revue Sénégalaise d'Histoire 1, 1: 39-69.

Clarence-Smith, W.G. (1977) "For Braudel: a note on the 'Ecole des Annales' and the historiography of Africa." History in Africa IV: 275-281.

Clark, T.N. (1967) "Marginality, eclecticism, and innovation." Revue Internationale de Sociologie 3, 12: 22.

———(1973) Prophets and Patrons: The French University and the Emergence of the Social Sciences. Cambridge, MA: Harvard University Press.

Cliffe, L. (1983) "Zimbabwe: political economy and the contemporary scene," in Southern Africa: Retrospect and Prospect, proceedings of a seminar of May 30-June 1, 1983. Edinburgh: Center of African Studies.

————and J. Saul [eds.] (1972) Socialism in Tanzania, vol. I. Nairobi: East African Publishing.

Cohen, D. W. (1977) Womunafu's Bunafu. Princeton: Princeton University Press.

————(1980) "Reconstructing a conflict in Bunafu: seeking evidence outside the narrative tradition," pp. 208-209 in J. C. Miller (ed.) The African Past Speaks. Folkestone: Dawson-Archon.

————(1983) "Food production and food exchange in the precolonial Lakes Plateau Region," pp. 1-18 in R. Rotberg (ed.) Imperialism, Colonialism and Hunger: East and Central Africa. Lexington, MA: Lexington Books.

Coifman, V. B. 1969. "History of the Wolof State of Jolof until 1860." Ph. D. dissertation, University of Wisconsin—Madison.

Collectif: Section ivoirienne de l' Association des Historiens Africains. (1977) "Pour une réelle africanisation des programmes d'histoire." Africa Zamani 6/7: 157-163.

Colvin, L. (1972) "Kajor and its relations with Saint-Louis du Senegal, 1763-1861." Ph. D. dissertation, Columbia University.

————(1977) "Theoretical issues in historical international politics: the case of Senegambia." Journal of Interdisciplinary History 8: 23-44.

Comeliau, C. and H. Leclerq (1978) Economie non-marchande et développement. Louvain-La-Neuve: Bibliothèque Internationale des Sciences du Développement.

Congress of Cultural Freedom (1962) The West African Intellectual Community. Ibadan.

Connah, G. (1981) Three Thousand Years in Africa. London.

Cooper, F. (1979) "The problem of slavery in African studies." Journal of African History 20, 1: 103-105.

————(1981a) From Slaves to Squatters. New Haven, CT: Yale University Press.

————(1981b) "Africa and the world economy." African Studies Review XXIV, 2/3: 1-86.

————(1984) "Urban space, industrial time, and wage labor in Africa," pp. 7-50 in F. Cooper (ed.) Struggle for the City. Beverly Hills, CA: Sage.

Copans, J. [ed.] (1975) Anthropologie et Imperialisme. Paris: Maspero.

————(1977) "A la recherche de la théorie perdue: marxisme et structuralisme dans l'anthropologie française," Anthropologie et Sociétés 1: 137-158.

————(1980a) "D'un africanisme à l'autre," pp. 53-68 in A. Schwartz (ed.) Les faux prophètes de l'Afrique, ou l'afr(eu)canisme. Québec: Presses de l'Université Laval.

————(1980b) Les marabouts de l'arachide: La confrérie mouride et les paysans du Sénégal. Paris: Le Sycomore.

————(1982) "Mode de production, formation sociale ou ethnie: les silences d'une anthropologie marxiste." Working paper, Centre d'Etudes Africaines, Ecole des Hautes Etudes en Sciences Sociales: Paris.

Coquery-Vidrovitch, C. 1972. Le Congo au temps de grandes compagnies concessionaires (1899-1930). Paris: Mouton.

————(1976a) "Changes in African Historical Studies in France," pp. 200-209 in C. Fyfe (ed.) African Studies since 1945. A Tribute to Basil Davidson. London: Longman.

————[ed.] (1976b) "L'Afrique et la crise de 1930-1938." Special Issue of Revue Française d'Histoire d'Outre-mer 63, 3/4.

————[ed.] (1978a) Connaissance du Tiers-Monde. Paris: U.G.E.

————(1978b) "Mode de production, histoire africaine et histoire comparée." Revue Française d'Histoire d'Outre-Mer 65: 355-360.

————(1985) Afrique noire. Continuités et ruptures. Paris: Payot.

————and H. Moniot (1984) L'Afrique noire de 1800 à nos jours. Paris: Presses Universitaires de France. (Originally published 1974)

Cornet, J. (1972) Art de l'Afrique noire au pays du fleuve Zaire. Bruxelles: Arcade.

Coulon, C. (1981) Le marabout et le prince: Islam et pouvoir au Sénégal. Paris: Pedone.

Coupez, A. (1983) "Etudes Africaines en Belgique," Africa Tervuren 29: 16-18.

Coupland, R. (1938) East Africa and its Invaders. London: Clarendon.

Coutau-Begarie, H. (1983) Le phenomène "Nouvelle Histoire." Paris: Economica.

Cowen, M. P. (1972) "Differentiation in a Kenya location." Presented to the East African University Social Science Council Conference, Nairobi.

————(1979) "Capital and household production: the case of wattle in Kenya's Central Province, 1903-1964." Ph.D. dissertation, Cambridge University.

————(1982) "The British state and agrarian accumulation in Kenya," in M. Franshan (ed.) Industry and Accumulation in Africa. London: Heinemann Educational Books.

Crook, R. (1978) "Local elites and national politics in Ghana: a case study of local politics and political centralization in Offinso, 1945-1966." Ph.D. dissertation, University of London.

Cruise O'Brien, D. (1971) The Mourides of Senegal. Oxford: Clarendon.

————(1975) Saints and Politicians. Cambridge: Cambridge University Press.

Cruise O'Brien, R. (1972) White Society in Black Africa: The French of Senegal. Evanston: Northwestern University Press.

————[ed.] (1979) The Political Economy of Underdevelopment: Dependence in Senegal. Beverly Hills, CA: Sage.

Crummey, D. (1980) "Abyssinian feudalism." Past and Present 89: 115-138.

————(1981) "State and society: nineteenth century Ethiopia," pp. 227-249 in D. Crummey and C.C. Stewart (eds.) Modes of Production in Africa. Beverly Hills, CA: Sage.

————(forthcoming) "Banditry and resistance: noble and peasant in nineteenth century Ethiopia," to appear in a forthcoming volume on social protest edited by D. Crummey. London: Heinemann.

————and C.C. Stewart [eds.] (1981) Modes of Production in Africa. Beverly Hills, CA: Sage.

Cultru, P. (1910) Histoire du Sénégal du XVIe Siècle à 1870. Paris: Larose.

Curtin, P. D. [ed.] (1967) Africa Remembered: Narratives by West Africans from the Era of the Slave Trade. Madison: University of Wisconsin Press.

————(1968) "Field techniques for collecting and processing oral data." Journal of African History 9, 3: 367-385.

————(1969) The Atlantic Slave Trade: A Census. Madison: University of Wisconsin Press.

————(1975) Economic Change in Precolonial Africa: Senegambia in the Era of the Slave Trade. (2 volumes). Madison: University of Wisconsin Press.

Dailly, C. (forthcoming) "Intellectuels Afro-Americains et intellectuels Africaines: Influences reciproques de la fin du XIXe siècle à la deuxième guerre mondiale." Ph.D. dissertation, Université de Paris III.

de Dampierre, E. (1967) Un ancien royaume Bandia du haut Oubangui Paris: Plon.

Danto, A. C. (1965) Analytical Philosophy of History. Cambridge: Cambridge University Press.

Dark, P.J.C. (1973) An Introduction to Benin Art and Technology. Oxford.

Darwin, J. (1984) "British decolonization since 1945: A pattern or puzzle?" Journal of Imperial and Commonwealth History 12: 187-209.

Davidson, B. (1952) Report from Southern Africa. London: Allison and Busby.

———(1957) Review of Hodgkin, 1956, in Universities and Left Review 1: 71-72.

———(1959) Old Africa Rediscovered. London: Gollancz.

———(1961) Black Mother. London: Gollancz.

———(1977) "Questions about nationalism," African Affairs 76: 39-46.

Davies, R. (1979) Capital, State and White Labour in South Africa, 1900-1960. An Historical Materialist Analysis of Class Formation and Class Relations. Brighton: Harvester.

Deblé, L. and P. Hugon [eds.] (1982) Vivre et Survivre dans les villes Africaines. Paris: Presses Universitaires de France.

Dee, J. H. (1978, 1979) "Levi-Strauss at the Theban Gates." Classical World 72: 257-261.

Delafosse, M. (1912) Haut-Sénégal-Niger. (3 volumes). Paris: Larose.

Deleuze, G. (1968) Différence et repétition. Paris: Presses Universitaires de France.

Delius, P. (1982) "Inboekselings and oorlams: the creation and transformation of a servile class." Journal of Southern African Studies 8, 2: 214-242.

———(1983) The Land Belongs to Us: The Pedi Polity in the Nineteenth Century. London: Heinemann.

Délivré, A. (1974) L'histoire des rois d'Imerina. Interprétation d'une tradition orale. Paris: Klincksieck.

Demunter, P. (1975) Masses rurales et luttes politiques au Zaire. Le processus de politisation des masses rurales au Bas-Zaire. Paris: Anthropos.

Denis, M. (1931) Histoire militaire de l'A.E.F. Paris: Imprimérie Nationale.

Denoon, D. (1983) Settler Capitalism: The Dynamics of Dependent Development in the Southern Hemisphere. Oxford: Clarendon.

———and A. Kuper (1970) "Nationalist historians in search of a nation: the 'New Historiography' in Dar es Salaam." African Affairs 69: 329-349.

Depelchin, J. (1975) "Towards a problematic history of Africa." Tanzania Zamani 18: 1-9.

———(1977) "African history and the ideological reproduction of exploitative relations of production." African Development 2, 1: 43-60.

———(1978) "The coming of age of political economy in African studies." International Journal of African Historical Studies 11, 4: 711-720.

Derrida, J. (1967) De la grammatologie. Paris: Editions de Minuit.

Deschamps, H. [ed.] (1970, 1971) Histoire Générale de l'Afrique. (2 volumes). Paris: Presses Universitaires de France.

Detienne, M. (1981) L'invention de la mythologie. Paris: Gallimard.

Devisch, R. (1981) Se re-créer femme. Manipulation semantique d'une situation d'infecondité chez les Yaka. Paris: Le Sycomore.

Devisse, J. (1976) "L'histoire de l'Afrique: Enseignement et recherche." Comptes rendus trimestriels de l'Académie des Sciences d'Outre-Mer 36: 611-618.

———(1981) "Recherche sur l'Afrique: l'histoire," pp. 630-647 in Etudes Africaines en Europe, I. Paris: Karthala.

d'Hertefelt, M. (1971) Les Clans du Rwanda ancien. Eléments d'ethnosociologie et d'ethnohistoire. Tervuren: Musée Royal de l'Afrique Centrale.

──── and A. Coupez (1964) La royauté sacrée de l'ancien Rwanda. Tervuren: Musée Royal de l'Afrique Centrale.

d'Hertefelt, M., A. A. Troubowrst, et J. Scherer (1962) Les anciens royaumes de la Zone Interlacustre méridionale: Rwanda, Burundi, Buha. Tervuren: Musée Royal de l'Afrique Centrale.

Diagne, P. (1967) Pouvoir politique traditionnel en Afrique noire. Paris: Présence Africaine.

──── (1977) "Renaissance et problèmes culturels en Afrique," pp. 213-307 in Introduction à la culture Africaine. Paris: UNESCO.

──── (1978) "Le néolithique dans l'aire Sénégambienne et dans les régions adjacentes: Contribution à la préhistoire de l'ouest africain." Ph.D. dissertation, Université de Paris.

Diallo, T. (1972) Les institutions politiques du Fouta Djalon au XIXe Siècle. Dakar: Institut Fondamental de l'Afrique Noire.

Diao, Y. (1933) "La Sénégal d'autrefois. Etude sur les cahiers de Nyoro Diao publiés par R. Rousseau." B.C.E.H.S. AOF 16, 2: 237-298.

Dike, K. O. (1956) Trade and Politics in the Niger Delta, 1830-1885. London.

──── and J. F. A. Ajayi (1968) "African Historiography," pp. 394-400 in D. L. Sills (ed.) International Encyclopedia of the Social Sciences. New York: Macmillan.

Diop, A. B. (1981) La société Wolof. Paris: Karthala.

Diop, C. A. (1955) Nations nègres et Culture. Paris: Editions Africaines.

──── (1960) L'Afrique noire précoloniale. Paris: Présence Africaine.

──── (1981) Civilisation et Barbarie. Paris: Présence Africaine.

Diouf, M. (1980) "Le Kajoor au XIXe siècle et la conquête coloniale." Ph.D. dissertation, Université de Paris-I.

Douglas, M. (1966) Purity and Danger. New York: Praeger.

Dozon, J. P. (1977) "Les leçons de l'histoire ou l'ethnologie dans tous ses états." Unpublished paper. Abidjan: ORSTOM.

Duby, G. and G. Lardreau (1980) Dialogues. Paris: Flammarion.

Dumont, L. (1966) Homo Hierarchicus: Essai sur le système des castes. Paris: Gallimard.

──── (1971) "Religion, politics and society in the individualistic universe," in Proceedings of the Royal Anthropological Institute for 1970.

──── (1977) Homo Aequalis: Genèse et épanouissement de l'idéologie économique. Paris: Gallimard.

Dunn, J. (1972) "But how will they eat?" Transactions of the Historical Society of Ghana 13: 113-124.

──── and A. F. Robertson. (1973) Dependency and Opportunity: Political Change in Ahafo. Cambridge: Cambridge University Press.

Durkheim, E. (1915) The Elementary Forms of Religious Life. New York: Macmillan.

Duviols, P. (1979) "La dinastia de los Incas: monarquia o diarquea? Argumentos heuristicos a favor de una tesis structuralista." Journal de la Société des Americanists 66: 67-83.

Echard, N. (1975) L'expérience du passé. Histoire de la société paysanne hausa de l'Ader. Niamey: Institut de Recherches en Sciences Humaines.

————and P. Bonté (1976) "Histoire et Histoires. Conception du passé chez les Hausa et les twareg Kel Gress de l'Ader (République du Niger)." Cahiers d'Etudes Africaines 16, 1/2: 237-296.

Eggan, F. (1967) "From history to myth: a Hopi example," pp. 33-53 in D. Hymes and W. Little (eds.) Studies in Southwestern Ethnolinguistics. Paris: Mouton.

Egharevba, J. (1956) A Short History of Benin. Ibadan. (Originally published 1934)

Eickelman, D. F. (1976) Moroccan Islam. Austin: University of Texas Press.

Ekechi, F. (1981) Missionary Enterprise and Rivalry in Igboland, 1857-1914. London.

Ekundare, R. O. (1973) An Economic History of Nigeria. London.

Ellis, G. (1980) "Feudalism in Ethiopia: a further comment on paradigms and their use." Northeast African Studies 1, 3: 91-97.

Elphick, R. (1974) Kraal and Castle. New Haven: Yale University Press.

————and H. Giliomee [eds.] (1979) The Shaping of South African Society, 1652-1820. London: Longman.

Equiano, Olaudah. (1789) The Interesting Narrative of the Life of Olaudah Equiano or Gustavus Vassa, the African, Written by Himself. London.

Etudes d'Histoire Africaine, VIII (1979) Special issue on Histoire de l'Enseignement en Afrique Centrale.

Etudes Rurales (1970) Special issue on "Terroirs Africains et Malagaches." No. 37-39.

Eynikel, H. (1984) Congo Belge. Portrait d'une société coloniale. Paris-Gembloux: Duculot.

Fabian, J. (1983a) "Missions and the colonization of African languages: development in the former Belgian Congo." Canadian Journal of African Studies 17: 165-187.

————(1983b) Time and the Other: How Anthropology Makes Its Objects. New York: Columbia University Press.

Fage, J. D. (1969) "Slavery and the slave trade in the context of West African history." Journal of African History 10, 3: 393-404.

————(1971) "Continuity and change in the writing of West African history." African Affairs 70: 236-251.

Fall, B. (1984) "Le travail forcé en Afrique occidentale française, 1900-1946: Cas du Sénégal, de la Guinée, et du Soudan." Ph.D. dissertation, Université de Dakar.

Fall, Y. (1982) L'Afrique et la naissance de la carthographie moderne. Paris: Karthala.

Fanon, F. (1961) Les damnés de la terre. Paris: Maspero.

Feierman, S. (1974) The Shambaa Kingdom: A History. Madison: University of Wisconsin Press.

————(1979) "Change in African therapeutic systems." Social Science and Medicine XIIIB, 4: 277-284.

————(1984) "The social origins of health and healing in Africa." Presented to the ASA Annual Conference: Los Angeles.

Feltz, G. (1981) "Une Introduction à l'histoire de l'enseignement en Afrique Centrale (XIXe - XXe siècles): idéologies, pouvoirs et sociétés." Bulletin de l'Institut Historique Belge de Rome 51: 351-399.

Fernandez, J.W. (1978) "African religious movements." Annual Review of Anthropology 7: 195-234.

————(1982) Bwiti: An Ethnography of the Religious Imagination in Africa. Princeton, NJ: Princeton University Press.

Ferro, M. (1983) Comment on raconte l'Histoire aux enfants à travers le monde entier. Paris: Payot.

Fetter, B. (1971) "African associations in Elizabethville, 1910-1935: their origins and development. Etudes d'Histoire Africaine VI: 205-233.

———(1983) Colonial Rule and Regional Imbalance in Central Africa. Boulder, CO: Westview.

Feyerabend, P. (1975) Against Method. London: Verso.

Finnegan, R. (1970) Oral Literature in Africa. Oxford: Clarendon.

Firth, R. (1981) History and Traditions of Tikopia. London: Wellington.

Fischer, R. (1970) Twilight Tales of the Black Baganda. London: F. Cass. (Originally published 1910)

Flint, J. (1983) "Planned decolonization and its failure in Africa." African Affairs 82: 389-411.

Foner, E. (1983) Nothing but Freedom. Emancipation and its Legacy. Baton Rouge: Louisiana State University Press.

Ford, J. (1971) The Role of Trypanosomiases in African Ecology: A Study of the Tsetse Fly Problem. Oxford: Clarendon.

Forde, D. (1956) Efik Traders of Old Calabar. London.

Foucault, M. (1973) The Order of Things: An Archaeology of the Human Sciences. New York: Random House (Originally published 1969)

Founou-Tchwiga, B. (1981) La surexploitation de la force de travail en Afrique: Considérations théoriques et études de cas. Paris: Silex.

Franceschi, P. (1977) Au Congo jusqu'au cou: Chez les pygmées de la forêt équatoriale. Paris: Hatier.

Frederickson, G. (1981) White Supremacy: A Comparative Study on American and South African History. Oxford: Clarendon.

Freund, B. (1983) "Labor and labor history in Africa." Presented to the ASA Annual Conference, Boston, MA.

Fyfe, C. [ed.] (1976) African Studies since 1945: A Tribute to Basil Davidson. London: Longman.

Gahama, J. (1983) Le Burundi sous l'administration Belge. La période du mandat 1919-1939. Paris: Karthala.

Gallagher, J. [A. Seal (ed.)] (1982) The Decline, Revival and Fall of the British Empire. Cambridge: Cambridge University Press.

———and R.E. Robinson (1953) "The Imperialism of Free Trade." Economic History Review (Series 2) 6: 1-15.

Gbadamosi, T.G.O. (1978) The Growth of Islam among the Yoruba, 1841-1908. London.

Geertz, C. (1973) The Interpretation of Culture. New York: Basic Books.

Gellar, S. (1976) Structural Changes and Colonial Dependency: 1885-1945. Beverly Hills, CA: Sage.

Le Genre Humain (1980) No. 3: Special issue on "Pensez, Classer." Paris: Complexe.

———(1982) No. 5: Special issue on "La rumeur." Paris: Complexe.

Gifford, P. (1982) "Misconceived dominion: the creation and disintegration of federation in British central Africa," pp. 387-416 in P. Gifford and W.R. Louis (eds.) The Transfer of Power in Africa. New Haven, CT: Yale University Press.

———and W.R. Louis [eds.] (1982) The Transfer of Power in Africa: Decolonization, 1940-1960. New Haven, CT: Yale University Press.

Gilkes, P. (1975) The Dying Lion. London: Julian Friedmann.

Godelier, M. (1984) L'idéel et le matériel. Pensées, économies, sociétés. Paris: Fayard.

Goldstein, L.J. (1976) Historical Knowing. Austin: University of Texas Press.

Goldsworthy, D. (1970) "Conservatives and decolonization." African Affairs 69: 278-281.

——(1971) Colonial Issues in British Politics, 1945-1961. Oxford: Clarendon.

Goody, J.R. (1961) "Religion and ritual: the definitional problem." British Journal of Sociology 12: 142-164.

——(1977a) The Domestication of the Savage Mind. Cambridge: Cambridge University Press.

——(1977b) "Mémoire et apprentissage dans les sociétiés avec et sans écriture: la transmission du Bagre." L'Homme 17, 1: 29-52.

——and I. Watt (1963) "The consequences of literacy." Comparative Studies in Society and History 5: 304-345.

Gorju, J. (1920) Entre le Victoria, l'Albert et l'Edouard. Rennes: Impriméries Oberthur.

——[ed.] (1938) Face au Royaume Hamite. Le Royaume frère de l'Urundi. Bruxelles: Vram.

Gorog-Karady, V. (1981) Littérature orale d'Afrique noire. Bibliographie Analytique. Paris: Larose.

Gramsci, A. (1949) "Note sul Machiavelli, sulla politica è sullo stato moderno," pp. 3-17 in Collected Works Volume 5. Turin: Einandi.

——(1971) Selections from the Prison Notebooks (edited and translated by G. Hoare and G.N. Smith). New York: International.

Gran. G. [ed.] (1979) Zaire: The Political Economy of Underdevelopment. New York: Praeger.

Gray, R. (1972) Review of M. Wilson and L. Thompson (eds.), The Oxford History of South Africa, in Race 14: 83-84.

——(1981) "Khalai-Khalai: people's history in Mozambique." People's Power in Mozambique, Angola and Guinea-Bissau 18: 3-17.

Greenberg, S.B. (1980) Race and State in Capitalist Development: Comparative Perspectives. New Haven, CT: Yale University Press.

Gueye, M. (1966) "La fin de l'esclavage à Saint-Louis et à Gorée en 1848," Bullétin de l'Institut Fondamental de l'Afrique Noire 28: 637-656.

——(1983) L'Afrique et l'esclavage. Paris: Martinsart.

Guiral, P. and E. Temine (1977) L'idée de race dans la pensée politique française contemporaine. Paris: Centre National de Recherche Scientifique.

Gutkind, C.W. (1977) "The Western academic abroad: an African response." Issue 7: 8-13.

Guy, J.J. (1979) The Destruction of the Zulu Kingdom. London: Longman.

Guyer, J. (1981) "Household and community in African studies." African Studies Review XXIV, 2/3: 87-137.

Hall, J. (1828) The Old Religion. London: W.S. Tansby.

de Halleux, G. et al. (1972/1973) Bibliographie Analytique pour l'Agronomie Tropicale: Zaire, Rwanda, Burundi. 2 volumes.

Halliday, F. and M. Molyneux (1981) The Ethiopian Revolution. London: Verso/ New Life.

Hardy, G. (1921) La mise en valeur du Sénégal, de 1817 à 1854. Paris: Larose.
———(1943) Histoire de la colonisation française. Paris: Larose.
Hargreaves, J. (1979) The End of Colonial Rule in West Africa. London: Macmillan.
———(1982) "Toward the transfer of power in British West Africa," pp. 117-140 in P. Gifford and W. R. Louis (eds.) The Transfer of Power in Africa. New Haven, CT: Yale University Press.
———(1983) Review of Gallagher, J. 1982. International Journal of African Historical Studies 16: 728-729.
Harris, G. (1978) Casting Out Anger. Cambridge: Cambridge University Press.
Harris, R. [ed.] (1975) The Political Economy of Africa. Boston, MA: Schenkman.
Hedges, D. (1978) "Trade and politics in Southern Mozambique and Zululand in the eighteenth and early nineteenth centuries." Ph.D. dissertation, University of London.
Heller, A. (1982) A Theory of History. London: Routledge and Kegan Paul.
Hemson, D. (1979) "Class consciousness and migrant labour: Dockworkers in Durban." Ph.D. dissertation, University of Warwick.
Henige, D. (1974a) "Reflections on early Interlacustrine chronology: an essay in source criticism." Journal of African History 15, 1: 27-41.
———(1974b) The Chronology of Oral Tradition: Quest for a Chimera. Oxford: Clarendon.
———(1974c) "Kingship in Elmina before 1869." Cahiers d'Etudes Africaines 14: 500-516.
———(1982a) "Truths yet unborn? Oral traditions as a casualty of culture contact." Journal of African History 23, 3: 395-412.
———(1982b) Oral Historiography. London: Longman.
de Heusch, L. (1954) "Autorité et prestige dans la société Tetela." Zaire 7: 1011-1027.
———(1972) Le roi ivre ou l'origine de l'Etat. Paris: Gallimard.
———(1982) Rois nés d'un coeur de vache. Paris: Gallimard.
Heyer, F. (1982) "Some aspects of dependence and independence of the Orthodox Church on the feudal class of Ethiopia." Northeast African Studies 4, 1: 35-38.
Hiernaux, J. (1970) "La Diversité biologique des groupes ethniques," pp. 53-62 in H. Deschamps (ed.) Histoire Générale de l'Afrique Noire, I. Paris: Presses Universitaires de France.
Hindess, B. and P. Q. Hirst (1975) Precapitalist Modes of Production. London: Routledge and Kegan Paul.
History and Theory (1981) "Bibliography of works in the philosophy of history, 1973-1977."
History Workshop Journal (1976) "Editorial." 1: 1-8; 2: 1-4.
Hiwet, A. (1975) "Ethiopia: from autocracy to revolution." Review of African Political Economy: Occasional paper No. 1: London.
Hoben, A. (1973) Land Tenure among the Amhara of Ethiopia. Chicago: University of Chicago Press.
———(1975) "Family, land and class in northern Europe and northern highland Ethiopia," pp. 157-170 in H. Marcus (ed.) Proceedings of the first U.S. conference on Ethiopian Studies. East Lansing: Michigan State University African Studies Center.
Hobsbawm, E. and T. Ranger [eds.] (1983) The Invention of Tradition. Cambridge: Cambridge University Press.

Hochegger, H. (1966) "Avant-Propos," in Le mariage, la vie familiale, et l'évolution coutumière chez diverses ethnies de la Province de Bandundu. Banningville: Publications du Centre Ethnologique.

Hodgkin, T. (1956) Nationalism in Colonial Africa. London: Muller.

———[ed.] (1960) Nigerian Perspectives: An Historical Anthology. London.

Holland, R. F. (1984) "The imperial factor in British strategies from Attlee to Macmillan, 1945-63." Journal of Imperial and Commonwealth History 12: 165-186.

———and G. Rizvi (1984) "Perspectives on imperialism and decolonization." Journal of Imperial and Commonwealth History 12: 1-209.

Holden, W. C. (1866) The Past, Present, and Future of the Kaffir Race. London: W. C. Holden.

Holton, G. (1973) Thematic Origins of Scientific Thought. Cambridge, MA: Harvard University Press.

Hoover, J. (1978a) "Mythe et remous historiques: A Lunda response to de Heusch." History in Africa 5: 63-80.

Hoover, J. J. (1978b) "The seduction of Ruwej: reconstructing Ruund history: The nuclear Lunda (Zaire, Angola, Zambia)." Ph. D. dissertation, Yale University.

Hopkins, A. G. (1973) An Economic History of West Africa. London: Longman.

———(1975) "On importing A. G. Frank into Africa," Economic History Review 2, 1: 13-21.

———(1980) "Africa's age of improvement." History in Africa 7: 141-160.

Horowitz, D. (1970) "Attitudes of British conservatives towards decolonization in Africa." African Affairs 69: 9-26.

Horowitz, R. (1967) The Political Economy of South Africa. London: Weidenfeld and Nicolson.

Houghton, H. (1964) The Economy of South Africa. Cape Town: Oxford University Press.

Houtondji, P. (1977) Sur la Philosophie Africaine. Paris: Maspero.

———(1981) "Que peut la philosophie?" Presence Africaine 119: 49-71.

Hulstaert, G. (1937) Le mariage des Nkundo. Bruxelles: Académie Royale des Sciences Coloniales.

Huybrechts, A. (1970) Transports et structures de développement au Congo: Etudes du progrès économique de 1900 à 1970. Paris: Mouton.

Idowu, H. O. (1969) "Assimilation in nineteenth century Senegal," Cahiers d'Etudes Africaines 9: 194-218.

———(1970) "The Conseil General in Senegal, 1879-1920." Ph. D. dissertation, University of Ibadan.

Ikime, O. (1979) "Through changing scenes: Nigerian history yesterday, today, and tomorrow." Inaugural address, 1979: Ibadan University.

———[ed.] (1980) Groundwork of Nigerian History. Ibadan: Longman.

Iliffe, J. (1969) Tanganyika under German Rule, 1905-1912. Cambridge: Cambridge University Press.

———[ed.] (1971) Modern Tanzanians. Nairobi: East African Publishing.

———(1979) A Modern History of Tanganyika. Cambridge: Cambridge University Press.

———(1983) The Emergence of African Capitalism. London: Macmillan.

Innes, D. (1984) Anglo-American and the Rise of Modern South Africa. London: Heinemann.

Institute of Commonwealth Studies. Collected seminar papers on the Societies of Southern Africa in the Nineteenth and Twentieth Centuries; produced annually from 1970. London: University of London.

Iroko, F. A. (1977) "Problèmes de périodisation en Histoire Africaine," Afrika Zamani 6-7: 103-140.

Irwin, P. (1981) Liptako Speaks: History from Oral Traditions in Africa. Princeton: Princeton University Press.

Isaacman, A. (1976) The Tradition of Resistance in Mozambique. Berkeley: University of California Press.

Isichei, E. [ed.] (1982) Studies in the History of Plateau State, Nigeria. London.

Izard, M. (1970) Introduction à l'histoire des royaumes Mossi. Paris: Centre national de la Recherche Scientifique.

Janzen, J. (1983) "Preface." African Studies Review XXIV, 2/3: v-vi.

Jefferson, T. (1955) "20 September 1787," in The papers of Thomas Jefferson. Princeton: Princeton University Press.

Jeffries, R. (1978) Class, Power and Ideology: The Railwaymen of Sekondi-Takoradi. Cambridge: Cambridge University Press.

————(1982) "Rawlings and the political economy of underdevelopment in Ghana." African Affairs 81: 307-317.

————(1983) "Beyond the Crisis in African Studies." West Africa 16: 1178-1180.

Jewsiewicki, B. (1972) "Notes sur l'histoire socio-économique du Congo, 1880-1960." Etudes d'Histoire Africaine III: 209-241.

————(1975) "Agriculture itinerante et économie capitaliste. Histoire des essais de modernisation de l'agriculture africaine au Zaire à l'époque coloniale." mimeographed manuscript: Lubumbashi.

————(1976) "La contestation sociale et la naissance du prolétariat Africaina au Zaire au cours de la prémière moitié du XXe siécle." Canadian Journal of African Studies 10, 1: 47-71.

————(1978) "Histoire économique d'une ville coloniale, Kisangani, 1877-1960." Les Cahiers du CEDAF 5.

————[ed.] (1979a) "Contributions à l'histoire de l'agriculture et de la pèche en Afrique Centrale." Special issue of African Economic History, VII.

————(1979b) "L'histoire en Afrique ou le commerce des idées usagées." Canadian Journal of African Studies, XIII, 1-2: 69-88.

————(1980) "Les Archives administratives zairoises de l'époque coloniale." Annales Aequatoria 1: 169-184.

————(1981a) "Histoire monument ou histoire conscience." Canadian Journal of African Studies 15, 3: 543-551.

————(1981b) "The production of history and social conscience, or how to 'civilize' the Other." History in Africa 8: 73-87.

————[ed.] (1984) Etat Independent du Congo, Congo Belge, République Démocratique du Congo, République du Zaire . . .? Québec: ACEA/SAFI.

————and J.-P. Chrétien [eds.] (1984) Sociétés rurales et technologies en Afrique Centrale et Occidentale au XXe Siècle. Québec: SAFI.

Jewsiewicki, B., Kilola Lema and J.-L. Vellut (1973) "Documents pour servir à l'histoire sociale du Zaire: Grèves dans le Bas-Congo en 1945." Etudes d'Histoire Africaine V: 155-188.

Jewsiewicki, B. and J. Létourneau [eds.] (1985) Mode of Production: the Challenge of Africa. Québec: SAFI.

Johnson, G. W. (1971) The Emergence of Black Politics in Senegal: The Struggle for Power in the Four Commmunes, 1900-1920. Stanford: Stanford University Press.

Johnson, J. 1974. "The Almanate of Futa Toro, 1770-1886: a political history." Ph. D. dissertation, University of Wisconsin—Madison.

Johnson, R. (1978) "Thompson, Genovese, and socialist-humanist history." History Workshop 6: 79-100.

Johnson, S. (1921) History of the Yorubas. London. (Originally published 1897)

Johnston, H. H. (1902) The Uganda Protectorate. London: Hutchinson.

Johnstone, F. A. (1970) "White prosperity and white supremacy in South Africa today." African Affairs 69: 124-140.

————(1976) Class, Race and Gold: A Study of Class Relations and Racial Discrimination in South Africa. London: Routledge and Kegan Paul.

de Jonghe, E. (1908) "L'activité ethnographique des Belges au Congo." Bullétin de la Société Belge d'Études Coloniales 5: 1-37.

————(1959) "Questionnaire ethnographique relatif au Congo Belge avec quelques indications bibliographiques." Congo 2: 1-37.

Journal of African History (1983) Special issue on "The family in Africa," XXIV, 2.

Journal of Southern African Studies. (1983) Special issue on "Women in southern Africa," X, 1.

Joutard, Ph. (1983) Ces voix qui nous viennent du passé. Paris: Hachette.

Judt, T. (1979) "A clown in regal purple: social history and the historian." History Workshop 7: 66-94.

K. W. [Tito Gabafusa Winyi] (1935, 1936, 1937) "The kings of Bunyoro-Kitara." Uganda Journal 3: 55-60; 4: 75-83; 5: 53-67.

Kaba, L. (1974) "Histoire Africaine et idéologie." Afrika Zamani 2: 10-20.

Kagame, A. (1956) La philosophie Bantu-Rwandaise de l'Etre. Bruxelles: Académie Royale des Sciences Coloniales.

Kagwa, A. (1971) The Kings of Buganda (trans.) M.S.M. Kiwanuka. Nairobi: East African Publishing. (Originally published 1901)

Kaké, I. B. (1982) Combats pour l'histoire Africaine. Paris: Presence Africaine.

Kandt, R. (1905) Caput Nili. Berlin: D. Reimer.

Kane, O. (1982) "L'Islamisation de la Sénégambie." Presented to a conference on the history of Senegal.

Kaniki, M. [ed.] (1980) Tanzania Under Colonial Rule. London: Longman.

Kaplan, D. E. (1977) "Class conflict, capital accumulation and the state: an historical analysis of the state in twentieth century South Africa." Ph. D. dissertation, University of Sussex.

Kapteijns, L. (1977) African Historiography written by Africans, 1955-1973: The Nigerian Case. Leiden: Afrika-Studiencentrum.

Karugire, S. R. (1979) A History of the Kingdom of Nkore in Western Uganda to 1896. Oxford: Clarendon.

Kayamba Badye. (1984). "Formation sociale et authenticité au Zaire," pp. 107-111 in B. Jewsiewicki (ed.) Etat Indépendent du Congo, République Démocratique du Congo, République du Zaire. Québec: SAFI.

Keegan, T. (1981) "The transformation of agrarian society and economy in industrialising South Africa: the Orange Free State grain belt in the early twentieth century." Ph. D. dissertation, University of London.

Kelle, E. J. (1981) "Revolution, class, and the national question: the case of Ethiopia." Northeast African Studies II, 3/III, 1: 43-67.

Kimambo, I. N. (1969) A Political History of the Pare of Tanzania, c. 1500-1900. Nairobi: East African Publishing.
———and A. J. Temu [eds.] (1969) A History of Tanzania. Nairobi: East African Publishing.
Kipre, P. (1979) "A propos de la conscience historique dans les sociétés de l'Afrique précoloniale." Afrika Zamani 10/11: 5-20.
Kitching, G. (1980) Class and Economic Change in Kenya: The Making of an African Petite-Bourgeoisie, 1905-1970. New Haven, CT: Yale University Press.
Kiwanuka, M.S.M. [translator] (1971) The Kings of Buganda, translation of Apolo Kagwa, Basekabaka be Buganda (1901). Nairobi: East African Publishing.
———(1977) "African precolonial history: a challenge to the historian's craft." Afrika Zamani 6/7: 23-35.
Ki-Zerbo, J. (1961) "L'histoire, lévier fondamental." Présence Africaine 2, 37: 144-147.
———(1972) Histoire de l'Afrique Noire. Paris: Hatier.
———[ed., UNESCO] (1980) Histoire Générale de l'Afrique, I. Paris: Hatier.
———(1983) "Nation, Justice et Liberté." Diogène 124: 73-82.
Kjeckshus, H. (1980) Ecology Control and Economic Development in East African History: The Case of Tanganyika, 1800-1950. London: Heinemann.
Klein, M. A. (1968) Islam and Imperialism in Senegal: Siné-Saloum, 1848-1914. Stanford, CA: Stanford University Press.
Klein, M. (1983) "Women in slavery in the western Sudan," in C. Robertson and M. Klein (eds.) Women and Slavery in Africa. Madison: University of Wisconsin Press.
Koelle, S. (1854) African Native Literature, or Proverbs, Tales, Fables, and Historical Fragments in the Kanuri or Bornu Language. London: Church Missionary House.
Kopytoff, I. (1979) "Indigenous African slavery: commentary one," pp. 62-77 in M. Craton (ed.) Roots and Branches: Current Directions in Slave Studies. New York: Pergamon.
Korn, F. (1965) Elementary Structures Reconsidered. London: Tavistock.
Kronenfeld, D. and H. W. Decker. (1979) "Structuralism." Annual Review of Anthropology 8: 505-513.
Kuper, L. and M. G. Smith [eds.] (1969) Pluralism in Africa. Los Angeles: University of California Press.
Laboratoire "Connaissance du Tiers-Monde." (1981) Actes du Colloque Entreprises et Entrepreneurs en Afrique (XIXe et XXe Siècles) (2 volumes). Paris: Universite de Paris VII.
———(1983) Entreprises et entrepreneurs en Afrique: XIXe et XXe Siècles. Paris: Harmattan.
Lacan, J. (1966) Ecrits. Paris: Seuil.
Lacroix, B. (1972) "Pouvoirs et structures de l'Université Lovanium." Les Cahiers du CEDAF: 2/3.
Lakroom, M. (1979) "L'essor du salariat au Sénégal dans l'entre deux guerres." Ph. D. dissertation, Université de Paris-VII.
Lakroum, M. (1983) Le travail inegal: paysans et salariés Sénégals face à la crise des années 30. Paris: Harmattan.
Lamar, H. and L. Thompson [ed.] (1982) The Frontier in History: North America and Southern Africa Compared. New Haven, CT: Yale University Press.

Lange, J. (1966) "The argument from silence." History and Theory 5: 288-301.

Lapeyre, H. (1971) "Retour à Croce." Revue Historique 245: 73-106.

Lapointe, C. and F. (1977) Lévi-Strauss and his Critics: An International Biography. New York: Garland.

Larzac, J. (1971) "Décoloniser l'histoire occitane." Les Temps Modernes 304: 676-696.

Law, R. (1984) "How truly traditional is our traditional history? The case of Samuel Johnson and the recording of Yoruba oral tradition." History in Africa 11: 195-224.

Le Goff, J. et al. (1978) La Nouvelle Histoire. Paris: Retz-CEPL.

Le Pape, M. and C. Vidal (1982) "Raisons pratiques Africaines." Cahiers Internationaux de Sociologie 73: 293-323.

Leclerc, G. (1972) Anthropologie et colonialisme. Paris.

Lefort, C. [ed.] (1982) Passé Present. Paris: Ramsay.

Legassick, M.J. (1971) "The Frontier Tradition in South African History." Institute of Commonwealth Studies 2: 1-33; republished in S. Marks and A. Atmore (1980): 44-79.

———(1974a) "Capital accumulation and violence in South Africa." Economy and Society 3, 3: 253-291.

———(1974b) "Ideology, legislation, and economy in post-1948 South Africa." Journal of Southern African Studies I, 1: 5-35.

———(1975) "South Africa: forced labour, industrialisation, and racial differentiation," pp. 227-270 in R. Harris (ed.) The Political Economy of Africa. Boston, MA: Schenkman.

Legendre, P. (1982) Paroles Poétiques échappées du Texte: Leçons sur la communication industrielle. Paris: Seuil.

Leonard, A. (1906) The Lower Niger and its Tribes. London.

Levine, D. (1966) Wax and Gold. Chicago: University of Chicago Press.

Lévi-Strauss, C. (1955) Tristes Tropiques. Paris: Plon.

———(1958) L'anthropologie structurale. Paris: Plon.

———(1963) Totemism. Boston, MA: Beacon.

———(1966) "The Philosophical attitude par excellence." Current Anthropology 7, 2: 112-123.

Lewis, G. (1855) Inquiry into the Credibility of the Early Roman History (2 volumes). London: J.W. Parker and Son.

Lewis, I.M. (1962) "Historical aspects of genealogies in north Somali social structure." Journal of African History 3, 1: 35-48.

Leys, C. (1975) Underdevelopment in Kenya: The Political Economy of Underdevelopment. London: Heinemann Educational.

———(1982) "Capitalist accumulation in the periphery: Kenya." pp. 170-192 in M. Franshen (ed.) Industry and Accumulation in Africa. London: Heinemann Educational.

Liegeois, L. (1941) "Notice sur le régime social des Basongo Meno de Kole." Bulletin des Juridictions Indigènes et du Droit Coutumier Congolais 9, 1: 13-23.

Linden, I. (1977) Church and Revolution in Rwanda. Manchester: Manchester University Press.

Lindsay, M. (1976) "Pistols shed light on famed duel." Smithsonian 7/8: 94-101.

Liniger-Goumaz, M. (1968) Pygmées et autres races de petite taille: Bibliographie générale. Geneva.

Loko ne Kongo. (1979) "Le Processus d'intégration nationale sous la deuxième République. Cas de l'ancienne Province de Léopoldville." Ph.D. dissertation, Université Nationale du Zaire-Lubumbashi.

Lonsdale, J. (1968) "Some origins of nationalism in East Africa." Journal of African History 9: 119-146.

———(1981) "States and social processes in Africa: a historiographical survey." African Studies Review 24, 2/3: 139-225.

———(1982) "A state of agrarian unrest: colonial Kenya." Presented to the Past and Present Conference, Oxford.

———(1983) "From colony to industrial state: South African historiography as seen from England." Social Dynamics 9, 1: 67-83.

Louis, W. R. (1976) Imperialism: The Robinson-Gallagher Controversy. New York: New Viewpoints.

Lovejoy, P. E. [ed.] (1981) The Ideology of Slavery in Africa. Beverly Hills, CA: Sage.

Low, D. A. (1982) "The Asian mirror to tropical Africa's independence," pp. 1-29 in P. Gifford and W. R. Lewis (eds.) The Transfer of Power in Africa. New Haven, CT: Yale University Press.

———and J. Lonsdale (1976) "Towards the new order, 1945-1963." in History of East Africa Vol. 3 [eds., D. A. Low and A. Smith]. Oxford: Clarendon.

Lowie, R. (1917) "Oral tradition and history." Journal of American Folklore 30: 161-167.

Luanda, N. N. (1979) "The negative mirror images of African initiative: colonial resistance and collaboration," mimeographed paper: Dar es Salaam.

Lucas, P. and J.-L. Vatin (1975) L'Algérie des Anthropologues. Paris: Maspero.

Lukes, S. (1973) "On the social determination of truth," pp. 230-248 in R. Horton and R. Finnegan (eds.) Modes of Thought. London: Faber.

Lumenga-Neso, K. (1982) Aux Origines de la ville de Kinshasa. Kinshasa: Centre de Recherches Pédagogiques.

Lutumba-lu-Vilu. (1972) Histoire du Zaire. L'administration centrale du Ministère belge des Colonies (1908-1940): structure et fonctionnement. Kinshasa: Okapi.

Ly, A. (1958) La compagnie du Sénégal. Paris: Présence Africaine.

McClelland, K. (1979) "Some comments on Richard Johnson, 'Edward Thompson, Genovese, and socialist-humanist history'." History Workshop 7: 101-115.

McLennan, G. (1982) "E. P. Thompson and the discipline of historical context," pp. 97-130 in R. Johnson et al. (eds.) Making Histories: Studies in History Writing and Politics. London: Hutchinson.

MacGaffey, W. (1970) Custom and Government in the Lower Congo. Los Angeles: University of California Press.

———(1978) "African history, anthropology, and the rationality of natives." History in Africa 5: 101-120.

———(1981) "African ideology and belief: a survey." African Studies Review 24, 2/3: 227-274.

———(1982) "The policy of national integration in Zaire." Journal of Modern African Studies 20, 1: 87-105.

———(1983) Modern Kongo Prophets. Bloomington: Indiana University Press.

Madden, F. and D. K. Fieldhouse [eds] (1982) Oxford and the Idea of Common-
    wealth. London: Croom Helm.
Mafeje, A. (1976) "The problem of anthropology in historical perspective." Cana-
    dian Journal of African Studies 10: 307-333.
de Mahieu, W. (1975) "A l'intersection du temps et de l'espace, du mythe et de
    l'histoire: Les généalogies, l'example Komo," Cultures et Développement 11:
    415-437.
Makwanza Batomisa (1984) "Histoire de l'évangelisation de l'ancien royaume
    Kongo, du XVIe au XVIIe siècles." Ph. D. dissertation, Université de
    Lubumbashi.
Malira Kakbuya (1974) "Regard sur la situation social de la citoyenne Lushoise
    d'avant 1950." Likundoli: Enquêtes d'Histoire Zairoise 2, 1: 63-71.
Mannheim, K. (1936) Ideology and Utopia. New York: Harcourt Brace Jovanovich.
Marcuse, H. (1955) Eros and Civilization. Boston, MA: Beacon Press.
Markakis, J. (1974) Ethiopia: Anatomy of a Traditional Polity. Oxford: Clarendon.
———(1981) "The military state and Ethiopia's path to 'socialism'." Review of
    African Political economy 21: 7-25.
———and N. Ayele (1978) Class and Revolution in Ethiopia. Nottingham:
    Spokesman/The Review of African Political Economy.
Marks, S. (1967) "The rise of the Zulu kingdom," pp. 85-91 in R. Oliver (ed.) The
    Middle Age of African History. London: Oxford University Press.
———(1978) "Natal, the Zulu royal family and the ideology of segregation." Journal
    of Southern African Studies 4, 2: 172-194.
———(forthcoming) "The drunken king and the nature of the state," in S. Marks,
    The Ambiguities of Dependence: State, Class and Nationalism in Early Twen-
    tieth Century Natal. Baltimore: The Johns Hopkins Press.
———and A. Atmore [eds.] (1980) Economy and Society in Preindustrial South
    Africa. London: Longman.
Marks, S. and R. Rathbone [eds.] (1982) Industrialisation and Social Change in
    South Africa, 1870-1930: African Class Formation, Culture and Consciousness.
    London: Longmans.
Marks, S. and S. Trapido (forthcoming) Ideology, Class, and Politics in Twentieth
    Century South Africa.
Marseille, J. (1984) Empire colonial et capital français (c.1880-c.1950): Histoire d'un
    divorce. Paris: A. Michel.
Marx, K. (1859) A contribution to the Critique of Political Economy.
Mashaury Kule, T. (1983) "Dynamique de l'action missionnaire Catholique chez les
    Yira occidentaux, 1906-1959." Ph. D. dissertation, Université Nationale du
    Zaire-Lubumbashi.
Matsetela, T. (1980) "The life story of Nkgono Mma Pooe: aspects of sharecropping
    and proletarianisation in the northern Orange Free State, 1890-1930," pp. 212-237
    in S. Marks and A. Atmore (eds.) Economy and Society in Preindustrial South
    Africa. London: Longman.
Mauny, R. (1961) Tableau Géographique de l'Ouest Africain au Moyen Age. Dakar:
    Institut Fondamental de Afrique Noire.
———(1962) "Perspectives et limites de l'ethnohistoire en Afrique." Bulletin de
    l'IFAN 24: 620-627.
Mazrui, A. (1970) "Epilogue." pp. 121-135 in Okot p'Bitek, African Religions in
    Western Scholarship. Nairobi: East African Literature Bureau.

Mbodj, M. (1978) "Un exemple d'économie coloniale, le Sine-Saloum (Sénégal), de 1887 à 1940: Culture arachidière et mutations sociales." Ph. D. dissertation, Université de Paris VII.

Mbokolo, E. (1981) "La formation de la bourgeoisie Zairoise, 1945-1980: éléments pour une recherche." Ecoles des Hautes Etudes en Sciences Sociales, Centre d'Etudes Africaines: Paris.

Mbonimana, G. (1981) "L'instauration d'un royaume chrétien au Rwanda (1900-1931)." Ph. D. dissertation, Louvain-la-Neuve.

Mbwiliza, J. F. (1978) "The struggle for ideological hegemony and the politics of the transition to socialism." Mimeographed paper: Dar es Salaam.

Meek, C. K. (1931) Tribal Studies in Northern Nigeria. London.

———(1937) Law and Authority in a Nigerian Tribe. London.

Meillassoux, C. (1963) "Histoire et institutions du Kafo de Bamako, d'après la tradition des Niare." Cahiers d'Etudes Africaines 4, 2: 186-227.

———(1964) Anthropologie économique des Gouro de la Côte-d'Ivoire. Paris: Mouton.

———[ed.] (1975a) L'esclavage en Afrique précoloniale. Paris: Maspero.

———(1975b) Femmes, greniers et capitaux. Paris: Maspero.

———(1980) Maidens, Meal, and Money. Cambridge: Cambridge University Press. (Originally published 1975)

Mémel-Foté, H. (1979) "Conscience et Histoire." Gado-Gado 45: 9-30.

Mercier, P. (1961) "Remarques sur la signification du 'tribalisme' actuel en Afrique." Cahiers Internationaux de Sociologie 31: 61-80.

———(1968) Tradition, changement, histoire. Les Somba du Dahomey septentrional. Paris: Anthropos.

Metegue N'nah, N. (1979) Economies et sociétés au Gabon dans la première moitié du XIXe Siècle. Paris: Harmattan.

Mettas, J. (1978) Repertoire des expéditions négrières françaises au XVIIIe siècle; Tome I: Nantes. Paris: Société Française d'Histoire d'Outre-Mer.

———(1984) Repertoire des expéditions négrières françaises au XVIIIe siècle; Tome II: Ports autres que Nantes. Paris: Société Française d'Histoire d'Outre-Mer.

Michel, M. (1982) "L'appel à l'Afrique." Contribution et réactions à l'effort de guerre en Afrique OHccid Occidentale Française (1914-1918). Paris: Publications de la Sorbonne.

Miller, J. C. (1973) "Requiem for the Jaga." Cahiers d'Etudes Africaines 49: 121-135.

———(1976) Kings and Kinsmen: Early Mbundu States in Angola. Oxford: Clarendon.

———(1980) "Listening for the African past," pp. 1-59 in J. C. Miller (ed.) The African Past Speaks. Folkestone: Dawson-Archon.

———(1982) "The significance of drought, disease, and famine in the agriculturally marginal zones of West Central Africa." Journal of African History 23, 1: 17-63.

———(1983) "Capitalism and slaving: the financial and commercial organization of the Angolan slave trade according to the accounts of Antonio Coehlo Guerreiro (1684-92)." International Journal of African Historical Studies XVII, 1: 17-61.

Miller, J. M. (1981) French Structuralism: A Multidisciplinary Bibliography. New York: Diho.

Mishambi, G. T. (1977) "The mystification of African history: a critique of Rodney's How Europe Underdeveloped Africa. Utafite 2, 2: 201-228.

Mlahabwa, J. (1978) "Towards a functional materialist history: the Dar es Salaam experience." mimeographed paper: Dar es Salaam.

Moniot, H. (1970) "Les sources de l'histoire africaine," pp. 123-147 in H. Deschamps (ed.) Histoire Générale de l'Afrique, vol. I. Paris: Presses Universitaires de France.

——— (1974) "L'histoire des peuples sans histoire," pp. 106-123 in Faire de l'histoire, I. Paris: Gallimard.

——— [ed.] (1976a) Le mal de voir. Paris: U.G.E.

——— (1976b) "L'anthropologie économique de langue française," pp. 85-124 in Questions à la sociologie française. Paris: Presses Universitaires de France.

Monnier, L. (1971) Ethnie et intégration régionale au Congo. Paris: ECEF.

Monteil, V. (1966) Esquisses Sénégalaises. Dakar: Institut Fondamental de l'Afrique Noire.

Moore, W. A. (1970) History of Itsekiri. London. (Originally published 1936)

Morgan, D.J. (1980) Official History of Colonial Development (5 volumes). London: Macmillan.

Morris, M. (1976) "The development of capitalism in South African agriculture: class struggle in the countryside." Economy and Society 3, 3: 292-344.

——— (1980) "The state and the development of capitalist social relations in the South African countryside: a process of class struggle." Ph.D. dissertation, University of Sussex.

Morrison, D.G. and H.M. Stevenson (1980) "Cultural pluralism, modernization, and conflict: an empirical anlaysis of sources of political instability in African nations," pp. 11-23 in J.N. Paden (ed.) Values, Identities, and National Integration: Empirical Research in Africa. Evanston, IL: Northwestern University Press.

Viscount Mountmorres (1906) The Congo Independent State. London.

Mudimbe, V. Y. (1973) L'autre face du royaume. Lausanne: L'Age d'Homme.

——— (1982a) L'odeur du père: Essai sur des limites de la science et de la vie en Afrique noire. Paris: Présence Africaine.

——— (1982b) "In memorium: Alexis Kagame (1921-1981)." Recherche, pédagogie et culture 56: 74-78.

——— (1984) "African gnosis: philosophy and the order of knowledge in Africa." Presented at the annual meeting of the African Studies Association, Los Angeles.

Mulambu Mvulaya (1971) "Contributions à l'étude de la révolte des Bapende." Cahiers du CEDAF, Serie 2.

——— (1974) "Le régime des cultures obligatoires et le radicalisme rural au Zaire (1917-1960)." Ph.D. dissertation, ULB-Bruxelles, published in Cahiers du CEDAF 617.

Mumbanza mwa Bawele (1974) "La contribution des Zairois à l'oeuvre d'évangelisation et à la prosperité des établissements missionnaires: la mission catholique de Libanda (1933-1960)," pp. 225-274 in Etudes d'Histoire Africaine VI.

——— (1978) "Les Ngombe de l'Equateur. Historique d'une identité," in Zaire-Afrique XVIII, 124: 229-249.

——— (1980) "Histoire des peuples riverains de l'entre Zaire-Ubangi. Evolution sociale et économique (c. 1700-1980)." Ph.D. dissertation, Université Nationale du Zaire-Lubumbashi.

————(forthcoming) "La piroque dans l'Ouest du bassin du Zaire au milieu du XIXe siècle: contribution à l'histoire de la navigation en Afrique Centrale coloniale," in Etudes d'Histoire Africaine, XI-XII.

Mutamba Makombo (1978) "Le Congo Belge (1940-1960): de l'émergence des évolués à l'indépendence." Ph. D. dissertation, Université de Paris.

Mworoha, E. (1976) "Développement et problèmatique du renouveau culturel au Burundi." Au coeur de l'Afrique (Bujumbura) X, 3: 104-105.

————(1977) Peuples et rois de l'Afrique des lacs. Dakar: Nouvelles éditions Africaines.

————(1981) "Redevances et prestations dans les domaines royaux du Burundi précolonial," pp. 751-768 in Le sol, la parole, et l'écrit: Mélanges en hommage à Raymond Mauny. Paris: Harmattan.

Nahimana, F. (1981) "Les principautés Hutu du Rwanda septentrional," pp. 115-137 in Centre de Civilisation Burundaise, La civilisation ancienne des peuples des Grands Lacs. Paris: Karthala.

Nairn, T. (1977) The Break-Up of Britain. London: New Left Books.

N'Daw, A. (1973) "The University of Dakar," in T. M. Yesufu (ed.) Creating the African University. Ibadan.

Ndaywel è Nzièm (1972) "Organisation sociale et histoire: Les Ngwi et Ding du Zaire." Ph. D. dissertation, Sorbonne.

————(1974) "Discours à l'ouverture du premier séminaire national des historiens zairois." Likundoli 2: 111-114.

————(1976) "La formation des historiens à la Faculte des Lettres." Likundoli Series C, I, 2: 1-42.

————(1976) "Le rapport d'enquête ethnographique: Un documentation pour servir à l'étude des populations du Zaire." Likundoli: Archives et Documents 4, 3: 34-42.

————(1980a) "Politique culturelle africaniste et libération Africaine," in V. Y. Mudimbe (ed.) La dépendence de l'Afrique et les moyens d'y remédier. Paris: Beger-Levrault.

————(1980b) "Histoire clanique et histoire ethnique: quelques perspectives méthod-ologiques." Cultures VII: 63-78.

Ndua Sold (1978) "Histoire ancienne des populations Luba et Lunda du plateau du Haut Lubilash dès origines au début du XXe siècle (Bena Nsamba, Bimpin, et Tuwidi)." Ph. D. dissertation, Université Nationale du Zaire-Lubumbashi.

Neale, C. (1981) "Pride and prejudice in African history: the idea of progress in African history, 1960-1970." Ph. D. dissertation, University of Sussex.

Newbury, D. (1973) Vers le passé du Zaire: quelques méthodes de recherche historique. Bukavu: IRSAC.

————(1978) "Bushi and the historians: historiographical themes in eastern Kivu." History in Africa V: 131-151.

————(1979a) "Kings and clans: Ijwi Island, c. 1780 - c. 1840." Ph. D. dissertation, University of Wisconsin—Madison.

————(1979b) "Kamo and Lubambo: dual genesis traditions on Ijwi Island, Zaire." Cahiers du CEDAF 5.

————(1980) "Lake Kivu regional trade in the nineteenth century." Journal des Africanists 50, 2: 6-36.

Neyt, F. (1981) "Traditional art and history in Zaire." Ph. D. dissertation, Université Catholique de Louvain-La-Neuve.

Nivison, D. S. (1983) "The dates of western Chou." Harvard Journal of Asiatic Studies 43: 481-580.

Nkadimeng, M. and G. Relly (1982) "Kas Maine: the story of a black South African agriculturalist," pp. 89-107 in B. Bozzoli (ed.) Town and Countryside in Transvaal. Johannesburg: Ravan.

Nkundabagenzi, F. (1962) Rwanda Politique, 1958-1960. Bruxelles: CRISP.

Northrup, D. (1978) Trade Without Rulers: Precolonial Economic Development in Southeastern Nigeria. London: Oxford University Press.

Nugent, D. (1982) "Closed systems and contradictions: The Kachins in and out of history." Man 17: 508-527.

Nyakatura, J. W. (1973) Anatomy of an African Kingdom: A History of Bunyoro-Kitara (ed., G. N. Uzoigwe). New York: Archon Press/Doubleday. (Originally published 1947)

Nzongola Ntalaja (1970) "The bourgeoisie and revolution in the Congo." Journal of Modern African Studies 8: 511-530.

Oakeshott, M. (1983) Experience and its Modes. Cambridge: Cambridge University Press.

Obenga, T. (1973) L' Afrique dans l'Antiquité: Egypte pharonique - Afrique noire. Paris: Présence Africaine.

———(1978) "Parenté linguistique génétique entre l'égyptien (ancien égyptien et copte) et les langues négro-africaines modernes," in Le peuplement de l'Egypte ancienne. Paris: UNESCO.

———(1980) Pour une nouvelle histoire. Paris: Présence Africaine.

Office National de Recherche et Développement (1973) "Programme general de Recherche de la Section de l'Homme." stencilled: Kinshasa.

O' Dowd, M. (1974) "South Africa in the light of the stages of economic growth," pp. 29-43 in A. Leftwich (ed.) South Africa: Economic Growth and Political Change. London: Jonathan Cape.

Ogot, B. (1964) "Kingship and statelessness among the Nilotes," pp. 284-302 in J. Vansina, R. Mauny, and L. Thomas (eds.) The Historian in Tropical Africa. Oxford: Clarendon.

———(1968) "The role of the pastoralist and the agriculturalist in African history," pp. 125-133 in T. O. Ranger (ed.) Emerging Themes in African History. Nairobi: East African Publishing House.

———(1976) "Towards a history of Kenya." Kenya Historical Review 4: 1-16.

———(1977) "Politics, culture and music in central Kenya: A study of Mau Mau hymns, 1951-1956." Kenya Historical Review 5, 2: 275-286.

Oliver, R. (1963) "Discernible developments in the interior, c. 1500-1840," pp. 169-211 in R. Oliver and G. Mathews (eds.) History of East Africa I. Oxford: Clarendon.

———and A. Atmore (1967) Africa Since 1800. Cambridge; Cambridge University Press.

Oliver, R. and J. D. Fage (1962) A Short History of Africa. Harmondsworth: Penguin.

Olivier de Sardan, J. P. (1969) Système des relations économiques et sociales chez les Wogo (Niger). Paris: Musée de l'Homme.

———[ed.] (1976) Quand nos pères étaient captifs: Récits paysans du Niger. Paris: Nubia.

O'Meara, D. (1975) "The 1946 African miners strike and the political economy of South Africa." Journal of Commonwealth and Comparative Politics 13, 2: 146-173.

——(1982) Volkskapitalism. Cambridge: Cambridge University Press.

Omer-Cooper, J. D. (1966) The Zulu Aftermath: A Nineteenth Century Revolution in Bantu Africa. London: Longman.

Onwuejeogwu, M. A. (1981) An Igbo Civilisation; Nri Kingdom and Hegemony. London.

Oroge, Adeniyi (1971) "The institution of slavery in Yorubaland with particular reference to the nineteenth century." Ph.D. dissertation, University of Birmingham.

Ottaway, M. (1976) "Social classes and corporate interests in the Ethiopian revolution." Journal of Modern African Studies 14, 3: 469-486.

Owusu, M. (1978) "Ethnography of Africa: the usefulness of the useless." American Anthropologist 80: 310-334.

Packard, R. (1981) Chiefship and Cosmology: An Historical Study of Political Competition. Bloomington: Indiana University Press.

——(1984) "Maize, cattle, and mosquitos: The political economy of malaria epidemics in colonial Swaziland." Journal of African History 25, 2: 189-212.

Palmer, H. R. [trans.] (1926) History of the first twelve years of the reign of Mai Idris Alooma of Bornu, 1571-1583.

Pankenier, D. W. (1981/1982) "Astronomical dates in Shang and western Chou." Early China 7: 3-37.

Pankhurst, R. [ed.] (1979) Tax Records and Inventories of Emperor Tewodros of Ethiopia, 1855-1865. London: University of London; School of Oriental and African Studies.

Park, M. (1979) Travels in the Interior Districts of Africa . . . in the years 1795, 1796, 1797. . . . London: W. Bulmer.

Parkin, D. (1968) "Medicine and men of influence." Man N. S. 3: 424-439.

Pauwels, M. (1958) Imana et le cultre des mânes au Rwanda. Bruxelles: Académie Royale des Sciences Coloniales.

Pearce, R. D. (1982) The Turning Point in Africa: British Colonial Policy, 1938-1948. London: Frank Cass.

Peemans, F. and P. Lefevre (1980) "Les sociétés coloniales belges: Archives et données bibliographiques (1885-1960)." Les Cahiers du CEDAF 3-4; 1980.

Peemans, J.-P. (1970) Diffusion du progrès et convergence des prix: Congo-Belgique, 1900-1960. Paris-Louvain: Nauwelaerts.

——(1975a) "The social and economic development of Zaire since independence." African Affairs 74: 151-165.

——(1975b) "Capital accumulation in the Congo under colonialism: the role of the state." pp. 165-212 in P. Duignan and L. Gann (eds.) Colonialism in Africa, 1870-1960; Vol. 4: The Economics of Colonialism. Cambridge: Cambridge University Press.

Peires, J. (1981) The House of Phalo. Berkeley: University of California Press.

Perrot, C.-H. (1982) Les Anyi-Ndenye et le pouvoir aux 18e et 19e siècles. Paris: Publications de la Sorbonne.

Person, Y. (1962) "Tradition orale et chronologie." Cahiers d'Etudes Africaines 7, 2/3: 462-476.

————(1968-1975) Samori: Une révolution dyula, 3 volumes. Dakar: Institut Fondamental de l'Afrique Noire.

————(1980) "Etat et nation en Afrique noire," in V. Y. Mudimbe (ed.) La Dépendance de l'Afrique et les moyens d'y remédier. Paris: Beger-Levrault.

————(1981) "Luttes nationales et luttes de classes." Les Temps Modernes 416: 1555-1577.

Pfordresher, K. (1984) "South African History Workshop." Radical Historians Newsletter 43: 1-3.

Phimister, I. R. (1984) Pasi ne (down with) class struggle? The new history for schools in Zimbabwe." History in Africa 11: 367-374.

Picon, G. (1970) "L'etudiant, Marx et le mois de mai," pp. 9-28 in J. Michelet (ed.) L'étudiant. Paris: Seuil.

Pilipili Kagabo (1974a) "Le premier séminaire national des historiens Zairois." Likundoli 2: 99-102.

————(1974b) "Histoire Zairoise et engagement national." Likundoli 2: 221-234.

Piskaty, K. (1957) "Ist das Pygmäenwerk von Henri Trilles eine zuverlässige Quelle?" Anthropos 52: 33-48.

Plisnier-Ladame, F. (1970) Les Pygmées: Enquêtes bibliographiques XVII. Brussels.

Poitou, J. P. (1981) "Une histoire à étages? Sur la notion de remploi idéologique," pp. 641-647 in Centre méridional d'histoire sociale, des mentalités et des cultures. Paris: Honore Champion.

Pollock, G. F. (1970) Civilizations of Africa: Historic Kingdoms, Empires, and Cultures. Middletown, CT: American Education Publication Unit.

Porter, B. (1980) "Aramaic letters: a study in papyrological reconstruction." Journal of the American Research Center in Egypt 17: 39-75.

Pouillon, F. (1978) "De l'idéologie: Introduction." L'Homme 18, 3/4: 7-16.

————(1979) "Remarques sur le verbe 'croire'," pp. 42-50 in M. Izard and P. Smith (eds.) La fonction symbolique Paris.

Pretorius, P. (1948) Homme de la brousse: Une autobiographie. Paris. (Originally published 1934)

Rabinow, P. (1984) "Anthropology and social sciences: an epistemological evaluation of methods." Presented to the ASA Annual Meeting: Los Angeles.

Raison, J.-P. (1978) "Continuité et comparaison dans les recherches Africanistes." Etudes Rurales 70: 5-8.

————(1981) "La géographie Africaine en France," pp. 591-629 in Etudes Africaines en Europe. Paris: Karthala.

Raison-Jourde, F. (1977) "L'échange inégal de la langue: La pénétration des techniques lingistiques dans une civilisation de l'oral." Annales: E.S.C. 32: 639-669.

————1985. "Les élites malgaches, XIXe-XXe siècles," in Labour, Capital, and Society 18 (forthcoming).

Ranger, T. O. [ed.] (1962) Historians in Tropical Africa. Salisbury: University College of Rhodesia and Nyasaland.

————(1968a) "Connexions between primary resistance movements and modern mass nationalism in East and Central Africa." Journal of African History 9: 437-453, 631-641.

————[ed.] (1968b) Emerging Themes of African History. Nairobi: East African Publishing House.

————(1969) "African reactions to the imposition of colonial rule in East and Central Africa," pp. 293-324 in L. H. Gann and P. Duignan (eds.) Colonialism in Africa, vol. I. Cambridge: Cambridge University Press.

————(1971) "The new historiography in Dar es Salaam: an answer." African Affairs 70: 50-61.

————(1975) "The Mwana Lesa movement of 1925," in T. O. Ranger and J. Weller (eds.) Themes in the Christian History of Central Africa. London: Heinemann Educational.

————(1976a) "Towards a usable African past," pp. 17-30 in C. Fyfe (ed.) African Studies Since 1945. New York: Africana.

————(1976b) "From humanism to the science of man: colonialism in Africa and the understanding of alien societies." Transactions of the Royal Historical Society, 5th Series, 26: 115-141.

Rathbone, R. (1968) "The government of the Gold Coast after the Second World War." African Affairs 67: 209-218.

————1973. "Businessmen to politics: party struggle in Ghana, 1949-1957." Journal of Development Studies 9: 391-401.

————(1983) "Parties, socio-economic bases and regional differentiation in the Rate of Change in Ghana," pp. 143-154 in P. Lyon and J. Manor (eds.) Transfer and Transformation: Political Institutions in the New Commonwealth. Leicester: Leicester University Press.

Raymaekers, R. et H. Desroches (1983) L'administration et le sacré. Discours religieux et parcours politiques en Afrique Centrale (1921-1957). Bruxelles: Académie Royale des Sciences d'Outre-Mer.

Recherches belges sur l'Afrique/Afrika-onderzoek in Belgie. (1976) Tervuren: Musée Royal de l'Afrique Centrale.

Reefe, T. Q. (1977) "Traditions of genesis and the Luba diaspora." History in Africa 4: 183-206.

Rehise, H. (1910) Kiziba. Land und Leute. Stuttgart: Strecker/Schaoder.

Revue Française d'Histoire d'Outre Mer (1981) Special issue on "Etat et société en Afrique noire."

Rey, P.-Ph. (1971) Colonialisme, néo-colonialisme, et transition au capitalisme. Exemple de la Comilog au Congo-Brazzaville. Paris: Maspero.

Richards, P. (1983) "Ecological change and the politics of African land use." African Studies Review 26, 2: 1-72.

Richardson, P. (1983) Chinese Mine Labour in Transvaal. London: Macmillan.

Ricoeur, P. (1983) Temps et récit, 1. Paris: Editions du Seuil.

Robertson, N. (1978) "The myth of the first sacred war." Classical Quarterly 72: 48-51.

Robinson, K. (1984) "Colonialism French-style, 1945-55: a backward glance." Journal of Imperial and Commonwealth History 12: 24-41.

Robinson, R. (1972) "Non-European foundations of European imperialism: sketch for a theory of collaboration," pp. 128-151 in W. R. Louis (ed.) Imperialism: The Robinson-Gallagher Controversy. New York: New Viewpoints.

————(1978) "Sir Andrew Cohen: Proconsul of African nationalism (1909-1968)," pp. 353-364 in L. Gann and P. Duignan (eds.) African Proconsuls. New York: Free Press.

————(1980) "Sir Andrew Cohen and the transfer of power in tropical Africa, 1940-1957," pp. 50-72 in W. H. Morris-Jones and G. Fischer (eds.) Decolonization and After: The British and French Experience. London: Frank Case.

————(1983) Review of Morgan, 1980. Journal of Imperial and Commonwealth History 12: 132-135.

————(1984) "Imperial theory and the question of imperialism after empire." Journal of Imperial and Commonwealth History 12: 42-54.

————and J. Gallagher (1961) Africa and the Victorians: The Official Mind of Imperialism. London: Macmillan.

————(1962) "The Partition of Africa," pp. 593-640 in F. H. Hinsley (ed.) The New Cambridge Modern History, vol. 9. Cambridge: Cambridge University Press.

Robinson, R. and A. Seal (1981) "Professor John Gallagher, 1919-1980." Journal of Imperial and Commonwealth History 9: 119-124.

Rodinson, M. (1980) La fascination de l'Islam. Paris: Maspero.

Rodney, W. (1972) How Europe Underdeveloped Africa. Dar es Salaam: Tanzania Publishing House.

Rosny, E. (1981) Les yeux de ma chèvre. Paris: Plon.

Ross, R. (1983a) Cape of Torments. Slavery and Resistance in South Africa. London: Routledge and Kegan Paul.

————(1983b) "The Cape gentry." Journal of Southern African Studies: 193-217.

Rossi, I. 1982. "Lévi-Strauss's theory of kinship and its empiricist critics: an anti-Needham position," pp. 42-67 in I. Rossi (ed.) The Logic of Culture. South Hadley, MA: Bergin.

Rowbotham, S. (1976) Hidden from History. New York: Vintage Books.

Runciman, W. G. (1970) Sociology in its Place. Cambridge: Cambridge University Press.

Runyan, W. R. (1981) Life Histories and Psychohistory. New York: Oxford University Press.

Ryder, A. F. C. (1969) Benin and the Europeans, 1845-1897. London.

Sabakinu Kivilu (1974) "Note sur l'histoire de la maladie du sommeil dans la région de Kisantu (1900-1912). Likundoli: Enquêtes d'Histoire II, 2: 151-162.

————(1981) "Histoire de la population et des conditions de vie à Matadi, 1891-1959." Ph. D. dissertation, Université Nationale du Zaire-Lubumbashi.

————(1984) "Population et santé dans le processus de l'industrialisation," pp. 94-98 in B. Jewsiewicki (ed.) Etat Indépendant du Congo, République Démocratique du Congo, République du Zaire. Québec: SAFI.

Sabatie, A. (1926) Le Sénégal: Sa conquête et son organisation (1914-1925). St. Louis: Imprimérie du Gouvernement.

Said, E. (1978) Orientalism. New York: Random House.

Saint-Martin, Y. (1967) L'empire toucouleur et la France: un demi-siècle de relations diplomatiques, 1846-1893. Dakar: Faculté des Lettres.

————(1970) L'empire toucouleur, 1848-1897. Paris: Le Livre Africain.

de Saint-Moulin, L. (1974) "L'histoire des villes du Zaire: Notions et perspectives fondamentales." Etudes d'Histoire Africaine 6: 137-167.

————(1976) "Contribution à l'histoire de Kinshasa." Zaire-Afrique 16: 461-473, 521-538.

————(1982) "L'organisation de l'espace en Afrique Centrale à la fin du XIXe siècle." Cultures et Développement 14: 259-296.

————(1983) "La population du Congo pendant la séconde guerre mondiale," pp. 15-50 in Le Congo Belge durant la séconde guerre mondiale: recueil d'études. Bruxelles: Academie Royale des Sciences d'Outre-Mer.

Sahlins, M. (1976) Culture and Practical Reason. Chicago: University of Chicago Press.

Samuel, R. (1975) The Village Labourer. London: Routledge and Kegan Paul.

————[ed.] (1981) People's History and Socialist Theory. London: Routledge and Kegal Paul.

Sanders, E. R. (1967) "The Hamitic hypothesis." Journal of African History 10: 521-532.

Saul, J. (1972) Socialism in Tanzania, I. Nairobi: East African Publishing House.

————and S. Gelb (1981) "The crisis in South Africa: class defense, class revolution." Monthly Review 33, 3: 1-160.

Sayer, D. (1975) "Method and dogma in historical materialism." The Sociological Review, 779-810.

Scheub, H. (1984) "A review of African oral traditions and literature." Presented to the ASA Annual Conference: Los Angeles.

Schmitz, J. (1982) "Le destin d'une classe clericale, les Toorobbe de Fuuta Tooro." Unpublished paper.

Schwarz, A. [ed.] (1980) Les faux prophètes de l'Afrique, ou l'afr(eu)canisme. Presses de L'Université Laval.

Sellassie, Bereket Habter (1980) Conflict and Intervention in the Horn of Africa. New York: Monthly Review Press.

Shepperson, G. (1961) "External factors in the development of African nationalism with particular reference to British Central Africa," pp. 317-332 in T. O. Ranger (ed.) Historians in Tropical Africa. Salisbury.

Shillington, K. (1981) "Land Loss, Labour and Dependence: the Impact of Colonialism on the southern Tswana, c. 1870-1900." Ph.D. dissertation, University of London.

Shivji, I. G. (1980) "Rodney and radicalism on the hill, 1966-1974," pp. 29-30 in Maji Maji 43 (Special Issue on Walter Rodney's Contribution to the Revolution).

Sikitele Gize (forthcoming) "Histoire de l'évolution de la dynamique socio-politique des Pende à l'époque coloniale." Ph. D. dissertation, Université de Lubumbashi.

Simons, J. and R. E. Simons (1969) Colour and Class in South Africa. Penguin: Harmondsworth Press.

Slater, H. (1981) "The production of historical knowledge at Dar es Salaam: mimeographed.

————(1981) "Africa and the production of historical knowledge." Kale 6: 1-33.

————(1982) "Shaka Zulu, apartheid, and the politics of the liberationist historiography of South Africa." Presented at the Fifth Annual Southern African Universities Social Science Conference: Lusaka.

————(1982) "The production of historical knowledge at Dar es Salaam." Presented at the Conference on Zimbabwe History: Retrospect and Prospect: Harare.

————(1983) "Marxist historiography and the teaching of history in Africa." Symposium on Marxist in Africa, Institute of Development Studies, University of Dar es Salaam.

Smith, A. (1979) "The contemporary significance of the academic ideals of the Sokoto 'Jihad'," in Y. B. Usman (ed.) Studies in the History of the Sokoto Caliphate. Lagos: Third Press International.

Smith, R. (1977) "Nigerian history is not mysterious: an eiremic reply to Professors Horton and Peel." Journal of the Historical Society of Nigeria 8, 4: 51-52.

Smith, T. (1978) "A comparative study of French and British decolonization." Comparative Studies in Society and History 20: 70.

Social Analysis (1980) Special issue on "Using Oral Sources: Vansina and Beyond," IV.

Soh, S. A. (1913) Chroniques du Fouta Sénégalais (trans. M. Delafosse and H. Gaden). Paris: Larose.

Soleillet, P. (1887) Voyage à Ségou, 1878-1879. Paris: Challamel Aine.

Spear, T. T. (1978) The Kaya Complex: A History of the Mijikenda Peoples of the Kenya Coast to 1900. Nairobi: Kenya Literature Bureau.

———(1981) "Whose history?" Journal of Pacific History 1: 133-148.

Sperber, D. (1974) Rethinking Symbolism. Cambridge: Cambridge University Press.

Staniland, M. (1977) The Lions of Dagbon. Cambridge: Cambridge University Press.

Stengers, J. (1957) Combien le Congo a-t-il couté à la Belgique? Bruxelles: Académie Royale des Sciences Coloniales.

———(1963) Belgique et Congo: l'élaboration de la charte coloniale. Bruxelles: Renaissance du Livre.

———(1974) "La Belgique et le Congo. Politique coloniale et décolonisation," pp. 391-440 in Histoire de la Belgique contemporaine, 1914-1970. Brussels: La Renaissance du Livre.

———(1978) "Une décolonisation précipitée: le cas du Congo Belge." Cultures et Développement 10, 4: 521-556.

———(1979a) "Belgian historiography since 1945," pp. 161-181 in P. C. Emmer and H. L. Wasseling (eds.) Reappraisals in Overseas History. Leiden: Leiden University Press.

———(1979b) "Les malaises de l'histoire coloniale." Bulletin des Séances de l'Académie Royale des Sciences d'Outre-Mer 4: 583-593.

Suret-Canale, J. (1958, 1964, 1972) Afrique noire (Occidentale et Centrale), T. I: Géographie, Civilisations, Histoire; ; T. II: L'ère coloniale (1900-1940); T. III: De la colonisation aux Indépendences (1945-1960). Paris: Editions Sociales.

Swai, B. (1977) "Local initiative in African history: a critique." Tanzania Zamani 20: 11-19.

———(1978) "The new Cinderella in African history." Tanzania Zamani 20: 11-19.

———(1980) "The use of history: towards the sociology of Africanist historiography." Unpublished paper: Dar es Salaam.

———(1982) "The contradictory past: historians and African history." Presented at the 1979 Southern African Universities Conference: Dar es Salaam.

———and A. Temu (1977) "Old and new themes in African history." Presented at the Workshop on the Teaching of History in African Universities: Lagos.

Swainson, N. (1980) The Development of Corporate Capitalism in Kenya, 1918-1977. London: Heinemann.

Talbot, P. (1926) The peoples of Southern Nigeria. London.

Tardits, C. (1958) Porto-Novo. Les nouvelles générations Africaines entre leurs traditions et l'Occident. Paris-La Haye: Mouton.

Temu, A. J. (1969) "The rise and triumph of nationalism," pp. 189-213 in I. Kimambo and A. Temu (eds.) A History of Tanzania Nairobi: East African Publishing House.

——and B. Swai (1981) Historians and Africanist History: A Critique. London: Zed.

Terray, E. (1969) L'organisation sociale des Dida de Côte d'Ivoire. Abidjan: Annales de l'Université.

——(1983) "Gold production, slave labor, and state intervention in precolonial Akan societies: a reply to Raymond Dumett." Research in Economic Anthropology 5: 95-129.

——(1984a) "Une histoire du royaume Abron du Gyaman. Dès origines à la conquête coloniale." Thèse d'Etat: Université de Paris I.

——(1984b) "L'anthropologie marxiste en France entre 1960 et 1980: essai de bilan," pp. 81-90 in R. Gallisot (ed.) Aventures du marxisme. Paris: Syros.

Tessman, G. (1913) Die Pangwe, Vol. 1. Berlin.

Thiam, I. (1983) "L'évolution politique du Sénégal, 1848-1930." Thèse d'Etat, Université de Paris I.

Thomas, L. L., J. Z. Kronenfild, and D. B. Kronenfeld. (1976) "Asdiwal Crumbles: A Critique of Lévi-Straussian Myth Analysis." American Ethnologist 3: 147-174.

Thompson, E. P. (1970) The Making of the English Working Class. Harmondsworth: Penguin. (originally published 1963)

——(1978a) "Folklore, anthropology and social history." Indian Historical Review 3: 247-266.

——(1978b) The Poverty of Theory and Other Essays. London: Merlin Press.

Thornton, J. (1977) "Demography and History in the Kingdom of Kongo, 1550-1750." Journal of African History 18, 4: 507-530.

——(1980) "The slave trade in eighteenth century Angola: effects on demographic structures." Canadian Journal of African Studies XIV, 3: 417-428.

——(1983a) The Kingdom of Kongo: Civil War and Transition, 1641-1718. Madison: University of Wisconsin Press.

——(1983b) "Sexual demography: the impact of the slave trade on family structure," in C. Robertson and M. Klein (eds.) Women and Slavery in Africa. Madison: University of Wisconsin Press.

Throup, D. (1982) "The Origins of Mau Mau." Institute of Commonwealth Studies seminar paper, 21.

——(1983) "The Kikuyu chief and the 'Second Colonial Occupation': another view of Mau Mau." African History seminar paper: School of Oriental and African Studies, London.

Tiers Monde (1980) "Secteur informel et petite production marchande dans les villes du Tiers Monde." Numéro Spécial 21: 82.

Trapido, S. (1971) "South Africa in a comparative study of industrialization." Journal of Development Studies 8, 3: 309-320.

——(1978) "Landlord and tenant in a colonial economy." Journal of Southern African Studies 5, 1: 26-58.

——(1980) "Reflections on land office and wealth in the South African Republic, 1850-1900," pp. 350-368 in S. Marks and A. Atmore (eds.) Economy and Society in Pre-Industrial South Africa. London: Longman.

————(1984) "Putting a plough to the ground: A history of tenant production on the Vereeniging estates, 1896-1920." Collected Seminar Papers on the Societies of Southern Africa, Vol. 13. London: Institute of Commonwealth Studies.

Trevor-Roper, H. (1963) "The rise of Christian Europe." The Listener, November 28, p. 871.

Trilles, H. (1898) "Chez les Fang." Missions catholiques 30.

————(1932) Les pygmées de la forêt équatoriale. Paris.

Trimingham, J.S. (1961) Islam in West Africa. Oxford: Clarendon.

Tshibangu Kabet M. (1980) "L'impact socio-économique de la grande crise économique mondiale des années 1929-1935 sur l'ancien Haut-Katanga industriel." Ph.D. dissertation, Université Nationale du Zaire, Lubumbashi.

Tshimanga wa Tshibangu (1976) Histoire du Zaire. Bukavu: CERUKI.

Tshund'olela Epanya (1980) "Politique coloniale, economie capitaliste, et sous-développement du Congo Belge: Cas du Kasai (1920-1952)." Ph.D. dissertation, Université Nationale du Zaire-Lubumbashi.

Tubiana, M.J. (1961) "Moyens et méthodes d'une ethnologie historique de l'Afrique orientale." Cahiers d'Etudes Africaines 2: 5-11.

————[ed.] (1981) Un patriote toundjour: le Faki Adam ab-Tisheka. Written notes accompanying the taped autobiography of Adam ab-Tisheka, "Tarikh Hayati". Valbonne: Laboratoire Peires.

Turrell, R. (1981) "Black Flag revolt on the Kimberly diamond fields." Journal of Southern African Studies 7, 2: 194-235.

————(1982) "Kimberly: labour and compounds, 1871-1888," pp. 45-76 in S. Marks and R. Rathbone (eds.) Industrialization and Change in South Africa. London: Longman.

————(1982) "Capital, class, and monopoly: The Kimberly diamond fields, 1871-1889." Ph.D. dissertation, University of London.

Twaddle, M. (1974) "On Ganda historiography." History in Africa 1: 85-100.

————(1975) "Rich Kenyans and poor Kenyans." Times Literary Supplement, December 26; p. 1545.

————(1976) "The politician as agitator in eastern Uganda," pp. 155-165 in W.H. Morris-Jones (ed.) The Making of Politicians: Studies from Africa and Asia. London: Athlone.

Tylor, E.B. (1871) Primitive Culture. London: J. Murray.

UNESCO (1981) Histoire Général de l'Afrique. Paris: Hatier.

University of Ibadan (1973) "The Department of History, 1948-1973." Commemorative Brochure.

Usman, Y.B. (1979) For the Liberation of Nigeria. London: New Beacon.

Valdelin, J. (1978) "Ethiopia 1974-1977: from anti-feudal revolution to consolidation of the bourgeois state." Race and Class 19, 4: 379-397.

Valensi, L. (1979) Histoire et anthropologie des pays d'Islam. Centre National de la Recherche Scientifique.

van Binsbergen, W.M.J. (1977) "Religious innovation and political conflict in Zambia," pp. 101-136 in W. van Binsbergen and R. Buijtenhuijs (eds.) African Perspectives: Religious Innovation in Modern African Society. Leiden: Afrika-Studiecentrum.

van Haeverbeke, A. (1970) "Remuneration du travail et commerce extérieur. Essor d'une économie paysanne exportatrice et termes de l'échange des producteurs d'arachides au Sénégal." Ph. D. dissertation, Université Catholique de Louvain.

van Helten, J. J. (1982) "Empire and high finance: South Africa and the international gold standard, 1890-1914." Journal of African History 23, 4: 529-548.

van Noten, F. (1981) "L'archéologie africaine en Belgique," pp. 100-104 in Etudes Africaines en Europe, I. Paris: Karthala.

van Onselen, C. (1976) Chibaro: African Mine Labour in Southern Rhodesia, 1900-1933. London: Pluto.

————(1982) Essays on the Social and Economic History of the Witwatersrand, 1886-1914; I: The New Nineveh; II: The New Babylon. London: Longman.

Vanderlinden, J. et al. [eds.] (1980) Du Congo au Zaire, 1960-1980. Brussels: Centre d'Etudes et de Documentation Africaines.

Vansina, J. (1960) "Recording the oral history of the Bakuba." Journal of African History I, 1: 43-57.

————(1961) De la tradition orale: Essai de méthode historique. Tervuren: Musée Royal de l'Afrique Centrale.

————(1962) L'évolution du royaume Rwanda des origines à 1900. Bruxelles: Académie Royale des Sciences d'Outre-Mer.

————(1963) Geschiedenis van de Kuba van Ongeveer 1500 tot 1904. Tervuren: Musée Royal de l'Afrique Centrale.

————(1965) Oral Tradition: A Study in Historical Methodology. Chicago: Aldine. (Originally published 1961)

————(1966a) Kingdoms of the Savannah: A History of the Central African States until European Occupation. Madison: University of Wisconsin Press.

————(1966b) Introduction à l'ethnographie du Congo. Bruxelles: C.R.I.S.P.

————(1968) "The use of ethnographic data as sources for history," pp. 97-124 in T. O. Ranger (ed.) Emerging Themes of African History. Dar es Salaam: East African Publishing.

————(1971a) "Once upon a time: oral traditions as history in Africa." Daedalus 100, 2: 442-468.

————(1971b) "Les mouvements religieux Kuba (Kasai) à l'époque coloniale." Etudes d'histoire Africaine 2: 157-189.

————(1972) The Tio Kingdom of the Middle Congo, 1880-1892. London: Oxford University Press.

————(1973) "Lukoshi Lupambula: Histoire d'un culte religieux dans les Régions du Kasai et du Kwango (1920-1970)." Etudes d'Histoire Africaine 5: 51-97.

————(1978a) The Children of Woot: A History of the Kuba People. Madison: University of Wisconsin Press.

————(1978b) "For oral tradition (but not against Braudel)." History in Africa 5: 351-356.

————(1980) "Lignage, idéologie et histoire en Afrique équatoriale." Enquêtes et Documents d'Histoire Africaine 4: 133-155.

————(1982) "Towards a history of lost corners in the world." Economic History Review 35: 165-178.

————(1983) "Is elegance proof? Structuralism and African history." History in Africa 10: 307-348.

————(1984a) Art History in Africa. London: Longman.

————(1984b) "Une approche dans le style de Braudel, sans Braudel." Revue Canadienne des Etudes Africaines 18, 1: 241-242.

————W. de Craemer, R. Fox (1976) "Religious movements in Central Africa: a theoretical study." Comparative Studies in Society and History 18: 458-475.

Veit-Brause, I. (1981) "A Note on Begriffsgeschichte." History and Theory 20: 61-67.

Vellut, J.-L. (1972) "Les Lunda et la frontière Luso-Africaine, 1700-1900." Etudes d'Histoire Africaine 3: 61-166.

————(1973) "Histoire et ethnie: Quelques reconsiderations récentes en Afrique Centrale." Likundoli I, 2: 56-62.

————(1974a) Guide de l'étudiant en histoire du Zaire. Kinshasa: Editions du Mont Noir.

————(1974b) "Pour une histoire sociale de l'Afrique centrale." Cultures et Développement 6, 1: 61-86.

————(1976) "Les cultures alimentaires en Afrique centrale ancienne. Suggestions pour une histoire africaine des sociétés agraires et de leur environnement." Presented to the Deuxième Journées d'Histoire Zairoise: Bukavu.

————(1977) "Rural Poverty in Western Shaba, c. 1900-1930," pp. 294-316 in R. Palmer and N. Parsons (eds.) The Roots of Rural Poverty in Central and Southern Africa. Berkeley: University of California Press.

————(1980) "Développement et sous-développement au Zaire. Notes préliminaires pour une perspective historique," in V. Y. Mudimbe (ed.) La dépendence de l'Afrique et les moyens d'y remédier. Paris: Berger-Levrault.

————(1981) "Les bassins miniers de l'ancien Congo Belge. Essai d'histoire économique et sociale (1900-1960). Les Cahiers du CEDAF 7.

————(1983) "Le Congo Belge dans la séconde guerre mondiale. Travaux Zairois," in Le Congo Belge durant la séconde guerre mondiale. Bruxelles: Académie Royale des Sciences d'Outre-Mer.

————(1983b) "Le Katanga industriel en 1944: Malaises et anxietés dans la société coloniale," in Le Congo Belge durant la séconde guerre mondiale. Bruxelles: Académie Royale des Sciences d'Outre-Mer.

Verdeaux, F. (1981) "L'Aizi pluriel. Chronique d'une ethnie lagunaire de Cote d'Ivoire." Ph.D. dissertation, EHESS.

Verhaegen, B. (1966, 1969) Rébellions au Congo, 2 volumes. Bruxelles: C.R.I.S.P.

————(1974) Introduction à l'histoire immédiate: Essai de méthodologie qualitative. Gembloux: Duculot.

————[ed.] (1975) Kisangani, 1876-1976. Histoire d'une ville. Kisangani-Kinshasa: C.R.I.D.E./Presses Universitaires du Zaire.

————(1977) "L'Histoire au Zaire: enseignement, recherches, publications." Revue Belge d'Histoire Contemporaine 8: 291-314.

————(1981) "Va et vient méthodologique entre la théorie, les faits, et les techniques de recherches: la question des relations entre méthode et technique." Notes, Travaux, Documents du CRIDE 2: 3-15.

Veyne, P. (1971) Comment on écrit l'histoire. Paris: Editions du Seuil.

Vidal, C. (1971) "Enquête sur le Rwanda traditionnel: Conscience historique et traditions orales." Cahiers d'Etudes Africaines 10, 4: 526-537.

————(1974) "Economie de la société féodale rwandaise." Cahiers d'Etudes Africaines 14, 1: 52-74.

————(1976) "L'ethnographie à l'imparfait: un cas d'ethno-histoire." Cahiers d'Etudes Africaines 16, 1/2: 397-404.

Villard, A. (1943) Histoire du Sénégal. Dakar: Ars Africae.

Vovelle, M. (1983) Idéologies et mentalités. Paris: Maspero.

Waane, S. A. C. (1981) "Ethnographic insights into the Iron Age of the Great Lakes Region: the production and distribution of iron, implements, salt, and pottery," in Centre de Civilisation Burundaise, La civilisation ancienne des peuples des grands lacs. Paris: Karthala.

Wallerstein, I. (1973) "Africa in a Capitalist World." Issue 3, 3: 1-11.

————(1974) The Modern World System I: Capitalist Agriculture and the Origins of the European World-Economy in the Sixteenth Century. New York: Academic.

————(1980) The Modern World System II: Mercantilism and the Consolidation of the European World Economy, 1600-1750. New York: Academic.

Wamba dia Wamba, E. (1980) "Brief theoretical comments on the quest for materialist history: concerning the article 'The Object of African History'." Unpublished paper: Dar es Salaam.

————(1981) "Concerning Henry Slater's paper 'Africa and the Production of Historical Knowledge': further considerations on the issue of history." Unpublished paper: Dar es Salaam.

————(1984) "L'histoire oui mais quelle histoire?" pp. 61-65 in B. Jewsiewicki (ed.) Etat Indépendent du Congo, République Démocratique du Congo, République du Zaire. Québec: SAFI.

Webster, J. B. [ed.] (1979) Chronology, Migration, and Drought in Interlacustrine Africa. London: Africana.

————(1983) "The high point of skepticism lost in a footnote fairyland." International Journal of African Historical Studies 15: 476-484.

Were, G. S. (1967) A History of the Abaluyia of Western Kenya, c. 1500-1930. Nairobi: East African Publishing.

White, P. T. (1983) "Tropical rain forests: nature's dwindling treasures." National Geographic Magazine 163, 1: 2-48.

Willan, B. (1979). Sol Plaatje. A Biography. London: Heinemann.

Williams, D. (1974) Icon and Image. London.

Williams, G. (1979) "In Defense of History." History Workshop 7: 116-125.

Willis, R. G. (1976) On Historical Reconstruction from Oral Traditional Sources. A Structuralist Approach. Evanston, IL: Northwestern University Press.

————(1981) A State in the Making: Myth, History and Social Transformation in Precolonial Ufipa. Bloomington: University of Indiana Press.

Wilson, J. L. (1856) Western Africa: Its History, Condition, and Prospects. New York.

Wilson, M. (1969) "Cooperation and conflict: the eastern Cape frontier," pp. 233-272 in M. Wilson and L. Thompson (eds.) Oxford History of South Africa I. Oxford: Clarendon.

————and L. Thompson [eds.] (1969, 1971) The Oxford History of South Africa, 2 volumes. Oxford: Clarendon.

Wolfe, A. (1961) In the Ngombe Tradition. Evanston: Northwestern University Press.

Wolpe, H. (1972) "Capitalism and cheap labour power in South Africa: from segregation to apartheid." Economy and Society 1, 4: 425-456.

Wondji, C. (1981) "L'histoire dans les sociétés lignagères de la Côte d'Ivoire," pp. 321-351 in Le sol, la parole et l'écrit: Mélanges en Hommage à Raymond Mauny. Paris: Harmattan.

——and J. N. Loucou (1976) "Histoire et développement." Africa Zamani 5: 76-87.

Woolf, S. J. (1982) "Appealing to the masses." Times Literary Supplement, 1982; pg. 1281.

Worden, N. (1982) "Rural slavery in the western districts of the Cape Colony during the eighteenth century." Ph. D. dissertation, Cambridge University.

Worger, W. (1982) "The Making of a Monopoly: Kimberly and the South African Diamond Industry, 1870-1895." Ph. D. dissertation, Yale University.

Wright, H. (1977) The Burden of the Present. Cape Town: David Phillips.

Wright, M. (1975) "Women in peril: life stories of captives in nineteenth century east Africa." African Social Research 20: 800-819.

——(1982) "Justice, women and the social order in Abercorn, Northeastern Rhodesia, 1898-1903," in J. Hay and M. Wright (eds.) African Women and the Law. Boston: Boston University Press.

——(1983) "Bwankiwa: consciousness and protest among slave women in Central Africa, 1896-1911," in C. Robertson and M. Klein (eds.) Women and Slavery in Africa. Madison: University of Wisconsin Press.

Wrigley, C. C. (1971) "Historicism in Africa: slavery and state formation." African Affairs 70: 113-124.

——(1974) "The Kinglists of Buganda." History in Africa 5: 129-139.

Young, M. C. (1965) Politics in the Congo. Princeton: Princeton University Press.

——(1976) The Politics of Cultural Pluralism. Madison: University of Wisconsin Press.

——(1982) "Patterns of social conflict: state, class, and ethnicity." Daedalus 111, 2: 71-98.

Yudelman, D. (1983) The Emergence of Modern South Africa: State, Capital and the Incorporation of Organized Labour on the South African Goldfields, 1902-1939. Westport, CT: Greenwood Press.

About the Contributors

E. J. Alagoa is Professor of History at the University of Port Harcourt (Nigeria). He received his Ph.D. from the University of Wisconsin and has since published widely on the history of the Niger Delta area and on the analysis of oral tradition. Among his works are *The Small Brave City-State: A History of Nembe-Brass in the Niger Delta* and *A History of the Niger Delta*.

Jean-François Bayart is a researcher at the Fondation Nationale des Sciences Politiques (Paris) and Editor of the journal *Politique Africaine*. He is the author of *L'état au Cameroon* and of many other works on the state and on populist modes of political activity in Africa.

Jean Bazin teaches social anthropology at the Ecole des Hautes Etudes en Sciences Sociales (Paris). His research focuses on the history of Segu (Mali). His latest work is *Guerres de lignages et guerres d'états en Afrique* (coedited with E. Terray).

Jean-Pierre Chrétien is associated with the Centre Nationale de Recherches Scientifiques (CNRS) in Paris and the Centre de Recherches Africaines at the Université de Paris I. His work deals primarily with the history of the East African Great Lakes area, especially with the history of Burundi.

Catherine Coquery-Vidrovitch is Professor of History and Director of the Laboratoire Tiers-Monde: Afrique, at the Université de Paris VII. Among numerous works on Africa her latest publications include *L'Afrique noire de 1800 à nos jours* (with H. Moniot, 1984) and *Afrique Noire: Permanences et Ruptures* (1985).

Mamadou Diouf, now teaching at the Université de Dakar, has published on the political history of Senegal, on the history of technology, and on demographic history. His research focuses primarily on the Wolof kingdoms of Senegal during the nineteenth century.

David Henige is African Bibliographer at the University of Wisconsin—Madison. He has published widely on the methodology of historical analysis, with a particular interest in the historian's use of oral sources. His latest work is *Oral Historiography.*

Bogumil Jewsiewicki taught at the University of Zaire (Lubumbashi) from 1969 to 1976 and now teaches at the Université Laval in Québec. He has published numerous works on the socioeconomic history of colonial Zaire.

Martin A. Klein teaches at the University of Toronto and has been doing historical research in Senegal for over 20 years. He has written extensively on Senegalese history and is currently working on a study of slavery and French colonial rule in West Africa. His latest work is *Women and Slavery in Africa* (coedited with C. Robertson).

Robert S. Love has worked for the Overseas Development Administration in London and as an economist in the Pacific. He formerly taught in Ethiopia, and he currently lectures in economics and development studies at Sheffield City Polytechnic. He has written on various aspects of development in Africa and the Pacific.

Paul E. Lovejoy is Professor and Chairman of the History Department at York University, Toronto. He has written extensively on West African history, focusing particularly on issues of slavery and trade diasporas. His latest works include *Caravans of Kola* and *Transformations in Slavery.*

Wyatt MacGaffey is Professor of Anthropology at Haverford College in Pennsylvania. He has published widely on religion and ideology, focusing especially on the societies of West Central Africa. Among his latest works is *Modern Kongo Prophets.*

Shula Marks is Director of the Institute of Commonwealth Studies at the University of London. She has published extensively on South African history.

Mohamed Mbodj, currently teaching at the Université de Dakar, has published on economic history and agricultural history in the Senegambia. His present research also includes technological innovations and historical demography.

Henri Moniot teaches on the history of black Africa and on the teaching of history at the Université de Paris VII. His works include *L'Afrique noire de 1800 à nos jours* (with C. Coquery-Vidrovitch), *Le mal de voir (Ethnologie et Orientalisme),* and *Enseigner histoire: Des manuels à la mémoire.*

Mumbanza mwa Bawele is Vice Doyen of the Faculté des Lettres and Professor of History at the Université de Lubumbashi (Zaire). He has published numerous articles on the socioeconomic history of the societies of the forest areas of central Zaire and on the cultural history of Zaire during the colonial period.

Caroline Neale was educated in anthropology and African history at the University of Sussex, and has taught in Tanzania. Her book *Writing "Independent" History: African Historiography, 1960-1980* is to be published in 1985. She has four children and lives in Melbourne, where she prepares teaching materials for the Victoria Education Department.

David Newbury has carried out research in Zaire and Rwanda. He has taught in Uganda and Zaire, as well as at the University of Wisconsin, Wesleyan University, and Bowdoin College (Maine).

Ndaywel è Nziem is Permanent Secretary of the Conseil d'Administration of the Université du Zaire. He teaches at the Institut Pédagogique National (Kinshasa) and is President of the Société des Historiens Zairois. He has written numerous articles on the history of Zaire.

Sabakinu Kivilu is Professor of History at the University of Kinshasa (Zaire). He has published many articles on demographic history and the history of health in colonial Zaire.

Henry Slater has taught for many years in the History Department at the University of Dar es Salaam. He has published on historical critique and on the conceptualization of historical issues in Africa.

Michael Twaddle teaches history and politics at London University's Institute of Commonwealth Studies; since 1974 he has been joint editor of the London-based journal *African Affairs*.

Jan Vansina teaches history at the University of Wisconsin—Madison. His publications focus particularly on the history, ethnography, and languages of Central Africa, Rwanda, and Burundi, as well as on methodological issues. Currently he is preparing a history of the forest areas of West Central Africa. His latest work is *Art History in Africa*.

Benoit Verhaegen is Dean of the Faculty of Social Sciences at Kisangani (Zaire), where he teaches research methodology and epistemology. He is also Director of the Centre d'Etudes et de Documentation Africaines (CEDAF) in Brussels. He is the author of *Rébellions au Congo* (2 volumes), among other works.

Christophe Wondji has taught for many years at the University of Abidjan (Ivory Coast). He now works with UNESCO. He has published numerous articles on the peoples of the Ivory Coast and is completing a work on resistance to colonial penetration in the Ivory Coast.